Environmental Politics and Policy

Fourth Edition

Environmental Politics and Policy

Fourth Edition

Walter A. Rosenbaum
University of Florida, Gainesville

A Division of Congressional Quarterly Inc.
Washington, D.C.

Copyright © 1998 Congressional Quarterly Inc.
1414 22nd Street, N.W., Washington, D.C. 20037

Printed in the United States of America

Cover design: Dennis Anderson

Library of Congress Cataloging-in-Publication Data

Rosenbaum, Walter A.
    Environmental politics and policy / Walter A. Rosenbaum.—4th ed.
        p.   cm.
    Includes bibliographical references and index.
    ISBN 1-56802-335-9
    1. Environmental policy--United States.   I. Title.
HC110.E5R665   1998
363.7'056'0973--dc21   98-8614

Contents

Tables, Figures, and Boxes

Boxes

Preface

Political prophecy is a notoriously risky business, but anyone who writes a book about contemporary environmental policy inevitably becomes a practitioner. One becomes acutely aware that education is a gamble with the future: a wager that what one teaches—or most of it—is what the next generation will need to know. This book is addressed in good part to an audience that will live mostly in the next century, its imagination and ambition resolutely fixed on tomorrow. Thus, writing thoughtfully about current environmental politics compels a fixed gaze on the horizon, a constant reflecting not only on what is but also on what may be—what will matter to those on the outward journey.

I intend that this new edition of *Environmental Politics and Policy*, at the very edge of a new century, reflect a sensitivity to the magnified importance of the future in weighing the state of current environmental affairs. I have retained from previous editions the fundamental conceptual and factual elements that colleagues and students have indicated through the years are especially useful, so readers will find considerable continuity between this edition and the three previous ones in content, organization, and style. As before, the book emphasizes the political context of environmental issues and the political implications of policy decisions by using the policy cycle and policy process as a conceptual framework. The use of substantive policy issues —air and water pollution, hazardous waste, and more—as an organizing principle remains as well. I continue to believe that a practical example is worth a paragraph of abstractions, so I have included an abundance of contemporary illustrations and case studies to keep the discussion fresh and interesting. I have also retained current appraisals of environmental quality in the analyses of specific policy domains, brief descriptions of the important substantive regulatory policies in each major policy area, and suggested readings. Of course, data and other information have been updated where necessary.

I have also made significant changes to this edition. The most important is the addition of Chapter 10, a wholly new discussion of the structure of international environmental politics and its growing importance to the United States. The inclusion of this chapter represents my belief that regional and global environmental politics will become increasingly important to Americans in the next century and, in the process, will profoundly alter the character of domestic environmental policy making. Other additions include an expanded discussion of environmental justice (in Chapter 4) and a review of economic alternatives to command-and-control regulation (in Chapter 5) in recognition of their growing importance in current policy debates. Associated with the discussion of economic approaches to regulation is an early appraisal of experience with emissions trading in air pollution. A new discussion of endocrine disrupters has been added to the chapter on hazardous and toxic substances to illuminate an emerging problem likely to increase in importance within the decade. In the same chapter, a discussion of Superfund—everyone's favorite regulatory disaster—emphasizes important improvements in recent years that may change the tenor of debate over this hugely expensive undertaking. Finally, the narrative now embraces events and issues arising from Bill Clinton's presidency.

I am indebted to my reviewers, Gordon Bennett, William R. Lowry, and Dennis Pirages, for their many constructive contributions to the new edition and to my editor, Tracy Villano, for her meticulous and thoughtful review of the manuscript. Mistakes of omission and commission are—alas!—still mine. Brenda Carter, as always, has been a source of continual encouragement and support for the book. This new edition marks a collaboration of almost twenty years with CQ Press for which I am most appreciative.

Environmental Politics and Policy

Fourth Edition

Chapter 1

The Politics of Regulatory Discontent

The difficulty of converting scientific findings into political action is a function of the uncertainty of the science and the pain generated by the action.
—William D. Ruckelshaus, former administrator
of the Environmental Protection Agency

Late in 1995 federal officials in Miami, Florida, announced an important milestone in their continuing fight against the illicit trade in controlled substances. Irma Henning, a Ft. Lauderdale shipping company executive, had been caught attempting to conceal 4,000 pounds of an illegal substance with a street value of $32 million—the largest single seizure of its kind in U.S. history. Her felony would cost her $250,000 in fines and five years in jail, but U.S. Customs agents acknowledged that such smuggling had become pervasive. "We know there are bigger people out there," observed one agent. Several months later, after four additional Miami smugglers were prosecuted on similar charges, the U.S. Attorney's Office admitted that Miami had become "a convenient location for this kind of trade. We are a major port and a major hub for the Central, Latin and South American markets."[1] To readers of *U.S.A. Today* and other wire services reporting the story, it all might at first have seemed familiar, a tired variation on *Miami Vice*. But this was different: the criminals were freon smugglers.

Prelude: "Operation Deep Freeze"

The illicit freon trade, already spreading along the Mexican and Canadian borders, is expected to increase as federal law gradually eliminates domestic freon production. Less than a decade ago, freon was a commonplace, an essential chemical with hundreds of industrial and

1

commercial uses and a component in practically every home refrigerator and automobile air conditioner. Now freon is a chemical contraband because environmental science has discovered that it is also an efficient, extraordinarily durable atmospheric pollutant.

The swift metamorphosis of freon from wonder chemical to global menace is one measure of how quickly and pervasively the social consciousness of Americans has been transformed by environmentalism. The politics of that transformation has profoundly affected our economic and political life. The powerful national and international forces that have emerged in the process are likely to shape American environmental policy into the next century. Awaiting them on the other side of that threshold are some of the most daunting challenges to environmental protection yet.

Federal officials estimate that the street value of freon smuggled through South Florida now approaches that of the region's narcotics trade. A massive crackdown on the illicit freon trade in 1995, known as Operation Cool Breeze, was the first of many such operations.[2] The soaring value of freon and the social repercussions that follow demonstrate how inextricably entwined the politics and science of national and international environmental management have become, and, in the process, how deeply and directly global and domestic ecological policies affect the average American economically.

From Wonder Chemical to Contraband

The domestic cost of freon is propelled upward by a U.S. agreement to join 140 other nations in an international treaty to eliminate rapidly the worldwide manufacture and use of chlorofluorocarbons (CFCs), now recognized as a principal cause of the destruction of the earth's stratospheric ozone layer. By the late 1980s atmospheric scientists, armed with convincing evidence that CFCs and related chemical compounds were dangerously reducing the ozone (most dramatically illustrated by the famous "ozone hole" over Antarctica), were warning world leaders that continued depletion of stratospheric ozone would mean sharp worldwide increases in skin cancer, eye diseases, crop failure, and other major ecological damage. In response, in 1987 140 nations signed the Montreal Protocol committing them to reduce CFC production by 50 percent by 1998. When evidence pointed conclusively to continuing rapid deterioration of stratospheric ozone, the developed nations agreed to eliminate all their CFC production by the year 2000. In 1992, they advanced this target date to 1996. Developing nations, however, were given an additional ten years to eliminate their CFC production in recognition of the greater technical and economic difficulties they would encounter in meeting this goal.

Global Protection Hits Home

The United States met its CFC emission control targets by rapidly eliminating the domestic production of new freon and by assessing a graduated tax on available domestically manufactured CFC-12 and closely related chemicals. The freon tax, introduced in 1990 at $1.37/lb., increased to $5.35/lb. in 1995 and has risen $ 0.45/lb. annually since. The average American is likely to feel the economic impact first in the garage. The rapid disappearance of domestic CFC-12 (or R-12) production, the freon used in all 80 million U.S. automobile air conditioners manufactured before 1992, means that motorists with older cars will have to replenish their freon by finding an existing stock of fresh CFC-12, by retrofitting the car to use a newer, substitute cooling agent, or by using recycled CFC-12. In the mid-1990s other regulated forms of CFC were also used in 160 million home refrigerators, 5 million commercial refrigerators, and more than 80,000 large commercial buildings. Additionally, CFCs were a major component in rubber insulating foam for commercial and home appliances and home construction, and for solvents widely used in the electrical industry. Newer, more expensive CFC substitutes, or costly retrofitting, will be required in virtually all instances.[3]

The U.S. Environmental Protection Agency (EPA) estimates that the $45 billion cost to rid the United States of CFC emissions is more than offset by the $32 trillion in crop damage, skin disease, and ecological ills averted. This may be scant comfort, however, for the average American motorist who must absorb much of this cost. In the latter 1990s, for example, the tax accounted for more than half the price of an average tank of new freon, inflating the cost from about $72 in 1995 to about $232 in the latter 1990s and more in following years. For the average American driving an older car or truck, this translates into a 300–350 percent price increase: an air conditioner recharge with new freon—if it is available—that cost 60 cents in 1992 cost more than $20 in 1998. Retrofitting the car to use a new CFC substitute instead cost between $200–450.[4] The motorist might decide instead to purchase recycled freon for the older auto. But recycled freon, often produced abroad, frequently contains impurities difficult to detect yet capable of destroying an auto air conditioning system at a replacement cost averaging about $1,000. In short, for the average American this is environmental protection with a bite. The discomfort is likely to increase as more than 10 million older cars are retrofitted with freon substitutes before the turn of the century.[5]

Smuggler's Gold From Gas

Meanwhile, freon smuggling has become a growth industry. Contraband freon, obtained in Russia, China, India, England, or other nations where CFC production is still legal, can be purchased at a fraction of the cost of domestic freon. Smuggled into the United States as "recycled" freon, it is sold at a handsome profit to auto services and consumers. Alternatively, freon produced abroad can be intentionally mislabeled as cargo headed through the United States to a foreign destination (such transit is still legal) and then diverted to domestic use. Either way, the U.S. government loses hundreds of millions in tax dollars annually. The U.S. Justice Department estimates that more than 20 million pounds of freon was smuggled into the United States in 1996, meeting, among other needs, about 90 percent of freon demand in South Florida. Auto mechanics, service centers, and other large freon consumers may resist the temptation to use smuggled products, but they risk angering customers by raising the freon charge, or losing their patrons to other, cheaper freon providers. Many auto service centers have already reported a consumer backlash. "Buyers are way off," observed a Los Angeles service center manager. "And the average customer gets upset at us, not the government," he lamented.

Are We Protecting the Ozone Layer? Yes . . . Maybe

A broad scientific consensus about the reality of stratospheric ozone depletion and scientists' ability to portray the consequences in vivid public images of grave human health and ecological damage contributed enormously in the latter 1980s in persuading national officials to act incisively on the issue. But it has been harder to produce equally persuasive ecological evidence to demonstrate the wisdom of the Montreal Protocol even though most scientists remain confident that CFC regulation is imperative and, in the long run, effective. While atmospheric studies in the early 1990s seemed to suggest a gradual improvement in the stratospheric ozone layer, particularly a significant reduction of the Southern hemispheric "ozone hole," later evidence sometimes seemed contradictory, as when the National Oceanic and Atmospheric Administration (NOAA) reported in late 1997 that the Antarctic ozone hole was "back, as big as ever."[6] Coming at a time when the economic costs of CFC reductions will be felt with increasing frequency by American industry and the average consumer, such reports diminish the scientific and regulatory credibility of CFC controls precisely when their political vulnerability increases.

The Realities of Environmental Governance

The struggle to regulate CFCs illuminates many important characteristics of U.S. environmental policy at the dawn of the twenty-first century. The rising cost of freon is one indication that American consumers can increasingly expect to pay a substantial and undisguised premium—measured not only in money but in personal convenience and creature comfort as well—for the quality of environmental protection they expect from their government. In Southern California, millions of residents are being asked to buy new lawn mowers or extensively repair their existing ones, to abandon the backyard barbeque or find alternatives to charcoal lighters, and to purchase auto fuel only from service stations with expensive new vapor controls on their gas pumps to enable Los Angeles and surrounding counties to comply with air quality standards required by the Clean Air Act Amendments of 1990. In Houston, Los Angeles, and Chicago, among many other major urban areas, local governments are considering placing limits on both the number of motor vehicles and vehicular access to business and commercial facilities in order to reduce urban smog. At the same time, concern over the relentlessly rising aggregate economic cost of environmental protection for the entire nation and for hundreds of vital economic sectors now virtually dominates the national debate on environmental policy.

The continuing scientific ambiguity about the ecological effectiveness of global freon regulation in tandem with the worldwide expansion of freon smuggling also highlight the persistent disputes about the ecological impact of existing environmental laws and the ongoing enforcement difficulties common to virtually all major domestic environmental laws. At the same time, the American public continues to believe firmly in the reality of environmental problems and in the necessity for an aggressive governmental response. And public officials routinely promise to deliver it. Moreover, Americans customarily expect a high quality of environmental management and repeatedly profess (at least in the abstract) a will to accept the costs and sacrifices necessary to achieve it. Federal and state governments struggle to translate this public mood into prompt, economical, and effective environmental governance even as the drumbeat of credible scientific warning about the increasing scope and severity of environmental ills and the imperative for incisive remedial action sounds on. The result is a volatile domestic political climate characterized by widespread public and governmental dissatisfaction with existing environmental laws, continuing national debate over the alternatives, a growing sense of scientific urgency to take effective action, and a critical searching of the nation's experience with environmental regulation over the last thirty years for a "learning curve" to direct policy reform into the next century.

Moreover, global issues like stratospheric ozone depletion increasingly crowd a national environmental agenda once almost exclusively confined to domestic problems. These international issues confront policy makers with the necessity for new policy skills, a new spatial and temporal perspective on ecological management, and new scientific sophistication appropriate to the new order of environmental problems they will confront.

The search for regulatory capability is also complicated because it is difficult, if not impossible, to know confidently how much responsibility for continuing environmental ills, or the appearance of new ones, is due to the failure of public institutions. The crabwise implementation and bloated costs of current environmental regulation nurture a petulant national mood that too easily blames public officials and institutions for almost all of the real or assumed failures of regulatory policy. Contemporary environmental controversy abounds, for instance, with implicit assumptions about how much Superfund—the legislation allocating grants to the states for cleaning up abandoned toxic waste sites—could accomplish *if* government were more effective, or how much better urban air quality would be *if* the Clean Air Act were adequately funded, or why newly discovered ground water pollutants wouldn't have appeared *if* the government had acted more wisely. Nature cannot so easily be held accountable to Congress. Persistent environmental problems may be inherently refractory under the best management, new problems may appear as a result of recently created technologies or may be discovered only with the gradual advance of scientific research. Additionally, existing regulations may be maligned for alleged failures with little consideration of how the environment would have fared had the laws not existed. It is important, therefore, to recognize that environmental problems often persist, or evolve, in spite of government and that judgments about environmental laws and institutions be tempered by an appreciation for the complexity of the ecological world.

Ecological Complexity: A Trio of Ecological Puzzles

In the last decade, the following three random events occurred in the United States. First, an outbreak of cryptosporidium, a potentially severe human intestinal infection caused by a water-borne parasite, occurred in Milwaukee, infecting 403,000 people and killing between 50 and 100 of them. At the time, Milwaukee's public water supply complied with all federal drinking water standards intended to protect the public from such well-known public health hazards, and public health officials were initially perplexed to explain the infestation. Second, fish samples taken from Florida's Everglades were found to contain as much as 4.4 parts per million (ppm) of methyl mercury—more than four times the level considered safe by the federal government and one of the highest concentrations ever recorded in the United States. Methyl mercury is rarely found in Florida's rural wetlands. Third, in Arkansas one of the nation's biggest poultry raisers had to destroy 400,000 chickens because they had become contaminated by the carcinogenic pesticide heptachlor, prohibited by the EPA for use on food crops since 1978.

In each case, explanations were found or suggested. Subsequent research implied that Milwaukee's epidemic of cryptosporidium was related to the turbidity of the city's drinking water, although turbidity in large public water systems had not previously been associated with microbial contamination. "Milwaukee was a wake-up call," observed one of EPA's drinking water experts in explaining why the agency would now carefully reevaluate its drinking water standards for turbidity.[7] The mercury contaminating the bass and warmouth of the Everglades might have come from Mexico, from illegal "midnight dumpers" of toxic wastes, or from the Everglades bottom muck where it had been deposited decades earlier, before mercury was banned from pesticides. There was no doubt about how the chickens had become contaminated. Poultry raisers had unknowingly fed them sorghum seeds that had been sprayed with heptachlor and sold illegally as feed grain.[8]

These events, while different in cause and consequence, have much in common. All were ecological surprises. Each involved a complex web of causality spanning great geographic distances, embracing different environmental media, and posing many alternative modes of explanation. Cause and effect could not easily be documented and sometimes spanned years or decades. Each event implied related problems not yet discovered, reminding those involved that ecology is a science rich in surprise and uncertainty. And each incident is one more revelation that large portions of the American environment are still seriously degraded almost thirty years after the nation's "environmental era" began. It is now clear that no simple and sovereign explanation for the nation's continuing environmental problems will suffice. Most ecological ills are the product of several factors in different, often interacting combinations involving government, technology, science, and the inherent character of the environment itself.

Implementation Obstacles

While practically every important environmental ill has been targeted by a major federal law, delay and difficulty in program implementation routinely impede enforcement. Implementation is frustrated frequently by decades of deficient agency staffing or budgets. In early 1993, for instance, the EPA was overwhelmed by the scientific and administrative complexity of its task and was able to reassess and register only 31 of more than 20,000 older pesticide products whose reevaluation had been ordered by Congress in 1972 and again in 1988. Despite a congressionally mandated deadline of 1997 to complete the job, the Government Accounting Office (GAO) reported that "the program may not be completed until 2006." Meanwhile, "most of these products may continue to be sold and distributed even though knowledge of their health and environmental effects is incomplete."[9] Enforcement of most environmental legislation also depends on voluntary compliance by regulated interests, public and private, but the responsible federal and state agencies quite often lack the resources to monitor compliance with the law. Few states, for example, routinely inspect public and private drinking water systems even though it is required by the Safe Drinking Water Act (1974). Half of the nation's 59,000 large water systems and one-fifth of the 139,000 small ones are not monitored to assure that water is uncontaminated by sewage or runoff with pesticides.[10] Quite often, information essential to effective regulation is missing or fragmentary, and the available information is often surprisingly haphazard. Many states, for instance, lack the technical resources to develop numerical standards for many groundwater contaminants and instead depend on evidence of environmental damage or public health risks before acting to control these substances.

Economic growth and population expansion often diminish the effectiveness of pollution controls over time. The automobile emission controls and reduced lead levels in gasoline required by the Clean Air Act together have lowered the average new car's hydrocarbon and carbon monoxide emissions by 90 percent and nitrogen oxide emissions by 75 percent since 1970.[11] But the number of automobiles in the United States has increased more than 53 percent, from 80.4 million in 1970 to 123.3 million in 1997, and more than 42 million new trucks have taken the road since 1970. This vehicle population explosion counteracts the emission reductions achieved for individual vehicles and leads eventually to widespread urban violations of federal air quality standards.

Scientific and Technological Innovation

Scientific and technical innovations also contribute to environmental problems by creating new substances or technologies with potentially serious environmental risks. Between 500 and 1,000 new chemical substances are created annually. Advances in biotechnology pose significant questions about the environmental risks associated with the products of recombinant deoxyribonucleic acid (DNA) techniques currently being used in academic, commercial, and governmental laboratories. New energy technologies based on fossil fuels or atomic energy always entail potentially adverse environmental consequences that must be weighed in decisions about the course of their development. Scientific and technical innovations, no matter how beneficial, almost always require trade-offs between environmental risks and social or economic benefits. Environmental regulation must continually struggle to keep pace with scientific and technical innovation.

Difficulties in environmental protection often arise from limited understanding of the causes and consequences of ecological degradation. Existing data on environmental quality are often scarce; environmental monitoring is often undervalued and underfunded. Data collection has only just begun in many environmental domains. Experience with many forms of environmental pollution is too recent to provide carefully tested evidence pointing to firm conclusions about causes, effects, and remedies. Toxic sludge, for example, is a recent problem resulting from vastly increased municipal waste-water treatment. Since 1972, municipal sludge has doubled in volume to about 7 million dry metric tons annually, and this volume is expected to double again within a decade. Little is known about the composition of these sludges and discovering a safe, economical disposal method remains a major problem.[12] Time may change scientific understanding of older environmental problems, as it has in the case of airborne particulates. When later research indicated that small particulates (those under ten microns) pose the most serious health risks, the EPA had to issue new ambient air standards in 1997 specifically to regulate small particulates.

Moreover, as the recent discoveries of acid precipitation and global ozone depletion demonstrate, nature can surprise science. Natural systems may absorb stress for long periods without overt evidence of damage. According to Sandra Postel of the Worldwatch Institute,

> a point comes ... when suddenly conditions worsen rapidly. Scientists may anticipate such sudden changes ... but rarely can they predict when they occur. As the scale and pace of human activities intensify, the risk of overstepping such thresholds increases.[13]

Widespread scientific concern with environmental quality is so recent that surprise is almost inevitable in ecological policy making.

Evolving Ecological Science

Finally, it has taken time for environmental scientists to comprehend the global scale of ecological processes and to educate policy makers into perceiving national problems in a world context. Throughout the 1970s, U.S. scientists and policy makers emphasized national environmental problems and solutions. The vocabulary of policy discussion now is considerably less parochial; policy makers are beginning to understand the interdependence of global environments. U.S. climate change is now perceived as one possible consequence of the depletion of Brazil's rain forest. Domestic exposure to pesticide residues on imported fruits and vegetables is now linked to U.S. exports worldwide of DDT and other hazardous pesticides. This growing awareness of pollution's global scope sharpens understanding of domestic environmental ills and at the same time delineates more clearly the limits of purely domestic policy responses to these ills. Dissatisfaction with current environmental programs, therefore, reflects scientific progress in defining more accurately the true scope of the problems policy makers must address.

In short, almost every significant environmental problem is fixed in a matrix of ecological, economic, political, and scientific causes and consequences that usually frustrates quick and simple solutions. This reality was not always apparent to environmental activists in the 1970s. Undaunted by scientific complexities and beguiled by a confidence that "pressing technology" could produce timely solutions to major environmental ills, many ecological activists expected unreasonably quick and thorough environmental restoration.[14] Much of this early optimism has been dissipated by experience with environmental regulation over the past twenty years, and the contemporary environmental movement is more realistic in its expectations about policy accomplishments. Nonetheless, there is ample reason for environmentalists, along with other Americans, to be deeply troubled about the state of the environment as the century ends and to press for more aggressive, resourceful public efforts at environmental restoration.

"Deeply and Fundamentally Flawed"

Rising apprehension about the capacity of existing institutions to manage the environment effectively was already evident in a 1993 report of the National Commission on the Environment, a private sector policy panel including four former administrators of EPA. Citing considerable evidence that the United States "is losing many battles" for environmental protection, a report by the Commission observed: "Regrettably, the U.S. statutory and regulatory system is woefully inadequate, cumbersome, and sometimes even perverse with respect to environmental issues." The Commission warned that "comprehensive reform is imperative to refocus the regulatory system on coherent policies that can bring about sustainable development, encourage environmentally benign technologies, and institute effective incentives for innovation and behavioral change."[15] This widely shared perception, raising fundamental questions about the adequacy of basic institutional structures and primary policies for environmental management, increasingly resonates through the environmental politics of the 1990s. By late 1997, for example, a three-year study of national environmental quality commissioned by the Andrew W. Mellon Foundation reluctantly ended its own comprehensive review by observing: "For all its accomplishments, we conclude that the pollution control regulatory system is deeply and fundamentally flawed." [16]

The nation's environmental politics in the last decade of the twentieth century have become as much a politics of governance as a politics of policy—a struggle to redefine how policy shall be made and to establish confidence in the institutions that must govern effectively, as well as a struggle to determine what shall be done. Proposals are now commonly debated to redesign the institutional framework, the incentive structure, and the goals of environmental regulation domestically and internationally. The dominating political cleavages in this politics of governance concern the scale and speed with which the basic processes and institutions on which environmental policy is grounded shall be reformed rather than disagreement about the need for such reform. As the capacity for environmental governance becomes an increasingly critical national issue, it accentuates a sharp shift in mood and substance between the environmental politics at the inception of the environmental era and its character two decades later. Nonetheless, the politics of the 1990s is a distillation of more than two decades of experience in environmental regulation. To understand the 1990s, one must begin with the legacy of the 1970s and 1980s.

From Era I to Era II

The Reagan years rise like a great divide between America's environmental eras. On the far side lies Environmental Era I, beginning in the 1960s and reaching into the latter 1980s. The Environmental Decade, as the 1970s were styled, created the legal, political, and institutional foundations of the nation's environmental policies. It promoted an enduring public consciousness of environmental degradation and fashioned a broad public agreement on the need for governmental restoration and protection of environmental quality that has become part of the American public policy consensus. It mobilized, organized, and educated a generation of environmental activists. The environmental movement prospered in a benign political climate assured by a succession of White House occupants tolerant, if not always sympathetic, to its objectives.

All this changed with the advent of the Reagan administration. Ronald Reagan and his advisors believed he had been elected to bring "regulatory relief" to the U.S. economy, and environmental regulations were an early priority on the hit list of laws needing "regulatory reform." The environmental movement regarded the Reagan administration as the most environmentally hostile in a half century and the president's regulatory reform as the cutting edge of a massive administrative assault on the institutional foundations of federal environmental law. The environmental movement, thrown on the defensive, expended most of its energies and resources through the 1980s in defending the legislative and administrative achievements of the Environmental Decade from the onslaught of President Reagan's regulatory relief.[17] The Reagan years severely tested the foundations of the environmental movement. The foundations held but little was done to advance the implementation of existing policy or to address new and urgent environmental issues. "The contest produced a standoff," concluded historian Samuel P. Hays:

> When the political force of public environmental desires became too great, the administration backed down, and when the administration became so zealous that it acted in disregard of established procedures or the intent of legislation, it was forced to change tactics. At the same time . . . the administration could effectively check most innovations in environmental policy that were ripe for action.[18]

To environmental leaders, the Reagan years meant, above all, dangerous drift and indecision, almost a decade of lost opportunities and intensifying environmental ills.

President George Bush awakened expectations of major reform from the environmental movement and brought to the White House a more sympathetic and active environmentalism. Bush's performance never vindicated his promise to be the "environmental president," but his administration ended the pernicious impasse of the Reagan years with important, if episodic, new policy initiatives and administrative reforms. EPA's morale and resources, severely depleted during the Reagan administration, were improved significantly by major funding and staff increases and by the appointment of a popular and politically skilled administrator. The Bush administration sponsored and adeptly promoted the Clean Air Act Amendments of 1990, among the most important and urgently needed environmental policy initiatives since 1970. The Department of Energy (DOE) finally ended decades of federal deception and negligence by acknowledging publicly the federal government's responsibility for the appalling environmental contamination at military nuclear weapons facilities.

Nonetheless, the backside of Bush environmentalism was equally conspicuous: a reluctance to address global environmental issues such as climate warming or the preservation of biodiversity, a progressively hardening resistance to any new domestic environmental regulation, a failure to increase EPA's staff and budget commensurate with its growing responsibilities, and low priority for environmentalism on the policy agenda, to name a few shortcomings. By the end of Bush's single term, it was apparent that his administration had restored only partially the resources essential for governmental management of the environment and had enacted only a few urgently needed policy initiatives. But the rush of history, abetted by science, politics, and economics, was carrying the nation into a new environmental era for which the glacial pace and cramped vision of Bush environmentalism seemed inadequate. Sometime deep in the twilight of the 1980s, the nation entered its second environmental era. Unlike Earth Day in April 1970, the media event that became the historic signature for the Environmental Decade, Environmental Era II arrived unproclaimed. But there have been portents, and freon smuggling is one.

Environmental Era II: A New Mood, a Different Agenda

On the threshold of the twenty-first century it is apparent that protecting the nation's environment is enormously more difficult, frustrating, and costly than had ever been imagined a few decades ago. The search for culprits always starts with government. The history of environmental policy making during the past two decades might seem like a conspiracy against lofty intentions and public planning, a testimony to incompetent policy design and administration, so often have major environmental laws fallen short of their objectives. However, the issues of environmental governance dominating the politics of the 1990s have no simple and sovereign explanation. In reality, many problems arise not from a failure of policy or institutions but from unanticipated events, from social, economic, and scientific forces created by environmental management itself, and from the lessons of experience. To understand the dominant issues of the 1990s, one must examine the confluence of forces creating them.

The Internationalization of Environmentalism

The first annual *Report* of the Council on Environmental Quality (CEQ) in 1970 assigned fewer than 10 of its 330 pages to international issues. The CEQ's 1992 *Report,* by contrast, assigned more than a third of its 200 pages to global issues including acid precipitation, stratospheric ozone depletion, global warming, biodiversity, coasts and oceans, fisheries, marine mammals, and more.[19] During the first environmental era, the movement's leaders spoke most often and relevantly to Americans about the nation's environmental ills. Environmental leaders now speak as naturally of the "Global Commons," a term denoting an international perspective hardened by a thirty-year accumulation of increasingly sophisticated scientific evidence about the global reach of environmental issues. Environmental scientist Barry Commoner once defined ecology as the awareness that in nature "everything is connected to everything else." [20] In this sense, the new rhetoric bespeaks a truly ecological understanding of policy problems.

Despite Reagan's opposition and Bush's ambivalence, U.S. involvement in regional and international environmental management has enlarged steadily since the 1980s as ecological realities compel the United States to acknowledge the interdependencies of national and international ecological issues. By the 1990s, the international environment had assumed a domestic importance far transcending its salience a decade earlier. The Clinton administration, committed to greater initiative and involvement in global environmental management, has enlarged further U.S. participation in treaties and other agreements on global ecological issues. No transformation in the domestic political conception of environmentalism has more profound future implications than this internationalization of ecological issues.

This transformation is expressed in two significant ways. First, there is growing recognition that national and global pollution are interdependent and, as a consequence, a purely domestic solution to most of the nation's major environmental problems is untenable. Second, there is an increasing perception that environmental protection is essential to the security of all nations in a world of environmental interdependence—in short, that environmental issues should be an inherent consideration in military, economic, and diplomatic policy. Awareness of this double bond between domestic and international environmentalism is evident in a recent report of the influential Carnegie Endowment for Peace:

> Preserving a habitable planet is an urgent addition to our foreign policy agenda. . . . America's well-being in turn depends as never before on the well-being of other countries. Global menaces to an American way of life may actually loom larger and more unpredictable in this crowded world than did the danger of nuclear conflagration during the Cold War. [21]

The increasing internationalization of U.S. environmental politics reverses a decade of official opposition to U.S. participation in most global environmental agreements by the Reagan and Bush administrations. During the Reagan years, this opposition frequently betrayed a reluctance to increase the U.S. contribution to the United Nations, which administered most global agreements, rather than hostility to the environmental principles involved in the treaties. Also, both the Reagan and Bush administrations cited the scientific controversies and uncertainties attending many issues, such as global warming and acid precipitation, to support their caution toward international agreements. Nonetheless, this disengagement was a repudiation of U.S. international leadership during the 1970s when, for example, the United States was a founder and leader of the United Nations Conference on the Human Environment in Stockholm, Sweden—the international meeting that established global environmentalism as a major international issue. With the important exception of the 1988 Montreal Protocol, the Reagan administration's ledger of global commitments was largely blank.

The Earth Summit, held at Rio de Janeiro in June 1992, dramatized the growing internationalization of environmental issues. The United States was among 179 states, and the president among 118 heads of state, attending the conference in which more than 7,000 nongovernmental organizations (NGOs) also participated in drafting Agenda 21, a five-hundred-page global environmental agenda for the next century. "The conference," Marvin S. Soroos observed, "was also remarkable for exposing how isolated the United States under the Bush administration had become on issues of global environmental governance."[22] The United States did sign the conference's Climate Change Convention and thereby committed itself to cooperate with 150 other nations in reducing air emissions that are blamed for promoting global climate warming. But the United States, a party to few other important agreements, was also the only participant refusing to sign the meeting's Biodiversity Convention involving the protection of endangered species.

Bill Clinton's presidential campaign, fortified with vice-presidential candidate Al Gore, a certified environmentalist, thrived on green politics. Courting the environmentalist vote, Clinton promised to reinvigorate the nation's global environmental leadership, to sign the global Biodiversity Convention, and to do much else that seemed to announce a resurgence of global activism in the White House. In reality, support for international global activism had been substantial, and growing, within Congress and among the public, if not in the White House, throughout the previous two decades. The internationalization of environmental politics, however, is also burdened with many of the problems inherent in domestic issues: scientific disagreement over the severity and character of global pollution, conflict about the allocation of costs for pollution control, a blatant weakness in international institutions for governance, and more. Whether the United States has the political imagination, will, and resources to achieve the goals it has declared under the Clinton administration in global environmentalism will be a recurring consideration throughout the chapters that follow.

Good Science, Confounding Science

The impact of scientific research on environmental regulation is paradoxical. Research creates new technologies to control environmental pollution, improves methodologies for estimating the scope and severity of exposure to environmental hazards, and devises new, environmentally benign substitutes for ecologically undesirable products. But scientific research also disrupts the regulatory process by illumining unanticipated environmental hazards, by exposing a scope and complexity to environmental pollution not previously understood, and by raising obstructive and politically divisive questions about the accuracy of scientific data on which existing regulations have been predicated. Regulatory discontinuities and controversies have become the inevitable price for environmentalism's success in accelerating and enriching ecological research. As with the nation, so also with the world. The importance of global environmental issues enlarges and environmental science becomes globally politicized. Disputes between nations and regional blocs over the credibility of the science undergirding various proposals for regional and global policies is now a commonplace. Which nation's scientific information shall be accepted as a basis of treaty negotiations? Whose science is more or less contaminated by political bias? How much information is necessary to compel action, or justify inaction, on global pollution? Whose scientists, or scientific methodologies, shall have priority when the experts disagree?

Indeed, the policy complexities created by environmental science are vividly exemplified by newly discovered global issues such as depletion of the stratospheric ozone layer, acid deposition, and global warming—issues hardly imagined little more than a decade ago. More mundane, but no less significant, are the numerous, continuing discoveries that may compel major changes in environmental policy. For example, studies by EPA and the Harvard School of Public Health in 1993 suggested that as many as 60,000 deaths annually were caused by inhalation of small particulates, no larger than 10 microns (a human hair is 75 microns in diameter) for which no air pollution standards currently exist and for which regulation would cost several billion dollars.[23] Other experts, citing the scarcity of controlled experiments on small particulates, argue that evidence is insufficient to justify such expensive regulation. In another instance, in 1985 Congress mandated that states and cities clean up, or remove, asbestos insulation in schools and public buildings following overwhelming evidence that asbestos is a potent carcinogen. After more than $15 billion had been spent in removing such insulation, EPA recommended the practice be discontinued when research revealed that removal could liberate dangerous quantities of asbestos fibers into the air.[24]

Moreover, increasingly sensitive technologies now reveal that toxic and hazardous substances are far more pervasive than previously assumed. Scientific monitoring has improved from an ability to detect substances in food, air, or water in concentrations of one part per million to one part per quadrillion (equivalent to one leaf among all the leaves on all the trees in the United States). As a result of this extraordinary precision, it can no longer be assumed that potentially dangerous substances can be removed completely from air, water, food, or other media. Thus, it appears extremely difficult, perhaps impossible, to eliminate some risk, however slight, of human exposure to potentially dangerous substances. However, many environmental laws, such as the Delaney Clause in the Food, Drug, and Cosmetic Act (1938) and some portions of the Safe Drinking Water Act were written under the assumption that dangerous substances could be eliminated entirely from food, air, and water—in effect, that a "no-risk" level of regulation could be achieved. "You can put a food substance in a process that can measure residues in parts per billion or parts per trillion," complained a spokesperson for regulated food manufacturers. "A zero-risk policy makes no sense because you are always chasing zero."[25]

Many regulatory problems are exacerbated because science is often silent when bidden to speak. Essential information is often missing or incomplete because activities such as environmental monitoring, statistical analysis, forecasting, and the tedious, expensive business of chemical risk assessment are underfunded, politically dull, time consuming, and belated. Often decades will elapse before enough information is available to provide scientifically satisfactory answers to important regulatory issues. Nonetheless, the impact of scientific research on environmental policy has been magnified by the mass media. The media have made environmentalism a populist science. Television, newspapers, and magazines monitor and interpret environmentally relevant science, then translate their findings into terms understandable to lay persons and package the information attractively for mass consumption. One only has to observe how suddenly the Greenhouse Effect became common media fare during the early 1990s to appreciate how rapidly new research enters public consciousness. Equally important, politically potent public moods also evolve in this manner. The media's political alchemy can transmute raw scientific revelations of environmental ills into widespread public anxiety to which governmental policy makers feel compelled to respond, while science simultaneously delays and confounds a solution to the problems it popularizes. Thus, unavoidable delays and difficulties (difficulties that often serve as a testament to the improved quality of research) nourish impatience with existing environmental policies. These problems would be less provocative, however, if they did not add to the steeply rising cost of environmental protection, which is now a major preoccupation to all sides of environmental policy issues.

How Much Should Regulation Cost?

During testimony before the Senate Governmental Affairs Committee, of which he was chair, Sen. John Glenn (D-Ohio) pondered. "The enormity of this thing just sort of overwhelms you," he remarked. Rapping his knuckles on the desk with each word, he continued: "One hundred ten billion, one hundred ten billion, one hundred ten billion, 'B,' billion. . . ."[26] Inspiring this contemplation was an estimate by the Department of Energy of the cost to clean up radioactive and chemical contamination at twelve sites across the United States at which the DOE had supervised negligently the manufacture of nuclear weapons. In fact, the estimate was not enormous enough, as later discoveries revealed. Rising costs are the norm in environmental regulation and a constant theme in all debate about future policy.

By most estimates, the national cost of environmental regulation does not seem excessive or recessionary. Currently, the United States spends about $120 billion annually for environmental control, or about 2 percent of the gross national product (GNP).[27] These total expenditures are less than half the national expenditures for clothing and shoes, a third of those for national defense, and about a third of those for medical care. These costs have decreased also from an average growth of 6 to 8 percent in the 1980s to about 3 percent in the 1990s.[28] Although aggregate expenditures have increased only moderately through the decade, these expenditures conceal very troublesome details. The cost of individual regulatory programs is soaring, often inflicting unanticipated heavy costs on specific economic sectors, depleting regulatory resources, and compelling a search for scarce new funding sources. After originally authorizing $1.6 billion for Superfund in 1980, for instance, Congress was compelled in the mid-1980s to increase spending to $15.2 billion, and EPA now estimates that costs may exceed $27.2 billion. Even minor regulatory actions can become major expenses. Digging a well to obtain samples of polluted groundwater can exceed $200,000; a single soil sample may run from $500 to $5,000 depending on how many contaminants are present. A third to half the cost of cleaning up a toxic waste site is in sampling, preparing applications for government permits, computer time for cleanup design, public relations, and other office work. The roster of inflationary programs has become a virtual catalog of the nation's major environmental laws.

Unanticipated environmental problems, unexpected scientific complexities, and inexperience with new regulation are common causes for massive cost overruns. Proponents of regulatory programs, particularly the congressional committees and staff writing the laws, are often ignorant (sometimes intentionally) about hidden costs. When Congress ordered EPA to issue regulations requiring communities to filter as well as to chlorinate their drinking water—a safeguard against giardiasis, a waterborne intestinal disease—it did not specify that the cost might approach $5 billion plus $500 to $700 million in annual operating expenses.[29] In another instance, the unanticipated difficulties in controlling the formation of low-level ozone and the emission of nitrogen oxides by trucks and automobiles are two major reasons achieving the Clean Air Act's goals is estimated to cost at least $80 billion more than the $60 billion already spent by federal, state, and local governments before the Act was amended in 1990.[30] The litany of other inflationary provocations includes administrative delay, litigation, bureaucratic bungling, waste, missing information, and political obstruction. Whatever the reasons, excessive costs divert public and private capital from more productive investment, promote economic inefficiency, impair competitiveness in some industries, and increase consumer costs. And bloated budgets become a cudgel in the hands of opponents eager to beat back demands for essential improvements in environmental management.

Environmentalists traditionally have approached discussions about the cost of environmental regulation with considerable wariness. They suspect, often correctly, that estimates of regulatory costs produced by business or other regulated interests are deliberately inflated. (However, they are not equally dubious about the considerably lower estimates they usually produce.) They also believe that cost-benefit comparisons applied to environmental policies are usually biased because it is much easier to monetize the costs of regulation than the benefits. Even more controversial is the problem of "ecological valuation"—assigning a value to wetlands, for example, when deciding whether to convert it to commercial development or to protect an endangered species whose habitat is threatened.

Moreover, many environmentalists consider it ethically irresponsible to allow economic costs to weigh heavily in making environmental regulations. Protecting human health and safety, and preservation of environmental quality for future generations, are assumed to be preeminent values when compared to any monetary costs that might be attached to their achievement.

But spiraling costs are changing traditional environmental attitudes. Leaving aside predictable and usually unresolvable arguments over the "real" cost of environmental regulations, the fact of sharply rising costs has compelled many major environmental leaders to seek creative strategies for reducing the expense and to collaborate in this effort with those businesses and industries being regulated. This has affected current policy debate in several ways. First, proposals to shift the primary objective of many current pollution laws, such as the Clean Air Act, from eliminating pollution to reducing exposure to the pollutants have become a major reform issue. This debate is explored in Chapter 6. Suffice it to note here that the proponents of reform believe that reducing the risk of exposure, rather than attempting to eliminate pollutants, is a far less expensive and more technologically feasible objective. Second, rising regulatory costs have encouraged more attention to eliminating pollutants ("pollution prevention") in production processes as an alternative to "end of the pipe" pollution treatment. Third, rising costs have encouraged all sides to give more attention to identifying the trade-offs between regulatory costs and benefits in an effort to identify where the limits of acceptability may be—in short, to identify the threshold of unacceptably high costs. Fourth, many environmental leaders and organizations have become more receptive to economic incentives and other market strategies as substitutes for traditional administrative procedures in securing compliance with environmental regulation on the assumption that market approaches may be more economically efficient and environmentally effective. Recently, national and international trading in "emission rights" has become an increasingly popular proposal by those favoring market-oriented strategies for pollution control.

Still, any debate about the importance of economic considerations in environmental regulation excites an ideological passion among many environmental leaders and groups who profoundly believe that environmental values must never be compromised by marketplace logic. The environmental movement will remain divided over the wisdom of economic reform. Reform will come anyway, albeit slowly and divisively.

The Debilitation of Regulation

The majority of important environmental laws have been implemented at a plodding pace and portions of all the laws exhibit regulatory rigor mortis. While practically all factions agree on the need for a remedy, a laggardly pace is the norm. One reason for this is the growing complexity of the regulatory process. The average size of major environmental statutes has inflated from about 50 pages in the 1970s to more than 500 pages in the 1990s. The original Clean Air Act (1970) was 68 pages; the Clean Air Act Amendments of 1990 weighed in at 788 pages and the regulations required for their implementation will exceed 10,000 pages. To create the elephantine regulations necessary to implement these complex laws and to apply the procedures in the appropriate instances can consume enormous time, as subsequent chapters will reveal. Toxics regulation provides an illustration. The average time required by the Toxic Substances Control Act (TSCA) for the complete testing of sixteen common chemicals (a small fraction of the total that must be evaluated under the law) from their initial selection through final EPA review of the test data has been eight years.[31]

Another important source of regulatory delay is the increasing mismatch between the responsibilities assigned to environmental agencies and the budgetary resources required for their accomplishment. While EPA's workload increased enormously in the 1980s, its budget failed to keep pace. Many deficiencies in current program implementation are the legacy of a decade of underfunding. Appropriations to monitor compliance with the Clean Air Act by stationary air pollution sources, for instance, declined 35 percent (in constant dollars—that is, after adjustment for inflation) and staff diminished by 14 percent between 1979 and 1990 while the number of regulation pollution sources increased from 27,000 to more than 30,000.[32] In 1992, a review panel of distinguished scientists noted that a major reason for EPA's lackluster research and development (R&D) program was inadequate funding: when adjusted for inflation, the R&D budget was 3 percent less than it had been in 1981, despite the growth in Agency responsibilities.[33]

Other potent impediments to program implementation include the litigation virtually predestined for any major regulation, difficult coordination between state and federal governments, bureaucratic infighting, and much else that shall become apparent in later chapters. Collectively, these implementation problems constitute one of the most urgent, and daunting, political and administrative tasks of the 1990s.

The Challenge of Information Integration

A major issue in Environmental Era II is solving the problem of how the diverse, complex information essential to effective environmental policy making can best be assembled and integrated into the policy process. Experience over more than two decades with different policy-making procedures has made it clear that too many different strategies are used and that many are flawed. Beyond this, disagreement prevails.

Environmental policy making is among the most complex in all government because it requires policy makers to arrange an extraordinarily diverse array of information into a coherent decision-making process. Usually, policy makers must be able to obtain and interpret scientific, economic, engineering, legal, and political information and to accord each its appropriate place in reaching policy decisions. For two decades, policy makers have struggled with various schemes for organizing and weighing this diverse information. The rule up to now seemed to be: every new law deserves a new strategy. The result has been a growing debate about which strategy, or strategies, is most desirable. Much of the current debate over institutional reform is promoted by dissatisfaction with the way information is now used in policy making.

The range of information officials are expected to obtain and integrate into environmental regulation is suggested by a few of the requirements EPA must fulfill in cleaning up abandoned hazardous waste sites according to the Superfund Amendments and Reauthorization Act of 1986 (SARA), a major revision of the 1980 Superfund legislation:

Scientific and Medical Information: EPA officials must determine that the degree of cleanup at the site will, at a minimum, be sufficient to protect human health and the environment.

Economic Information: After choosing how much to clean up a site, EPA officials must decide the most cost-effective approach to the cleanup.

Engineering Information: At the same time EPA officials are wrestling with the scientific and economic issues, they must also assure that the cleanup method they choose will create a *permanent* solution and use alternatives to the dumping of hazardous materials at the site "to the maximum extent practicable."

Legal Information: EPA is expected to come up with a "permanent" solution to site cleanup, but the law does not clarify how long "permanent" means. A few decades? A century? Forever? Suppose no proposed solution will last forever. How much less than forever is acceptable?

Political Information: EPA may make financial grants to individuals or groups affected by the cleanup for the purpose of helping them obtain technical help in understanding the problem and weighing the alternative solutions. Who should get these awards? Is it wise to make them?

One major problem, discussed in Chapter 4, is that federal law is notoriously inconsistent in mandating what kinds of information should be considered when deciding whether a substance should be regulated. The same substance may be regulated by different criteria, depending on whether it is found in food, water, air, or food crops. Among the thirty-four current federal laws regulating public exposure to hazardous or toxic substances, regulators have many alternative criteria for deciding when a substance should be controlled: seven laws require consideration only of health risks, two require a comparison of the available remedies, and twenty-five mandate some kind of balancing of risks and costs.

Another problem is packaging information to make it useful to officials. Quite often, controversy over scientific issues produces such a welter of conflicting and controversial information that policy makers cannot easily decide what information, if any, is valid. In the end, as scientist and government consultant Allan Mazur observed, "a dispute itself may become so divisive and widespread that scientific advice becomes more of a cost than a benefit to the policy maker." [34] Cost-benefit analysis provokes one of the great holy wars in environmental politics because many within the environmental movement believe such analysis seldom (some would say *never*) provides decision makers with an accurate accounting of all benefits and costs involved in environmental regulations. This problem has long been an issue in the preparation of Environmental Impact Statements (EISs). The National Environmental Policy Act of 1970 (NEPA) requires federal agencies to prepare EISs for any proposed program or decision "significantly affecting the quality of the human environment." Many critics believe the EISs have become too bloated with detail and technical information to clarify for decision makers the important environmental impacts of their decisions.

Arguments continue over when information is best introduced into the policy-making process. This problem provoked some of the most important controversies in environmental politics during the 1980s. One long-running battle concerns how early the public should be given an opportunity for participation and when the public should be excluded in making environmental regulations. A second controversy, running throughout the Reagan and Bush administrations and sure to reappear, concerns at what point, if at any, in environmental regulation it is proper for the president and the administration to attempt to influence agency regulation writing.

No issue incites more emotion in environmental decision making than the question of what information should weigh most heavily. Should cost-benefit data be accorded greater importance than health and safety data in deciding how much to control a potentially dangerous substance? How important are the political impacts of a regulation in comparison to its cost or its environmental impact? One reason for this controversy is the congressional habit of writing environmental laws thick with criteria to be considered in making policy decisions but thin with enlightenment on how to weigh them. For example, TSCA leaves practically no detail of regulation unmentioned, yet offers no help in deciding what factors are most important when instructing EPA on what to consider in deciding whether the risks from exposure to a substance are "unreasonable":

> The type of effect (chronic or acute, reversible or irreversible); degree of risk; characteristics and number of humans, plants, and animals, or ecosystems, at risk; amount of knowledge about the effects; available or alternative substances and their expected effects; magnitude of the social and economic costs and benefits of possible control actions; and appropriateness and effectiveness of TSCA as a legal instrument for controlling the risk.[35]

In such situations, administrators often must assume the responsibility for deciding how much weight to accord different factors and how to defend their decisions against political and legal attacks.

Even if a law is clear about the relative importance of different criteria in environmental policy making, controversy is likely over whether various participants were biased or prejudiced in the way they created or considered information. In recent years, a growing body of research suggests that scientists and other technical specialists may be influenced by political, economic, or other social values when making apparently professional judgments concerning the extent to which a substance may constitute a hazard to humans or to the environment. Almost everyone involved deplores this bias, but devising a risk assessment process that eliminates it is difficult. The quest for laws and institutional arrangements that reduce or eliminate the influence of undesirable factors in environmental policy making continues with unabated fervor in Environmental Era II—a sign of how difficult it has proven to engineer the legal and institutional arrangements that assure that only the right factors affect decisions at the right time.

The Governmental Setting

The politics of Environmental Era II are shaped not only by current issues but also by inherited laws, governmental institutions, and court decisions that have evolved over the past thirty years. Governmental institutions become vested interests and actors in the policy process. Laws, administrative regulations, and court decisions create precedents and define limits on existing policy choices. The political, financial, and institutional investments in the current structure of environmental policy making become substantial "sunk costs" that must be taken into account when deciding whether to change existing policies. Many aspects of this governmental setting will be discussed in later chapters. But it is useful first to examine the setting in broad and brief perspective in order to illuminate the range and complexity of the political forces involved in the environmental policy process.

The Administrative Setting

Nearly thirty federal agencies have a mission or authority affecting some aspect of the environment. This bureaucracy is a pastiche of numerous agencies with overlapping and sometimes conflicting authority, of agency rivalries and unceasing turf wars, of institutions with differing congressional and interest group clienteles. The two agencies bearing the heaviest burden of responsibility for environmental protection and regulation are EPA and the Occupational Safety and Health Administration (OSHA). EPA, created by an executive order of President Richard Nixon in 1970, is the largest federal regulatory agency in terms of budget and personnel. Its responsibilities embrace an extraordinarily large and technically complex set of programs ranging across the whole domain of environmental management. (EPA's political and administrative problems will be discussed in Chapter 3.) This staggering range of responsibilities is one major reason why EPA has been chronically overworked and repeatedly proposed as a candidate for major organizational reform.

OSHA was created by the Occupational Safety and Health Act (1970) and lodged within the Department of Labor. Its responsibilities include creating and enforcing standards to protect employers and employees in the workplace, creating and maintaining a system to keep records and report job-related injuries and illnesses, encouraging the states to develop and enforce their own workplace health and safety programs, and numerous other duties that routinely plunge the agency into political controversy. OSHA often shares with EPA a responsibility for risk assessment and enforcement of regulations intended to protect humans and the environment from hazardous or toxic substances.

The Statutory Setting

Current federal environmental legislation is a patchwork of several hundred congressional enactments written over the last half century. Legal scholar Christopher Schroeder's verdict about federal toxic substance laws—he said that they have "resulted not in a well-designed cabin, but in a pile of logs"—applies as well for the whole of federal environmental legislation.[36] Many controversies prominent in Environmental Era II result from the inconsistencies, contradictions, confusions, and inadequacies of this statutory welter. At the same time, each law memorializes the success of a major environmental coalition in waging a battle for environmental protection that may have lasted decades. Each law acquires a politically vocal and potent constituency from congressional factions, private interests, bureaucratic agencies, and program beneficiaries. A huge volume of judicial opinions girding each law with court-derived interpretations and justifications further institutionalizes the legislation. These laws are the legal edifice on which environmental policy has been erected.

An idea of the variety and range of these congressional enactments can be gleaned from Table 1-1, which summarizes the major legislative enactments currently on the federal statute books relating to just one category of environmental pollutant, toxic substances. Since the vocabulary of policy conflict is fashioned from these laws, many of the laws will be discussed further in subsequent chapters. However, cataloging even a few types of law should be sufficient to emphasize two realities about today's environmental policy controversies: (1) the existing law becomes a conservative force in policy debate because it is difficult to change; and (2) the incompatibilities and omissions in current environmental legislation are a continuing cause of difficulties in policy implementation and enforcement.

Economic Investments

Public and private institutions in the United States are now spending annually more than $150 billion for pollution abatement and control. By far the largest portion of this spending is made by the private sector—currently, about four of every five dollars. While this spending represents a relatively small portion of the federal budget or the annual capital outlays of most businesses, the total annual expenditure is only slightly less than the combined U.S. budget for health, veterans' benefits, and education. Most economists predict that this level of spending will prevail, and probably increase, throughout the rest of this century.

The economic burden of environmental regulation varies greatly among U.S. industries. Table 1-2 indicates the non-farm sector of the U.S. economy is estimated to have spent a relatively modest 2.8 percent of total capital outlays for pollution abatement in the early 1990s, and this figure is expected to diminish to an annual average between 1.7 and 1.9 percent, depending on how fully existing pollution regulations are implemented. But the petroleum and primary metals industries spent an annual average of more than 10 percent in the late 1980s and may have spent as much in the first half of the 1990s as well.[37] Most economists do not now consider U.S. expenditures for pollution abatement to be a significant deterrent to U.S. economic growth or capital investment in most U.S. economic sectors. But the magnitude of this spending in the past and its likely continuation well into the next century do affect current policy debates in several important ways.

Numerous industries, having invested heavily for many years in required pollution control technologies, strongly resist new regulations compelling them to modify previously installed technologies or to spend more than anticipated on future pollution abatement. Many regulated public and private interests believe this spending can be reduced significantly by new forms of regulation based on marketplace principles, such as "marketable pollution permits" that enable regulated firms to trade government pollution allowances, like other commodities, to achieve the lowest cost of pollution abatement. Many industries believe that their

Table 1-1 *Major Toxic Chemical Laws Administered by the EPA*

Statute	Provisions
Toxic Substances Control Act	Requires that EPA be notified of any new chemical prior to its manufacture and authorizes EPA to regulate production, use, or disposal of a chemical
Federal Insecticide, Fungicide, and Rodenticide Act	Authorizes EPA to register all pesticides and specify the terms and conditions of their use, and remove unreasonably hazardous pesticides from the marketplace
Federal Food, Drug, and Cosmetic Act	Authorizes EPA in cooperation with FDA to establish tolerance levels for pesticide residues on food and food products
Resource Conservation and Recovery Act	Authorizes EPA to identify hazardous wastes and regulate their generation, transportation, treatment, storage, and disposal
Superfund (Comprehensive Environmental Response, Compensation, and Liability Act)	Requires EPA to designate hazardous substances that can present substantial danger and authorizes the cleanup of sites contaminated with such substances
Clean Air Act	Authorizes EPA to set emission standards to limit the release of hazardous air pollutants
Clean Water Act	Requires EPA to establish a list of toxic water pollutants and set standards
Safe Drinking Water Act	Requires EPA to set drinking water standards to protect public health from hazardous substances
Marine Protection, Research, and Sanctuaries Act	Regulates ocean dumping of toxic contaminants
Asbestos School Hazard Act	Authorizes EPA to provide loans and grants to schools with financial need for abatement of severe asbestos hazards
Asbestos Hazard Emergency Response Act	Requires EPA to establish a comprehensive regulatory framework for controlling asbestos hazards in schools
Emergency Planning and Community Right-to-Know Act	Requires states to develop programs for responding to hazardous chemical releases and requires industries to report on the presence and release of certain hazardous substances

Source: Environmental Protection Agency, *Environmental Progress and Challenges: EPA Update* (Washington, D.C.: Environmental Protection Agency, 1988), 113.

Table 1-2 *Estimated Total Capital Expenditures for Pollution Control by U.S. Non-Farm Industries, 1972–2000 (as percent of total capital investment)*

Pollution control capital investment	1972	1987	1990	2000 Present	2000 Full
In billions of 1986 dollars	20	30	41	30	39
In billions of 1990 dollars	23	35	47	35	45
As percent of total capital investment	2.5	2.3	2.8	1.7	1.9

Source: Environmental Protection Agency, *Environmental Investments: A Summary* (Washington, D.C.: Environmental Protection Agency, 1990), 2–5.

expenditures on pollution abatement are a major damper to future plant expansion and market exploration. Finally, many regulated interests are convinced that their own costs for pollution abatement, and perhaps those of many other economic sectors, are unacceptably high when compared with the benefits.

The Environmental Movement

The many groups marching under the environmental banner continue to grow in number, sophistication, and political aggressiveness. Organization is the bedrock of U.S. environmentalism on which the politics of Era II is mounted. To the media and public surprised by Earth Day 1970, the environmental movement seemed to materialize from a political vacuum. In fact, between 1960 and 1970 the national groups sponsoring the event had already grown from 123,000 to almost 820,000 members.[38] As always, behind the public politics of environmentalism was the driving force of calculated organizational action and adroit media manipulation—the evidence of skilled political advocacy.

The environmental movement is also changing. Membership growth has enlarged the political clout of environmental interests at the state and local level. The proliferation of organizations manifests an increasingly divisive pluralism within the movement as well—ideologically, organizationally, and tactically. In the 1990s, ideological cleavages between moderates and radicals, and between the national leaders and local grassroots constituencies, have widened and hardened.

Ideological Consensus and Cleavage

Environmentalism has never been a church of one creed. The reformist politics of the 1990s have exacerbated ideological, programmatic, and tactical disagreements that have always existed among the faithful. While pluralism, and conflicts born of it, are inherent to environmentalism, this pluralism is still bounded by general values, attitudes, and beliefs—a way of looking at nature, humanity, and U.S. society— widely shared with many nuances by environmental leaders and activists. While it lacks the coherence of an ideology, it sets environmentalists apart from mainstream American culture.

Core Values

Reduced to essentials, environmentalism springs from an attitude toward nature that assumes that humanity is part of the created order, ethically responsible for the preservation of the world's ecological integrity and ultimately vulnerable, as are all earth's other creatures, to the good or ill humans inflict on nature. In the environmentalist perspective, humans live in a world of limited resources and potential scarcities; like the good stewards of an inheritance, they must use their scientific genius to manage global resources. An enlightened approach to managing nature, the environmentalists argue, should stress the interdependency of all natural systems (the ecosystem concept), the importance of ecological stability, resource sustainability, and the enormously long time span across which the impact of ecological change occurs. In its approach to nature, environmentalism emphasizes the sanctity of the created order as a warning against the human assumption that we stand above and apart from the created order by virtue of our intelligence and scientific achievements. All this is summed up for many ecologists in the metaphor of "spaceship earth," the image of a unique and vulnerable ecosystem traveling through space and time, dependent on its crew for survival.

In its cultural stance, environmentalism sharply criticizes marketplace economics generally and capitalism particularly, and denigrates the growth ethic, unrestrained technological optimism, and the political structures supporting these. Such an attitude places environmentalists on a collision course with dominant American values. Environmentalism challenges U.S. confidence in market mechanisms to allocate scarce resources for several reasons. Environmentalists assert that market economics esteem economic growth and material consumption above concern for ecological balance and integrity. Therefore, the market cannot be relied on to "signal" resource scarcity efficiently enough to prevent possibly catastrophic resource exhaustion. Many, like William Ophuls, believe marketplace economies are ecologically reckless:

> An unregulated market economy inevitably fosters accelerated ecological degradation and resource depletion through ever higher levels of pro-

duction and consumption. Indeed, given the cornucopian assumptions upon which a market system is based, it could hardly be otherwise; both philosophically and practically, a market economy is incompatible with ecology.[39]

Environmentalism is less hostile to technology itself than to blind faith in the power of technology to cure whatever ecological ills it begets and to bland confidence in technological expertise to meet humanity's material and spiritual needs. Environmentalists regard the public's confidence in American know-how as responsible for many of the nation's most difficult environmental problems, such as the management of commercial nuclear technologies. The environmental movement's initial political agenda arose from these attitudes toward the natural world and contemporary culture. From its inception, the movement has expressed an ambivalence toward the nation's dominant social structures that frequently translates into calls for major institutional as well as policy reforms. Many environmentalists believe that the nation's dominant political institutions and processes must be reformed because they are committed to the preservation of ecological, economic, and technological values that are hostile to prudent ecological management. For some, this is summed up as suspicion of the "establishment" and the traditional institutions and processes associated with it. A. Susan Leeson argues, "if American political ideology and institutions have been successful in encouraging the pursuit of happiness through material acquisition, they appear incapable of imposing the limits which are required to forestall ecological disaster."[40] Many fear the power of an interlocking economic and political structure committed to controlling technology in environmentally reckless ways.

Until the 1980s, the national organizations representing the environmental movement were largely untroubled by impassioned, divisive ideological cleavages. During the 1980s, however, an emergent radicalism and ideological discensus within the movement cohered into a multitude of newly dissident organizations and opened acrimonious schisms within many older, established groups. By the 1990s, the environmental movement had become an uneasy alliance of numerous, often discordant, political camps spread across a widening ideological terrain.

The Ideological Mainstream

Organized environmentalism today is divided into several ideological enclaves. The movement's dominant ideological and political style has been crafted by *pragmatic reformers,* the largest, most politically active and publicly visible organizations represented by national groups such as the Sierra Club and the National Wildlife Federation. These large membership organizations emphasize political action through government, traditional styles of politics such as bargaining and coalition-building, and national environmental agendas focusing on pollution, resource conservation, and land use. Their priorities are "influencing public policy in incremental steps, forging pragmatic alliances issue by issue with those with whom they could agree," explained Michael McCloskey, a previous executive director of the Sierra Club. McCloskey emphasized that the pragmatists do not believe "that the entire political or economic system needed to be changed and were confident that environmental protection could be achieved within the framework of existing institutions of governance." [41]

The robust ideological diversity among the pragmatists, however, makes them appear more an ecumenical movement than a denomination. One important factional conflict divides "preservationist" groups, such as the Sierra Club or Wilderness Society, which emphasize the preservation of resources rather than their economic or recreational exploitation, against such groups as the Izaak Walton League or National Wildlife Federation, which favor prudent resource development for public use and economic growth. Another significant cleavage exists between the pragmatists and anti-establishment groups such as Friends of the Earth and Environmental Action, impatient at the moderation and slowness of political action among the leading national groups but still committed to traditional forms of political activity. These critics, who agree on little else, complain about the amount of foundation money flowing into the coffers of pragmatic environmental groups. Such generous underwriting—often by very large donors such as the Pew Memorial Trusts and the Heinz Foundation—altogether exceeds $400 million annually and, in the opinion of the critics, compels mainline environmentalism to compromise programs and tactics to suit its foundation patrons. "It's like throwing a huge steak in among a bunch of starving lions," complained a spokesman for Oregon's Native Forest Council. "The lions will jump on it even if it is laced with arsenic." [42] Undoubtedly, foundations do prod their environmentalist clientele toward political moderation, but such influence is highly variable. The hardliners, moreover, have their own foundation angels, such as the Turner Foundation, created by broadcast entrepreneur Ted Turner, which contributes millions of dollars annually to aggressive anti-establishment environmental organizations. And many "odd couple" alliances exist between relatively moderate foundation sponsors and aggressive environmental activists such as that between the Ford Foundation and the Environmental Defense Fund. Even without these other provocations, differing organizational agendas and constituencies are themselves divisive to environmentalism. Which organizational agendas shall prevail in the competition among environmental organizations for political primacy? Shall the movement's priorities be air or water pollution, land preservation, hazardous waste management, national land use planning, species preservation, global environmental problems, recreational development, indoor air pollution, or something else?

Deep Ecologists

Another highly vocal faction within environmentalism is constituted from individuals and groups ideologically committed to *deep ecology* or *lifestyle transformation*. Deep ecologists believe humans are, at best, only a part of nature and not necessarily the most significant part. They believe that all forms of life have an equal claim on existence, that social, political, and economic institutions should promote the ecological vitality of all created orders, that fundamental changes in national institutions and lifestyles are essential to preserve global ecological integrity. The fundamental political problem, from the deep ecologist's perspective, is that social institutions have become instruments for human exploitation of the created order for the primary benefit of humans, often through technologies that threaten to destroy essential aspects of the natural order. Deep ecology inherently challenges the fundamental institutional structures and social values on which governments, economies, and societies presently are constituted. Thus, between deep ecologists and what they call the "shallow" ecology of mainstream environmentalism there abides a profound philosophical tension, nourished by antagonistic principles and a sharply disparate political imagination.[43]

Deep ecologists, lacking the political leverage of organizational or numerical strength, are presently a vocal, aggressive, and dissenting minority within the environmental movement. Many within the movement, preferring social to political action, have adopted individual and collective lifestyles outside conventional American culture. Nonetheless, deep ecologists continue to be politically active, often to greatest effect at the state and local levels. They also constitute a persistent, opportunistic minority in many national environmental organizations with considerable potential to become a creative as well as a disruptive influence in national environmental politics.

Radical Environmentalism

Militant and alienated from the movement's organizational mainstream, radical environmentalism emerged in the 1980s among environmentalists disillusioned with establishment styles and accomplishments. According to Bill Devall, the radical environmentalists "were discouraged by the compromising attitude of mainstream groups, by the bureaucratization of the groups, by the professionalization of leaders and their detachment from the emerging concerns of grassroots supporters, and by the lack of success of mainstream organizations in countering the Reagan anti-environmental agenda." [44]

Radical environmentalists favor "direct action" tactics, including the street politics of civil disobedience, nonviolent demonstrations, and political obstruction. To environmental radicals, the harassment of commercial whaling vessels on the high seas by Greenpeace protest vessels, carefully orchestrated to attract media attention worldwide, was better politics than the inhibited, reformist style of the mainline organizations.

Radical environmentalists share a common sensibility that all life is mortally threatened by an ecological degeneration created by advanced modern cultures. Thus, radicals espouse a fundamental cultural transformation that rejects the dominant political and economic institutions of most advanced societies as incompatible with global ecological vitality. This preoccupation with transformational politics usually involves a belief in "bearing witness" by lifestyle changes emphasizing harmony with nature, conservation of resources, and cooperative living in reconstructed, ecologically sensitive societies. [45]

Despite a commitment to nonviolence, radicals betray an ambivalence, if not a tolerance, about forms of violence—"ecotage" or "monkey-wrenching" are euphemisms—condemned from within and without the environmental movement. The small but aggressive movement Earth First!, created by former staff members of mainstream environmental groups, epitomizes this tendency despite its many other conventional activities. For instance, Earth First! spokespersons sometimes assert that in defense of nature, and to save old growth trees from the lumberyards, it may be permissible to spike these trees with metal rods likely to fragment viciously when shattered by commercial logging chain saws.

Other groups, such as Greenpeace and the Sea Shepherd Society, have been accused of nonviolent "direct action" that provokes violence, such as disabling the nets of commercial fishing vessels that refuse to protect dolphins during deep-sea tuna harvesting. In light of the profound cultural alienation inherent in many radical ideologies, an ambivalence about political violence is inevitable, although radical environmentalism's political strategies still remain—sometimes barely—within the tradition of nonviolent "direct action."

Organizational Structures and Strategies

The number and size of environmental organizations expanded through the mid-1990s, but membership subsequently declined, evidence of a familiar up-and-down cycle common to environmental organizations as public perceptions of environmental crises ebb and flow. Table 1-3 indicates strong membership growth throughout the early 1990s, largely a response to aggressive organizational recruiting and the highly publicized confrontations between White House and environmentalists during the Reagan-Bush period. By the latter 1990s, however, the largest organizations had collectively lost more than a million members. Nonetheless, the major national organizations retain the numbers and resources to ensure their influential presence in national policy making. Moreover, to the national membership rolls should be added thousands of grassroots state and local groups—one national organization concerned with solid waste, for instance, identifies 7,000 collaborating state and local groups. Altogether, the number of national, state, and local environmental organizations is estimated to exceed 10,000.

Membership.   While social support for environmentalism is broadly based in the United States, the organizational membership is mostly middle- to upper-class, white, well educated, and well off. Robert Cameron Mitchell found in his 1978 survey of four major environmental organizations that half the members had two years or more of graduate education—an achievement found among only 7 percent of the entire population.[46] Such a socially select membership exposes environmentalists to the frequent criticism that the so-called greens are too white and too well off, that they are racists or elitists indifferent to minorities and the economically disadvantaged. To support these accusations, critics argue that environmentalism fights for clean air, not for equal employment opportunity; promotes wilderness preservation for upscale recreationists, not better schools for the disadvantaged; condemns pollution in national parks but not inner-city decay—in short, the agenda of environmentalism is largely a wish list from the book of middle-class, white lifestyles. Mainstream environmental organizations, increasingly sensitive to such criticism, have struggled to broaden their social constituency and policy agendas. One casualty of the struggle is the Audubon Society's egret, once the organization's traditional logo. Concerned that the organization's image was becoming timeworn and elitist, the leadership in 1991 dispatched the bird in an effort to appeal to a younger membership (the average member was then in his or her mid-40s). "Members of the staff have been asked to refrain from overusing 'bird images.'"[47] A number of national organizations have initiated joint action with labor and minority groups intended to make environmentalism relevant to the workplace

Table 1-3 *Reported Membership in Seven Environmental Interest Groups,
1989, 1992, and 1997*

	Membership		
Interest group	1989	1992	1997
Audubon Society	516,000	600,000	600,000
Environmental Defense Fund	125,000	200,000	300,000
Friends of the Earth	NA	50,000	35,000
National Wildlife Federation	5,800,000	6,200,000	4,400,000
Natural Resources Defense Council	170,000	NA	170,000
Sierra Club	553,000	575,000	550,000
Wilderness Society	330,000	310,000	270,000
Total	7,424,000	7,935,000	6,525,000

Source: Robert Cameron Mitchell, "From Conservation to Environmental Movement: The Develop-
ment of Modern Environmental Lobbies," in *Government and Environmental Politics: Essays on
Historical Development Since World War II,* ed. Michael J. Lacey (Lanham, Md.: University Press of
America, 1990); "Power of the Earth," *Congressional Quarterly Weekly Report,* Jan. 20, 1990, 146;
Carol A. Schwartz, ed., *Encyclopedia of Associations,* 28th ed. (New York: Gale Research, 1994);
and Sandra Jaszczak, ed., *Encyclopedia of Associations,* 31st ed. (New York: Gale Research, 1997).

Note: N/A = Not available.

and neighborhood. The Natural Resources Defense Council, for
instance, recently joined with grassroots organizations in predominantly
Hispanic, low-income east Los Angeles to oppose a large-scale toxic
waste incinerator located there. Most national environmental organizations, responding to initiatives from minority groups, also have supported the emerging "environmental equity" movement intended to end
discrimination toward the economically disadvantaged in environmental
policy making.

The Organizational Mainline.   The movement's national leadership
is concentrated in a small number of highly visible, politically skilled, and
influential organizations. Most of these are included in the Group of Ten,
an informal alliance of mainline organizations that often collaborate on
national issues. These include the National Wildlife Federation, Sierra
Club, National Audubon Society, Wilderness Society, Friends of the
Earth, Environmental Defense Fund, National Parks and Conservation
Association, the Izaak Walton League, the Natural Resources Defense
Council, and the Environmental Policy Institute. The large mainline
groups, the movement's political pragmatists, are today thoroughly professionalized and sophisticated in their staffs and organization, as well
armed with the high-technology tools and modern techniques of policy
advocacy as any other powerful national lobby. The large membership
rolls of the national organizations demonstrate an aptitude for direct mail
solicitation as good as can be found in Washington, D.C.

The growing professionalization of leadership among mainline groups has provoked accusations from many environmentalists that the national organizations have lost their fire and vision. The critics charge that the national leadership is more bureaucratic than charismatic, that it lacks touch with the movement's grassroots since it has become preoccupied with bargaining and compromise. "Increased professionalization," Robert Cameron Mitchell, Riley Dunlap, and Angela Mertig observed in their study of national environmental organizations, "carries with it the dangers of routinization in advocacy, careerism on the part of staff members, and passivity on the part of volunteers, all of which have been detected in the national organizations."[48]

Factional infighting may be an inevitable price for professional advocacy. Controversy within environmentalism over the political loyalty of the professionalized leadership now frequently erupts into nasty media brawls. A typical incident was the public street fight between environmental organizations over the North American Free Trade Agreement (NAFTA), supported by such establishment regulars as the National Wildlife Federation and the National Audubon Society. Groups opposing NAFTA, including the Sierra Club, Friends of the Earth, Greenpeace, Public Citizen, and the Rainforest Action Network, prepared newspaper advertisements asking, "Why are some 'green' groups so quick to sell off the North American environment? Maybe they are too cozy with corporate funders."[49] This is increasing disaffection with the national leadership is one reason for the increase in state and local environmental organizations as well as for the growth of radical environmentalism. Another important reason for the growth of grassroots organizations has been Washington's continuing devolution of regulatory authority to state and local governments, a trend initiated by the Reagan administration.

The Essential Politics of Procedure.   Representative John Dingell (D-Mich.), a legislator of legendary political skill, once shared a lesson gleaned from thirty years in Congress: "I'll let you write the substance on a statute and you let me write the procedures, and I'll screw you every time."[50] Dingell's axiom illuminates a law as fundamental to policy making as gravity is to physics: the decision-making rules, as much as the policy outcomes, enlarge or diminish group power. The environmental movement, always respectful of Dingell's axiom, has been as aggressive in promoting advantageous policy procedures as in creating substantive environmental laws.

The politics of procedure is always a fundamental consideration in environmentalist political agendas. Indeed, the movement's power flows, in good part, from success in procedural politics, from aggressively exploiting advantage through the intricate manipulation of policy process. Because so many environmental laws are implemented largely through bureaucracy and the courts, environmental organizations have been especially sensitive to the importance of protecting, or enhancing, decision-making procedures that work to their benefit in these institutions. The success of this strategy depends on securing these procedural advantages through law—statutory, administrative, or judicial. The public politics of environmentalism could not have succeeded so well, and perhaps not at all, had not environmentalism's political power been anchored in procedural law during the movement's rise to influence in the 1970s. "To a great extent, environmental group power . . . was legal power," observed George Hoberg, and environmentalism survived because the new legal arrangements "granted environmental groups institutional and legal foundations that to a large extent solidified their power status within the regime." [51]

Environmental groups have benefited especially from changes in law and administrative procedure that enhance their access to information and their opportunities to participate in the implementation of environmental laws. A major environmental reform was the enactment of NEPA in 1970, requiring federal agencies to prepare environmental impact statements that have become a major source of substantive information and procedural influence in federal environmental policies. Other important reforms include provisions in almost every major environmental law to greatly expand citizen participation in administrative decision making and to make it easier for citizens to sue administrative agencies for failure to implement environmental laws. Equally important has been increased activism among federal judges in critically reviewing the regulatory decisions of environmental agencies—the so-called "hard look" doctrine—that often works to the environmentalists' advantage.

Environmentalism and Its Critics

National environmental organizations prefer the image of political outsiders but the mainline groups are now acknowledged Washington insiders, part of the interest group establishment. While environmentalist organizations are committed to defending the "public interest" and public values, they also represent a constituency with its own ideological and material interests. As environmentalism becomes increasingly organized and politicized nationally, critics assert that it has also assumed the narrow, self-interested viewpoint of every other interest group while promoting policies that often serve no public ends.

Public Interest or Self-Interest?

Critics frequently allege that environmentalism is largely the voice of a social elite hostile to American capitalism, distrustful of science, and obsessed with imagined or exaggerated ecological problems. In one such indictment, the editors of the *Detroit News* complained that environmentalists were "a small band of environmental doomsayers, mostly upper middle-class whites, who are quick to forecast disaster but never see an upside to technology and economic progress."[52] To fortify such arguments, critics assert that the environmentalists' passion for controlled economic growth will deprive the economically disadvantaged domestically and internationally, that wilderness preservation usually benefits a handful of naturalists but deprives the average American of access and enjoyment of wilderness resources, that locking up resources costs jobs and inhibits economic progress. To such critics, environmentalism speaks not for *the* public interest but for *a* public interest that excludes millions of Americans.

The white, comfortably middle-class ambiance of most environmental organizations does nothing to diminish such criticism, as the executive director of the Natural Resources Defense Council, John H. Adams, acknowledged. "There is much to criticize—the predominantly white staffs, the cultural barriers that have damaged and impeded joint efforts with activists of color."[53] Many environmental organizations are striving diligently for greater social diversity in membership and programs but the stigma of social exclusivity still clings to the movement. Additionally, increased professionalization and competition among environmental groups breeds a preoccupation with organizational needs. "There's tremendous competition out there for money," observed Les Line, a former editor of *Audubon Magazine*. "And we've gotten top-heavy with bureaucrats and accountants and fund-raisers who are all good professionals but I don't think you'd catch them sloshing through the marsh."[54] Critics frequently add that environmentalism's hidden agenda is economic revolution. "One must recognize," wrote the lawyer and legal scholars Marc Landy and Mary Hague, "that their goals are not limited to environmental quality . . . environmentalists are part of a broader reform movement . . . the 'Public Lobby' . . . that is anti-business."[55]

Environmental leaders do resort to the rhetoric of crisis so habitually that environmentalism's mother tongue may seem to be the Apocalypse. This hyperbolic style begets the kind of misstatements on which critics often seize to demonstrate environmentalism's distorted vision. There have certainly been errors, as later discussion of the controversies over the pesticide Alar and the chemical dioxin will demonstrate. In addition, the seriousness of many ecological issues declared to be "crises" may be, at most, a matter of unresolved scientific controversy. Nonetheless, environmentalists have aroused an appropriate sense of urgency about numerous ecological issues, such as air and water pollution, groundwater contamination, radioactive wastes, and surface mining, to cite but a few. And the movement maintains substantial public credibility and support despite some glaring lapses in judgment. The crisis style, however, will eventually become trite and unappealing if it becomes habitual. The environmental movement risks its credibility unless it persistently works at discriminating intelligently between a serious problem, a potential crisis, and a real emergency.

The mainline environmental organizations are also condemned as shrewd opportunists, promoting policies that enlarge their own political power at public expense. The environmentalist attitude toward the Superfund program is often cited as a flagrant case in point. The major environmental groups generally insist on the strictest possible standards for all Superfund site cleanups, as required in the original law. Others have suggested that some relaxation of standards would enormously shrink the huge program costs and greatly facilitate site cleanups without significantly increasing risks to public health. But, the critics assert, environmentalists insist on the stringent standards because it draws to their side the waste treatment industry and the legal profession for whom the strictest standards assure the greatest income.

Constructive Opposition or Destructive Obstruction?

It is a political axiom of organized environmentalism that only unremitting pressure on government will assure that environmental laws are implemented effectively. This informal ideology of countervailing power is animated by the conviction that government officials cannot be trusted to implement environmental regulations without the coercive force of pressure politics. Bureaucratic distrust runs so deeply through environmentalism that, next to saving nature for humanity, environmentalists often seem most dedicated to protecting the public from its public servants. This sour assault on environmental regulators, for instance, comes not from regulation's embittered foes but from Michael McCloskey, the executive director of the Sierra Club:

> [Regulatory programs] need endless follow-through and can go wrong in a thousand places. The relevant bureaucracies have minds of their own and very little loyalty to the ideas of those who lobbied the programs through. Although the bureaucracies are somewhat responsive to Presidential direction, they are not very responsive to outside lobbying and are subject to no self-correcting process if they fail to be productive.[56]

The reliance by those within organized environmentalism on countervailing power is manifest in their resistance to the relaxation of very strict pollution standards such as the "zero risk" now required for food additives by the Food and Drug Act—a resistance that critics consider "stonewalling." Countervailing power also means continual resort to litigation, administrative process, citizen involvement, and any other procedures that equate with group pressure on government. More than half of all litigation initiated against federal agencies involving compliance with NEPA and the majority of all legal challenges to the EPA regulations originate with environmental organizations, often in collaboration with labor unions, consumer groups, and private interests. Environmental organizations are extremely aggressive in challenging federal, state, and local agencies over compliance with Superfund cleanup standards and over licensing of hazardous waste disposal sites and nuclear utilities, among many other issues. Citizen involvement activities at all governmental levels are exploited, if not dominated, by environmental groups and their allies to considerable advantage.[57]

The skilled exploitation of these and other political processes has invested environmentalists with political power they would probably not otherwise possess. Moreover, countervailing power often forces administrative agencies and their regulated interests to comply with laws they might prefer to ignore and frequently improves the quality of regulatory decision making. But countervailing power has also produced enormous delay in the implementation of regulations and increased significantly the cost of environmental regulation through litigation and administrative process. Moreover, countervailing power at state and local levels can virtually immobilize the process of licensing hazardous facilities. Whether the use of countervailing power has become dangerously disruptive to environmental governance is a concern to many within the environmental movement as well as to its critics, for such power can be subverted into chronic obstruction of the processes it was intended to safeguard.

The continuing controversy over environmentalism, whatever its admitted merits, reveals some political realities: that environmentalist organizations do have institutional dogmas and self-serving agendas that may not always be comparable with the larger interests of the movement or even with their own professed goals. While environmental organizations do frequently speak in the name of an encompassing public interest and may unselfishly pursue it, they also speak for a distinctive social and ideological constituency that often does not include the whole public, and often not even a majority of the public. Environmentalism itself is increasingly divided over the goals and social constituencies to which it should be responsive. The rancorous pluralism already inspired by these conflicting convictions will continue to expand into the next century. In addition, the professionalization of national organizational leadership—inevitable if environmentalism is to survive the fiercely competitive struggle among interest groups for political resources—is also likely to breed a growing disunity between national leadership and grassroots environmentalism.

The Public and Environmentalism

Contrary to early predictions that environmentalism would be a trendy and transient public enthusiasm, support for the movement and its political agenda has been broad and vigorous among Americans since the inception of the first environmental era in 1970. This support has been politically crucial for the movement, counterbalancing the advantage enjoyed by the opposition in financial resources and governmental access. Environmental organizations have proven to be extremely adept at arousing public concern on environmental matters and turning it into political advantage.

A "Core Value"

"The transformation of the environment from an issue of limited concern to one of universal concern is now complete," observed opinion analyst Everett Carll Ladd in mid-1996.[58] The strength of public support for environmental protection throughout the 1990s, as measured by public opinion polls, certainly appears vigorous and widespread. Opinion polls report that substantial majorities in almost all major socioeconomic groups support the environmental movement and governmental programs to protect the environment and have supported them since the onset of Environmental Era I. It might even appear that Americans are becoming a nation of environmentalists. In late 1997, for example, about 68 percent of Americans "place[d] themselves squarely in the pro-environmental camp." This finding was similar to a Gallup Poll conducted two years earlier which reported that 63 percent of respondents considered themselves "to be an environmentalist."[59] Opinion analyst Ladd, like many opinion experts, concluded that environmentalism has become a "core American value," one of those issues now firmly rooted in a national political consensus.[60] The supportive public includes racial minorities to whom environmentalism is often presumed to be unappealing because the environmentalists' agenda seldom attacks social and economic discrimination in education, employment, or politics, areas in which minorities often experience the most severe political deprivations. Numerous studies reveal no significant differences between black and white Americans in environmental concern, although whites are much more politically active in environmental matters.[61] It would seem, moreover, that most Americans will commit their wallets, as well as their hearts, to environmental protection. Over the years since 1970, public opinion studies have often revealed public sentiments similar to a 1997 opinion poll report that 76 percent of the respondents believed environmental improvements should be made "regardless of the cost." [62]

So long as environmental questions are lofty abstractions, the public answers can easily imply that environmentalism's roots go deeply as well as broadly across America. Certainly when the political bedrock of environmental regulation seems threatened—when fundamental laws such as the Clean Air Act or Clean Water Act seem imperilled—public support for environmentalism can be impressive. The most politically powerful demonstration of such support occurred during the bitter confrontation between the Reagan administration and environmental organizations in the early 1980s. The Reagan administration sabotaged its own political agenda by failing to appreciate the strength of public support for environmental protection in the face of sweeping reforms aimed directly at major environmental programs in the early 1980s. Environmental interests effectively turned public opinion against much of the Reagan reform agenda, thereby greatly limiting its scope and effectiveness. Environmental organizations were able to demonstrate their public appeal to particular advantage by successfully mobilizing public opinion against early Reagan initiatives in Congress to severely weaken by amendment the Clean Air Act and the Toxic Substances Control Act.

Environmentalists have also accomplished what amounts to a massive raising of the public's ecological consciousness through mass education about environmental issues facing the United States and the world. Less than twenty years ago, ecology and the environment were issues foreign to most Americans. Today many Americans have a rudimentary understanding of many basic ecological precepts, including the importance of resource conservation and the global scale of environmental problems. The movement has educated the public and itself into embracing a progressively larger conception of "the environment." Before the 1960s, most environmental groups were concerned primarily with land and wildlife management, not air or water pollution or hazardous waste. The goals of the early environmentalists betrayed a nearsighted vision, focused mostly on domestic issues, and the supporting science was unsophisticated in its lack of sensitivity to the complex interrelationships among environmental problems. By the late 1980s, viewpoints were more global, ecologically informed, and expansive. In 1959, for instance, the Defenders of Wildlife were defending individual animals, not species survival, and then mostly zoo animals. Today, the organization stresses, among other issues, worldwide habitat protection and conservation of endangered species.

Environmental organizations also have encouraged greater public skepticism about the credibility and managerial skills of the scientists, technicians, and other spokespersons for science and technology involved in public affairs. Over the past two decades, environmental organizations repeatedly have challenged the competence of scientific experts and the quality of science supporting opponents in political and administrative battles. These unrelenting technical controversies over the management of commercial nuclear power, the regulation of pesticides, the setting of appropriate air- and water-quality standards, and much else have educated the public on the limits of scientific expertise. Many environmental groups have promoted effectively local citizen involvement in decisions about the siting of real or potential environmental hazards, such as hazardous waste sites. Critics charge that these groups are entirely too successful at grassroots activism. They blame environmentalists for the rapid spread of NIMBYism (Not In My Backyard)—the uncompromising public opposition to living next to any potentially hazardous facility. This will be discussed more fully in Chapter 7.

But Is Public Environmentalism Deep?

Despite the public's ecological concern, environmentalism's public impact still may be restricted in important ways. Environmentalism may now be a consensual value in American politics, but it is what public opinion analyst Riley Dunlap calls a "passive consensus"—a situation of "widespread but not terribly intense public support for a goal [in which] government has considerable flexibility in pursuing the goal and is not carefully monitored by the public." [63] Carll Ladd is blunter: Americans, having affirmed their environmentalism, "have turned to other things." [64]

The "other things" to which Americans are turning do not appear to include sustained interest or reflection about environmental issues at home, at work, or at the voting booth. Even though the public consistently rates Democrats much higher than Republicans on environmental stewardship, being green doesn't appear to help Democrats get to the White House. Environmentalism, in fact, has so far had little impact upon presidential voting. In none of the last four presidential elections, for instance, did more than 11 percent of voters ever state that the environment was the most important issue in casting their ballots. [65] Despite Bill Clinton's efforts in 1996 to wrap his campaign in an environmentalist mantle with the presence of self-proclaimed environmentalist Al Gore as his running mate, fewer than 1 percent of those who voted for him cited environmentalism as the most important reason and fewer than 10 percent cited environmentalism among *any* reason for supporting him.[66] Conversely, the public may have disliked Ronald Reagan's assault on environmental regulation, but it did not hurt him at the polls. It seems environmental values are linked weakly to candidate or party preference for most voters at national elections but they may play a more important role in state and local elections—sometimes. In congressional elections among nine western states in 1994, for instance, opinion polls suggested that the Clinton administration's public land policies were a significant consideration in voter support for Republican candidates. However, fewer than 4 percent of Virginians voting in their 1997 gubernatorial election said the environment was the most important consideration in choice, including only 7 percent of those who voted for the self-proclaimed "environmentalist" Democratic candidate.[67]

Elections aside, environmental issues seldom arouse intense or sustained concern for most Americans. In 1995, fewer than 1 percent of Americans listed the environment among any of the nation's most important problems. After the 1996 presidential elections, one national poll revealed that fewer than 1 percent of registered voters believed the environment should be a high priority during Clinton's second term.[68] Sudden surges of public interest or apprehension about the environment do predictably rise in the aftermath of widely publicized environmental disasters or emergencies, but public concern is usually evanescent unless the issue is repeatedly dramatized and personalized.

Also, Americans frequently resist policies essential to implementing the environmental programs they claim to support, especially when personal cost or inconvenience may be involved. Environmentalism may be at greatest political risk as regulation strikes ever more intimately at the average American's everyday life. Consider California's lawn mowers. The average lawn mower emits in one hour as much smog-creating hydrocarbons as a modern automobile. The California Air Resources Board adopted new rules in 1994 that require installation of catalytic converters (and presumably inspection and maintenance) on gas-powered mowers by 1999, with additional modifications to prevent the converters from igniting the grass. How will millions of Californians react to environmentalism's costly and inconvenient invasion of their backyards? How will other Americans respond when they must pay a premium to purchase cleaner burning auto fuel by the end of the decade? It is not apparent, either, how the public might react when confronted by a choice between environmental protection and energy supply, or more cancer research, or greater defense spending, or other difficult trade-offs. Nor has environmentalism yet proven its political toughness by surviving the most brutal test of enduring public commitment: an economic depression.

Conclusion

In calendar time, 1990 marked the start of the third decade of the environmental era proclaimed in the 1970s. In political time, it is the midday of Era II. The momentum of Environmental Era I, begun with the fervor and optimism of Earth Day 1970, dissipated amid the bitter partisan conflicts and policy paralysis of the Reagan administration. Environmental Era II began when the environmental movement regained the initiative in the closing days of the Reagan administration. Americans seemed in the early 1990s to have reawakened to the gravity of the nation's ecological problems in the aftermath of numerous highly publicized environmental crises and the increasingly confident predictions by environmental scientists of impending global climate changes worldwide. In the United States, the political climate was indeed changing. For the first time in nearly a decade, the White House and Congress were prepared to collaborate on a new agenda of major environmental policies. But the sense of malaise has not lifted, and new policy initiatives have not brought the anticipated reinvigoration of environmental regulation. A disappointment darkening to disillusion has grown at the policy implementation failures even a more benign White House regime could not alleviate. By the mid-1990s, environmental policy making was facing a crisis of institutional capacity in which the design of the fundamental policy instruments and their organizational settings increasingly were questioned.

Concern with problems of institutional capacity is the most conspicuous evidence that the politics of Era II are different from Era I. But there is other testimony. The environmental movement's policy agenda is different: globalism, radical reform of existing institutions and laws, increased cost consciousness, and great awareness of limits and problems in achieving regulatory goals have assumed much greater prominence on this agenda. Many environmental groups have become more moderate and pragmatic tactically, less confrontational and ideologically rigid in dealing with the opposition. The movement has become much more pluralistic and divisive ideologically, more publicly argumentative within, and—for the mainstream organizations, at least—more akin to other major political interest groups in its tactics and increasingly professional management.

Indeed, the environmental movement in Era II now commands the greatest political resources in its history. In the mid-1990s most national organizations were reporting the largest membership and employing the biggest, most skilled staff in their histories. The movement has money, direct-mail technology, politically seasoned organizers—all the trappings of the politically privileged. The movement continues to enjoy broadly based public approval and agreement with its major policy goals, even if it has only lately begun to examine the problem of minority discrimination implicit in much environmental policy making. All these political resources may still seem inadequate at times in light of the ambitious political tasks the movement has undertaken, but these resources now far exceed those with which Environmental Era I began.

Questions remain—many and profound—about the intensity and political impact of public support for environmental values, even as polls in the 1990s report a broad public consensus on the need for environmental regulation. Yet to be tested is how important ecological values will be in public priority if the public has to choose between environmental policies and other issues claiming limited public resources, such as fighting drug addiction, crime, and AIDS. Neither is it clear that most Americans will vote ecologically when it comes to candidates for public office. What is clear is that Americans are still reluctant to accept many of the personal costs and to bear many of the inconveniences that are essential if we are to make environmental protection the reality the public professes to wish.

Notes

1. Victor Chase, "Contraband in the Stratosphere," *Environmental Health Perspectives* 103, no. 12 (December 1995).
2. Rae Tyson, "Freon-Smuggling the Latest Miami Vice," *USA Today,* December 26, 1995.
3. U.S. Department of Energy, Energy Information Administration, "Emissions of Greenhouse Gases in the United States 1995: Halocarbons and Other Gases" October 22, 1996 (Washington, D.C.: Government Printing Office, October 22, 1996); H. Josef Herbert, "U.S. Targets Smuggling of Banned Chemical," *Detroit News,* January 10, 1997.
4. Jack Cheevers, "Deep-Sixing CFCs; As Ban Looms, Companies and Consumers Feel Pinch," *Los Angeles Times,* November 8, 1994.
5. Donna Lawrence, "Complaints About Freon-Free A/C Expected to Mount: The Supply of Old Refrigerant Is Likely to Run Out Between 1998 and 2000, the EPA Says," *Atlanta Constitution,* March 29, 1996.
6. "NOAA Releases New Data on South Pole Hole," *New York Times,* October 12, 1997.
7. "Turbid Tap Water May Be Source of Unexplained Intestinal Ailments," *New York Times,* November 4, 1997.
8. *New York Times,* July 12, 1988; March 14 and 16, 1989.
9. Government Accounting Office (GAO), "Pesticide Reregistration May Not Be Completed Until 2006." Report No. GAO/RCED 93-94 (May 1993), iii.
10. *New York Times,* April 15, 1993; GAO, "Widening Gap Between Needs and Available Resources Threatens Vital EPA Program," Report No. GAO/RCED 92-184 (July 1992).
11. *New York Times,* February 21 1993.
12. Environmental Protection Agency (EPA), Office of Policy Planning and Evaluation, *Environmental Progress and Challenges: EPA's Update* (Washington, D.C.: EPA, 1988), 70.
13. Sandra Postel, *Altering the Earth's Chemistry* (Washington, D.C.: Worldwatch Institute, 1986), 7.

14. John E. Boninak, "The Evolution of 'Technology Forcing' in the Clean Air Act," *Environmental Reporter,* Monograph No. 21, July 25, 1975. See also Charles O. Jones, *Clean Air* (Pittsburgh: University of Pittsburgh Press, 1975), chaps. 7 and 8.

15. National Commission on the Environment, *Choosing A Sustainable Future* (Washington, D.C.: Island Press, 1993), xv, 8.

16. J. Clarence Davies and Jan Mazurek, *Regulating Pollution: Does The U.S. System Work?* (Washington, D.C.: Resources for the Future, 1997), 2.

17. Jonathan Lash, Katherine Gillman, and David Sheridan, *A Season of Spoils* (New York: Pergamon, 1984); Susan Tolchin and Martin Tolchin, *The Rush To Deregulate* (Boston: Houghton Mifflin, 1983); Norman J. Vig and Michael E. Kraft, eds., *Environmental Policies in the 1980s* (Washington, D.C.: CQ Press, 1984).

18. Samuel P. Hayes, *Beauty, Truth and Permanence: Environmental Politics in the United States, 1955–1985* (Cambridge: Cambridge University Press, 1987), 525.

19. Council on Environmental Quality (CEQ), *Environmental Quality: The First Annual Report of the Council on Environmental Quality* (Washington, D.C.: Government Printing Office, 1970); CEQ, *Environmental Quality, 1993* (Washington, D.C.: CEQ, 1994).

20. Barry Commoner, *The Closing Circle: Nature, Man and Technology* (New York: Knopf, 1971), chap. 1.

21. Christopher Madison, "Juggling Act," *National Journal,* January 9, 1993, 64.

22. Marvin S. Soroos, "From Stockholm to Rio: The Politics of Global Environmental Governance," in *Environmental Policy in the 1990s,* 2d ed., ed. Norman J. Vig and Michael E. Kraft (Washington, D.C.: CQ Press, 1994), 371.

23. *New York Times,* July 19, 1993.

24. Ibid.

25. *New York Times,* October 12, 1988. See also John J. Cohrssen and Vincent T. Covello, *Risk Analysis: A Guide to Principles and Methods for Analyzing Health and Environmental Risks* (Washington, D.C.: Council on Environmental Quality, 1989), chap. 4.

26. *New York Times,* July 14, 1988.

27. U.S. Department of Commerce, Bureau of the Census, *Statistical Abstract of the United States, 1996* (Washington, D.C.: Government Printing Office, 1997).

28. EPA, Office of Policy Planning and Evaluation, *The Costs of a Clean Environment* (Washington, D.C.: EPA, 1990), v–viii.

29. *New York Times,* August 5, 1993.

30. *New York Times,* July 28, 1988.

31. GAO, "Status of EPA's Reviews of Chemicals Under the Chemical Testing Program," Report No. GAO/RCED 92-31FS (October 1991), 27.

32. GAO, "Improvements Needed in Detecting and Preventing Violations," Report No. GAO/RCED 90-155 (September 1990), 20.

33. *New York Times,* March 20, 1992.

34. Allan Mazur, *The Dynamics of Technical Controversies* (Washington, D.C.: Communications Press, 1981), 29–30.

35. CEQ, *Environmental Quality, 1979* (Washington, D.C.: CEQ, 1980), 218.

36. Christopher Schroeder, "The Evolution of Federal Regulation of Toxic Substances," in *Government and Environmental Politics: Essays on Historical Development Since World War II,* ed. Michael J. Lacey (Lanham , Md.: University Press of America, 1990), 114–140.

37. EPA, *Environmental Investments: A Summary* (Washington, D.C.: EPA, 1990), 2–5.

38. Robert Cameron Mitchell, Angela G Mertig, and Riley E. Dunlap, "Twenty Years of Environmental Mobilization: Trends Among National Environmental Organizations," in *American Environmentalism: The U.S. Environmental Movement, 1970–1990,* ed. Riley E. Dunlap and Angela G Mertig (Philadelphia: Taylor and Francis, 1991), 24.

39. William Ophuls, *Ecology and the Politics of Uncertainty* (San Francisco: W. H. Freeman, 1977), 171.

40. A. Susan Leeson, "Philosophic Implications of the Ecological Crisis: The Authoritarian Challenge to Liberalism," *Polity* 11 (Spring 1979): 305.
41. Michael McClosky, "Twenty Years of Change in the Environmental Movement: An Insider's View," in *American Environmentalism*, ed. Dunlap and Mertig, 78–89.
42. Scott Allen, *Boston Globe*, October 20, 1997.
43. Bill Devall, "Deep Ecology and Radical Environmentalism," in *American Environmentalism*, ed. Dunlap and Mertig, 51–61; G. Sessions, "The Deep Ecology Movement," *Environment Review* 11 (June 1987): 105–125; Rick Scarce, *Eco-Warriors: Understanding the Radical Environmental Movement* (Chicago, Ill.: Noble Press, 1992).
44. Devall, "Deep Ecology and Radical Environmentalism," 55.
45. David Foreman, *Ecodefense* (Tucson: Ned Ludd Books, 1988); G. Grossman, *And On The Eighth Day We Bulldozed It* (San Francisco: Rainbow Action Network, 1988); S. Obst Love and D. Obst Love, ed., *Ecotage* (New York: Bantam Books, 1972); and D. Day, *The Environmental Wars: Reports from the Front Lines* (New York: St. Martin's Press, 1989).
46. Robert Cameron Mitchell, "From Conservation to Environmental Movement: The Development of the Modern Environmental Lobbies," in *Government and Environmental Politics*, ed. Lacey, 213–236.
47. *New York Times*, August 5, 1993.
48. Robert Cameron Mitchell, "Public Opinion and the Green Lobby," in *Environmental Policy in the 1990s*, ed. Norman J. Vig and Michael E. Kraft (Washington, D.C.: CQ Press, 1990), 81–102.
49. *New York Times*, September 16, 1993.
50. George Hoberg, *Pluralism by Design: Environmental Policy and the American Regulatory State* (New York: Praeger, 1992), ix.
51. Ibid., 198–199.
52. Warren T. Brookes, "Here Comes Flat Earth Day," *Detroit News*, March 8, 1990.
53. John H. Adams, "The Mainstream Environmental Movement," *EPA Journal* 18, no. 1 (1992): 25–26.
54. *New York Times*, June 9, 1993.
55. Marc K. Landy and Mary Hague, "The Coalition for Waste: Private Interests and Superfund," in *Environmental Politics: Public Costs, Private Rewards*, ed. Michael S. Greve and Fred L. Smith (New York: Praeger, 1992), 75.
56. Michael McClosky, "Twenty Years of Change in the Environmental Movement," in *American Environmentalism*, ed. Dunlap and Mertig, 86.
57. Michael J. McCann, "Public Interest Liberalism and the Modern Regulatory State," *Polity* 21 (Winter 1988): 373–400.
58. Everett Carll Ladd and Karlyn Bowman, "Public Opinion on the Environment," *Resources* 124 (Summer 1996): 5.
59. Jerry Spangler, "Survey Shows Environmental Values Deeply Rooted," *Desert News*, October 9, 1997; "The Environment," *USA Today*, April 20, 1995.
60. Everett Carll Ladd, "Clearing the Air: Public Opinion and Public Policy on the Environment," *Public Opinion* 5, no. 1 (February–March 1982): 16–20.
61. Paul Mohai, "Black Environmentalism," *Social Science Quarterly* 71, no. 4 (1990): 744–765.
62. Gallup Poll, *The Gallup Poll* (Wilmington, Del.: Scholarly Resources, Inc., 1997).
63. Riley E. Dunlap, "Public Opinion and Environmental Policy," in *Environmental Politics and Policy: Theory and Evidence*, ed. James P. Lester (Durham, N.C.: Duke University Press, 1989), 131.
64. Carll Ladd and Bowman, "Public Opinion on the Environment."
65. Ibid.
66. Gallup Poll, *The Gallup Poll*.
67. Ibid.
68. Carll Ladd and Bowman, "Public Opinion on the Environment," 7.

Suggested Readings

Cahn, Matthew A. *Environmental Deceptions: The Tensions Between Liberalism and Environmental Policymaking in the United States.* Albany: State of New York University Press, 1995.

Davies, J. Clarence, and Jan Mazurek. *Regulating Pollution: Does the U.S. System Work?* Washington, D.C.: Resources for the Future, 1997.

Howard, Philip K. *The Death of Common Sense.* New York: Random House, 1994.

National Commission on the Environment. *Choosing A Sustainable Future.* Washington, D.C.: Island Press, 1993.

Ophuls, William, and A. Stephen Boyan, Jr. *Ecology and the Politics of Scarcity Revisited: The Unraveling of the American Dream.* New York: W. H. Freeman, 1992.

Vig, Norman J., and Michael E. Kraft, eds. *Environmental Policy in the 1990s.* 3d ed. Washington, D.C.: CQ Press, 1997.

Chapter 2

The Politics of Environmental Policy

Mr. Bush told the environmentalists, "I know there is some skepticism about my commitment, but it is real and I am going to surprise you in a good way."
— *New York Times*, December 1, 1988

The White House confirmed today that it had censored Congressional testimony on the effects of global warming by a top Government scientist, but it insisted that the changes reflected policy decisions, not scientific conclusions.
— *New York Times*, May 9, 1989

The Bush administration had been in office less than six months when it blundered into a controversy that seemed to reduce the president's earnest professions of environmental concern to campaign fluff. The occasion was the scheduled testimony of James E. Hansen, director of the Goddard Institute for Space Studies, National Aeronautics and Space Administration (NASA), before the Senate Subcommittee on Science, Technology, and Space on May 8, 1989. Hansen's previous testimony that the Greenhouse Effect was imminent had made him a minor political celebrity. His new testimony on climate warming was expected to draw considerable congressional and media attention again.

But the attention came a day earlier and concerned what Hansen was *not* supposed to say. Newspapers learned that Hansen's testimony had been edited—against his strong objections—by the Office of Management and Budget (OMB), which often reviews proposed congressional testimony by important agency spokespeople. The editing transformed many of Hansen's originally confident predictions about global warming into cautious conjecture. He had intended to tell the subcommittee: "We believe it very unlikely that this overall conclusion . . . [that there will be] drought intensification at most middle- and low-latitude land areas, if

50

greenhouse gases increase rapidly . . . will be modified." [1] Instead, the officials at the OMB insisted that he say:

> Again, I must stress that the rate and magnitude of drought, storm, and temperature change are very sensitive to the many physical processes mentioned above, some of which are poorly represented in . . . models. Thus, these changes should be viewed as estimates from evolving computer models and not as reliable predictions.

He had intended to assure the subcommittee that he and his NASA colleagues who prepared the testimony were "confident that greenhouse gases are primarily of human origin." But the OMB again insisted he state that the relative contribution of human and natural processes to changing climate patterns "remains scientifically unknown."

This was not the first time Hansen and the White House had crossed swords on this issue. Earlier, he had given congressional testimony as a private citizen rather than agree to the insistence of the Reagan White House that he omit from his testimony any recommendation for increased funding for research on climate transformation. This time, however, Hansen went public with his complaints. "It distresses me that they put words in my mouth. They even put it in the first person," he observed. "I should be allowed to say what is my scientific position; there is no rationale by which OMB should be censoring scientific opinion. I can understand changing policy, but not science." [2]

White House representatives quickly asserted that the changes in Hansen's speech reflected policy decisions, that they were not tampering with science, and argued that Hansen's original conclusions were "not necessarily those of all scientists who have considered this matter" and that "there are many points of view on the global warming issue and many of them conflict with those stated by Dr. Hansen." [3] In fact, there was disagreement within the scientific community over many aspects of the climate warming issue. There was little doubt, however, that OMB's guiding inspiration was a determination that Hansen's testimony square with current White House policy stressing the uncertainty of climate warming.

Conflict between the White House and agency scientists over where science ends and politics begins is not peculiar to the Bush administration. Presidents of both parties have usually insisted on a White House prerogative to review all major policy statements before senior bureaucrats deliver them officially. And many scientists in the bureaucracy have objected. Hansen, politically skilled and seasoned, knew how to turn his quarrel into a media event. Moreover, Democrats on the Senate subcommittee seized on the incident to criticize the administration robustly during the committee hearings. Subcommittee Democrats also provided

Hansen with ample opportunity in his subsequent testimony to chastise the OMB for its scientific and ethical bungling.

The event embarrassed the White House. It armed George Bush's critics with new ammunition, appeared to contradict the president's professions of concern for an environmental movement whose goodwill he was cultivating, and revealed confusion in the administration's policy management. While environmental policies usually develop less clumsily, this incident featured some characteristics common to environmental policy making. First, policy making is a process that involves a number of related decisions originating from different institutions and actors ranging across the whole domain of the federal government and private institutions. As Hugh Heclo observed, policy is "a course of action or inaction rather than a specific decision or action."[4] Moreover, policy making is continuous; once made, decisions rarely are immutable. Environmental policy is in some respects fluid and impermanent, always in metamorphosis. Second, policy makers—whether they are of the legislative, White House, or bureaucratic type—can seldom act without restraint. Their discretion is bounded and shaped by many constraints: constitutional separations of power, institutional rules and biases, statutory laws, shared understandings about the "rules of the game" for conflict resolution, inherited culture, and more. These restraints collectively are given in the policy setting, which means government resolves almost all issues in a predictable style. Third, environmental policy making is a volatile mixture of politics and science that readily erupts into controversy among politicians, bureaucrats, and scientists over their appropriate roles in the process, as well as over the proper interpretation and use of scientific data in policy questions.

One useful way to understand public policy, and environmental policy specifically, is to view the process as a cycle of interrelated phases through which policy ordinarily evolves. Each phase involves a different mix of actors, institutions, and constraints. While somewhat simplified, this approach does illuminate particularly well the interrelated flow of decisions and the continual process of creation and modification that characterizes governmental policy development.

The Policy Cycle

Public policies usually develop with reasonable order and predictability. Governmental response to public issues—the business of converting an issue into a policy—customarily begins when an issue can be placed on the governmental agenda. Successful promotion of issues to the agenda does not ensure that public policies will result, but this step initiates the policy cycle. An environmental issue becomes an environmental policy as it passes through several policy phases.

Agenda Setting

Charles O. Jones aptly called this "the politics of getting problems to government."[5] It is the politics of imparting sufficient importance and urgency to an issue so that the government will feel compelled to place the matter on the "official agenda" of government—that is, the "set of items explicitly up for the serious and active consideration of authoritative decision-makers."[6] This means getting environmental issues on legislative calendars, before legislative committees, on a priority list for bill introduction by a senator or representative, on the schedule of a regulatory agency, or among the president's legislative proposals. In brief, getting on the agenda means placing an issue where institutions and individuals with public authority can respond and feel a need to do so. Especially if an environmental issue is technical and somewhat esoteric, its prospects for making the agenda are bleak unless political sponsors are attracted to it. Clarence Davies, a veteran environmental activist and EPA administrator, observed, "New technical information by itself does not significantly influence the political agenda. It must be assisted by some type of political propellent"—an interest group, congressional committee, or the president, for example.[7]

Congressional attention to climate warming was largely produced by astute issue positioning and timing. Hansen's declaration to a congressional committee in mid-1988 that climate warming had already begun immediately vested the issue with prestigious scientific endorsement, instant media exposure, and an air of urgency—a potent political combination. "I've never seen an environmental issue mature so quickly, shifting from science to the policy realm almost overnight," a representative from a major environmental group remarked. "It took a governmental forum during a drought and a heat wave and one scientist . . . saying loudly and clearly what others were saying privately. That's mighty important in the public policy business."[8]

Formulation and Legitimation

The governmental agenda also can be a graveyard for public problems. Few issues reaching the governmental agenda, environmental or otherwise, reach the stage of policy formulation or legitimation. Policy formulation involves setting goals for policy, creating specific plans and proposals for these goals, and selecting the means to implement such plans. Policy formulation in the federal government is especially associated with the presidency and Congress. The State of the Union message and the avalanche of bills annually introduced in Congress represent the most obvious examples of formulated policies. Policies once created must also be legitimated—invested with the authority to evoke public acceptance. This usually is done through constitutional, statutory, or administrative procedures, such as voting, public hearings, presidential orders, or judicial decisions upholding the constitutionality of laws—rituals whose purposes are to signify that policies have now acquired the weight of public authority.

Implementation

Public policies remain statements of intention until they are translated into operational programs. Indeed, the impact of policies largely depends on how they are implemented. What government is doing about environmental problems relates in large part to how the programs have been implemented. Eugene Bardach has compared implementation of public policies with "an assembly process." He writes that it is "as if the original mandate . . . that set the policy or program in motion were a blueprint for a large machine that has to turn out rehabilitated psychotics or healthier old people or better educated children. . . . Putting the machine together and making it run is, at one level, what we mean by the 'implementation' process."[9] Policy implementation involves especially the bureaucracy, whose presence and style shape the impact of all public policies.

Assessment and Reformulation

All the procedures involved in evaluating the social impact of government policies, in judging the desirability of these impacts, and in communicating these judgments to government and the public can be called "policy assessment." Often the federal courts assume an active role in the process, as do the mass media. The White House, Congress, and the bureaucracy continually monitor and assess the impacts of public policy also. As a consequence, once a policy has been formulated, it may pass through many phases of "reformulation." All major institutions of government may play a major role in this process of reformulation.

Policy Termination

The "deliberate conclusion or succession of specific governmental functions, programs, policies or organizations," amounts to policy termination, according to Peter deLeon.[10] Terminating policies, environmental or otherwise, is such a formidable process that most public programs, in spite of intentions to the contrary, become virtually immortal. Policies usually change through repeated reformulation and reassessment.

Policy Making Is a Combination of Phases

Because policy making is a process, the various phases almost always affect each other, an important reason why understanding a policy often requires considering the whole development pattern. For instance, many problems encountered by the EPA when enforcing the Federal Water Pollution Control Act (passed in 1956) arose from congressional failure to define clearly in the law what was meant by a "navigable" waterway to which the legislation explicitly applied. Congress deliberately built in this ambiguity in order to facilitate passage of the extraordinarily complicated legislation. In turn, the EPA sought early opportunities to bring the issue before the federal courts—to compel judicial assessment of the law's intent—so that the Agency might have reliable guidance for its implementation of the provision. Also, many aspects of environmental policy may occur simultaneously. While the EPA was struggling to implement portions of the Superfund legislation allocating grants to the states for cleaning up abandoned toxic waste sites, Congress was considering a reformulation of the law to increase funding authorization to support more state grants.

Constitutional Constraints

The design of governmental power intended two centuries ago for a nation of farmers still rests heavily upon the flow of policy making in a technological age. Like other public policies, environmental programs have been shaped, and complicated, by the enduring constitutional formula.

Checks and Balances

The Madisonian notion of setting "ambition against ambition," which inspired the constitutional structure, creates a government of countervailing and competitive institutions. The system of checks and balances disperses power and authority within the federal government among legislative, executive, and judicial institutions and thereby sows tenacious institutional rivalries repeatedly encountered in discussions of specific environmental laws. Yet, as Richard E. Neustadt observed, these are separated institutions sharing power; effective public policy requires that public officials collaborate by discovering strategies to transcend these institutional conflicts.[11]

The U.S. federal system disperses governmental power by fragmenting authority between national and state governments. Despite the growth of vast federal powers, federalism remains a sturdy constitutional buttress supporting an edifice of authority—shared, independent, and counter-vailing—erected from the states within the federal system. "It is difficult to find any governmental activity which does not involve all three of the so-called 'levels' of the federal system."[12] No government institution monopolizes power. "There has never been a time when it was possible to put neat labels on discrete 'federal,' 'state' and 'local' functions."[13]

Regulatory Federalism

Federalism introduces complexity, jurisdictional rivalries, confusion, and delay into the management of environmental problems. Authority over environmental issues inherently is fragmented among a multitude of different governmental entities. Moreover, almost all new federal regulatory programs since 1970 permit, or require, implementation by the states. Thirty-five states, for instance, currently administer water pollution permits under the Clean Water Act. State implementation of federal laws may vary greatly in scope and detail. Management of water quality in the Colorado River basin, for instance, is enormously complicated because seven different states have conflicting claims on the quantity and quality of Colorado River water to which they are entitled. No overall plan exists for the comprehensive management and protection of the river, and none can exist in this structure of divided and competitive jurisdictions. The federal government often attempts to reduce administrative complications in programs administered through the states by the use of common regulations, guidelines, and other devices to impose consistency in implementation. However, the practical problems of reconciling so many geographic interests within the arena of a single regulatory program often trigger major problems in implementing the programs.

Federal and state collaboration in environmental regulation is often amiable but just as often contentious. Many state authorities believe that numerous environmental problems now federally regulated are best managed by state and local governments. Many such state authorities also resent the expense and administrative difficulty they must endure to implement the numerous environmental laws and regulations they believe the federal government negligently has piled on them. During the 1980s, for example, almost a third of all major federal legislative mandates affecting the states related to environmental issues. During that decade, the EPA regulations to implement these laws are estimated to have cost the states more than $24 billion in state capital expense and operating costs, while federal financial support for these state activities was diminishing.[14]

Organized Interests

The Constitution encourages a robust pluralism of organized interests. Constitutional guarantees for freedom of petition, expression, and assembly promote constant organization and political activism at all governmental levels among thousands of economic, occupational, ethnic, ideological, and geographic interests. To make public policy in the United States requires public officials and institutions to reconcile the conflicting interests of organized groups whose claims not only to influence but to authority in making public policy have resulted in an unwritten constitutional principle. The constitutional architecture of the U.S. government also provides numerous points of access to public power for such groups operating in a fragmented governmental milieu. The political influence broadly distributed across this vast constellation of organized private groups clouds the formal distinction between public and private power.[15] Instead, the course of policy making moves routinely and easily between public institutions and private organizations mobilized for political action.

These constitutional constraints have important implications for environmental policy. It is easier to defeat legislation and other governmental policies than to enact them, to frustrate incisive governmental action on issues than to create it. Further, most policy decisions result from bargaining and compromise among institutions and actors all sharing some portion of diffused power. Formulating policy usually means coalition-building in an effort to engineer consensus by reconciling diverse interests and aggregating sufficient strength among different interests to support effective policies. James DeLong observed:

> Agencies like to achieve consensus on issues and policies. If they cannot bring everyone into the tent, they will try to get enough disparate groups together so as to make the remainder appear unreasonable. If the interested parties are too far apart for even partial consensus, then the agency will try to give everybody something. . . .[16]

Bargaining and compromise often purchase consensus at the cost of disarray and contradiction in the resulting policies. "What happens is not chosen as a solution to a problem but rather results from compromise, conflict and confusion among officials with diverse interests and unequal influence," notes Graham Allison.[17]

Incrementalism

Public officials strongly favor making and changing policy incrementally. "Policy making typically is part of a political process in which the only feasible political change is that which changes social states by relatively small steps," writes Charles A. Lindblom. "Hence, decision makers typically consider, among all the alternative policies that might be imagined to consider, only those relatively few alternatives that represent small or incremental changes from existing policies."[18] In general, such incrementalism favors relying on past experience as a guide for new policies, carefully deliberating before changing policy, and rejecting rapid or comprehensive policy innovation.

Incrementalism is politically seductive. It permits policy makers to draw on their own experiences in the face of unfamiliar problems and encourages the making of small policy adjustments "at the margins" to reduce anticipated, perhaps irreversible, and politically risky consequences. But incrementalism also can become a prison to the imagination by inhibiting policy innovation and stifling new solutions to issues. Especially when officials treat new policy issues as if they were familiar ones and deal with them in the accustomed ways, a futile and possibly dangerous repetition of the past in the face of issues requiring a fresh approach can result.

The Clean Air Act (1970), the National Environmental Policy Act (NEPA) of 1970, and the other innovative legislation of the early 1970s came only after Congress repeatedly failed in dealing with environmental issues incrementally.[19] Beginning with the Water Pollution Control Act of 1956, the first significant effort to define a role for the federal government in pollution abatement, Congress and the White House continued into the late 1960s to write legislation that treated pollution management as a "uniquely local problem" in which a "partnership" between federal and state governments was considered the appropriate model. This deference to the states was a prescription for inaction; few states voluntarily wrote or enforced effective pollution controls. In the Water Quality Act (1965) and the Air Quality Act (1967) Congress prodded the states a bit more vigorously by setting compliance deadlines for state pollution control plans, yet the legislation was so burdened with ambiguities and constraints on federal action that the legislation was ineffective.

By the early 1970s Congress felt compelled to break with this incrementalism. The environmental movement had grown rapidly in political strength. Although to many observers environmentalism appeared to have swept to political prominence in a few months, its rise on the national policy agenda had been prompted by years of increasingly skilled, patient, and persistent promotion by a multitude of groups. The Clean Air Act, for instance, had been supported for almost five years by a national environmental alliance, the Clean Air Coalition, before it achieved national attention. Also, the growing severity of environmental degradation was creating a climate of opinion congenial to aggressive new approaches to pollution abatement. Environmentalists were aided powerfully in their quest for new federal approaches to pollution abatement by the presence of veteran conservationists who assumed crucial congressional positions during this period: Sen. Edmund S. Muskie (D-Maine), Sen. Henry M. Jackson (D-Wash.), Sen. Philip A. Hart (D-Mich.), Rep. Morris Udall (D-Ariz.), Rep. Paul McCloskey (R-Calif.), Rep. Paul Rogers (D-Fla.), and many others. Equally important, environmentalism had become a major media preoccupation.

The time consumed in attempts to attack problems incrementally, the degree of environmental damage necessary to convince Congress that new approaches were needed, and the effort invested by the environmental movement in political action all testify to the tenacity of incrementalism in the policy process. Indeed, one risk in the new environmental programs of the 1970s is that with time they also may settle into an incremental mold resisting necessary changes.

Interest-Group Liberalism

It is an implicit principle in American politics, assumed by most public officials as well as those groups seeking access to them, that organized interests affected by public policy should have an important role in shaping those policies. Few special interests enjoy such a pervasive and unchallenged access to government as business, for reasons soon to be elaborated, but almost all major organized groups enjoy some measure of influence in public institutions. Many officials, in Theodore Lowi's terms, conduct their offices "as if it were supposed to be the practice of dealing only with organized claims in formulating policy, and of dealing exclusively through organized claims in implementing programs." [20]

Structuring Groups into Government

Arrangements exist throughout governmental structures for giving groups access to strategic policy arenas. Lobbying is accepted as a normal, if not essential, arrangement for ensuring organized interests a major role in lawmaking. More than 1,000 advisory committees exist within the federal bureaucracy to give interests affected by policies some access and voice in agency deliberations. Hundreds of large, quasi-public associations bring together legislators, administrators, White House staff, and private group representatives to share policy concerns, thereby blurring the distinction between public and private interests. The National Rivers and Harbors Congress, for example, looks after water resource projects; the Highway Users Federation for Safety and Mobility diligently promotes the Interstate Highway System; and the Atomic Industrial Forum pursues the interests of commercial nuclear power corporations. Successful, organized groups so effectively control the exercise of governmental power that, in Grant McConnell's words, significant portions of American government have witnessed "the conquest of segments of formal state power by private groups and associations." [21] In effect, group activity at all governmental levels has been practiced so widely that it has become part of the constitutional order.

Business: An Unusual Kind and Degree of Control

No interest has exploited the right to take part in the governmental process more pervasively or successfully than has business. In environmental affairs, the sure access of business to government assumes enormous importance, for business is a major regulated interest whose ability to represent itself and secure careful hearing before public agencies and officials often delays or complicates such regulation. But historically and institutionally the influence of business on government has transcended the agencies and officials concerned with environmental affairs. Business traditionally has enjoyed what Lindblom has called a "special relationship" with government.

Business weighs especially heavy in the deliberations of public officials because its leaders collectively manage much of the economy and perform such essential economic functions that the failure of these businesses would produce severe economic disorder and widespread suffering. According to Lindblom

> Government officials know this. They also know that widespread failure of business . . . will bring down the government. A democratically elected government cannot expect to survive in the face of widespread or prolonged distress. . . . Consequently, government policy makers show constant concern about business performance.

So great is this concern that public officials usually give business not all it desires but enough to ensure its profitability. Out of this grows the privileged position of business in government, its widely accepted right to require that government officials often "give business needs precedence over demands from citizens through electoral, party, and interest-group channels." [22]

Business also enjoys more practical political advantages in competition with other interests for access and influence within government: far greater financial resources, greater ease in raising money for political purposes, and an already existing organization available for use in political action. These advantages in strategic resources and salience to public officials do not ensure business uncompromised acceptance of its demands on government nor do they spare it from defeat or frustration by opponents. But business often, if not usually, is able to exploit its privileged status in American politics to ensure that its views are represented early and forcefully in any policy conflicts, its interests are pursued and protected carefully at all policy stages, and its forces are mobilized effectively for long periods of time. These are formidable advantages, often enough to give a decisive edge in competitive struggles with environmental or other interests that do not have the political endurance, skill, or resources to be as resolute in bringing pressure on government when it counts.

Environmentalism's Enlarging Access

Prior to the 1970s environmentalists were at a considerable disadvantage in achieving effective access to government when compared with environmentally regulated interests, particularly business. The environmental lobby could claim, with considerable justification, to be political outsiders when compared to business. However, environmental groups—along with public interest groups, consumer organizations, and others advocating broad public programs—were quick to promote a number of new structural and legal arrangements that enlarged their governmental influence, as noted in Chapter 1. Indeed, these structural and legal arrangements often were created deliberately for the advantage of environmental interests by Congress and administrative agencies. These new arrangements, defended ferociously by environmental organizations against continuing assaults by their political opposition, have diminished greatly the disparities in political access and influence that once so conspicuously distinguished environmentalists from their political opponents. The political season has turned. In the rough calculus of governmental influence, environmentalists may not yet claim parity with organized business. But environmentalism no longer wears comfortably the rags of the politically disadvantaged and the establishment outsider. In the vernacular of Washington, D.C., environmentalists are now a "major player."

Political Feasibility

Veteran Washington, D.C., observer Ralph Huitt asked, "What considerations enter into the selection of priorities and the specific program designed to meet them?" The answer is political feasibility. That means, noted Huitt, "Will it 'go' on the Hill? Will the public buy it? Does it have political 'sex appeal'?"[23] Policy deliberations involve more than calculations of political feasibility, but there is often a large component in them. Political feasibility involves an intuitive and often highly subjective judgment by public officials concerning what policies and programs can be enacted and implemented in some reasonably effective way, given the political realities as they are understood. It is often a judgment quite different from determinations of rationality, economy, or fairness to a policy. The irrationality, vagueness, and apparently sloppy drafting in legislation, environmental or otherwise, are often explicable as efforts to make the laws feasible. Calculations of political feasibility affect presidents, judges, and administrators, as well as legislators in policy making. In short, political feasibility is another test, and another constraint, on policy.

Examples of this constraint abound in environmental policy. Political feasibility convinced Congress, when it enacted the original $18 billion federal sewage treatment grant program in 1972, that it must also provide a statutory allocation formula ensuring every state, regardless of size or need, a guaranteed and substantial minimum authorization to enforce the program. Political feasibility, in the guise of congressional opinion, dissuaded the Reagan administration from attempting to abolish the $20 billion synthetic fuels program authorized under President Carter. Uncounted thousands of executive orders, presidential addresses, congressional bills, and agency regulations have perished unissued because they bore the stigma of political infeasibility.

Policy makers are influenced not only by these general constraints but also by the characteristics of the various governmental institutions that make policy. Each institution has its own characteristic constraints on policy. This is particularly important in understanding environmental policy making in Congress, the bureaucracy, and the courts, in which different institutional constraints—known as "policy styles"—prevail.

The Political Seasons

The political climate of policy making is inconstant, powerful, often fickle. Opportunities to make or change policy shift continually, often unpredictably, with a transformed political season. At any given time, there will be differences between what policy makers want and what they can accomplish, between what they are compelled to do and what they would prefer to do, between what is feasible and what is not. This ebb and flow of opportunity is created by different circumstances. The most important include changes in the partisan control of governmental institutions, transient shifts of public mood, and major economic change. These can be called the changing "seasons" of policy making.

Changing Party Majorities

The balance of party strength within Congress and between Congress and the White House powerfully shapes the substance and opportunities for environmental policy making. In theory, opportunities to make or change policy are greatest when the White House and Congress are controlled by the same party. However, since 1970 Republicans have usually occupied the White House and Democratic majorities have controlled both congressional chambers. The floodtide of environmental legislation originating in Washington, D.C., during the 1970s was, in large part, the result of a broad, bipartisan environmental coalition in both chambers that strongly supported innovative environmental programs proposed or accepted by both Republican and Democratic presidents. The political climate for environmentalists darkened markedly with Reagan's election and remains unsettled ever since. The eight years under Reagan were made up of conflict and impasse between a president and Congress dominated by different parties and committed to radically different policy agendas.

During the early Reagan era, Democratic control of the House of Representatives largely prevented the administration from passing in that chamber the manifold changes in existing environmental laws it had pledged to accomplish in the name of "regulatory relief." Even when the Republicans enjoyed a brief, tenuous Senate majority from 1980 through 1984, Democrats controlling the major House environmental committees mounted a fierce campaign of investigations, budget reviews, and other forays against Secretary of the Interior James Watt, EPA administrator Anne Burford, and other important Republicans in environmentally sensitive positions; this threw the Republicans on the defensive and turned much of the media and public opinion against Reagan's most ambitious attempts at regulatory relief. The return of a Democratic Senate majority in 1984 again vested committee control in that chamber to Reagan's opposition. So effective was the congressional Democratic majority in frustrating Reagan's environmental agenda that by the end of Reagan's first term the administration largely had abandoned the legislative strategy for regulatory relief and relied instead on achieving what it could of its reforms through the administrative channels available to the president as the chief executive.

Reagan's enormous impact on environmental policy making in the 1980s is evidence, however, that in the hands of a politically skilled president with a clear policy agenda, White House resources can be fashioned into a potent policy-making instrument, with or without congressional cooperation. Reagan's impact on environmental policy was achieved largely by an aggressive, imaginative use of the executive powers inherent in the presidential office, a strategy followed as well by his successor, George Bush. Presidential authority to appoint upper- and middle-level administrators of agencies with major environmental responsibilities, such as the EPA and the Department of the Interior, was used to place administrators committed to regulatory reform in policy-sensitive positions in which they could affect daily administrative implementation of environmental laws through their discretionary authority. During the Reagan years, especially, these administrators were able to obstruct and revise many environmental regulations so effectively that the administration's environmental goals were at least partially achieved without any congressional cooperation. Further, Reagan used the budget and the OMB to reduce personnel and financial resources available for many environmental programs and to change priorities among them through shifting budget allocations.

With the exception of EPA administrator William K. Reilly, the Bush administration's environmentally important appointments generally went to persons sympathetic to the Reagan-Bush regulatory reform agenda and thereby objectionable to most environmental organizations. As with Reagan, Bush used the authority of the executive office, especially the OMB, to revise, delay, or defeat numerous environmental regulations ideologically unacceptable to the administration. Among the Bush cabinet and staff, the EPA's Reilly was the odd-man-out on environmental issues. The chill blowing toward the EPA from the White House was unmistakable, a continuing and effective obstacle to many environmental policy initiatives from Congress or the bureaucracy. Thus, President Bush, like his predecessor, used to great advantage a strategy of selective neglect to delay or prevent the advance of many environmental issues to national importance by denying them a place on his legislative agenda, by discouraging their promotion in legislative priority, and by ignoring them in his public presentations.

The Democrat's return to the White House with Bill Clinton's 1992 presidential victory became less the prelude to the brightening political future anticipated by environmentalists than a false dawn. Much of the explanation lay in the stunning Republican congressional victories of 1994 that returned a Republican majority to both congressional chambers and elevated to its leadership a cadre of Republicans outspokenly unsympathetic to most of the major environmental legislation created by Congress in the previous two decades. Fortified with comfortable majorities in both chambers, and cheered on by a large delegation of newly elected congressional Republicans, especially from the West, who attributed their victories to their virulent anti-environmentalism, the Republican leadership sponsored a multitude of new legislative proposals—part of what they called their "Contract With America"—which would have radically recast, and usually enfeebled, most of the major environmental laws written during the 1970s and 1980s.

These early Republican initiatives failed, largely because more moderate voices in both parties, as well the public opinion polls, convinced the Republican leadership that radical anti-environmentalism would ultimately be politically disastrous for the party image and for its 1996 congressional candidates. Nonetheless, Republican militants were articulating a genuine, if more restrained, congressional and public dissatisfaction with the progress of environmental governance that seemed to demand some kind of significant reform. The immediate impact of the 1994 congressional elections was several years of unusually malevolent, and ultimately unproductive, confrontation between the congressional critics of most existing federal environmental legislation and environmentalists, their congressional allies, and the Clinton White House. Environmentalists were again on the defensive. The president, facing a Republican-controlled Congress and unable or unwilling to promote an aggressive environmental agenda, seemed content to protect existing environmental programs rather than to advance vigorously a new environmental agenda. The 1996 national elections did little to change the president's strategic position with Congress. The Republican militants moderated their congressional agenda but the White House maintained a largely passive, reactive stance in environmental matters even as the president continued to assert vigorously his commitment to environmentalism. While many environmentalists repeatedly criticized Clinton and Vice President Al Gore for an indifferent environmental record through 1997, one major reason for the president's apparently lackluster environmental performance was the constraints imposed upon him by the congressional impotence of his own party.

Shifting Public Moods

"When President Nixon and his staff walked in the White House on January 20, 1969, we were totally unprepared for the tidal wave of public opinion in favor of cleaning up the nation's environment that was about to engulf us," John C. Whittaker, one of Nixon's close advisors, remembered. Congress was quicker to read the political prophecy in the polls.[24] By Earth Day, recalled the same advisor, "so many politicians were on the stump that Congress was forced to close down."[25] The Nixon administration's ecological indifference evaporated when the White House discovered the political capital to be made from environmentalism. The administration's many legislative proposals and executive acts intended to promote environmental protection, such as creating the EPA and issuing executive orders to halt public works projects alleged to be environmentally dangerous, were strongly influenced by surging public interest in environmental protection. This has been the political reality since. Presidents and Congress alike feel enormous political pressure to respond when confronted by broad public majorities demonstrating a strong interest, or apprehension, about an environmental issue.

The pressure to do something, or to look as if something is being done, is irresistible when sudden spikes of public apprehension rise in the aftermath of a well-publicized environmental crisis. Many major environmental laws and regulations are direct responses to environmental disasters, real or threatened. The Three Mile Island nuclear reactor accident of 1978 begot new regulations from the Nuclear Regulatory Commission (NRC) increasing the requirements for emergency planning at commercial nuclear power plants; the Love Canal toxic waste discoveries inspired the Superfund legislation. The tragic 1984 chemical plant disaster at Bhopal, India, in which 5,000 nearby residents and plant workers lost their lives, almost alone produced the 1986 community "right to know" amendment to the Superfund legislation requiring that industries using dangerous chemicals disclose the type and amount of these chemicals to individuals living within an area likely to be affected by an accident on site. "The Bhopal train was leaving the station," observed one environmental lobbyist about Congress, "and we got the kind of legislation we could put on the train." [26]

This hypersensitivity to public opinion is criticized frequently because it sometimes results in hastily written laws difficult to implement. According to economists Robert W. Crandall and Paul R. Portney, "Congress bears a large share of the responsibility for the problems of environmental regulation. Congress has passed enabling statutes containing unrealistic deadlines and an unnecessary degree of specificity with respect to the standards that [agencies] must issue." [27] The congressional penchant for writing environmental legislation bristling with mandatory deadlines and "hammer" clauses that appear to demonstrate toughness about pollution often has hobbled governmental efforts to deal with environmental ills. Nonetheless, it is difficult for presidents and legislators to take a longer time and more deliberate approach to ecological problems when issues acquire the guise of a public crisis.

Opinion can also become an obstacle to environmental policy making when the public mood is inhospitable to action. The disappearance of gasoline and petroleum shortages in the late 1970s, and other evidence that the "energy crisis" was passing, quickly removed energy problems from public concern and thwarted efforts by the Carter administration to pass new energy regulatory programs after mid-1978. By the time the Reagan administration finished its first term, Congress no longer felt pressure to continue mandatory plans for national fuel rationing, to require increased fuel economy standards for automobiles after 1986, or to promote solar technologies and other fuel conservation measures. Advocates of environmental issues often must wait until the opinion climate is ripe in order to move the White House or Congress to action. Crisis or disaster may sometimes be the only force that moves the political will.

Economic Change

In all environmental policy making, economics is the counterpoint to ecology. The impact of environmental policies on the economy is a continual preoccupation of both environmental regulators and the regulated. Economic conditions, in turn, influence environmental policy making.

The economic impact of environmental regulations is a continual issue in all discussions of environmental policy. Concern most often focuses on whether environmental regulation will inhibit expansion of the gross national product (GNP), how regulations will affect business investments and the market position of firms or industries, and whether regulatory costs are inflationary. Regulated interests frequently assert that specific policies will have most, or all, of these negative effects, while proponents of regulation usually claim no such negative effects will occur. Data wars erupt: each side summons its economists and econometrics to vindicate its position and discredit the opposition. While the result of these conflicts is often inconclusive, the issues are vitally important. Policies that appear (or can be made to appear) to adversely affect economic growth, market positions, or business investment are likely to command greater and more critical attention from policy makers than those appearing more economically benign. In times of economic recession or depression, the economic impact of policies can become the major determinant of their survival.

Environmental regulations, in any case, do create major public and private costs. Between 1980 and 1989, U.S. public and private expenditures for pollution abatement and control exceeded $546.4 billion. About 60 percent of this bill was paid by the private sector.[28] In general, studies suggest that new capital spending for pollution control by public and private sectors has not significantly deterred growth of the GNP or contributed much to inflation or a rise in the Consumer Price Index (CPI). For most industries, spending for pollution control has been a gradually diminishing portion of new capital investment over the past two decades. In 1990, spending on pollution control by businesses was estimated at 2.8 percent of all capital investment, a figure expected to diminish to 1.7 percent by the year 2000.[29]

Economic conditions affect environmental policy making in several ways. Most important, the mix of economic activities in the United States largely determines the character and magnitude of the nation's pollution problems and the kinds of stress placed on its resource base. As the U.S. economy moves away from heavy dependence on manufacturing, the mix of environmental stresses changes. Between 1950 and the late 1980s, employment in U.S. manufacturing declined from 50 percent of the work force to 32 percent, while employment in service and high-technology sectors climbed to about 51 percent of the labor force. This manufacturing decline reduced the air pollution emissions from U.S. industry, but increased the volume of solid and hazardous waste generated nationally. In the past two decades, the greatest stress on regional resources produced by economic growth has occurred in the South and West.

Perhaps no technology has created more environmental stress than the automobile. In the United States there is one automobile for every two Americans, the highest density of automobiles to people in the world; each auto will be driven on average 10,000 miles annually. The U.S. transportation sector accounts for approximately 63 percent of the nation's petroleum consumption. It is a major source of air pollution emissions and contributes significantly to water pollution through groundwater contamination from leaks at refineries and service stations, creates major solid waste problems, and encourages urban blight and growth management difficulties.

It is assumed by most theorists that a major economic recession, depression, or serious bout with inflation would profoundly affect environmental regulation. The United States has experienced no major depression and only a few short recessions since the 1970s. The serious inflation of the 1978–1983 period, intensified by rising energy prices associated with the so-called energy crisis of the mid-1970s, did not appear to create a political climate hostile to environmental regulation. However, the economic recession beginning in 1989 and the sluggish recovery in the early 1990s affected the environmental agendas of the Bush and Clinton administrations. The economic malaise all but extinguished the Bush administration's mild enthusiasm for environmental policy innovation after 1990 and—much to the disappointment of environmentalists—inhibited the scope of environmental reforms initiated by the Clinton administration despite the president's campaign commitment to aggressive environmentalism.

The Institutional Setting

In the United States the tasks of policy formulation, implementation, and assessment are invested largely in the White House, Congress, bureaucracy, and courts. Because the latter three institutions play such a prominent role in environmental policy making, the institutional bias characteristic of each assumes a crucial role in explaining the federal response to environmental issues.

Congress: Policy Formulation by Fragmentation

The Constitution invests Congress with the principal legislative powers in the federal government. While twentieth-century realities compel the president, bureaucracy, and courts to share these powers, Congress remains preeminent in policy formulation and legitimation. Despite the panoply of party organizations, legislative leaders, and coordinating committees, Congress remains largely an institution of fragmented powers and divided geographic loyalties. Legislative power is dispersed in both chambers among a multitude of committees and subcommittees; local or regional concerns often tenaciously claim legislative loyalties. The electoral cycle intrudes imperiously on policy deliberations. The public interest and legislative objectivity compete with equally insistent legislative concerns to deliver something, if possible, from Washington to the "folks back home." In environmental affairs, Congress is an assembly of scientific amateurs that must enact programs of great technical complexity to ameliorate scientifically complicated environmental ills most legislators dimly understand.

Committee Decentralization. Congress has been described as a "kind of confederation of little legislatures." [30] In both chambers the committees and subcommittees—those little legislatures wielding the most consistently effective power in the legislative system—are dispersed and competitive in environmental matters. William Ruckelshaus, the EPA's first administrator, complained in the early 1970s that he had to deal with sixteen different congressional subcommittees. [31] The situation has gotten worse. Today, fourteen of twenty-two standing House committees share some jurisdiction over environmental policy.

In the Senate, eleven committees and several dozen subcommittees share jurisdiction over environmentally sensitive energy issues. Water policy is even more decentralized: seventy congressional committees and subcommittees share some jurisdiction. (The array of committees and their environmental jurisdictions are indicated in "Congressional Committees and their Jurisdictions.") With authority over environmental policy fragmented among a multitude of committees in each chamber, competition and jurisdictional rivalry commonly occur as each committee attempts to assert some influence over environmental programs. The result is that, as a rule, environmental legislation evolves only through protracted bargaining and compromising among the many committees. This time-consuming process often results in legislation that is vague or inconsistent. Divided jurisdictions, however, provide different interest groups with some point of committee access during environmental policy formulation, and consequently these groups resist efforts to reduce the number of committees with overlapping jurisdictions and concentrate authority in a few major committees.

Localism.   During a crucial Senate vote on funding the highly controversial, multimillion-dollar Tennessee-Tombigbee Waterway, a reporter was impressed by what he called "the unabashed display of horse trading among Senators not wanting to endanger their own project."[32] Funding finally passed because many senators of both parties had bartered their support for the project in return for assurances that project proponents would return the favor when other projects were considered. "But that's nothing new," according to Sen. Howell Heflin (D-Ala.). "It's happened in the United States Senate since the beginning."[33]

The Senate's unapologetic loyalty to reciprocity in voting for local public works projects, known as political pork, is driven by a powerful tradition of localism in congressional voting. In American political culture, legislators are treated by constituents—and regard themselves—as ambassadors to Washington, D.C., from their own geographic areas. They are expected to acquire skills in the practice of pork-barrel politics, capturing federal goods and services for the constituency. They are also expected to be vigilant in promoting and protecting local interests in the national policy arena. Congressional tenure is more likely to depend on a legislator's ability to serve these local interests than on other legislative achievements. While not the only influence on congressional voting, such politics is deeply rooted and probably the single most compelling force in shaping voting decisions.

This localism affects environmental policy in different ways. By encouraging legislators to view environmental proposals first through the lens of local interests, it often weakens sensitivity to national needs and interests. At worst it drives legislators to judge the merits of environmental policies almost solely by their impact on frequently small and atypical constituencies. The Reagan administration learned about the costs of failing to recognize legislators' instinctive localism when, through the Department of the Interior, in late 1981 it proposed the approval of two lease applications for oil exploration in the Los Padres National Forest near Big Sur, one of California's most spectacular coastal vistas. The White House found itself confronting united opposition—

regardless of party affiliation—from the entire twenty-two-member California House delegation. Geographic loyalty, therefore, awakened by fear of environmental devastation to Big Sur, united California Republicans with the opposition Democrats and against their own party.

Localism also whets the congressional appetite for federal distributive programs freighted with local benefits. An aroma of political pork can add appeal to an environmental program, especially if other important local issues are involved. This lesson is not lost on the environmental bureaucracies. For instance, when opposition by the powerful House Ways and Means Committee appeared to threaten defeat for the initial Superfund legislation, a program strongly supported by the EPA, the Agency worked with sympathetic congressional staff members to create a list of prospective Superfund sites in each committee member's district. The committee members were thereby reminded of the "ticking time bombs" in their districts *and* of the potentially great financial benefits from cleanup activities—an almost irresistible double-dose of localism.[34] It is not surprising that federal grants to build pollution control facilities, such as sewage treatment plants, also have instant appeal. Even the comparatively tiny federal program for such grants to the states in the mid-1960s had great appeal. "The program was immensely popular. . . . Congressmen enjoyed the publicity and credit they received every time they announced another grant for another community in their district."[35] The huge $18 billion waste treatment facilities program authorized in 1972, the second largest public works program in U.S. history, was even more popular. After ten years, the $10.5 billion obligated under the program had generated 4.5 million worker-years of employment supporting about 7.3 million Americans. The EPA estimated that for every $1 billion spent, about 50,900 worker-years of employment would be generated in plant and sewer construction.[36]

Elections.   The electoral cycle also dominates the legislative mind. The constitutionally mandated electoral cycles of the federal government—two years, four years, six years—partition the time available for legislative deliberation into periods bound by different elections. Within these time frames, policy decisions are continually analyzed for their electoral implications and often valued largely for electoral impacts. This affects congressional policy styles in several ways. First, the short term becomes more important than the long term when evaluating programs; legislators often attribute more importance to a program's impact on the next election than to its longer-term effects on unborn generations. Second, policies are tested continually against public opinion. While a weak or badly divided public opinion often can be ignored, a coherent majority opinion related to an environmental issue usually wields significant influence on congressional voting, especially when legislators can associ-

Congressional Committees and Their Jurisdictions

The following are congressional committees with jurisdiction over environmentally related programs for which each committee is responsible.

House of Representatives, 105th Congress

House Committee on Agriculture
  Subcommittee on Department Operations, Nutrition, and Foreign Agriculture
  Subcommittee on Resources Conservation, Research, and Forestry
House Committee on Appropriations
  Subcommittee on VA, HUD, and Independent Agencies
House Committee on Commerce
  Subcommittee on Commerce, Trade, and Hazardous Materials
  Subcommittee on Energy and Power
  Subcommittee on Health and Environment
House Committee on Government Reform and Oversight
  Subcommittee on National Economic Growth, Natural Resources, and Regulatory
    Affairs
House Committee on Resources
  Subcommittee on National Parks, Forests, and Lands
  Subcommittee on Fisheries, Wildlife, and Oceans
  Subcommittee on Energy and Mineral Resources
  Subcommittee on Water and Power Resources
  Subcommittee on Native American and Insular Affairs
House Committee on Science
  Subcommittee on Energy and the Environment
House Committee on Transportation and Infrastructure
  Subcommittee on Coast Guard and Maritime Transportation
  Subcommittee on Surface Transportation
  Subcommittee on Water Resources and Environment

Senate, 105th Congress

Senate Committee on Agriculture, Nutrition, and Forestry
  Subcommittee on Forestry, Conservation, and Rural Revitalization
  Subcommittee on Research, Nutrition, and General Legislation
Senate Committee on Appropriations
  Subcommittee on Veterans' Affairs, HUD, and Independent Agencies
Senate Committee on Commerce, Science, and Transportation
  Subcommittee on Surface Transportation and Merchant Marine
  Subcommittee on Oceans and Fisheries
  Subcommittee on Science, Technology, and Space
Senate Committee on Energy and Natural Resources
  Subcommittee on Energy Production and Regulations
  Subcommittee on Energy Research and Development
  Subcommittee on Forests and Public Land Management
  Subcommittee on Parks, Historic Preservation, and Recreation
Senate Committee on Environment and Public Works
  Subcommittee on Transportation and Infrastructure
  Subcommittee on Superfund, Waste Control, and Risk Assessment

Subcommittee on Clean Air, Wetlands, Private Property, and Nuclear Safety
Subcommittee on Drinking Water, Fisheries, and Wildlife
Senate Committee on Governmental Affairs
Subcommittee on Oversight of Government Management and the District of Columbia

Total number of committees with jurisdiction over EPA: 13
Total number of subcommittees with jurisdiction over EPA: 31

Source: National Academy of Public Administration, *Setting Priorities, Getting Results: A New Direction for EPA* (Washington, D.C.: National Academy of Public Administration, 1995), 124–125.

ate the opinion with their own constituencies. Hazardous waste cleanup programs, for example, are hard to oppose whatever their actual merits because the "ticking time bomb" has become a durable, powerful public metaphor in practically every constituency.

Bureaucracy: Power Through Implementation

Federal agencies concerned with environmental affairs and closely related matters such as energy, consumer protection, and worker health have grown explosively in the past three decades. More than 150 major new federal laws, most concerned with broad regulation of business and the economy in the interest of public health and safety, have been enacted since 1970. More than twenty new regulatory agencies have been created to implement these programs, including the EPA, the Occupational Safety and Health Administration (OSHA), and the Department of the Interior's Office of Surface Mining Reclamation and Enforcement.

The Power of Discretion. The significance of the environmental agencies mentioned in the previous section rests less on their size and budget than on the political realities obscured by a constitutional illusion. The Constitution *appears* to vest the power to formulate policy primarily in Congress, while leaving to the president and the executive branch the task of seeing that the laws are "faithfully executed." Although implemented and enforced principally in the bureaucracy, public policy actually develops in both branches of the government.

Delegated authority and administrative discretion are the wellsprings of bureaucratic power. Congress routinely invests administrators with responsibility for making a multitude of decisions it cannot or will not make itself about the implementation of policy; often this becomes legislative power delegated to the executive branch. Even when delegation is not clearly intended, administrators assume the power to make public

Federal Agencies with Environmental Regulatory Responsibility

The following federal agencies share regulatory responsibility in matters concerning environmental and occupational health.

Agricultural Stabilization and Conservation Service. Administers various voluntary land-use programs to protect, expand, and conserve farmlands, wetlands, and forests. *(Agriculture Department)*

Army Corps of Engineers. Regulates all construction projects in navigable waterways; promulgates regulations governing the transportation and dumping of dredged materials in navigable waters; develops, plans, and builds various structures to protect areas from floods, supply water for municipal and industrial use, create recreational areas, improve water and wildlife quality, and protect the shorelines of oceans and lakes. *(Defense Department)*

Bureau of Land Management. Administers public lands located mainly in the western United States and Alaska. Resources managed include timber, minerals, oil and gas, geothermal energy, wildlife habitats, endangered plant and animal species, rangeland vegetation, recreation areas, wild and scenic rivers, wild horses and burros, designated conservation and wilderness areas, and open-space lands. *(Interior Department)*

Consumer Product Safety Commission. Establishes mandatory safety standards governing the design, construction, contents, performance, and labeling of consumer products; develops rules and regulations to enforce standards. Hazard-related programs include acute chemical and environmental hazards.

Federal Aviation Administration. Establishes and enforces rules and regulations for civil aviation safety standards, including noise and exhaust emissions from aircraft (in cooperation with the EPA). *(Transportation Department)*

Federal Energy Regulatory Commission. Issues licenses for hydroelectric power; provides for recreational opportunities, flood control, and the efficient and safe operation of project dams. *(Energy Department)*

Federal Highway Administration. Sets functional safety standards for the design, construction, and maintenance of highways; establishes safety standards for commercial motor carriers in interstate or foreign commerce; regulates the movement of dangerous cargoes on highways and administers programs to reduce motor carrier noise. *(Transportation Department)*

Federal Maritime Commission. Certifies the financial responsibility of vessels that carry oil or other hazardous material to cover costs of cleaning up spills in navigable waters.

Federal Trade Commission. Protects the public from false and deceptive advertising, particularly involving food, drugs, cosmetics, and therapeutic devices. Issues report on tar and nicotine contents of cigarettes.

Food and Drug Administration. Administers laws to ensure the purity and safety of foods, drugs, and cosmetics. Develops programs to reduce human exposure to radiation; conducts research on the effects of radiation exposure and toxic chemical substances found in the environment. *(Health and Human Services Department)*

Materials Transportation Bureau. Develops and enforces operating safety regulations for the transportation of all materials by pipeline; carries out inspection, compliance, and enforcement actions for transport of all hazardous materials (including radioactive materials) by air, water, highway, and rail. *(Transportation Department)*

Mine Safety and Health Administration. Develops, promulgates, and ensures compliance with mandatory mine safety and health standards. *(Labor Department)*

National Bureau of Standards. Researches and provides technical information on the protection of public health and safety, environmental quality, industrial productivity, and the promotion of better materials use. *(Commerce Department)*

National Institute for Occupational Safety and Health. Researches and develops occupational safety and health standards. *(Department of Health and Human Services)*

National Oceanic and Atmospheric Administration. Describes, monitors, and predicts conditions in the atmosphere, ocean, sun, and space environment; disseminates environmental data through meteorological, oceanographic, geophysical, and solar-terrestrial data centers; manages and conserves living marine resources and their habitats, including certain endangered species and marine mammals. *(Commerce Department)*

National Park Service. Administers programs to conserve the scenery, natural and historic objects, and wildlife in the nation's parks. *(Interior Department)*

National Transportation Safety Board. Investigates and reports on the transportation of hazardous materials. *(Transportation Department)*

Nuclear Regulatory Commission. Licenses the construction and operation of nuclear reactors and other facilities; licenses the possession, use, transportation, handling, and disposal of nuclear materials.

Office of Conservation and Renewable Energy. Directs energy conservation programs; expands use of biomass, alcohol fuels, and urban waste; studies effects of acid rain and carbon dioxide associated with coal burning. *(Energy Department)*

Office of Surface Mining Reclamation and Enforcement. Protects against the adverse effects of coal mining operations; establishes minimum standards for regulating effects of surface coal mining; promotes reclamation of previously mined lands. *(Interior Department)*

Office of Water Research and Technology. Supervises the nation's water quality and quantity; researches controls for the quality and quantity of groundwater and surface water, conservation techniques and technologies, protection of fragile water ecosystems, and water management planning. *(Interior Department)*

Soil Conservation Service. Administers program to develop and conserve soil and water resources; offers technical assistance on agricultural pollution control and environmental improvement projects. *(Agriculture Department)*

U.S. Coast Guard. Works with Materials Transportation Bureau to ensure that shipowners clean up oil or hazardous materials discharged into navigable waters. *(Transportation Department)*

U.S. Fish and Wildlife Service. Regulates the development, protection, rearing, and stocking of wildlife resources and their habitats; protects migratory and game birds, fish and wildlife, endangered and threatened species; enforces regulations for hunters of migratory waterfowl; preserves wetlands as natural habitats. *(Interior Department)*

U.S. Forest Service. Manages the national forests and grasslands; regulates the use of forest resources and the activities of commercial foresters working in national forests. *(Interior Department)*

U.S. Geological Survey. Classifies and manages mineral and water resources on federal lands, including the outer continental shelf. Maintains the Earth Resources Observation System Data Center which conducts and sponsors research to apply data findings in mapping, geography, mineral and land resources, water resources, rangeland, and wildlife and environmental monitoring. *(Interior Department)*

Water and Power Resources Service. Develops and manages water and power resources in the western states. Projects include flood control, river regulation, outdoor recreation, fish and wildlife enhancement, and water-quality improvement. *(Interior Department)*

Source: Environment and Health (Washington, D.C.: Congressional Quarterly, 1981), 130–131.

policy when they choose how to implement policies permitting different options—hence the existence of administrative discretion. Consider, for instance, how delegated authority and administrative discretion coalesce as the Forest Service deals with routine responsibilities. In recommending approval of leases for mining exploration in Los Padres National Forest, the U.S. Forest Service must decide if roads to drilling sites are "potentially erodible," and whether each drilling site lies in "unstable bedrock." The Forest Service landscape architects and area supervisors must also approve the location of drilling and other exploration equipment, the routes of all drilling roads, and the types of vehicle used.[37]

Congress and the president, using a variety of constitutional and statutory powers, attempt to discipline the exercise of administrative discretion. Congress usually includes with its grants of delegated authority a great many statutory guidelines intended to give administrators various criteria for the exercise of authority. Congress may assert its inherent powers of legislative oversight, budget review and authorization, legislative investigation, as well as other powers to ensure administrative responsibility in program implementation. The White House staff, drawing on the president's powers as chief executive and many congressionally delegated powers, can influence administrative discretion. Still this oversight holds no certain rein on administrative discretion, particularly in light of the vast number and complexity of environmental programs, the elephantine size of the bureaucracy, and competing demands on presidential and congressional time.

A commonplace example can illustrate the pervasive problem of controlling administrative discretion. In 1981, President Reagan ordered all federal administrative agencies to prepare a "Regulatory Impact Analysis" (RIA)—a type of benefit/cost assessment—for most of their new regulatory proposals and left to his own administrative management agency, the OMB, the responsibility to draft guidelines for the agencies. The OMB, in turn, interpreted the president's order as requiring the responsible agencies, such as EPA, to include in each of its assessments an evaluation of alternatives to the proposed regulation. The EPA, for its part, issued guidelines to each of its offices recommending that at least four alternatives be considered for each proposed new regulation. A review of RIAs prepared by one EPA office in mid-1997 suggests that the intent of the original White House directive had been significantly adulterated by this trickle-down of discretionary authority from White House to EPA. Of the twenty-three assessments studied, six examined only one alternative to the proposed regulation. The rest compared two or more alternatives to the proposed regulation but weren't always clear about how many alternatives or which types were involved. In no instance had any agency in the chain of command violated law, nor was there evidence of intent to do so.[38] Still, the documents ultimately prepared by EPA appeared to disregard in many respects the intent of the original White House directive. Whatever the interpretation, the flow of discretionary authority and its compounding influence throughout government, for good and ill, will be reality, in all seasons, for all presidents, all parties. The federal bureaucracy, assured of generous discretionary authority well into the future, will continue to be an independent and largely self-regulated influence in environmental policy.

Bureaucratic Competitiveness.   The bureaucracy is no monolith. Its powers in environmental affairs, although collectively vast, also are dispersed and competitive. One source of this fragmentation is the federalizing of environmental administration. Many major environmental laws enacted in Washington, D.C., are administered partially or wholly through state governments; others give states an option to participate. Under the Federal Water Pollution Control Act, for instance, twenty-seven states currently administer their own water pollution permit systems; all but six states and the District of Columbia administer the Safe Drinking Water Act. The Clean Air Act permits the states to participate in several major aspects of the program, including the control of pollutants and the establishment of emission standards for stationary sources.

Another cause of fragmented administrative authority is the chronic division and overlapping responsibility for environmental programs among federal agencies. Twenty-seven separate federal agencies share major regulatory responsibility in environmental and occupational health (see "Federal Agencies with Environmental Regulatory Responsibility"). Regulating even a single pollutant often necessitates what might appear to be a bureaucratic convention. Toxic substances currently are regulated under twenty different federal statutes involving five agencies. To address all the problems in human exposure to vinyl chloride, for example, would require the collaboration of all five agencies working with fifteen different laws.[39]

Dispersed authority breeds conflict and competition among agencies and their political allies over program implementation, authority, and resources—the "turf fighting" familiar to students of bureaucracy. While collaboration is common, it is never dependable. State environmental agencies often disagree with federal agencies and among themselves over the proper implementation of the same program. Such a disagreement prompted nine states to sue the EPA in mid-1993 in order to compel the Agency to issue overdue regulations defining the standards the states must follow in issuing pollution permits. No state wanted to take the initiative.[40]

Federal agencies are notoriously fitful collaborators in environmental affairs. The Department of Energy (DOE), for instance, resisted for decades efforts by the EPA and the Nuclear Regulatory Commission to regulate the military nuclear weapons facilities under its jurisdiction. In 1993, the DOE ended years of bureaucratic bickering and litigation by agreeing to pay a $500,000 fine to the EPA for failing to meet a deadline in cleaning up its Fernald, Ohio, nuclear weapons facility—an unusual instance of the government fining itself.[41] Historic conflicts have prevailed between the Forest Service in the Department of Agriculture and the Bureau of Land Management in the Department of the Interior over forest management practices on public lands.

Among environmental bureaucracies, as elsewhere in the executive branch, turf fights are as common as paper clips. In this milieu of dispersed and competitive agency authority, policy implementation often becomes a continual process of collaboration and conflict between coalitions of agencies and their allies shaping and reshaping policy as the relative strengths of the conflicting alignments change. Moreover, administrative conflict crosses the institutional divisions of the federal government, spreads downward through the federal system to state and local governments, and outward from government to organized private groups. Indeed, agencies failing to enlist diverse and active allies in their policy struggles may frustrate their own missions and leave their futures hostage to more politically skilled opponents.

The Courts: The Role of Appraisal

Federal judges actively participate in the environmental policy process in several ways. They continually interpret environmental law, an inevitable task in light of the ambiguities and silences common to environmental legislation. This statutory interpretation often amounts to policy making by the judicial branch. Judges also attempt to ensure that agencies discharge their mandated responsibilities under environmental legislation and otherwise comply with administrative obligations. In addition, the federal courts enforce the Administrative Procedures Act (1946), the code of administrative procedures applicable to all federal agencies. Finally, the courts ensure that environmental laws and their administrative implementation comply with constitutional standards. As the volume of environmental litigation expands relentlessly, federal judges find themselves increasingly at the pulse points of environmental policy making. While critics have argued that federal judges are not prepared by a legal education for this pivotal role in adjudicating complex scientific and economic issues, the trend seems inexorable.

The Courts and Environmental Policy.   The impact of the federal courts on environmental policy has changed over the decades since the inception of the Environmental Era. In the 1970s, federal court decisions in both substantive and procedural issues generally worked to the advantage of environmental interests. During this period, the federal judiciary often was seen by environmentalists as the Great Equalizer, offsetting the previously enormous advantage enjoyed by regulated interests in administrative and judicial forums. Environmental organizations, aggressively exploiting the procedural advantages they had gained during the 1970s to compel federal enforcement of new regulatory programs, achieved some of their most significant judicial victories during this period.

The federal courts, particularly the Supreme Court, made several significant contributions to environmental policy during Environmental Era I. During the 1970s the courts greatly expanded opportunities for environmental groups to bring issues before the bench by a broadened definition of "standing to sue," a legal status that permitted individuals or organizations the right to sue governmental agencies for failure to enforce environmental legislation. Beginning with the Scenic Hudson case in 1966, the federal courts broadened for more than a decade the criteria by which citizens could acquire such "standing" to sue federal agencies over enforcement of environmental regulations.[42] In more recent years the courts have not always been consistent or generous in their definitions of standing. Nonetheless, the earlier decisions enabled environmental interests to use litigation effectively to bring pressure on Congress, administrative agencies, and regulated interests for more effective environmental policies during a crucial decade when major environmental laws were being written.[43]

The substantive interpretations of environmental laws by the federal courts during the 1970s also had a major impact in strengthening the scope and impact of many programs. The 1972 decision of the federal district court in *Sierra Club v. Ruckelshaus* interpreted the goals of the Clean Air Act to require that all states prevent the degradation of any airsheds with ambient air quality higher than national standards.[44] This decision in effect forced the EPA and Congress to create the Prevention of Significant Deterioration (PSD) policy to protect all high-quality airsheds throughout the United States. According to R. Shep Melnick, "PSD was born in the courtroom and has resided there almost constantly for the past decade."[45] Indeed, as Melnick's meticulous study of the federal courts and the Clean Air Act indicates, the courts have been major players in the evolution of extremely stringent air pollution control standards by Congress and the EPA.[46] Environmentalists, impatient with the faltering pace of the EPA's development of a priority list of hazardous pollutants for examination as required under the Toxic Substances Control Act (TSCA), used the federal courts—particularly the District Court for the District of Columbia, an especially sympathetic forum for environmentalists—to force the EPA to speed up its priority setting.

The federal courts also were instrumental in enforcing strict procedural compliance and reasonable adherence to the intent of the law in enforcing the requirement of the National Environmental Policy Act for environmental impact statements (EISs) in the federal bureaucracy. The EIS process has been particularly useful to environmentalists by disclosing the implications of administrative issues that otherwise might not have been apparent, by serving as an early warning system to alert environmental groups to impending new issues, and by compelling federal agencies to give environmentalists an opportunity to influence decisions with environmental consequences.

Shifting Fortunes: Environmental Era II. Beginning in the late 1970s, business and other regulated interests began to use the federal courts far more effectively than they had previously. In addition, the ideological climate of the federal judiciary shifted during the 1980s as an increasing number of federal judges far less sympathetic to environmentalist viewpoints sat as appointees of the Reagan and Bush administrations. The increased effectiveness of business interests also bespeaks the great growth in number and activity of specialized not-for-profit legal foundations representing regulated industries in environmental litigation. Reasoning that the devil should not have all the good tunes, business patterned these associations after the very successful public interest legal foundations created in the 1970s to represent environmental interests. As do environmental public interest groups, these business associations maintain they are suing the government in the public interest and enjoy tax-exempt status. However, business public interest groups are financed principally by organizations, such as the Adolph Coors Company and the Scaife Foundation, that have fought vigorously against most of the major environmental regulatory programs that have been passed during the past three decades. "There is no mistaking the fact . . . that the Reagan-Bush appointees look with disfavor on most demands made by environmental litigants," legal scholar Lettie Wenner concluded. "Reagan policy makers reduced the severity of many of the regulations originally drafted by regulatory agencies. Many of these new regulations have now been appealed to the courts, and there have been few victories for environmental groups."[47]

During the 1980s and early 1990s, the increasing number of cases initiated by regulated interests against laws advantageous to environmental interests restricted environmentalists' standing to sue, limited the freedom of environmental agencies in writing environmental regulations, and elevated the importance of property rights and economic considerations in determining the extent to which businesses should be regulated environmentally. Environmental groups, thrown on the defensive, found the federal courtroom increasingly inhospitable. And the pressure continues: "With their superior legal and economic resources, major corporations and trade associations have asked the courts to reinterpret environmental laws in a more probusiness light. . . . In addition, industry and property owners are making intense demands on federal courts . . . arguing that the laws themselves should be declared unconstitutional and unenforceable."[48]

The benefit to business interests from this growing strength in environmental litigation does not depend solely on winning cases. Exhaustive and relentless challenges to federal regulation can delay enforcement of environmental laws for many years and throw environmental groups on the defensive, compelling them to invest scarce resources in protracted legal battles. Often battles are won not by the side with the best case but by the side with the most endurance.

Litigation as a Political Tactic.　The impact of the courts on policy, as the previous discussion suggests, arises not only from the substance of court rulings but also from the use of litigation as a tactical weapon in policy conflict—a weapon used by all sides. The courts become another political arena in which losers in prior policy battles fought among Congress, the bureaucracy, and the White House can launch yet another campaign. It is not surprising that environmental groups specializing in litigation, such as the Environmental Defense Fund, increased their activity during the Reagan administration in an often unsuccessful effort to counteract through the courts what they alleged to be massive regulatory resistance to their interests within the administration.

Litigation is also a stall in the policy process, a frustration to the opposition. Litigation creates a bargaining chip to be bartered for concessions from the opposition. Both environmentalists and their opposition have used the obstructive capacities of litigation to good advantage. When the Department of the Interior attempted in late 1981 to sell for energy exploration 111 tracts of offshore land in California's coastal zone, the state of California and numerous environmental groups joined in litigation blocking the sale of 32 tracts, among the most desirable, thereby freezing sale of the others also. This persuaded the Department to reconsider the leases rather than risk a prolonged freeze on the sale of all valuable tracts. Litigation initiated in the mid-1970s by environmentalist opponents of the Seabrook, New Hampshire, nuclear power plant cost the facility owners almost $15 million monthly in delay and almost succeeded in closing the facility permanently.

Many critics have pegged NEPA's requirement for EISs as an especially productive source of lawsuits working to the advantage of environmentalists, but the data suggest otherwise. The number of lawsuits challenging agency actions under NEPA has been steadily diminishing in number and importance. One important reason is that the federal courts in the 1980s were increasingly disinclined to sustain challenges as long as the judges were convinced that agencies had prepared and reviewed EISs properly. Another reason is that EISs are fast becoming a bureaucratic rite, meticulously observed while often substantively ignored.

The Administrative Setting

In the political conflicts of environmentalism, the federal bureaucracy is rapidly displacing Congress as the strategic heartland. A great diversity of administrative agencies share increasing responsibility for environmental administration and, with it, the enormous delegated and discretionary power inherent in implementing the law. By far the most important, most visible, and largest of the environmental regulators is the Environmental Protection Agency.

The Environmental Protection Agency

Asked if his job had been rewarding, a former administrator for the EPA replied that it was "like beating a train across a grade crossing—if you make it, it's a great rush. If you don't, you're dead." [49] An insider's guide to Washington, D.C., ranked the job of administrator for the EPA among the 100 toughest positions in the city. Created by an executive order of President Richard Nixon in 1970 and repeatedly scheduled for elevation to Cabinet status, the EPA is the federal government's largest regulatory agency in budget and personnel. Its responsibilities embrace extraordinarily complicated and technical programs running across the whole domain of environmental management and touching almost all major sectors of the U.S. economy. Under these conditions, political controversy is the daily bread of EPA's leadership. "The Administrator rarely goes to the President with good news and is more often the bearer of bad news," observed Lee Thomas, the EPA's administrator from 1985 to 1988. "You almost never have a decision where many people applaud it." [50]

The size of the EPA's regulatory burden is suggested in "Major Responsibilities of the EPA," which summarizes the EPA's current statutory responsibilities. These regulatory programs represent the major environmental legislation of the past two decades, including the Clean Air Act; the Clean Water Act; the Noise Control Act; the Safe Drinking Water Act; the Resource Conservation and Recovery Act; the Toxic Substances Control Act; the Marine Protection, Research, and Sanctuaries Act; the Federal Insecticide, Fungicide, and Rodenticide Act; the Superfund legislation; and the Superfund Amendments and Reauthorization Act. Beginning with a staff of approximately 8,000 and a budget of $455 million in 1972, the EPA steadily grew to almost 13,000 employees and a budget of $1.35 billion until 1981, when the Reagan administration severely reduced its budget and personnel. The Agency recovered somewhat in the late 1980s and presently has about 18,000 employees and an annual budget of approximately $7.6 billion, of which less than half actually supports its administrative activities (most of the money underwrites water treatment and Superfund grants). The Agency, whose administrator is appointed by the president, consists of a Washington, D.C., headquarters and ten regional offices, each headed by a regional administrator. Unlike most regulatory agencies, the EPA administers both regulatory and distributive programs such as the huge federal waste treatment grants, the Superfund program, and various research activities.

Notwithstanding some significant achievements, the EPA has confronted a daunting array of problems in the 1990s: an unmanageable burden of continually growing regulatory responsibilities, a politically toxic inheritance of congressional distrust and disruptive oversight born of bitter controversies surrounding the Reagan administration in the 1980s and resurrected by the 1994 Republican congressional takeover, a chronically inadequate budget, and the administrative complexities inherent in complex environmental regulations. The growing disparity between the EPA's administrative responsibilities and its resources has reached a point at which many observers believe the Agency is, or will soon be, mired in "a pathological cycle of regulatory failure." [51] Even less pessimistic observers suspect that the EPA's job may have become impossibly difficult.

By the mid-1980s it was already obvious, as the Council on Environmental Quality (CEQ) observed, that "the Environmental Protection Agency cannot possibly do all the things its various mandates tell it to do," and conditions have not improved.[52] The Agency is years, or decades, behind in complying with many of the most important requirements in its ten major statutory programs and new jobs are always ahead. The 800-page Clean Air Act Amendments of 1990, for instance, required the EPA to hire 200 new employees and to write 55 major regulations within two years (which it could not accomplish).[53] Enforcement of TSCA, the Resource Conservation and Recovery Act (RCRA) of 1976, and the Superfund program have been especially difficult. Of the estimated 3,700 businesses that are required by RCRA to control their environmental releases of toxic substances, for example, by the late 1990s less than 9 percent had actually created the cleanup measures required by EPA.[54]

One reason for the Agency's chronic compliance problems is the congressional penchant for packing legislation with a multitude of demanding deadlines, detailed management instructions, and "hammer clauses"

Major Responsibilities of the EPA

The following are the major regulatory tasks assigned to EPA in each important pollution control program.

In the area of air quality, the EPA:
• Establishes national air quality standards.
• Sets limits on the level of air pollutants emitted from stationary sources such as power plants, municipal incinerators, factories, and chemical plants.
• Establishes emission standards for new motor vehicles.
• Sets allowable levels for toxics like lead, benzene, and toluene in gasoline.
• Establishes emission standards for hazardous air pollutants such as beryllium, mercury, and asbestos.
• Supervises states in their development of clean air plans.

In the area of water quality and protection, the EPA:
• Issues permits for the discharge of any pollutant into navigable waters.
• Develops "effluent guidelines" to control discharge of specific water pollutants, including radiation.
• Develops criteria that enable states to set water quality standards.
• Administers grants program to states to subsidize the cost of building sewage treatment plants.
• Regulates disposal of waste material, including sludge and low-level radioactive discards, into the oceans.
• Cooperates with the Army Corps of Engineers to issue permits for the dredging and filling of wetlands.
• Sets national drinking water standards to ensure that drinking water is safe.
• Regulates underground injection of wastes to protect purity of groundwater.
• With the Coast Guard, coordinates cleanup of oil and chemical spills into U.S. waterways.

To control the disposal of hazardous waste, the EPA:
• Maintains inventory of existing hazardous waste dump sites.
• Tracks more than 500 hazardous compounds from point of origin to final disposal site.
• Sets standards for generators and transporters of hazardous wastes.
• Issues permits for treatment, storage, and disposal facilities for hazardous wastes.
• Assists states in developing hazardous waste control programs.
• Maintains a multibillion-dollar fund ("Superfund") from industry fees and general tax revenues to provide for emergency cleanup of hazardous dumps when no responsible party can immediately be found.
• Pursues identification of parties responsible for waste sites and eventual reimbursement of the federal government for Superfund money spent cleaning up these sites.

To regulate chemicals, including pesticides and radioactive waste, the EPA:
• Maintains inventory of chemical substances now in commercial use.
• Regulates existing chemicals considered serious hazards to people and the environment, including fluorocarbons, PCBs, and asbestos.
• Issues procedures for the proper safety testing of chemicals and orders them tested when necessary.
• Requires the registration of insecticides, herbicides, or fungicides intended for sale in the United States.
• Requires pesticide manufacturers to provide scientific evidence that their products will not injure humans, livestock, crops, or wildlife when used as directed.

- Classifies pesticides for either general public use or restricted use by certified applicators.
- Sets standards for certification of applicators of restricted-use pesticides. (Individual states may certify applicators through their own programs based on the federal standards.)
- Cancels or suspends the registration of a product on the basis of actual or potential unreasonable risk to humans, animals, or the environment.
- Issues a "stop sale, use, and removal" order when a pesticide already in circulation is found to be in violation of the law.
- Requires registration of pesticide-producing establishments.
- Issues regulations concerning the labeling, storage, and disposal of pesticide containers.

- Issues permits for pesticide research.
- Monitors pesticide levels in the environment.
- Monitors and regulates the levels of radiation in drinking water, oceans, rainfall, and air.
- Conducts research on toxic substances, pesticides, air and water quality, hazardous wastes, radiation, and the causes and effects of acid rain.
- Provides overall guidance to other federal agencies on radiation protection matters that affect public health.

In addition, the EPA:
- Sets noise levels that are acceptable for construction equipment, transportation equipment (except aircraft), all motors and engines, and electronic equipment.

that threaten dire consequences should the EPA fail to comply with various statutory deadlines. All this micromanagement is but one manifestation of a profound legislative distrust permeating almost all of the Agency's congressional relationships, an inheritance of the EPA's bitter political confrontations with Congress during the Reagan years. During the first Reagan administration, the White House attempted to move the Agency's concerns sharply away from its environmentalist constituency and toward business and other regulated interests. The Agency's enforcement activities and regulatory budget were sharply curtailed and its leadership, headed by EPA administrator Anne Burford, was perceived by most congressional representatives to be hostile to the regulatory programs Congress had enacted. The resulting political controversies badly demoralized the Agency, fortified congressional determination to exercise unusually strict oversight of EPA activities, and initiated a continuing period of rigid legislation intended to reduce to a minimum the Agency's discretion in implementing regulatory programs. Subsequent efforts by the Reagan and Bush administrations to restore a measure of effectiveness and credibility to EPA programs did not generally compensate for the political and programmatic damage sustained by the EPA.

By 1988, the Agency had met approximately 20 percent of the 800 statutory deadlines it had inherited and evidence of continuing congressional problems abounded into the 1990s.[55] The EPA continues to experience what is probably the most relentless legislative oversight of any federal agency. (So habitually does Congress investigate activities of the EPA that the General Accounting Office, the congressional watchdog agency, has a permanent branch at EPA headquarters.) The EPA's budget continues to lag behind its continually growing responsibilities: employees in research and development, for instance, whose work is essential to creating an adequate science base for regulatory rule making, decreased from 2,300 to 1,800 between 1981 and 1991.[56]

The Agency's image and morale have improved significantly since 1988 under the leadership of administrators William K. Reilly and Carol Browner and with the advent of an environmentally involved Democratic White House since 1993. But many of the EPA's difficulties elude political resolution. They appear to arise from inherent and serious flaws in its organizational structure and policy design and they are not easily eradicated. The EPA is now into its third decade, and it is apparent that the administrative flexibility and political independence essential to its effective operation have not grown appropriately with its enormously expanded authority, nor has its organizational structure adapted well to its increasing responsibilities. One salient environmental issue of the late 1990s is likely to be reform and restructuring of the EPA as the imperative for action becomes increasingly obvious.

The Council on Environmental Quality

The National Environmental Policy Act included a provision for the establishment of a commission to advise the president on environmental matters. To be headed by three members appointed by the president, the Council on Environmental Quality was to be part of the president's staff. Among the major responsibilities prescribed for the Council in Section 203 of NEPA were (1) to gather for the President's consideration "timely and authoritative information concerning the conditions and trends in the quality of the environment both current and prospective"; (2) "to develop and recommend to the President national policies to foster and promote the improvement of environmental quality"; and (3) "to review and appraise the various programs and activities of the Federal Government" to determine the extent to which they comply, among other things, with the requirement for writing EISs.[57] The CEQ was created, then, as were other major presidential advisory commissions, to provide policy advice and evaluation from within the White House directly to the president.

Since its first year of operation in 1971, the CEQ has published a widely distributed and densely documented annual report, a periodic appraisal of major environmental trends, issues, and new developments.

The Council also administers the process for writing and reviewing EISs within the federal government. The CEQ is a small agency with no regulatory responsibilities or major environmental programs beyond modest research activities, but it has assumed symbolic importance and political value to environmental interests. Its presence within the White House implies a high national priority to environmental programs, and the Council's opportunities to influence the president directly means that it might act, in the words of environmental leader Russell Peterson, as "the environmental conscience of the executive branch." Nonetheless, as with all other presidential advisory bodies, the CEQ exercises no more influence in White House decisions than the president cares to give it; it may carry on its NEPA-mandated activities, but the president is free to ignore any of its recommendations or other initiatives.

The CEQ's rapid decline in status since the Carter administration illustrates how much its effectiveness depends on presidential favor. The Council enjoyed considerable influence under President Carter, a strong environmentalist, but its influence plummeted rapidly during the Reagan administration. One of Reagan's earliest acts after his inauguration was to reduce the CEQ's staff from forty-nine to fifteen and to reduce its budget by 50 percent; that sent a message.[58] The CEQ's publications and other research activities immediately declined in number and quality. Throughout the remainder of the Reagan administration, the CEQ seemed to inhabit a White House nether region from which it was seldom seen or heard. President Bush's pledges of environmental concern did not, to the disappointment of environmentalists, portend better days for the CEQ, nor did the arrival of the Clinton administration in 1992. President Clinton's proposal to replace the CEQ with a White House environmental policy advisor appointed by the president shocked the environmental community and seemed virtually an obituary for the Council. Even should the CEQ remain, it has clearly ceased to be a major player in White House politics.

The Department of the Interior

Established as a cabinet-level department in 1845, the Department of the Interior has acquired responsibilities over more than a century that leave few national environmental issues untouched. The Department's important environmental responsibilities include (1) protection and management of more than 549 million acres of public land—roughly 28 percent of the total U.S. land area—set aside by Congress for national parks, wilderness areas, forests, and other restricted uses; (2) administration of Native American lands and federal Native American programs, including authority over western tribal lands containing a very large proportion of the coal, petroleum, uranium, and other largely unexploited energy resources in the western United States; (3) enforcement of federal surface mining regulations through its Office of Surface Mining, Reclamation and Enforcement; (4) conservation and management of wetlands and estuarine areas; and (5) protection and preservation of wildlife, including endangered species. Headed by a cabinet secretary appointed by the president, the Department's programs historically have been a primary concern to environmentalists; the interior secretary, although not always identified with the environmental or conservationist movements, in recent decades has been compatible with their interests.

At the beginning of the Reagan administration, the Department of the Interior—and particularly Reagan's first choice as the Department's secretary, James Watt—was a source of continual controversy as a result of its efforts to make sweeping changes in personnel and programs. Critics charged that the Department's programs to protect the environment had been placed on the agenda for an administration "hit list" applied by Secretary Watt. The secretary, more than any other official, epitomized to environmentalists all that seemed wrong with the Reagan administration's environmental record; he became the movement's arch villain. These controversies were rooted in strong environmentalist convictions about the nature of the Department that shape their organizational response to any departmental leadership. Environmentalists maintain that the Department of the Interior's leadership, as with the EPA's, should be acceptable to the environmental movement and reasonably supportive of the Department's programs. Watt's political associations prior to his appointment, including especially his leadership of a conservative public interest law firm representing many corporations and state governments opposing federal regulation, seemed enough to disqualify him for office in the environmentalists' view. Watt's subsequent actions seemed to vindicate the environmentalists' worst premonitions.

The Department has always been a battleground between interests seeking to conserve the resources in the public domain and those seeking generous access to them. The Department's mandate to ensure "balanced use" of resources between conservation and development—a mandate that continually propels the Department and its secretary into a storm of controversy concerning which use shall dominate—is a certain source of trouble for every secretary. Moreover, the Department's programs serve a clientele including not only environmentalists, but also the timber and cattle industries, mining companies, sports enthusiasts, a multitude of private corporations, and many other interests who expect the Department to be solicitous of their viewpoints. Finally, the western states historically have maintained that they have not been given sufficient voice in the administration of the federal lands that often constitute the vast majority of land within their boundaries. The desire of these states to assume greater control over the public domain within their jurisdictions and the resulting tensions with the federal government will outlive any administration.

Watt's strident conflicts were unusually nasty, even for a public office rich in controversy, and he was forced to resign in October 1983 after becoming a political liability for the White House. Watt's successors during the Reagan administration successfully removed the Department from the headlines and took a more conciliatory approach to its environmental critics. But environmentalists, convinced that only the leadership style had changed, continued to assert that the Department was hostile to conservation values and the regulatory programs intended to promote them. The Bush administration did little to appease these critics by appointing former New Mexico representative Manuel Lujan, Jr., as secretary. Lujan and his management team seemed to embrace essentially the same viewpoint as their Reagan-appointed predecessors. Congress generally frustrated the Bush administration's efforts to open vast tracts of public domain for oil exploration and commercial timbering but Lujan continued to provoke environmentalist ire by attacking many important environmental regulations under his jurisdiction, such as the Endangered Species Act. "Of course, I'm the protector of endangered species," he declared with an ambivalence that suffused most of his Department's resource policies, "but by the same token, I must make resources available to the public."[59] Lujan's combat with the Mount Graham red squirrel, an endangered species blocking construction of an astronomical observatory, became a minor *cause célèbre*. "Do we have to save every subspecies?" he complained. "The red squirrel is the best example. Nobody's told me the difference between a red squirrel, a black one or a brown one."[60] The head of the Bureau of Mines did not improve the Department's environmental image by subsequently declaring to a conference of miners, loggers, and other resource developers that environmentalists were "a bunch of nuts."[61]

While environmentalists were generally delighted with President Clinton's selection of former governor Bruce Babbitt to be secretary of the Department of the Interior, they were not so satisfied with many of Babbitt's early policy initiatives, including the scope of the Department's efforts to restrict timbering and other resource development on public lands. The Clinton administration's agenda of slow and cautious environmental reform, especially grating on grassroots environmentalists who expected a bold display of environmental initiative, seemed certain to nurture continuing controversy, albeit much more temperate than in the 1980s, between the Department and its environmentalist constituency.

The Nuclear Regulatory Commission

The Nuclear Regulatory Commission (NRC) was created by Congress in 1976 to assume the regulatory responsibilities originally vested in the Atomic Energy Commission (AEC). An independent agency with five commissioners appointed by the president, the NRC regulates most non-military uses of nuclear facilities and materials. The commission's major activities related to the environment include the (1) regulation of the site choice, construction, operation, and security of all civilian nuclear reactors; (2) designation and supervision of all nuclear waste repositories; (3) regulation of uranium mining and milling facilities; and (4) closing of civilian nuclear facilities after they discontinue production (called decommissioning). In 1997, the NRC employed about 3,100 individuals and had a budget of approximately $477 million.

Environmental groups have been most concerned with the NRC's supervision of nuclear power plants and repositories for radioactive wastes. Although 123 nuclear plants were operating or approved for construction by 1996, the majority of these have been criticized by environmental groups for alleged deficiencies in structural safety, control of radioactive emissions, and waste storage.[62] In addition, environmental groups have often been very aggressive in seeking NRC safety reviews of operating plants and personnel training procedures. The NRC has assumed a major responsibility for the review of site selection and the supervision of waste disposal at the nation's first permanent nuclear waste repository at Yucca Flats, Nevada. Environmental groups regard the process of site construction and waste disposal a major issue of the 1990s.

The NRC and environmental groups have been both adversaries and allies. The environmental movement generally has supported the NRC's stricter enforcement and review of regulations for operating nuclear facilities and its increasingly rigorous standards for new facility licensing. Yet environmentalists also have criticized the NRC for allegedly siding too often with the nuclear power industry against its critics, for bureaucratic inertia and conservatism, and for ignoring technical criticism and data from sources not associated with the nuclear power industry or the Commission. As with other regulatory agencies, the NRC is bound to its own clientele—the nuclear power industry—by professional associations, common technical and economic concerns, and historical sympathies; it is also committed to regulating the industry in the public interest while maintaining sufficient objectivity and disengagement from the nuclear power movement to do that job. These often conflicting responsibilities lead the NRC into controversies with environmental interests. Nonetheless, the NRC and its mission remain among the most environmentally significant elements in the executive branch.

The Department of Energy

Despite its size and importance, the Department of Energy has been the stepchild of the executive branch. Widely criticized and burdened with difficult, unpopular programs throughout the 1980s, the Department began the 1990s confronting immense new problems—legal, political, economic, and technical—created by disastrous mismanagement of the military nuclear weapons facilities under its jurisdiction since the late 1970s. These unprecedented difficulties constituted more high-profile bad news for an agency with a talent for collecting misfortune.

The DOE finished the 1990s still mired in high-visibility controversy, struggling against the stigma of flagrant mismanagement and saddled with responsibility for unpopular policies. The DOE's problems seem almost inevitable in light of its history. The Department was created in 1976 when Congress combined a number of independent agencies with programs already operating in other departments in order to bring the federal government's sprawling energy activities within a single bureaucratic structure. Under the DOE's jurisdiction are regulatory activities and energy programs strongly affecting the environment. The more important of these include (1) promotion of civilian nuclear power activities; (2) regulation of military nuclear facilities and radioactive wastes; (3) administration of the federal government's research and development programs in energy production and conservation; (4) regulation of price controls for domestic petroleum and natural gas; and (5) administration of federal research and development grants for commercial synthetic fuels production in the United States. With approximately 18,200 employees and a budget of $15.4 billion in 1997, the DOE is the principal executive agency involved in the regulation and production of many different energy technologies with significant environmental impacts. Also by design it is expected to undertake a volatile agenda of frequently contradictory and inconsistent missions destined to set it at odds with itself and with the environmental community: to promote environmentally risky energy technologies and to minimize the environmental risks; to promote energy use and energy conservation; to stimulate research and development of new energy-consuming technologies and energy-saving ones; to control energy prices in emergencies; to avert energy shortages and stimulate long-range energy planning.

From its inception, the DOE lacked strong leadership and internal stability. Its important research and development programs were plagued by delays, maladroit administration, and controversy. Constant internal reorganizations left the agency's staff demoralized and confused about its mission and viability. With its substantial commitment to promoting fossil fuel and nuclear energy technologies throughout the 1980s, the DOE's relationship with the environmentalist community was more often confrontational than conciliatory. Only after years of resistance, for example, did the DOE finally permit the EPA and OSHA to supervise worker safety at its nuclear weapons sites in the early 1990s. Throughout the Reagan and Bush years, the DOE's internal environmental watchdogs were understaffed and usually outgunned politically by bureaucratic proponents of fossil fuel and nuclear energy development. The Clinton administration, determined to reconstruct the DOE's image and policy priorities, initiated measures intended to strike a better balance between energy promotion and environmental concern.

By far the most politically and financially costly problem confronting the DOE is still the environmental contamination of the nation's nuclear weapons facilities. In the early 1990s it became apparent that a half century of negligent, often reckless mismanagement of the military weapons sites by earlier federal agencies and their private contractors had left the DOE with an inheritance of sick and endangered workers, environmental contamination, legal and political liability, and technical cleanup problems of staggering proportions. Led by Secretary of Energy Hazel R. O'Leary, the Clinton administration aggressively sought to discover the full extent of the human and environmental damage and to confront the cost of its remediation. Cleanup at the seventeen major military weapons facilities in twelve states was estimated initially to cost between $28 and $50 billion for the first five years.[63] Overall, more than 122 nuclear weapons manufacturing and laboratory sites in thirty states, the Marshall Islands, and Puerto Rico have to be made safe. Most experts, however, now believe the early cost estimates are unrealistically low. Numerous studies indicate that the DOE's military weapons cleanup program will probably exceed $250 billion and take perhaps a half century or more to accomplish—if it can be accomplished, for no public or private agency has any experience in cleaning up radioactive contamination of such scale and complexity.[64] Spending for the cleanup of these nuclear weapons sites and for other related programs could transform involuntarily the DOE into the nation's largest environmental agency and launch it on the most expensive public works program in U.S. history (see Chapter 8).[65]

Conclusion

In an important sense, environmental degradation is a twentieth-century problem resolved according to eighteenth-century rules: fundamental government arrangements such as institutional checks and balances, interest group liberalism, congressional localism, and much else reviewed in this chapter are explicitly created by the Constitution or implicit in its philosophy. In contrast, bureaucracy has imparted to environmental policy making, as to other federal policies, a distinctly twentieth-century character; administrative politics now play as fundamental a part in shaping environmental policy as any other, older element in the Constitution.

The explosive growth within the past few decades of federal environmental legislation, together with a specialized environmental bureaucracy, has added distinctly new elements to the federal policy cycle and indicates that environmental management has become a permanent new policy domain within federal and state governments with its own set of institutional and political biases.

Notes

1. *New York Times,* May 8, 1989.
2. Ibid.
3. *New York Times,* May 9, 1989.
4. Hugh Heclo, "Issue Networks and the Executive Establishment," in *The New American Political System,* ed. Anthony King (Washington, D.C.: American Enterprise Institute, 1979), 89.
5. Charles O. Jones, *An Introduction to Public Policy* (North Scituate, Mass.: Duxbury Press, 1978), chap. 2.
6. Roger W. Cobb and Charles D. Elder, *Participation in American Politics* (Baltimore, Md.: Johns Hopkins University Press, 1972), 86.
7. J. Clarence Davies III, "Environmental Regulation and Technical Change," in *Keeping Pace with Science and Engineering: Studies in Environmental Regulation,* ed. Myron F. Uman (Washington, D.C.: National Academy Press, 1993), 255.
8. Quoted in *New York Times,* July 23, 1988.
9. Eugene Bardach, *The Implementation Game* (Cambridge, Mass.: MIT Press, 1971), 36.
10. Peter deLeon, "A Theory of Termination in the Policy Process: Rules, Rhymes and Reasons" (Paper delivered at the annual meeting of the American Political Science Association, Washington, D.C., Sept. 1–4, 1977), 2.
11. Richard E. Neustadt, *Presidential Power* (New York: Wiley, 1960).
12. Morton Grodzins, "The Federal System," in *American Federalism in Perspective,* ed. Aaron Wildavsky (Boston: Little, Brown, 1967), 257.
13. Ibid. See also Charles E. Davis and James P. Lester, "Federalism and Environmental Policy," in *Environmental Politics and Policy: Theories and Evidence,* ed. James P. Lester (Durham N.C.: Duke University Press, 1989), 57–86; and James P. Lester, "A New Federalism? Environmental Policy in the States," in *Environmental Policy in the 1990s,* ed. Norman J. Vig and Michael Kraft (Washington, D.C.: CQ Press, 1990), 59–80.
14. U.S. Advisory Commission on Intergovernmental Regulations, *Federal Regulation of State and Local Governments: The Mixed Record of the 1980s* (Washington, D.C.: Advisory Commission on Intergovernmental Relations, July 1993), Publication A-126, 44–45, chaps. 4, 8.
15. This mingling of private and public power is well explored in Grant McConnell, *Private Power and American Democracy* (New York: Vintage Books, 1967). See also Helen M. Ingram and Dean E. Mann, "Interest Groups and Environmental Policy," in *Environmental Politics and Policy,* ed. Lester, 135–157.

16. James V. DeLong, "How To Convince an Agency," *Regulation* (Sept./Oct. 1982): 31.
17. Graham Allison, *The Essence of Decision* (Boston: Little, Brown, 1971), 163.
18. Charles A. Lindblom, "The Science of Muddling Through," *Public Administration Review* (Spring 1959): 86.
19. The reasons for this departure are examined carefully in J. Clarence Davies III and Charles F. Lettow, "The Impact of Federal Institutional Arrangements," in *Federal Environmental Law,* ed. Erica L. Dolgin and Thomas G. P. Guilbert (St. Paul, Minn.: West Publishing, 1974), 26–191.
20. Theodore Lowi, "The Public Philosophy: Interest Group Liberalism," *American Political Science Review* (March 1967): 18.
21. McConnell, *Private Power and American Democracy,* 162.
22. Charles A. Lindblom, *The Policy Making Process,* 2d ed. (Englewood Cliffs, N.J.: Prentice-Hall, 1980), 73.
23. Ralph Huitt, "Political Feasibility," in *Policy Analysis in Political Science,* ed. Ira Sharkansky (Chicago: Markham Publishing, 1970), 410.
24. John C. Whittaker, "Earth Day Recollections: What It Was Like When the Movement Took Off," *EPA Journal* 14, no. 6 (July/Aug. 1988): 14.
25. Ibid.
26. Quoted in Margaret Kriz, "Fuming over Fumes," *National Journal,* Nov. 26, 1988, 3008.
27. Robert W. Crandall and Paul R. Portney, "Environmental Policy," in *Natural Resources and the Environment: The Reagan Approach,* ed. Paul Portney (Washington, D.C.: Urban Institute Press, 1984), 14.
28. U.S. Department of Commerce, Bureau of the Census, *Statistical Abstract of the United States, 1992* (Washington, D.C.: Government Printing Office, 1993), 217. Figures are given in dollar values of 1982, corrected for inflation.
29. Environmental Protection Agency (EPA), *Environmental Investments: The Cost of a Clean Environment: A Summary* (Washington, D.C.: EPA, 1990), vi.
30. Huitt, "Political Feasibility," 414.
31. Barry G. Rabe, *Fragmentation and Integration in State Environmental Management* (Washington, D.C.: Conservation Foundation, 1986), 16–17. See also Michael E. Kraft, "Congress and Environmental Policy," in *Environmental Politics and Policy,* ed. Lester, 179–211.
32. *New York Times,* Nov. 5, 1981.
33. Ibid.
34. Mark J. Landy and Mary Hague, "The Coalition for Waste: Private Interests and Superfund," in *Environmental Politics: Public Costs, Private Rewards,* ed. Michael S. Grave (New York: Praeger, 1992), 72.
35. R. Douglas Arnold, *Congress and the Bureaucracy* (New Haven, Conn.: Yale University Press, 1979), 133.
36. Lawrence Mosher, "Clean Water Requirements Will Remain Even if the Federal Spigot Is Closed," *National Journal,* May 16, 1981, 874–878.
37. *National Journal,* Nov. 21, 1981.
38. General Accounting Office (GAO), "Improving EPA's Regulatory Impact Analysis," Report No. GAO/RCED 97-38 (1997).
39. David D. Doniger, *The Law and Policy of Toxic Substances Control* (Baltimore, Md.: Johns Hopkins University Press, 1978), 3.
40. *New York Times,* April 25, 1993.
41. GAO, "Cleaning Up Nuclear Facilities—An Aggressive and United Federal Program Is Needed," Report no. GAO/EMD 82-40 (May 25, 1982), v. See also *New York Times,* May 15, 1993.
42. *Scenic Hudson Preservation Conference v. Federal Power Commission,* 354 F.2d 608 (2d Cir. 1965).
43. Werner J. Grunbaum, *Judicial Policy Making: The Supreme Court and Environmental Quality* (Morristown, N.J.: General Learning Press, 1976), 31. See also Lettie McSpadden Wenner, "The Courts and Environmental Policy," in *Environmental Politics and Policy,* ed. Lester, 261–288.

44. *Sierra Club v. Ruckelshaus,* 344 F. Supp. 253 (D.D.C. 1972), *upheld sub. nom. Fri v. Sierra Club,* 412 U.S. 541 (1973).
45. R. Shep Melnick, *Regulation and the Courts: The Case of the Clean Air Act* (Washington, D.C.: Brookings Institution, 1983), 73.
46. Ibid. See especially chap. 4.
47. Lettie M. Wenner, "Environmental Policy in the Courts," in *Environmental Policy in the 1990s,* 2d ed., ed. Norman J. Vig and Michael E. Kraft (Washington, D.C.: CQ Press, 1994), 156.
48. Ibid., 149.
49. Quoted in John H. Trattner, *The Prune Book: The 100 Toughest Management and Policy-Making Jobs in Washington* (Lanham, Md.: Madison Books, 1988), 250.
50. Ibid., 249.
51. Richard J. Lazarus, "The Tragedy of Distrust in the Implementation of Federal Environmental Law," *Law and Contemporary Problems 54* (Autumn 1991): 334. See also Marc K. Landy, Marc J. Roberts, and Stephen R. Thomas, *The Environmental Protection Agency: Asking the Wrong Questions* (New York: Oxford University Press, 1990); and Paul R. Portney, ed., *Public Policies for Environmental Protection* (Washington, D.C.: Resources for the Future, 1990), chaps. 1, 8.
52. Council on Environmental Quality (CEQ), *Environmental Quality, 1985,* (Washington D.C.: CEQ, 1986), 14. See also Walter A. Rosenbaum, "Into the Nineties at EPA: Searching for the Clenched Fist and the Open Hand," in *Environmental Policy in the 1990s,* 2d ed., ed. Vig and Kraft, 121–143.
53. GAO, "EPA's Chemical Testing Program Has Not Resolved Safety Concerns," Report no. GAO/RCED 91-136 (June 1991), 2.
54. GAO, "Hazardous Waste: Progress Under the Corrective Action Program Is Limited, but New Initiatives May Accelerate Cleanups," Report no. RCED 98-3 (October 1997).
55. Richard J. Lazarus, "The Tragedy of Distrust," *Law and Contemporary Problems 54* (Autumn 1991): 323.
56. EPA, Environmental Indicators and Forecasting Branch, *Managing for Environmental Results: A Status Report on EPA's Environmental Indicator Program* (Washington, D.C.: EPA, 1991).
57. NEPA, Title II, 42 U.S.C. sec. 4321 et seq. (1970).
58. Lawrence Mosher, "Environmental Quality Council Trims Its Sails in Stormy Budget Weather," *National Journal,* July 24, 1982, 1306–1307.
59. Quoted in *New York Times,* May 26, 1990.
60. Quoted in *New York Times,* May 12, 1993.
61. Quoted in *New York Times,* March 23, 1991.
62. The environmentalist viewpoint is summarized in Michelle Adoto, "The Union of Concerned Scientists," in *Safety Second: The NRC and America's Nuclear Power Plants* (Bloomington: Indiana University Press, 1987).
63. *New York Times,* July 4, 1990.
64. GAO, "Department of Energy: Cleaning Up Inactive Facilities Will Be Difficult," Report no. GAO/RCED 92-149 (June 1993); see also GAO, "Much Work Remains to Accelerate Facility Cleanups," Report no. GAO/RCED 93-15 (Jan. 1993).
65. See Christopher Madison, "The Energy Department at Three—Still Trying to Establish Itself," *National Journal,* Oct. 4, 1980.

Suggested Readings

Cohen, Richard E. *Washington At Work: Back Rooms and Clean Air.* New York: Macmillan, 1992.
Hayes, Samuel P. *Beauty, Health and Permanence: Environmental Politics in the United States, 1955–1985.* New York: Oxford University Press, 1987.
Hoberg, George. *Federalism By Design: Environmental Policy and the American Regulatory State.* New York: Praeger, 1992.

Jones, Charles O. *An Introduction to Public Policy.* 2d ed. North Scituate, Mass.: Wadsworth, 1984.
Lindblom, Charles A., and Edward J. Woodhouse. *The Policy-Making Process.* 3d ed. Englewood Cliffs, N.J.: Prentice-Hall, 1993.

Chapter 3

Making Policy:
Institutional Challenges

> . . . [O]ne of the two Deputy Regional Administrators in EPA's Boston
> office said that staff in that office are already being pushed beyond
> their limits because they are doing both traditional and reinvention
> activities. This official observed that some of the agency's initiatives
> are extensions of efforts that are about 15 years old and suggested
> that the agency review all of its reinvention-related initiatives. . . .
> —U.S. General Accounting Office's review of EPA's
> "Reinventing Regulation" Initiatives, 1997

The echoes of Earth Day barely had faded when the writers of the first
annual report of the Council on Environmental Quality (CEQ), so far
unbruised by experience, looked ahead from 1970 and saw the future of
environmental policy. "We already know what problems are most pressing," the writers of the report concluded. "Clearly, we need stronger
institutions and financing. We need to examine alternative approaches to
pollution control . . . better monitoring and research . . . to establish priorities and comprehensive policies."[1] That first CEQ report made no
mention of acid precipitation, atmospheric ozone depletion, the Greenhouse Effect, biotechnology, preservation of biological diversity, estuarine pollution, groundwater contamination, or growth management,
among many other currently important environmental issues. History
defies prophecy. Environmental degradation now looks quite different—
more comprehensive, more intractable, more subtle—than it appeared at
the beginning of Environmental Era I. Time also chastens and changes
assumptions. Today what seems most urgently needed is not stronger
institutions but *different* ones, not alternative policies but *newer* ones,
not only better monitoring and research but also *better ways to use* the
resulting data.

Problems in environmental policy making have become the quiet
crises of the contemporary environmental movement, as serious as any

97

global ecological derangement apparent at the beginning of Era II. In the years since 1970, environmental regulation has become thoroughly institutionalized through numerous laws, regulatory agencies old and new, and the development of political structures linking governing institutions, regulatory agencies, states, environmental groups, regulated interests, and others in a continuing policy-making network. The policy-making process institutionalized in this way appears as much a problem as an accomplishment.

When the Conservation Foundation asserted in 1989 that the foremost domestic problem in environmental policy making was "an overarching need to rethink the whole structure of the apparatus that we have in place for solving the problem of pollution and waste," it captured a pervasive sentiment within the environmental movement.[2] In this chapter, institutional design will be discussed. In Chapter 4, we will look closely at the complex procedures and problems created by risk assessment—as well as "environmental justice." In Chapter 5, we will look at the economic logic of regulation. These matters have become priority items on any reform agenda for contemporary environmental policy.

Institutional Problems

The institutional problems in environmental policy making often appear to be not a failure of institutions to perform as designed but a misconception of institutional forms themselves. In effect, government often seems to be mounting a war on modern ecological degradation armed with policy muskets and bureaucratic cavalry. This disparity between means and ends is apparent in the style of congressional policy making on environmental issues, in the EPA's current organizational structure, in the impact of federalism on policy implementation, and in the continuing bureaucratic pluralism and competition in environmental policy implementation.

Congress: Too Much Check, Too Little Balance

In a Madisonian government of separated institutions sharing powers, environmental administrators have good reason to look warily toward Congress. The Constitution invests the Congress with enormous authority over the daily conduct of the president and the executive branch. Congress may enact, rescind, or amend an environmental law. It can use its appropriations authority to alter levels of funding or staff in a regulatory program; it can reward or punish environmental agencies at annual budget reviews, congressional committee hearings, and investigations. It may use its inherent "oversight" powers to delay or speed a program's implementation.

Congress further enlarges its influence through numerous understandings, informal arrangements sanctified by tradition, and assertions of prerogative that administrators ignore at their peril. Members of Congress, for instance, believe that they are guardians of their constituencies' interests in federal programs such as pollution regulation. Thus, Congress collectively and legislators individually become involved relentlessly in the implementation of almost all environmental programs affecting "the folks at home."

Congress has become, as the constitutional framers anticipated, the most potent institution in the intricate structure of "checks and balances" erected around the president and the executive branch. Congress has also become a rich source of delay, confusion, and waste in both making and implementing environmental policy. These problems arise from excesses and exaggeration in the authority the constitutional framers prudently invested in Congress—a case of checks and balances gone awry. Many of these difficulties could be eliminated or mitigated by a self-imposed discipline of which Congress may be incapable.

"Ready, Fire, Aim": Crisis Decision Making. The congressional response to environmental problems is highly volatile, waxing and waning according to changing public moods, emerging environmental crises, economic circumstances, or today's front page ecological disasters. Congress easily falls into a "pollutant of the year" mentality, mandating new programs or sudden changes in existing ones according to what pollution problems currently seem most urgent or according to the public's current mood. Thus, the 1978 Love Canal disaster hastened enactment of the Comprehensive Environmental Response, Compensation, and Liability Act of 1980 (CERCLA, known popularly as "Superfund"), and the 1984 chemical plant explosion in Bhopal, India, assured passage of the "community right-to-know" provision in the 1986 Superfund Amendments and Reauthorization Act (SARA).

The Ocean Dumping Act of 1988 is the very model of crisis-inspired legislation at its worst. During the summer of 1988, popular bathing beaches along New York's eastern coast frequently were fouled with medical wastes, raw sewage, and other dangerous debris apparently washed ashore from New York City sewage dumped more than 100 miles offshore. Closed beaches and public revulsion at the widely publicized pollution quickly persuaded Congress to pass, without one dissenting vote, the Ocean Dumping Act prohibiting further ocean disposal of urban waste within a few years. Congress was unmoved by expert testimony that held the real cause of the contamination to be the continual overflow from New York City's antique sewer system, whose repair would be hugely expensive. Nor was Congress in the mood to evaluate alternatives. "There is no question," argued the chief engineer of the regional waste management agency, "that the New York City sewer system is the greatest cause of water pollution in the region. But a sewer system isn't sexy. It's expensive to fix, and nobody wants to hear about it. So people focused on what they understand . . . and they understand that sewage and the sea don't seem nice together."[3] Local representative Thomas J. Manton (D-Queens), initially opposed to the act, soon capitulated to political realities. "Nobody wanted to discuss the relative risks or merits," he later explained. "It had been a bad summer, and we all wanted to be able to say we did something. So we passed a law. I tried to have a debate. And it was like I was trying to destroy the planet."[4] As a result of the Act, the City of New York will spend $2 billion on facilities to convert sewage into fertilizer and $300 million annually for a decade to dispose of its sludge, although many experts believe an equally effective and much cheaper solution would have been possible if Congress had not ordained that ocean dumping be entirely eliminated.

Environmental policies are seldom so poorly conceived, but this reactive policy making assures an environmental agenda in which place and priority among programs depend less on scientific logic than on political circumstance. Often, the losers are scientifically compelling environmental problems unblessed with political sex appeal. Moreover, once a program is legislatively attractive, it usually acquires a mandated budget that virtually ensures survival. Most environmental scientists, for instance, consider indoor air pollution a more compelling health risk than abandoned hazardous waste sites or even some forms of air pollution currently regulated, but most of the EPA's air pollution budget is mandated for ambient air regulation, and Congress lacks enthusiasm to tackle indoor air pollution in the absence of a crisis.[5]

Another result of this crisis mentality is administrative overload. The EPA and other environmental agencies have often had to implement quickly a multitude of new programs, hastily enacted without sufficient time or resources provided for the tasks. In one six-year period, for instance, Congress required the EPA to implement the Clean Air Act (CAA) of 1970; the Federal Water Pollution Control Act Amendments (FWPCAA) of 1972; the Safe Drinking Water Act (SDWA) of 1974; the Toxic Substances Control Act (TSCA) of 1976; and the Resource Conservation and Recovery Act (RCRA) of 1976. Congress felt no urgency, however, about providing the EPA with the resources commensurate with this avalanche of new responsibilities. As a result, the Agency has struggled continually and unsuccessfully to find the means to carry out all the program mandates. This crisis mentality also begets constantly mandated changes in regulatory priorities and program deadlines. One example is the sudden congressional decision in 1977, dignified as a "midcourse correction," to switch emphasis of the FWPCAA away from controlling industrial pollutants (such as suspended solids or oxygen-demanding materials) and toward control of pollutants whose dangers were then becoming obvious. Such changes, however imperative they seem at the moment, are highly disruptive to the orderly implementation of existing laws.

Guidance: Too Much and Too Little. Behind the facade of high purpose and ambitious action of every major environmental law there is likely to stretch a terrain mined with muddled language, troublesome silences, and inconsistent programs. Some of this is inevitable. Mistakes in statutory design occur because federal environmental regulations address problems of great scientific and administrative complexity with which legislators have had no prior experience. Moreover, members of Congress are typically lawyers, business executives, or other nonscientific professionals who depend on the expertise of administrators to clarify and interpret the law appropriately in regard to specialized environmental programs. The constant pressure of legislative affairs discourages most members of Congress from giving considerable attention to environmental issues, or developing an adequate understanding of them. "It's tough to get Congress to focus on bills with sufficient time to develop an adequate depth of understanding," observed John A. Moore, former acting deputy director for the EPA. "You've got 1 or 2 Congressmen who truly know it; there are 400 others that are going to vote on it." [6]

Environmental legislation is often vague and contradictory because Congress cannot or will not resolve major political conflicts entailed in the law. Instead, Congress often papers over the conflict with silence, confusion, or deliberate obscurity in the statutory language. This results in a steady flow of political hot potatoes to the bureaucracy, which must untangle and clarify this legal language—often to the accompaniment of political conflict and legislative criticism—or leave the job to the courts. The EPA becomes enmeshed in protracted litigation and political bargaining, and program regulations essential to implementing the laws often are held hostage to these procedures. Moreover, many regulations can be formulated competently only after research that might require years or decades.

Congressional frustration with the continual delay in implementing environmental laws has led to the habitual use of extravagant, extraordinarily detailed, and inflexible language in new environmental laws, to the constant mandating of precise deadlines for completing various programs, and to prescription, in exquisite detail, of how administrators are to carry out program activities—in effect, to a cure as bad as the disease.

SARA is a monument to overcontrol. In SARA's five sections, Congress mandated 150 deadlines:

> EPA is solely responsible for 59 deadlines . . . and jointly responsible . . . for 5 others. The law imposes 14 deadlines on [other] nonspecified federal entities . . . 9 other federal entities are tasked with 48 specific deadlines. The law also imposes 5 deadlines on states, 8 deadlines on local community government groups, and 11 deadlines on private sector business facilities that handle hazardous substances.[7]

One section of SARA contains a provision concerning how local communities are to implement required emergency planning for facilities using highly dangerous chemicals. This requires the EPA to set a threshold quantity for the release of these toxic chemicals that will automatically trigger community emergency procedures. If the EPA fails to set this threshold, however, the law mandates that the threshold will automatically be two pounds—no matter what the chemical. A threshold this low would almost assure a local emergency response to every toxic chemical release in a community.

"An Odd and Intricate System of Checks-and-Balances."   Republican victories in the 1994 congressional elections only perpetuated the fractious relationship between EPA and Congress. The new Republican majority in both legislative chambers, ideologically hostile toward the Agency and its programs, at first enthusiastically assaulted the Agency's budget and regulatory authority in a comprehensive effort to severely diminish both. Among those leading the Republican charge was Rep. Jerry R. Lewis (R-Calif.), the new chairman of the House appropriations committee with jurisdiction over the EPA. "This is an agency that needs some serious shaking," he warned in the bellicose style of the new legislative majority.[8] The Reagan administration had learned, at considerable political cost, that frontal assaults on the statutory bulwark of environmental regulation invite a public backlash and soon unnerve legislative Republicans themselves—even ardent congressional opponents of environmental laws usually wish to avoid the public stigma of being "anti-environmental." Congressional Republicans re-learned the lesson between 1994 and 1998 and eventually abandoned their initial sweeping assault in preference to persistent, quieter, and less publicly risky campaigns aimed selectively at portions of various environmental laws and segments of EPA budgets vulnerable to antiregulatory strategies. This did not produce the "serious shaking" the new Republican majority had promised but Republican antipathy did slow appreciably the growth of EPA's budget, the passage of new environmental legislation, and the revision of older laws, much to the dissatisfaction of most environmental organizations. As the decade closed, it seemed by a per-

verse political logic that friends and critics of environmental regulation had unwittingly collaborated to assure that legislative overcontrol of EPA, and the administrative distrust nourishing it, would be virtually institutionalized in Congress. "Pro-environment members of Congress fear that the agency will not be ardent enough in defending the environment; members more sympathetic to business concerns fear that the agency will be too ardent," concluded Resources for the Future's comprehensive review of federal regulatory programs. "The pro-environment members (and the pro-business members) write detailed instructions into law; the pro-business members try to ensure that the agency will not have enough resources to fully implement the laws and that the courts will have authority to second guess any agency decisions. EPA is thus the focus of an odd and intricate system of checks-and-balances."[9]

In the end, congressional overcontrol seldom satisfies either critic or proponent of environmental regulation. Because it does not leave enough flexibility in the law when justifiable delays may be essential, overcontrol practically ensures frequent agency failures to meet some deadlines, thereby eroding the credibility of programs and agencies. In addition, overcontrol often drives agencies to set up their own informal, unannounced timetables for completing assigned programs and to set their own program priorities in an effort to deal with the law more realistically. Finally, agency failures to conform to congressional overcontrol are provocations to litigation and further congressional oversight of the programs involved, delaying and complicating rather than hastening implementation. And all these complications are expensive.

The Legislative Bluff.   Congress has written into major environmental laws a multitude of sanctions, many ostensibly severe, intended to encourage compliance with environmental regulation and to arm regulators with the power to compel it. The CAA, for instance, authorizes the EPA to impose a moratorium on the construction and operation of any new stationary source of air pollution in any urban area that fails to attain federally required air-quality standards by the mandated deadlines; this, in effect, gives the Agency the authority to stop major urban economic development. The CAA also empowers the EPA to issue documents halting all federal highway construction funds and other major federal grants to any state with urban areas failing to meet deadlines for compliance with federally required air-quality standards. The Superfund legislation authorized federal and state regulators to sue the creators of abandoned hazardous waste sites to recover all the costs of removal and remedy involved in making abandoned sites safe. The RCRA empowers the EPA to secure a court injunction stopping any activity by any person or firm that endangers public health or safety by failing to comply with the Act's requirements for the handling of dangerous substances.[10] And so forth.

Tough penalties cannot be used routinely. Effective regulation requires that the sustaining sanctions be varied and selectively used. Regulators often need both authority and opportunity to bargain about when and how penalties will be applied to regulated interests failing to comply with the laws. Nonetheless, a powerful sanction merely threatened will eventually become a rusty regulatory blunderbuss, its power more apparent than real.

Congress has diminished the credibility of many tough sanctions written into environmental legislation by repeatedly extending compliance deadlines for regulations, thereby sidestepping the sanction problem. Consider, for example, the deadline of the CAA for the nation's metropolitan areas to meet national air-quality standards for ozone or face a moratorium on new factory construction and loss of federal highway funds. Congress first set the deadline for 1976, then extended it to 1982, then to 1987, then to late 1988, then to 1990—extensions granted to save more than sixty metropolitan areas from sanctions. Once Congress authorized the EPA to extend the CAA deadlines, the message was clear. According to R. Shep Melnick, "Congress and the EPA once again showed that they would not stand behind the standards and deadlines previously announced with great seriousness. Every major participant knows that loopholes will always appear in the nick of time, thus obviating the need to impose sanctions in areas that fail to meet air quality standards." [11] Continuing congressional setbacks in compliance deadlines have also been made for automobile emission requirements in the CAA, in water-quality standards for municipal waste treatment systems regulated under the FWPCAA, and many other programs in other environmental laws.

Among the many plausible reasons customarily given for this congressional habit are the legislators' concerns about the adverse economic impact of sanctions on the local and national economy, the alleged difficulties in developing the technologies needed to meet compliance deadlines, and the administrative and judicial delays that impede program implementation. Equally important is a lack of political will to face the consequences of the commitments the Congress has made to enforce the law. In effect, the toughest sanctions in environmental legislation often amount to little more than impotent legislative make-believe.

Subgovernments

One of Washington's most venerable institutions is the subgovernment, sometimes described as a "policy whirlpool" or "iron triangle." The classic subgovernment is a trinity comprised of a congressional committee, agency personnel, and an interest group, all united by a common commitment to a narrow policy objective, most often the implementation of some portion of major federal law and the promotion of the interests it serves.[12] Subgovernments vary in durability and membership, but many tenaciously preserve a large measure of influence, if not control, over routine policy making in their own domains. Subgovernments often facilitate communication, negotiation, and consensus building among the different institutional interests involved in policy making. They bridge the gap between separated governmental institutions and private interests, often promoting policy implementation and appraisal. Subgovernments often become helpful, even essential, cogs in the political infrastructure in Congress's daily struggle to carry out its constitutional responsibilities.

Among the most important subgovernments involved with environmental policy making are those joining congressional committees with the agencies over which they have jurisdiction and with the interest group constituencies for those agencies. A number of congressional committees, for instance, possess significant oversight or budgetary authority over the EPA, including the House Energy and Commerce Committee; the House Government Operations Committee; the House Science, Space, and Technology Committee; the Senate Environment and Public Works Committee; and the Appropriations Committee in each chamber. As with all congressional committees, those concerned with environmental agencies such as the EPA, Department of the Interior (DOI), the Nuclear Regulatory Commission (NRC), and the Occupational Safety and Health Administration (OSHA) have acquired a strong political stake in maintaining their jurisdictions and their working relationships and understandings with the agencies involved in their oversight. Indeed, the chairs of many congressional environmental committees and subcommittees—people such as Rep. John D. Dingell (D-Mich.), Rep. Henry A. Waxman (D-Calif.), Sen. John H. Chafee (R-R.I.), and Sen. George J. Mitchell (D-Maine)—became national figures in great measure through their environmental activities.[13]

The congressional committees anchoring environmental subgovernments also have a strong vested interest in perpetuating their jurisdictions over specific agencies and programs. The committees are likely to resist vigorously any effort to reorganize environmental agencies, or the congressional committee structure, or the environmental laws over which they exercise oversight when such change threatens to diminish committee influence over the agencies involved. This perpetuates the multitude of committees and fragmented authority over environmental affairs in Congress and erects almost insurmountable obstacles to major reorganization of agencies and programs when fundamental change may be essential to better regulation. A case in point is the "integrated environmental management" now advocated by many environmental policy reformers. Using this approach, regulators would decide on the best strategy for regulating a pollutant after tracking its movement through all the ecosystem—air, water, and land, for example—rather than segmenting its control into different methods according to whether it is found in land, water, or air. The environmental subgovernments were "responsible for undermining various consolidation proposals in environmental and conservation management during the early and middle 1970s . . . [and] effectively blocked enactment in 1979 of the proposed Integrated Environmental Assistance Act, which had offered some promise as a source of environmental integration."[14]

These problems are not peculiar to environmental policy. They reveal historic political values and institutional processes nurtured by the constitutional design of Congress and two centuries of American political culture. Tyranny of the immediate—the congressional tendency to respond to the most compelling problem at hand and to be preoccupied with the short-term consequences—is inevitable in a legislature whose entire lower chamber and a third of its upper one is elected every two years. Preoccupation with the next election easily constricts the congressional time horizons of most importance to a period of a few years and compels attention to the problems most likely to be on the public's mind at that time. A desire to sidestep possibly intractable legislative conflicts by shifting them to administrators, or to avoid the threatening political and economic consequences of enforcing the law, is instinctive to all politicians. So is the impulse to hold fast to whatever legislative arrangements give one power and influence. Behaviors so strongly inspired by the fundamental political order become all but immutable.

Some improvement may be possible through relatively moderate reforms, such as reorganization of the congressional committee structure and better legislative drafting in the laws. Perhaps, as will be elaborated later, fundamental institutional redesign may be the only solution. But at least two reforms merit brief mention because they deal not with changes in congressional design or habit but with how legislators have been taught to think about the natural order. First, many congressional obstacles to better environmental regulation might be reduced greatly if Congress were convinced that the nation's present environmental ills constituted a crisis of such extraordinary order as to threaten national security and community survival. Second, many legislators might be more willing to forgo their customary approaches to environmental policy making if they were individually better educated about the character of environmental problems and about how public institutions are helping to solve the problems or to exacerbate them.

EPA's Organizational Structure

Critics and defenders of current environmental regulation may disagree about solutions, but almost all agree that the EPA is not implementing its regulatory responsibilities well. A vocal but small clan of critics favor abolishing the Agency altogether. A larger, more influential group advocates abandoning exclusive reliance on the "command-and-control" philosophy presently guiding most Agency programs and placing greater reliance on marketplace incentives—of which much will be said in later chapters. Most reform proposals, however, range from modest alterations in the Agency's existing resources and mandate to radical restructuring of the Agency's organization and mission.

Administrative Overload

Economist David Vogel wrote, "By requiring the EPA to accomplish so much, Congress has virtually ensured that the Agency's rule-making and enforcement efforts will be inadequate. The price the EPA has paid for its successful effort at strict enforcement in selected policy areas— such as control of automobile emissions . . . has been the virtual neglect of its regulatory responsibilities in a whole host of other areas." [15] The evidence of the EPA's current administrative overload is written in the statistics of missed deadlines, lagging research, and impossibly distant completion dates for existing program responsibilities. The doleful litany includes the following:

- The Federal Insecticide, Fungicide, and Rodenticide Act (FIFRA) requires the EPA to evaluate more than 50,000 individual pesticide products containing more than 600 active ingredients and 900 inert ingredients. "If EPA has to prepare interim registration standards for all 600 active ingredients," the General Accounting Office (GAO) concluded, "then the Agency may finish the first round reviews in about 2004." [16]
- The average time for EPA to clean up Superfund sites placed on the fast-track National Priority List (NPL), reserved for the most dangerous sites, had increased from 6.3 years in the mid-1980s to more than 8 years by the mid-1990s. The EPA, according to a GAO study in late 1997, would be unlikely to meet its own estimate of 8 years to clean up Superfund sites added in the future to the NPL.[17]
- In 1987, Congress passed amendments to the Clean Water Act mandating that the EPA establish rules and take other actions necessary to assure that the states would create a permit program to regulate stormwater runoff from industrial and municipal sites. The EPA issued the first of the state guidelines twenty-one months after the statutory

deadline. Because of this delay, Congress extended the deadline from 1992 to 1994 for small cities to comply with the guidelines.[18] At the end of 1994, EPA had still not issued the guidelines for small cities. The Agency now expects to issue the required small cities guidelines by 1999.

Confronted with a daunting multitude of program responsibilities, data requirements, testing needs, and program deadlines, the EPA frequently resorts to improvised strategies for deciding which programs and pollutants will get priority. Sometimes it depends on litigation initiated by private interests—most often environmental groups—to force its attention to specific programs. The Agency was able to give priority to a TSCA requirement that it act within one year on recommendations from its experts concerning whether a substance merited testing for carcinogenicity only because the Natural Resources Defense Council sued the EPA and obtained a judicial order for the Agency to speed up the review process. Sometimes the Agency ignores portions of the law to make its workload manageable. In order to cope with the otherwise impossible task of screening 60,000 chemicals presently in commercial use, as in one instance involving TSCA, Edward Woodhouse observed that the EPA "simply misinterpreted the law: the agency placed its focus exclusively on new uses of new chemicals. . . . EPA apparently decided (probably implicitly) that its staff and funds were inadequate to cover tens of thousands of existing chemicals."[19] Sometimes Agency managers explicitly establish their own priorities among programs.

Program Integration Problems

The EPA has come to resemble a regulatory holding company, a conglomerate of offices, each focused narrowly on problems in a single environmental medium (such as air, land, or water) or on one kind of pollutant (such as toxic waste). Further, each office is responsible for numerous regulatory laws written with little attention to their compatibility. "Each program has staked out an environmental problem that it is required to 'fix,' according to the peculiar rules embodied in its statutory mandate," observed the CEQ.[20] The EPA originally was conceived very differently. The advisory council recommending the EPA's creation to President Nixon had argued that environmental policy had a unique character because there were "interactions and trade-offs inherent in controlling different types of pollution." The EPA was expected to be the means to "rationalize the organization of environmental efforts" and "give focus and coordination to them."[21] In short, the EPA was intended to synthesize approaches to specific environmental problems into an "integrated and holistic approach"—which is precisely what the EPA has *not* done.

Circumstances conspired against this integrated approach from the EPA's inception. Its most grievous fault was lack of political allure. Congress and the White House, under intense public pressure to do something quickly about specific pollution problems, needed to promote what seemed the quickest solution to what appeared to be the most urgent problem of the moment. Integrated management, in contrast, seemed strange and complicated, too difficult to explain and too unpredictable in results to appeal to Congress or the public.[22] Also, the program offices concerned with air, water, and land quickly dominated the EPA and defeated most efforts to create more integrated programs; these offices had powerful constituencies while the multimedia programs did not. Barry Rabe noted, "Each environmental medium and the separate programs within each medium have attracted politically potent constituencies that are likely antagonists toward any attempt to transform—or integrate—the existing system. They include environmental professionals and agencies, representatives of business and industry, and various policy-making committees and subcommittees that operate in Congress and state legislatures."[23] Environmental groups were usually unsympathetic, perhaps because they feared that integrated management would subvert existing programs. Moreover, environmental law usually regulates the impact of specific pollutants, such as threats to public health or groundwater quality, and legislative pressure to produce results gives regulators little incentive to take the longer time necessary to develop more holistic approaches to pollution management.

The segmented approach to pollution management embodied in EPA's organization and programs is often unsatisfactory because it does not effectively deal with cross-media pollution and interactive pollutants. Consider the example of regulating the hazardous wastes from the nation's more than 3,500 electroplating firms. If such firms are permitted to flush their wastes into municipal waste treatment systems, these wastes (including heavy metals such as cadmium, copper, and nickel) can kill the bacteria essential for municipal water treatment. If the heavy metals are removed from the wastes before they are flushed into the municipal system, a toxic sludge remains. In 1984, the EPA decided to phase out the use of landfills for the disposal of these sludges. If electroplating firms then decided to stabilize the waste sludge by mixing it with other agents such as cement kiln dust, the poisons may be secured and acceptable for landfills but the metals then cannot be recycled and the wastes create much greater bulk in landfills rapidly filling to capacity. Under present law, these toxic metals will be managed differently according to which medium is affected. Regulating these wastes by one approach creates a new form of pollution and transfers costs from one program to another. At the present time, no federal law empowers the EPA to manage these toxic sludges by calculating the costs and risks involved in their migration from one environmental medium to another and by selecting a strategy that creates the least total cost, or risk, when all the different media are considered.

The problem of interactive pollutants is illustrated by the increased health risks that may be associated with metals exposed to acid precipitation. Studies of regions with heavy acid precipitation indicate that metals in soil and lake sediment (such as aluminum, cadmium, mercury, and lead) become more soluble as the acidity increases in the water. Acidified water can "leach metals from soils and lake sediments into underground aquifers, streams, and reservoirs, potentially contaminating edible fish and water supplies. It can also dissolve toxic metals from the pipes and conduits of municipal or home water systems, contaminating drinking water." [24] No current federal program or office of the EPA exists with the authority to manage acid precipitation through comprehensive study of its multimedia effects and interactive consequences. Instead, acid precipitation is regulated by different methods, according to different criteria, depending on whether it is airborne or deposited in soil, and whether its chemical products affect surface waters.

Developing an integrated approach to pollution management would take considerable time. One obstacle is the lack of reliable, accurate scientific models explaining cross-media pollution processes and identifying the costs and risks involved. In addition, few scientific professionals are trained in integrated management, and few resources currently are invested in developing such training programs. But integrated management has much to recommend it. It would produce regulatory methods that create significant cost reduction, and perhaps quicker results than the segmented approaches currently applied to pollution problems. For example, removing sulfur from electric power plant air emissions usually results in toxic sludges that must then be treated by land disposal, which in turn often creates groundwater contamination. Greater control of sulfur air emissions at their source, however, might require more costly air pollution control technologies yet result in far less overall expense and greater reduction of health and ecological risks than regulating sulfur in air, soil, and groundwater separately.[25]

Needed: More Money, More Staff

The EPA was underfunded and understaffed seriously throughout the 1980s. Many of the Agency's current problems with missed deadlines and laggard enforcement are a continuing inheritance from the Reagan administration's severe budget reductions in the early 1980s. Between 1980 and 1983, the Agency lost almost one-third of its budget and more than one-fifth of its personnel.[26] Congress subsequently rejected many additional budget and personnel cuts, but the Agency's budget failed to keep pace with its growing regulatory responsibilities throughout the 1980s. By the late 1990s, the EPA's budget had apparently recovered from the austerity of the 1980s, yet the convalescence was deceptive. While the Agency's FY 1998 budget of $7.36 billion represented an 8.5 percent increase over the prior year and a more than 20 percent increase over its budget a decade before, comparatively little was actually allocated for EPA's basic operations. More than two-thirds of the budget was dedicated to Superfund and waste treatment grants largely destined for state and local governments. In contrast, less than a third of the total budget supported the EPA's operating expenses—regulatory program management, enforcement and research—the real sinews of pollution regulation and prevention. The Agency's work force has remained largely unchanged since 1992, averaging about 18,500 employees. Agency officials generally assert this is not enough to provide the personnel required to administer the continuing accumulation of new responsibilities inherited by EPA throughout the 1990s.

Missing Priorities

Like the man who mounted his horse and galloped off in all directions, the EPA lacks a constant course. With responsibility for administering nine separate statutes and parts of four others, the EPA has no clearly mandated priorities, no way of allocating scarce resources among different statutes or among programs within a single law. Nor does the EPA have a congressional charter, common to most federal departments and agencies, defining its broad organizational mission and priorities. While the Agency has had to make informal, ad hoc decisions about program priorities to survive, these are much less satisfactory legally and politically than a clear, congressionally mandated agenda.

Congress has shown little inclination to provide the EPA with a charter or mandated priorities, in good part because the debate sure to arise on the relative merit and urgency of different environmental problems is an invitation to a political bloodletting most legislators would gladly avoid. Intense controversy would be likely among states, partisans of different ecological issues, and regulated interests over which problems to emphasize; the resulting political brawl would upset existing policy coalitions that themselves were fashioned with great difficulty. Moreover, setting priorities invites a prolonged, bitter debate over an intensely emotional issue: should the primary objective of environmental protection be to reduce public risks associated with environmental degradation as much as seems practical or—as many environmentalists fervently believe—is the goal to eliminate all significant forms of pollution altogether? Many experts inside and outside the EPA have argued that unless Congress sets priorities enabling the Agency to concentrate its resources on a relatively few feasible, measurable objectives, the nation will be dissipating its environmental resources among a multitude of different programs and objectives with few significant results.

The Reform Struggle

EPA's administrators have been acutely aware of the Agency's managerial problems and have initiated many programs throughout the 1990s to encourage greater administrative efficiency and effectiveness when opportunities arose. The difficulties involved in implementing these internal reforms arise, quite often, from conflicts among the Agency's numerous stakeholders, both inside and outside the organization, whose "buy-in" to reform is frequently essential to its success. Even politically skilled administrators, armed with a vigorous reform agenda and administrative expertise, have struggled to overcome the divisive pluralism of interest often evident among the EPA's multiple constituencies.

In 1995, for example, EPA administrator Carole Browner launched more than forty management initiatives intended, among other things, to encourage more "integrated" pollution management between the Agency's various media offices, to facilitate better cooperation with state and local governments, to speed the regulatory process, and to accomplish a multitude of other desirable objectives. But few results are readily observable. Among the major impediments to reform are the difficulty in convincing the Agency's own rank-and-file to "buy-in" to a new, integrated approach to pollution regulation; the opposition of state regulatory officials to many reforms; the confusion among numerous interest groups involved with Agency programs concerning the intention and impact of the proposed reforms; and disagreement between headquarters and regional EPA offices over their respective responsibilities in the reform process.[27] Browner's experience, shared by all EPA administrators, illustrates that EPA's administrative afflictions cannot be blamed upon a single villain, however much Congress may be involved in specific problems. The Agency's own internal factions, as well as its own nominally supportive interest group constituency, share responsibility with other federal and state bureaucracies as well as with EPA's ideological opponents in erecting obstacles to needed reform.

The Impact of Federalism

The Constitution created more than a government of countervailing and competitive institutions. The tenacious institutional rivalries inherent in the U.S. constitutional system are moderated because, as Richard E. Neustadt observed, the institutions share power.[28] Effective policy requires that public officials collaborate by discovering strategies to transcend these institutional conflicts. So it is with the federalism through which environmental regulations are usually implemented.

Federalism disperses governmental power by fragmenting authority between national and state governments. Despite the historical enlargement of federal powers, federalism remains a sturdy constitutional buttress supporting the edifice of authority—shared, independent, and countervailing—erected for the states within the federal system. An observer has said, "It is difficult to find any government activity which does not involve all three of the so-called 'levels' of the federal system." Yet no one level monopolizes power. "There has never been a time when it was possible to put neat labels on discrete 'federal,' 'state,' and 'local' functions."[29]

Environmental programs usually are federalized, and sometimes regionalized, in their implementation, thereby introducing another political dimension to the policy process. For instance, federal air and water pollution legislation is administered through the Washington headquarters of the EPA, its ten regional offices, and the majority of state governments, which assume the responsibility for issuing to pollution dischargers a permit specifying the acceptable control technologies and emission levels. In the mid-1990s, for instance, thirty-eight states had authority to issue water permits and forty-nine certified pesticides under federal authority. This two- and three-tiered design ensures that state and regional interests take part in the regulatory process and that, consequently, state and local governments, together with their associated interests, actively pursue their individual, often competitive objectives during program implementation. Even if the states are not formally included in the administration of federal environmental regulations, they are likely to insist on some voice in decisions affecting them. For example, states with Department of Defense (DOD) nuclear weapons processing facilities insisted they be consulted when the DOD determined the priority list for site cleanup after widespread mismanagement of nuclear materials was discovered at more than twenty sites in the late 1980s.[30]

Federalism in environmental regulation guarantees voice and influence to the multitude of different states involved, providing an essential representation for various geographic interests affected politically and economically by federal environmental laws. Federalism also encourages diversity and experimentation in program administration, at times producing valuable innovation in program implementation. Often, it has been aggressive state pressure that forced the EPA's policy implementation and innovation. Nine Northeastern states, for instance, sued EPA in mid-1993 to compel the Agency to issue long-delayed regulations for state air pollution permit programs. The Northeastern states and California have pushed vigorously the recalcitrant Agency to assume greater initiative in implementing its responsibilities for developing cleaner automobile fuels. Often, state environmental programs have been models for federal legislation.

But federalism also complicates and delays program implementation when, for instance, it multiplies the number of local government environmental agencies issuing permits. In Washington state, for example, there were until recently six state permitting agencies, a regional air pollution authority, five county permitting agencies, and three municipal agencies.[31] Regulated interests often complain about the time and difficulty required to collect all the necessary permits and plea for the creation of a "one-stop" system that would enable them to obtain permits through one coordinating agency. Federalism also encourages bargaining between federal, regional, and state agencies when writing and enforcing regulations. State governments have a habit of using their congressional representatives to influence federal environmental regulation to their own advantage. Much of the delay, conflict, and confusion in program implementation also arises because state governments have been so adept in persuading their congressional delegations to intervene in the regulatory process on behalf of a state interest.

Few issues arouse state concern more than federal aid and administrative discretion for the states in program management. Federal aid comes in many forms: grants for program administration, staff training, salary supplements, program enforcement, and pollution control facilities; technical assistance in program development or enforcement; research cost sharing; and much more. In the latter 1990s, the EPA provided about one in every five dollars spent by the states on major pollution control programs and an additional $2.5 billion in grants for the construction of waste treatment facilities. The states understandably favor generous federal cost-sharing in the administration of federally mandated environmental programs. Many proponents of environmental regulation believe that the amount of federal aid directly affects the quality of environmental protection, particularly in those states lacking adequate staff and technical resources to implement programs on their own.

Another fertile source of controversy in regulatory federalism are the many regional conflicts deeply embedded in the nation's history. Disagreements between the Western states, where most of the federal public lands reside, and Washington over the management of the public domain west of the Mississippi—almost a third of the nation's land area—repeatedly erupt in the course of federal environmental regulation. The "Sagebrush Rebellion" of the early 1980s exemplified the western states' perennial grievance against administration of the public lands within their boundaries by a distant Department of the Interior. More than half of Alaska, Idaho, Nevada, Oregon, Utah, and Wyoming is federally owned, as is more than a third of Arizona, California, Colorado, and New Mexico. The western governors and their allies launched a determined campaign to persuade Congress and the White House to grant the states a much greater voice in deciding how these lands, and particularly their economic resources, should be developed. Both President Reagan and his first secretary of the interior, James Watt, enthusiastically embraced the Sagebrush Rebellion and promised to use their administrative powers to give the states more voice in the DOI's management of western lands. The rebellion proved little more than a skirmish, however, when Congress and the federal courts blocked early Reagan administration efforts to make most of the promised changes and the western states grew apprehensive about the environmental destruction that might accompany massive economic development on the public lands.[32] The Bush administration succeeded in pacifying the Sagebrush rebels but a new rebellion never lurks far from any confrontation between the West and Washington over public lands management.

A newer, but equally contentious, regional conflict first appeared in the mid-1980s when scientific evidence began to validate the existence of acid rain and the transport of acid rain precursors across national, regional, and state boundaries. It soon became apparent that much of the considerable acid deposition falling in Northeastern states originated among the extensive smokestack industries along the Ohio River valley. Northeastern governors soon took the initiative in demanding that the EPA compel Ohio River states to impose stricter emission controls on their smokestack industries. The offending states resisted this onslaught, thrusting the EPA into the middle of an increasingly acrimonious dispute between Ohio River valley states, intent on defeating new EPA emission controls on the region's fossil-fuel burning industries, and Northeastern states supporting the controls to limit the airborne pollution from Ohio River sources. In mid-1993, nine Northeastern states sued the EPA to compel the Agency to issue long-delayed regulations for state air pollution control permits which, it was assumed, would accomplish the desired emission controls. EPA subsequently issued the delayed regulations, but they did not abate the offending stack emissions to the satisfaction of the Northeastern states, who have increasingly, but so far unsuccessfully, pressed Congress for a remedy through legislative amendments to the Clean Air Act.

Even without regionalism, the amount of discretion permitted the states when interpreting and enforcing federal regulations within their own borders would be a matter of ceaseless controversy in American environmental administration. In general, the states prefer the federal government to leave state administrators with enough discretion to adapt federal environmental regulations to unique local conditions and to be responsive to local economic and political interests. Assailing the federal government for imposing regulations on the states without respect for local interests is a political mantra among state officials, but the criticism has grown increasingly strident as the states' competence and resources for pollution regulation have improved throughout the 1990s. States now commonly complain that federal regulations force them to conform to rules that are inappropriate, economically wasteful, or politically unfair to local interests—a mood aggravated by mounting regulatory responsibilities imposed by Washington along with diminishing financial support for their implementation. These confrontations occur over many different issues in many political venues, as the following illustrate:

• In mid-1997 West Virginia's principal air pollution regulatory official declared the state's intention to fight newly proposed federal air quality standards for nitrogen oxide because "they impose an unwarranted hardship on our citizens." A lawyer representing state electric utilities who helped prepare these remarks added a regional spin to the conflict: "We're being set up by the Northeast and we're being set up by EPA. If we don't resist they're going to have us for lunch."[33]

• Massachusetts Governor William Weld in 1995 withdrew his state's support for a new motor vehicle emissions testing program intended to help the state comply with federal air pollution control regulations because similar programs in other states "provoked motorist outrage." The Massachusetts legislature was unable to pass a newer emissions control law before the deadline expired in late 1997.[34]

• Wyoming Senator Mike Enzi (R) introduced a bill in Congress to prohibit the EPA from withholding environmental regulatory authority from Wyoming because the state recently passed a law allowing companies that identify and correct their environmental problems to avoid civil penalties. EPA had "harassed" the state, complained Enzi. "I think it is a tragedy that EPA has been so obstructive in giving the states a chance to test reasonable and innovative solutions to a cleaner environment," he observed.[35]

As the West Virginia incident demonstrates, major state industries and other locally important economic interests affected by environmental regulation often join the crusade for generous administrative discretion to the states in which their political clout may be much greater than in Washington. The rising discontent in regulatory federalism is particularly worrisome to proponents of environmental protection because voluntary, well-intentioned cooperation is essential to effective pollution control in the U.S. constitutional structure. Conflict over the respective roles of federal and state governments will always occur in the federalized administration of environmental laws, a certain inheritance for any new White House administration. Still, such progress as has been achieved in the nation's environmental programs has resulted, in large measure, from a productive, largely dependable federalism in program design and implementation.

Bureaucratic Pluralism and Competition

Regulatory politics involves not only bargaining and conflict among federal, regional, and state regulatory agencies, but also recurrent competition among different regulatory agencies. Few environmental problems lie within the jurisdiction of a single agency. Several agencies—sometimes as many as nine or ten—will share responsibility for some aspect of environmental management. Organized interests with a stake in an environmental issue will promote, if possible, a major role for whatever relevant agency is most sympathetic to their viewpoints. Also, various interests will fight tenaciously to keep sympathetic agencies from losing their regulatory influence on crucial issues. American farmers fought long but largely in vain to prevent Congress from investing the newly created EPA with the Agriculture Department's former authority for pesticide regulation. The farmers reasoned correctly that the Agriculture Department would be considerably more sympathetic to the viewpoint of pesticide users and hence less inclined to restrict agricultural chemicals than would the EPA. More successful was the Pentagon's campaign to prevent the NRC from inheriting authority to regulate military reactors and nuclear fuel facilities when the Atomic Energy Commission was abolished in 1976. Instead, authority went first to the Energy Research and Development Administration and later to the new Department of Energy—both of which the Pentagon assumed to be more responsive to military interests than the NRC.

Often, regulating environmental pollutants becomes primarily a struggle between federal bureaucracies—perhaps state agencies as well—each with a different viewpoint and constituency. Chemical regulation requires a bureaucratic convention. Twelve different federal laws concern some aspect of chemical safety, dispersing major authority for their implementation among twelve federal agencies, including the Department of State and the U.S. Agency for International Development. Many chemicals are regulated by multiple agencies: "Federal control of all exposures from the manufacture, use, and disposal of vinyl chloride would have required the participation of five federal agencies and involvement of 15 separate laws," Barry Rabe noted.[36]

Even when conflict is unintended, bureaucratic disagreement and inconsistency over environmental regulation often leads to time-consuming litigation, leaving the courts to sort out the respective jurisdictions and the appropriate interpretations of law affecting water pollution discharges, pesticide management, or the multitude of other environmental matters subject to multiple bureaucratic authorities. Congress is seldom disposed to eliminate some of this bureaucratic competition by vesting regulatory authority more parsimoniously among fewer agencies. Congressional committees and subcommittees with existing authority over various regulatory agencies are loath to permit any erosion of authority among agencies over which they have oversight, lest the committee's influence suffer as well. Moreover, organized interests will quickly rush to the defense of agencies with whom they have useful working relationships. And bureaucratic managers are quick to mobilize their allies against formidable assaults on the agency's jurisdiction or authority.

Conclusion

To most Americans, the nation's environmental troubles are epitomized by polluted air, fouled water, dangerously unregulated hazardous and toxic wastes, and a multitude of other ecological derangements. This chapter illuminates a less obvious dimension of the environmental crisis that is equally dangerous in its ecological implications: the institutional and economic obstacles to implementing environmental policy effectively. In many critical respects, the institutions and policies the nation now depends on to reverse its ecological degradation are failing, sometimes badly. Equally as imperative as new technological solutions to ecological ills are new economic and institutional solutions. Finding these solutions will require critical, difficult debate within the environmental movement and among public policy makers at all governmental levels concerned with ecological restoration.

These problems are especially refractory because they often originate in the fundamental constitutional design of the political system, or in deeply rooted political traditions. Among these problems are congressional overcontrol of the agencies implementing environmental policy, legislative reluctance to create clear mandates and priorities within regulatory programs, the excessive fragmentation of committee control over environmental policy, and the resistance of subgovernments to structural and policy reform. While federalism is essential to the political architecture of any environmental regulatory program in the United States, it also complicates policy implementation by introducing competitive, pluralistic interests.

Other problems arise from the excessive dependence on traditional policy approaches to environmental problems, particularly the standards-and-enforcement method of regulation and the single-media approach to controlling specific pollutants. While other approaches often seem more appropriate, and in some cases have been tried experimentally, they are strongly resisted by a multitude of institutional, professional, and economic interests with a stake in the status quo. Often, the environmental movement itself has been excessively conservative in resisting policy innovation.

Among the significant economic problems arising from environmental regulation, none is more often debated than the high cost of environmental regulation. As costs continually rise well above expectations, the need to find cost-effective, cost-saving approaches to policy making grows more apparent. While cost-benefit analysis is sometimes a useful strategy for reducing regulatory costs, its serious political and economic deficiencies suggest that other approaches, involving more economic incentives for pollution abatement in the private sector, are likely to be more broadly effective. None of the problems now associated with regulatory incapacity are likely to be solved easily or quickly.

Notes

1. Council on Environmental Quality (CEQ), *The First Annual Report of the Council on Environmental Quality* (Washington, D.C.: Government Printing Office, 1970), 232.
2. Conservation Foundation, *Newsletter,* no. 1 (1989): 1.
3. Quoted in *New York Times,* March 22, 1993.
4. Ibid.
5. General Accounting Office (GAO), "Indoor Air Pollution: Federal Efforts Are Not Effectively Addressing a Growing Problem," Report no. GAO/RCED 92-8 (Oct. 1991), 6.
6. Quoted in Margaret E. Kriz, "Pesticidal Pressures," *National Journal,* Dec. 12, 1988, 3, 125–126.
7. GAO, "Superfund: Missed Statutory Deadlines Slow Progress in Environmental Programs," Report no. GAO/RCED 89-27 (Nov. 1988), 3.
8. *New York Times,* September 23, 1995. On the Republican reform agenda generally, see Bob Benenson, "GOP Sets the 104th Congress on New Regulatory Course," *Congressional Quarterly Weekly Report,* June 17, 1995, 1693–1703; "House Panel Takes Quick Action on Risk Assessment Provisions," *Congressional Quarterly Weekly Report,* February 11, 1995, 450–452; and "Bipartisan Rewrite Breezes Through Committee," *Congressional Quarterly Weekly Report,* March 25, 1995.

9. Clarence Davies and Jan Mazurek, *Regulating Pollution: Does The U.S. System Work?* (Washington, D.C.: Resources for the Future, 1997), 6–7.
10. Richard N. L. Andrews, "Environment and Energy: Implications of Overloaded Agendas," *Natural Resources Journal* 19, no. 3 (July 1979): 487–504.
11. R. Shep Melnick, "Pollution Deadlines and the Coalition of Failure," *Public Interest,* no. 75 (Spring 1984): 125.
12. R. Shep Melnick, *Regulation and the Courts* (Washington, D.C.: Brookings Institution, 1983), 378.
13. Louis Fisher, *The Politics of Shared Power,* 2d ed. (Washington, D.C.: CQ Press, 1987), 222–223.
14. Barry G. Rabe, *Fragmentation and Integration in State Environmental Management* (Washington, D.C.: Conservation Foundation, 1986), 128–129.
15. David Vogel, *National Styles of Regulation* (Ithaca, N.Y.: Cornell University Press, 1986), 167.
16. GAO, "Pesticides: EPA's Formidable Task to Assess and Regulate Their Risks," Report no. GAO/RCED 86-125 (April 1986), 35.
17. GAO, "Duration of Superfund Process," Report no. GAO/RCED 97-20 (March 1997).
18. *New York Times,* April 25, 1992.
19. Edward J. Woodhouse, "External Influences on Productivity: EPA's Implementation of TSCA," *Policy Studies Review* 4, no. 3 (Feb. 1985): 500.
20. CEQ, *Environmental Quality, 1985* (Washington, D.C.: CEQ, 1986), 12–13.
21. Richard A. Harris and Sidney M. Milkis, *The Politics of Regulatory Change* (New York: Oxford University Press, 1989), 228.
22. Peter W. House and Roger D. Shull, *Regulatory Reform: Politics and the Environment* (Lanham, Md.: University Press of America, 1985), 106ff.
23. Rabe, *Fragmentation and Integration,* 126.
24. Sandra Postel, *Altering the Earth's Chemistry: Assessing the Risks* (Washington, D.C.: Worldwatch Institute, 1986), 36.
25. Conservation Foundation, *State of the Environment: An Assessment at Mid-Decade* (Washington, D.C.: Conservation Foundation, 1984), chap. 9.
26. Norman J. Vig and Michael E. Kraft, "Environmental Policy from the 1970s to the 1990s: Continuity and Change," in *Environmental Policy in the 1990s,* 2d ed., ed. Michael E. Kraft and Norman J. Vig (Washington, D.C.: CQ Press, 1994), 19 and app. 3.
27. GAO, "Reinventing Environmental Regulation," Report no. GAO/RCED 97-155 (1997), 6.
28. Richard E. Neustadt, *Presidential Power* (New York: Wiley, 1960), 33.
29. Morton Grodzins, "The Federal System," in *American Federalism in Perspective,* ed. Aaron Wildavsky (Boston: Little, Brown, 1967), 257.
30. Conservation Foundation, *Newsletter* (Sept. 1986): 6.
31. Rabe, *Fragmentation and Integration,* 26–27.
32. David R. Beam, "New Federalism, Old Realities: The Reagan Administration and Intergovernmental Reform," in *The Reagan Presidency and the Governing of America,* ed. Lester M. Salamon and Michael S. Lund (Washington, D.C.: Urban Institute Press, 1984), 440.
33. Ken Ward, *Charleston Sunday Gazette-Mail,* Oct. 17, 1997.
34. Peter Howe, *Boston Globe,* Oct. 29, 1997.
35. *Billings Gazette,* Nov. 2, 1997.
36. Rabe, *Fragmentation and Integration,* 14.

Suggested Readings

Greve, Michael S., and Fred L. Smith, eds. *Environmental Politics: Public Costs, Private Rewards.* New York: Praeger, 1992.

Landy, Marc K., Marc J. Roberts, and Stephan R. Thomas. *The Environmental Protection Agency: Asking the Wrong Questions From Nixon to Clinton.* Expanded ed. New York: Oxford University Press, 1994.

National Academy of Public Administration. *Setting Priorities, Getting Results: A New Direction for the Environmental Protection Agency.* Washington, D.C.: National Academy of Public Administration, 1995.

Chapter 4

To Govern Is to Choose:
Risk Assessment and
Environmental Justice

I just had an eight-hour briefing on fine particulate standards. . . .
Our scientists told me we can defend any standard between 150 and
250 parts per million. So pick a number.
  —William Ruckelshaus, former administrator
    of the Environmental Protection Agency

Risk assessment means never having to say you're certain.
  —Humor among professional risk assessors

In February 1989, the Environmental Protection Agency alarmed Americans, including most of the nation's commercial apple growers, with the ominous announcement that daminozide, a chemical ripening agent used on red apples, posed "a significant risk of cancer to humans."[1] The EPA estimated that the chemical could cause cancer in 5 of 100,000 persons exposed to it over a seventy-year period—a risk unacceptable under current law—and pose higher risks to children. Then came confusion. The EPA announced that it would not suspend the use of daminozide, known by the trade name Alar, for eighteen months, even though it had the authority to suspend immediately the use of any agricultural chemical posing an immediate threat to public health, because test results "did not show conclusively that [daminozide] posed an imminent hazard to human health."[2] The Agency explained that it was making the announcement in advance of the actual suspension date to speed the process for removing Alar. Presumably, the aroused media attention and congressional alarm were the desired political propellents in this instance.

The Alar Scare

Although Alar was used on only 5 percent of red apples grown in this country, getting it off the market would not be easy. Food processors and retail food chains might promise to accept no more apples treated with Alar, but the chemical was impossible to detect on apple skins because it penetrates the surface and is absorbed. In addition, Alar could not be removed from, or readily detected in, apple juice or other processed foods made with treated apples.

The EPA's announcement provoked a battle over the scientific and administrative wisdom of the decision. The controversy followed a scenario highly predictable in such pesticide issues. Uniroyal Corporation, the pesticide manufacturer, challenged the scientific basis for the EPA decision and announced that it "completely disagreed" with the pronouncement because independent laboratories used to evaluate Alar had found it posed "no significant risk to public health."[3] Representatives for environmental groups denounced the EPA for not banning Alar immediately and charged that the announced policy "would not be protective of children's or the public's health."[4] The president of a grower's trade group, the International Apple Association, protested that "available data have not confirmed any health threat"[5] from Alar. Finally, the experts weighed in with their opinions. Early on in the scare, Bruce Ames, a biochemist with the University of California and an expert on the genetic effects of chemicals, dismissed the EPA estimates as "worst case piled on worst case and none of it true."[6] Nonetheless, many schools and other institutions feeding children were removing red apples from their menus and consumers were avoiding them.

A few days after the EPA announcement, the Natural Resources Defense Council (NRDC), a public interest law firm, inflamed the Alar controversy by issuing a report alleging that 5,500 to 6,200 children, roughly 5 in every 20,000 children among the current preschool population, "may eventually get cancer solely as a result of exposure before 6 years of age" to chemical residues on fruits and vegetables.[7] A public relations firm, hired by the NRDC to publicize its pesticide study, offered the report as an exclusive to the highly popular CBS television program *60 Minutes*. On February 26, 1989, the program broadcast a report anchored by Ed Bradley in which Alar was characterized as "the most potent cancer causing agent in the food supply today."[8] At that point Alar had been captured in a high-powered, professionally managed campaign to stamp the pesticide into national consciousness. The president of the public relations firm explained: "Our goal was to create so many repetitions of NRDC's message that average American consumers (not just the policy elite in Washington) could not avoid hearing it. . . . The idea was for the 'story' to achieve a life of its own, and continue for weeks and months to affect policy and consumer habits."[9]

The Alar scare did achieve a public life of its own, notwithstanding the outspoken scientific opposition. "Voodoo statistics," concluded the executive director for the American Council on Science and Health. "No evidence [has been found] of even one case of human cancer in children and adults linked to exposure to the minute pesticide residue in food."[10] No matter; sales in the apple industry, usually a $1.1 billion annual business, were reduced significantly. The apple was further embattled when the Consumers Union reported in late March that 75 percent of the apple juice samples it examined from store shelves contained Alar.[11] The Processed Apple Institute, the trade association representing a majority of apple juice producers, retorted that its own testing of 4,623 samples from a cross-section of brands produced only eight with detectable levels of Alar. The Consumers Union asserted that its tests were more sensitive to Alar. The Processed Apple Institute responded that Consumers Union's tests were inaccurate and unapproved by the federal government. The thrust and parry continued for months, one risk assessment countering another.

The one certain loser was the apple industry. By mid-1991, most scientists had concluded that the public risks posed by Alar never justified the alarm aroused by the Alar controversy a few years earlier. But apple growers in upstate New York, Michigan, and the Pacific Northwest had been badly damaged economically: during the first six months of the Alar scare the nation's growers had lost an estimated $125 million in income and only in 1992 did the market again approach normal conditions. Some family farms were lost permanently in the depressed market. Following another tradition in environmental politics, representatives of the apple growers sued the NRDC, its public relations firm, CBS news, and others for recovery of damages inflicted by the Alar controversy.

The true extent of public risk from exposure to Alar, or to many other agricultural chemicals, still remains uncertain. The adversaries still disagree about the evidence and its inferences, and about the wisdom of the EPA's solution. The EPA's decision itself was complicated by many circumstances. The Agency first received studies in the mid-1970s suggesting that daminozide might cause human cancers, and by 1985 was considering a proposal for daminozide's cancellation. But the EPA's own science advisory board, arguing that data were still insufficient, urged more testing at that time.[12] Further tests on laboratory animals produced both cancerous and noncancerous tumors in mice—but daminozide did not produce tumors in rats. This posed an interpretation problem because both animals were used to assess risks of human exposure to carcinogens. Further, the carcinogenic risk was not Alar itself but a chemical by-product left on food when Alar was heated. And Alar was only one of more than one hundred chemicals used on apple trees in the United States. An average grower might use between six and twenty chemicals in a single growing season. Thus, Alar might not be the most dangerous among these chemicals. Moreover, the EPA and its congressional watchdogs confronted an apparently rising tide of public anxiety, propelled by astute public relations management, over food safety. From a political standpoint, inaction was virtually impossible.

It is ironic to note that the EPA would have had an easier decision if Alar had been a new chemical. The Toxic Substances Control Act (TSCA) would have placed the burden of proving Alar's safety on its manufacturer and the EPA could have suspended its use with the evidence it already had available. Since Alar was a chemical already in use, the burden of *proving* its toxicity to humans rested with the EPA.

The final decision was a fabric of suppositions. The EPA had to assume that its animal data were accurate and applicable to human beings with the probabilities it had calculated. The Agency had to assume it had enough data to create a strong presumption that daminozide was carcinogenic to humans, even when the data were inconsistent. It had to assume it had sufficient information to prove it was better to accept the risks and costs in suspending daminozide than to tolerate the risks associated with continuing public exposure to the chemical—even though those risks were estimates, at best. And the EPA had to assume that public concern, once incited, would not quickly abate. These problems are not unique to Alar. They appear in various guises in most decisions to regulate toxic or hazardous substances. The Alar controversy is one episode in a continuing conflict over the proper means for measuring the risks and costs from exposure to a wide range of substances suspected to be environmentally hazardous. This chapter explores the reasons why these conflicts arise and persist.

Risk Assessment and the Limits of Science

Risk assessment in different guises has become a common component of environmental policy making. In recent years, the EPA alone has annually written more than 7,500 risk assessments in various forms to carry out its regulatory responsibilities.[13] In 1993, President Clinton further elevated the importance of risk assessment by requiring in Executive Order 12866 that all regulatory agencies, not only environmental ones, "consider, to the extent reasonable, the degree and nature of risks posed by various substances or activities within its jurisdiction" and mandating that each proposed regulatory action explain how the action will reduce risks "as well as how the magnitude of risk addressed by the action relates to other risks within the jurisdiction of the agency." [14]

Yet risk assessment grows increasingly controversial even as its influence expands, until it now incites among the environmental community the impassioned conflicts once confined to such Holy Wars as the benefit-cost debate. A major reason for the controversy is that risk assessment lies in the treacherous zone between science and politics where practically all environmental policies reside and where collaboration between public officials is both essential and difficult. A scientific issue—and usually a controversy—is almost always embedded in the political conflict over environmental policy. The enlarging debate over the reality of global climate warming and the appropriate U.S. policy response, for instance, is in good measure a disagreement among policy makers and scientists themselves about the accuracy of various and often inconsistent atmospheric models used by climate experts to predict the onset and scale of the predicted warming. What public officials and scientists involved in policy making want from each other is quite often unobtainable. Public officials seek from scientists information accurate enough to indicate precisely where to establish environmental standards and credible enough to defend in the inevitable conflicts to follow. Scientists want government to act quickly and forcefully on ecological issues they believe to be critical.[15] Yet science often cannot produce technical information in the form and within the time desired by public officials. Indeed, science often cannot provide the information at all, leaving officials to make crucial decisions from fragmentary and disputable information. Scientists often discover that public officials and agencies are unwilling, or unable, to await the slow testing and validation of data before reaching decisions about scientific issues; data are needed now, or tomorrow. Policies often are made, and unmade, without resort to the scientific materials supposed to govern such decisions.

In short, environmental issues often raise difficult scientific and political questions. They compel public officials to make scientific judgments and scientists to resolve policy issues for which neither may be trained. The almost inevitable need to resolve scientific questions through the political process and the problems that arise in making scientific and political judgments compatible are two of the most troublesome characteristics of environmental politics.

Science Issues in Political Settings

The growth of environmental legislation in the past two decades is evidence of the federal government's increasing concern with science and technology since World War II. Legislation concerning atomic power, air and water pollution, workplace and consumer safety, and hazardous wastes all have put before public officials and agencies the need to make determinations of public policy by depending heavily on scientific evidence and scientific judgments. Indeed, environmental issues routinely require administrative agencies, Congress, judges, the White House staff, and even the president to make these determinations.

The range of scientific judgments required of administrative agencies in implementing environmental programs seems to embrace the whole domain of ecological research. For instance, the Coast Guard is authorized "in order to secure effective provisions . . . for protection of the marine environment . . . to establish regulations for ships with respect to the design and construction of such vessels . . . and with respect to equipment and appliances for . . . the prevention and mitigation of damage to the marine environment." [Ports and Waterways Act of 1972, Pub. L. No 92-340]

The EPA is to set effluent standards for new sources of water pollution so that each standard reflects "the greatest degree of effluent reduction . . . achievable through application of the best available demonstrated control technology, process, operating methods, or other alternatives, including, where practicable, a standard permitting no discharge of pollutants." [Federal Water Pollution Control Act of 1972, Pub. L. 90-500]

The EPA is required to establish "standards of performance" for classes and categories of new air pollution sources "which contribute significantly to air pollution or contribute to endangerment of public health or welfare." [Clean Air Act, Pub. L. 84-159 (1955), Pub. L. 90-148 (1970), Pub. L. No. 101-549 (1990)]

Congress, and particularly the congressional committees writing legislation, also may have to resolve a multitude of technical issues. When regulating hazardous substances, for instance, what is a reasonable period to specify for chemical manufacturers to produce reliable data on the human effects of potentially dangerous substances? Is it necessary to regulate air emissions from diesel trucks in order to reduce harmful air pollutants? Is it appropriate to include heavy metals in the list of water pollutants for which standards must be created by the EPA? Eventually judges will be compelled to weigh scientific evidence and render judgment on environmental issues. Did the Department of the Interior have sufficient information to file a valid environmental impact assessment on a proposed coal mining lease on federal lands? Do federal standards for nuclear reactors adequately protect public safety as required by law? The fabric of environmental policy is so interwoven with scientific issues that it is impossible to exclude them at any stage of the policy process.

Policy Pressures and Scientific Method

Few public officials are scientists. Faced with the technical questions inherent in environmental policy, officials customarily turn to scientists and technicians for answers or, at least, for definitions of alternative solutions to clarify choices. As a matter of practical politics, solving issues by resorting to credible scientific evidence can also deflect from officials the criticism they might otherwise endure—sometimes science alone legitimatizes policy. But the politician and the scientist live in fundamentally different decision-making worlds.

There are significant differences in the time frames for problem solving. "In his search for truth," Roger Revelle observed, "the scientist is oriented toward the future; the politician's orientation is usually here and now. He desires quick visible pay-offs for which he often seems willing to mortgage the future. For the politician in a democratic society, infinity is the election after the next one." [16] Often, public officials are compelled to act swiftly. The Clean Air Act (CAA), for example, required the EPA administrator to set standards for sulfur oxides and nitrogen oxides within two years. The Superfund Amendments and Reauthorization Act (SARA), passed in 1986, included among its 150 deadlines a requirement that the EPA issue a plan to implement SARA's radon research program, produce an annual report on radon mitigation demonstration programs, and provide a report on its national assessment of the radon problem in less than two years after the legislation was passed. [17]

If a crisis erupts—a newly discovered leaking hazardous waste dump or a potentially catastrophic oil spill—information is needed immediately. But scientific information rarely appears on demand, even in urgent situations, and especially when it must be sufficiently accurate to point a clear direction for policy.

Public officials, moreover, often must craft environmental policies amid continuing disagreement between experts and the public over the degree of risk associated with various environmental problems. Table 4-1 compares how the EPA's risk experts and the public evaluated various environmental hazards. For instance, while the public rated chemical waste disposal as the highest environmental risk, the experts ranked it considerably lower. In contrast, the experts assigned much greater risk to stratospheric ozone depletion and indoor radon than did the public. Chemical plant accidents were rated a major risk by the public, but not by the experts. In effect, these differences amount to two different agendas of priority for environmental regulation. Critics of current environmental regulation, pointing to these disparate views of ecological risk, often argue that public opinion has intimidated policy makers into following the wrong environmental priorities. Many argue that the public

Table 4-1 How Experts and the Public Estimate Environmental Risks

Experts	Public
High to medium risk	
Criteria air pollutants from mobile and stationary sources (includes acid precipitation)	Chemical waste disposal
	Water pollution
	Chemical plant accidents
Stratospheric ozone depletion	Outdoor air pollution
Pesticide residues in or on foods	Oil tanker spills
Hazardous/toxic air pollutants	Exposure to pollutants on the job
Indoor radon	Eating pesticide-treated food
Indoor air pollution other than radon	Other pesticide risks
Tap water used for drinking	Contaminated drinking water
Exposure to consumer products	
Worker exposure to chemicals	
Low risk	
Hazardous waste sites—active	Indoor air pollution
Hazardous waste sites—inactive	Exposure to chemicals in consumer products
Other municipal and industrial waste sites	Biotechnology (genetic engineering)
Underground storage tanks	Strip-mine wastes
Contaminated sludge	Nonnuclear radiation
Accidental releases of toxic chemicals	Greenhouse Effect
Accidental oil spills	
Biotechnology (genetic engineering)	

Source: Adapted from *EPA Journal* 13, no. 9 (Nov. 1987): 11.

needs a much better education with respect to environmental risks. For elective public officials, especially, the reality is that what the public believes to be a significant environmental risk can be ignored only at great political peril. In fact, it is difficult for most policy makers to weigh expert and public assessments of risk equally—and even more difficult to yield to the experts when these experts disagree with an aroused public. Public opinion often intimidates even scientific professionals in government.

Still, decisions must be made, thus confronting policy makers with an unsettling choice between a scientifically risky decision or a politically risky decision.[18] Consider, for example, the decision in September 1997 by officials of the National Institute for Environmental Health Sciences (NIEHS) and the Minnesota Pollution Control Agency (MPCA) to announce publicly that samples of Minnesota surface and groundwater had produced severe abnormalities in native frogs. Asserting that they did not know what compound in the water might cause the deformities or what human health effects might follow, the agencies offered bottled water to residents with drinking wells in the affected areas, a pronouncement quickly reported and amplified by state and national news media. Little more than a month later, the NIEHS and MPCA endured withering criticism from scientific colleagues who accused the agencies of a rushed and inept decision that unduly alarmed the public without scientific justification. Researchers in EPA's Minnesota research laboratory, as well as other research scientists, asserted that their own evidence contradicted the agency conclusions, that the deformities resulted from a chemical imbalance common to Minnesota water and not particularly worrisome. "Now federal scientists are going to look like idiots, even ones who are ultimately proven right," complained the director of another federal research lab. Nonetheless, both NIEHS and MPCA defended their decision. "We had no intention of going public until we were further along in interpreting the data," explained an NIEHS official, but a public announcement became unavoidable. The MPCA research scientist who made the decision to alert the public insisted she would still make the same decision. Knowledge about the frog deformities was spreading among the public, she explained, and any attempt by her agency to distribute bottled water without a public explanation would incite a panic, she noted. "We felt as a public agency we needed to let people know exactly where research was at," she concluded.[19]

The Minnesota incident was especially discomfiting for scientific professionals because the scientist prefers to measure the correctness of a policy by the standards of experimentation and empiricism. For example, the appropriate standard for an air pollutant would be determined by careful dose-response studies involving animals and perhaps human beings. The public official, in contrast, has to calculate a standard's correctness using several additional criteria. Will it satisfy enough public and private interests to be enforceable? Can it be enforced with existing governmental personnel and budget? Does the standard appear credible? (It must not be so controversial as to shake public confidence.) The public official may be content to set environmental standards within a range of acceptable figures, according to what will best balance political, economic, and administrative considerations. But the scientist may measure acceptability by the single standard of precision; accuracy, not acceptability, matters. Under these circumstances, it is understandable that policy makers and their scientific consultants often disagree about what data should be used, and in what manner, in policy decisions.

Derelict Data and Embattled Expertise

Controversy among experts commonly arises in environmental policy making. Contending battalions of experts—garlanded with degrees and publications and primed to dispute each other's judgment—populate congressional and administrative hearings about risk assessment. Policy makers are often left to judge not only the wisdom of policies but also the quality of the science supporting the policies.

Missing Data. Why is controversy so predictable? Frequently there is a void of useful data about the distribution and severity of environmental problems or possible pollutants. Many problems are so recent that public and private agencies have only just begun to study them. Many pollutants—hazardous chemicals, for instance—have existed only a few decades; their ecological impacts cannot yet be reliably measured. Quite often the result is that nobody has the information "somebody should have." For example, no information is available on the toxic effects of an estimated 79 percent of chemicals used in commerce. Fewer than one-fifth have been tested for acute effects, fewer than one-tenth for chronic (for example, cancer causing), reproductive, or mutagenic effects. In late 1985 the EPA's assistant administrator for pesticides and toxic substances stated that the databases for many previously registered pesticides were "woefully inadequate and the existing data have not been evaluated by current standards."[20] Very little information is available to provide accurate estimates of the volume of hazardous waste generated by location. State estimates are so disparate, concluded the General Accounting Office (GAO), that they "preclude any conclusive statements about how much waste is being generated within a state."[21] It is difficult to determine whether the federal Construction Grants Program has significantly reduced discharges from waste-water treatment plants because "little methodologically defensible work has been done to determine the program's effects on in-stream characteristics and other aspects of water quality."[22]

A federal government study of coal waste concluded: "Much of the information presented on coal wastes was speculative and not universally agreed upon. . . . Although coal has been around longer than nuclear [power], its environmental and health effects are not as fully understood. In fact, coal wastes were not even recognized as potentially hazardous until recent years."[23]

Lacking high quality data, experts often extrapolate answers from fragmentary information; plausible disputes over the reliability of such procedures are inevitable. The scarcity of fundamental information on ecological trends and pollutant characteristics is a major reason why environmental monitoring is essential to prudent policies.

Late and Latent Effects. Disagreement over the severity of environmental problems also arises because the effects of many substances thought to be hazardous to humans or the environment may not become evident for decades or generations. The latency and diffusion of these impacts also may make it difficult to establish causality between the suspected substances, or events, and the consequences. Asbestos, a hazardous chemical whose malignancy has been documented recently, illustrates these problems.[24] Since World War II, approximately 8 million to 11 million U.S. workers have been exposed to asbestos, a mineral fiber with more than 2,000 uses; its heat resistance, electrical properties, immunity to chemical deterioration, and other characteristics made it appear ideal to a multitude of major industries. It has been used widely to manufacture brake and clutch linings, plastics, plumbing, roofing tile, wall insulation, paint, paper, and much else. Asbestos is highly carcinogenic. Among those exposed to significant levels of asbestos, 20 to 25 percent died of lung cancer; 7 to 10 percent perished from mesothelioma (cancer of the chest lining or stomach); and another 8 to 9 percent died from gastrointestinal cancer.[25] The toxicity of asbestos has become apparent only recently because cancers associated with it do not become clinically evident until fifteen years to forty years after exposure; illness may appear from two years to fifty years later. Added to the incalculable cost of human suffering is the immense economic impact of these delayed effects. By 1993 more than 17,000 liability suits had been filed against almost 300 companies involved in the past use or manufacture of asbestos. One major manufacturer, the Johns Manville Company, has been involved in more than 100,000 lawsuits, with claims in excess of $8 billion.

Many other substances used in American commerce, science, and domestic life are suspected of producing adverse impacts on humans or the environment. These impacts may be diffuse and latent; conclusive evidence might not appear for decades. Yet government officials must decide whether to regulate these substances now. In effect, experts are estimating the risks from continued use of a substance when the actual effects on humans and the environment are largely unknown. Difficult as such calculations are, a failure to act, as in the case of asbestos, eventually may prove so costly in human suffering and economic loss that scientists may be reluctant to wait for conclusive data. Experts also must weigh in their risk calculus the possible irreversibility of anticipated future impacts. These complex and often tenuous determinations lead to honest disagreements over the validity of most risk assessments associated with hazardous substances. These issues are vividly illustrated by the federal government's continuing problems with the chemical dioxin.

The Risks in Risk Assessment: The Case of Dioxin.   The controversy over dioxin entails problems—political, scientific, and economic—common to regulatory science. And something more. The issue may prove to be a political time bomb, for it has evolved to the point at which it raises compelling scientific doubts about the reliability of the fundamental experimental methods used by all federal agencies in chemical risk assessment.

Early in the 1990s, the EPA was persuaded by growing scientific evidence to initiate a searching reevaluation of its twenty-year-old exposure standards for the chemical dioxin, which it had characterized earlier as one of the most lethal substances on earth.[26] The most dangerous among the seventy-five varieties of dioxin was thought to be 2,3,7,8-tetra-chlorodibenzodioxin, known as TCDD, considered so harmful that the EPA's maximum exposure standards had limited human ingestion of TCDD to .006 trillionth of a gram per day for every kilogram (2.2 pounds) of body weight over an average lifetime—in other words, an average-sized man was limited daily to an amount equal to a grain of sand sliced one billion times.

The EPA's original exposure standard for dioxin, as with most risk assessments made by federal agencies, was largely extrapolated from animal experiments. Throughout the 1970s and 1980s, however, accumulating scientific evidence delivered an ambiguous verdict about the dangers inherent in dioxin even while its lethal public reputation increased. In the late 1970s, the EPA ordered an end to production of the weed killer 2,4,5-T, also a dioxin, on the basis of its own earlier studies and additional, if circumstantial, evidence of great harm to persons exposed to high concentrations of the herbicide. When concentrations of dioxin far exceeding levels considered safe were discovered during 1981 in the soil of Times Beach, a small Missouri community, the EPA decided that public safety required the permanent evacuation of the whole town. All 2,240 residents were removed to a new residence and reimbursed for their property at a cost exceeding $37 million, while an additional $100 million was spent to clean up other nearby contaminated sites. During the 1980s, hundreds of lawsuits were filed against the federal government by Vietnam veterans for alleged health impairment from exposure to dioxin in the defoliant Agent Orange. Meanwhile, major industries, such as chemical manufacturers, were spending millions of dollars to eliminate their dioxin emissions. The EPA's strict standards, for instance, were expected to cost the paper and pulp industry about $2 billion for pollution control.

But a growing number of scientific experts began to question publicly not only the EPA's exposure standards for dioxin but also the reliability of all animal studies for determining safe levels of human exposure to hazardous substances.[27] A particularly damning public indictment of the EPA's own standard appeared in 1991 when the federal scientist who had ordered the evacuation of Times Beach admitted to a congressional committee that he made the wrong decision. "Given what we know now about this chemical's toxicity," then assistant surgeon general Vernon N.

Houk stated, "it looks as if the evacuation was unnecessary."[28] In 1991, the World Health Organization delivered another assault on the EPA's dioxin assessment when it declared its support for a new standard increasing the permissible human exposure by 1,600 percent above the EPA's limits.

Further complications arose in 1992 when a panel of experts convened by the EPA concluded that while dioxin was a significant cancer threat only to people exposed to unusually high levels in chemical factories, it also wreaked biological havoc among fish, birds, and other wild animals even in minute doses.[29] Thus, a decision about the dioxin standard apparently confronted the EPA with a perverse choice: keep the standard and sacrifice potentially huge regulatory savings for the American economy *or* lower the standard, save the money, and vastly increase the future risk of serious ecological derangement—a clear-cut choice between the economy and the environment. In early 1993, another blow against the science undergirding federal toxic regulations was delivered by the director of the National Institute of Environmental Health Sciences, the federal agency supervising all federal animal studies used in toxics regulation. The director released portions of a report from a panel of leading toxicologists that concluded that many of the assumptions driving the animal research "did not appear to be valid."[30] Animal studies alone, concluded most of the experts, were not reliable means for judging the exposure risks to human beings in toxics research. While some leading experts disagreed with these conclusions, it appeared from the report that most of the experts had some serious reservations about the reliability of the tests on which current regulations were based. Alternative approaches to animal testing that avoid the errors criticized by the panel did exist, the report noted, but these tests took two to eight years to conduct and therefore seemed an impractical remedy.

Environmental organizations have resisted any relaxation of the EPA's current dioxin standard. Scientific experts speaking for these organizations assert that the new evidence creates no compelling case for a new standard. "Nothing that has been learned about dioxin since 1985 when EPA first published its risk assessment findings on dioxin . . . supports a revision of science-based policy or action," Ellen K. Silbergeld, a pathologist and expert witness for environmental organizations, argued.[31] Nonetheless, the Clinton administration has demonstrated considerable unease with existing exposure standards for many regulated toxics and the issue is far from settled.

If the unfolding controversy seriously diminishes the credibility of risk assessment methods, the whole scientific underpinning of federal risk assessment, and probably its legal defensibility, will be eroded. This would then become one of the most scientifically and politically devastating events in the history of federal toxic substance regulation.

Animal and Epidemiological Experiments. As the dioxin controversy testifies, estimates of health risks from suspected toxics are a rich source of controversy. But, having rejected most controlled human studies as ethically repugnant, scientists are left with no certain alternatives in arriving at risk estimates. They may attempt to characterize a substance's danger based on existing knowledge of how chemical carcinogens affect human cells. But little knowledge exists about the precise way in which these chemicals alter the structure and chemistry of cells. The common alternative is the controlled animal experiments in which test animals are exposed to substances, the effects monitored, and the risks to human beings extrapolated from the findings.

These animal studies are particularly controversial when estimating the human effects from low levels of chemical exposure—for instance, a dose of a few parts per million or billion of a pesticide or heavy metal in drinking water over thirty years. The human risks of cancer or other serious illnesses will be small, but how small?[32] And how reliable is the estimate? Animal studies do not and cannot use enough animals to eliminate possibilities of error in estimating the human effects of low-level exposure. To demonstrate conclusively with 95 percent confidence that a certain low-level dose of one substance causes less than one case of cancer per million subjects would require a "mega-mouse" experiment involving 6 million animals.[33] Instead, researchers use high doses of a substance with relatively few animals and then extrapolate through statistical models the effect on humans from low-level exposure to the tested substance. But these models can differ by a factor of as much as 100,000 in estimating the size of the dose that could produce one cancer per million subjects. A whole litany of other problems attend small animal studies. Failure to observe any response to a substance among a small group of animals does not imply a substance is safe. Animals, moreover, differ greatly in their sensitivity to substances; dioxin is 5,000 times more toxic to guinea pigs than to hamsters, for example.[34]

Epidemiological studies depend on surveys recording the relationship between known human exposure to suspected hazardous substances and the known effects; the investigator does not deliberately expose humans to possibly dangerous substances but does attempt to capitalize on exposure when it occurs. Such after-the-fact studies have been used to establish the cancer risks of exposure to cigarette smoke and asbestos, for example. Epidemiological studies can establish statistical relationships between exposure to suspected hazardous substances and adverse effects, but they cannot prove causality; as a consequence, they are open to dispute. Challenges often are raised because such studies cannot be controlled scientifically to eliminate other possible factors affecting the results. Some connections between exposure to substances and effects often can be drawn for the general population, but, as David Doniger observed, "humans are exposed to too many different substances at unknown doses for unknown periods to permit statistically reliable conclusions to be drawn. Moreover, there are synergistic and antagonistic interactions between chemicals that drastically complicate drawing conclusions about the effects of each chemical." [35]

The Limited Neutrality of Scientific Judgment

Perhaps fifty opportunities exist in a normal risk assessment procedure for scientists to make discretionary judgments. Although scientists are presumed to bring to this task an expertise untainted by social values to bias their judgments, they are not immune to social prejudice, especially when their expertise is embroiled in a public controversy. "The more an issue is in the public eye, the more expert judgments are likely to be influenced unconsciously by pre-existing policy preferences or by supposedly unrelated factors such as media presentations, the opinions of colleagues or friends, or even the emotional overtones of certain words used in the debate," according to physicist Harvey Brooks, a veteran of many public controversies. [36]

Scientific judgment on environmental issues can be influenced by one's beliefs about how government should regulate the economy, by one's institutional affiliation, or by other social and political attributes. For example, a study of 136 occupational physicians and industrial hygienists working in government, industry, and academia examined the link between their political and social backgrounds and their opinions about a proposed standard by the Occupational Safety and Health Administration (OSHA) for carcinogens. Scientists employed in industry were more politically and socially conservative than those employed by universities or government. The industry scientists were more likely to favor scientific assumptions about identifying carcinogens that would decrease the probability that a substance would be deemed a risk to human health—in effect, they favored scientific premises that made regulation of a substance less likely. [37]

In another study, political scientists Thomas M. Dietz and Robert W. Rycroft interviewed 228 risk professionals involved in federal environmental policy making to determine if a relationship existed between their professional judgments in risk assessment and their social, political, and institutional backgrounds. Among the many links discovered, they found that "place of employment is significantly linked to differences in . . . the use of both risk and cost-benefit analysis," and that once risk professionals became involved in policy making there was "a weakening of disciplinary perspectives and a strengthening of viewpoints based on politics and ideology." [38] In general, Dietz and Rycroft concluded that risk professionals working for corporations or trade associations differed from those working for government or academic institutions in their technical judgments about how risk should be determined and when substances should be regulated, as well as in broader attitudes about governmental regulation.

Social or political bias can be particularly pernicious when unrecognized or unadmitted by the experts. Yet no barrier can be contrived to wholly insulate science from the contagion of social or economic bias. Knowledge that such bias exists, however, has important implications for risk assessment and its related controversies. The existence of this bias is a strong argument for keeping scientific and technical determinations open to examination and challenge by other experts and laypersons. There should be no domain of science quarantined from public inquiry. Scientists working in the public sector have a professional and personal responsibility to encourage rigorous self-examination of their own technical judgments in light of their vulnerability to social bias. The myth of a socially neutral science should not be unchallenged within the scientific professions. Moreover, it is now evident that many technical controversies in policy making may not be resolvable by resort to scientific evidence and argument because "scientific" solutions will be permeated with social, political, or economic bias. Indeed, political controversy often subverts scientific integrity. Experts can be readily, even unintentionally, caught up in the emotionally and politically polarizing atmosphere of such disputes, their judgment so badly compromised that, as Dorothy Nelkin remarked, their expertise "is reduced to one more weapon in a political arsenal." [39]

The Value of Science in Environmental Policy Making

Despite the scientific disputes attending environmental policy making, it remains important to recognize how often science provides useful and highly reliable guidance to policy makers. Often the scientific data relevant to an issue clearly point to the adverse impacts of substances and define the magnitude of their risks; this was certainly evident in the data leading to the federal government's decision to ban most domestic agriculture uses of the pesticides DDT, aldrin, and dieldrin, for instance. Furthermore, even when one set of data does not alone provide definitive evidence of human risks from exposure to chemicals, numerous studies pointing to the same conclusion together can provide almost irrefutable evidence; such was the case in the epidemiological evidence indicting asbestos as a human carcinogen. Often the reliability of data will be routinely challenged by those opposed to the regulation of some substance regardless of the ultimate merit—or lack of it—to their case. In the end, public officials must make decisions on the basis of the best evidence available. For all their limitations, scientific data often enable officials to define more carefully and clearly the range of options, risks, and benefits involved in regulating a substance even when the data cannot answer all risk questions conclusively.

Even if indisputable data were available on the risks of human exposure to all levels of a substance, controversy would continue over the acceptable level. It is asserted sometimes that science should be responsible for determining the magnitudes of risk from exposure to chemicals and that government should define the acceptability—that is, defining acceptable risk is largely a political matter. Such a division of labor is rarely possible. Scientists, too, are often drawn into the nettlesome problem of determining what levels of exposure to substances ultimately will be acceptable.

What Risks Are Acceptable?

Risk assessment for environmental policy making is also difficult because no clear and consistent definition of "acceptable risk" exists in federal law. The EPA, with several other federal agencies, wrestles daily and inconclusively with the problem of defining "acceptable risk." Discretionary judgment permeates the process, inviting pressure and counterpressure from contending sides struggling to influence official decisions to their advantage. The EPA, uneasy with the enormous scientific uncertainties inherent in determining acceptable risk, frequently has shrouded its discretionary decisions in a fog of verbal mystification. Nonetheless, determining acceptable risk remains an intensely discretionary—and often political—affair, however much the language of the law may try to conceal it.

Defining acceptable risk would be less contentious if Congress provided environmental regulators with a clear and consistent statutory standard. Acceptable risk is usually defined in environmental regulation by statutory criteria—that is, standards written into law to guide regulators in determining when to regulate a substance. Despite repeated congressional efforts at clarification, the only consistency in these statutory standards is their inconsistency.[40]

A Multitude of Risk Criteria

A multitude of different congressional standards guide regulatory agencies in making determinations of acceptable risk. Different substances often are regulated according to different standards. The same agency may have to use as many as six or seven standards depending on which substances, or which laws, are involved. The same substance may be subject to one regulatory standard when dumped into a river and another when mixed into processed food. Statutory risk standards are commonly vague and sometimes confusing; congressional intent may be muddled, often deliberately.

In general, regulatory agencies encounter one or more of the following statutory formulas in determining the permissible exposure levels to various substances.[41] The examples are drawn from existing legislation.

1. *Health-based Criteria.* Regulatory agencies are to set standards based upon risks to human health from exposure to a hazard. These standards are usually "cost oblivious" because they seldom permit agencies to use the cost of regulation as a consideration in standard setting. Health-based criteria, however, can involve different levels of acceptable health risk. Federal regulators must prove that a pesticide poses "an unreasonable adverse effect" on human health or the environment before it can be removed from the market *and* they must also weigh the unreasonable effects against the economic benefits to farmers and consumers. [Federal Insecticide, Fungicide and Rodenticide Act (1990)] In contrast, the Food and Drug Act, until recently modified, had established a "no risk" standard for public health: "No additive shall be deemed to be safe if it is found to induce cancer when ingested in man or animal, or if it is found, after tests which are appropriate for the evaluation of the safety of food additives, to induce cancer in man or animal. . . ." [Food, Drug and Cosmetic Act (1938)] In contrast, the Clean Air Act instructs the EPA to determine acceptable health risks with an adequate "margin of safety." The national primary ambient air quality standards, mandates the CAA, ". . . shall be . . . in the judgment of the Administrator, based on [air quality] criteria and allowing an adequate margin of safety . . . requisite to protect human health." [Clean Air Act (1970)] The EPA is also left to determine the magnitude of this margin, and for whom it applies.

2. *Technology-based Criteria.* EPA is instructed to assure that pollution sources will use "the best available" or "the maximum achievable" technology, or some other specified technology criteria, to control their hazardous emissions. The Safe Drinking Water Act and the Federal Water Pollution Control Act both use technology-based standards. In effect, "acceptable" risks are defined by whatever residual risks to public health may exist after the prescribed control technologies are applied to a pollution source. From EPA's perspective, the regulatory task is somewhat eased because the Agency does not have to assess the actual

public health risks from exposure to a specific pollutant. Instead, it has to assure that the prescribed technology is applied to the pollution source.

3. *Balancing Criteria.* Congress mandates that an agency consider, to varying extent, the costs of regulation, or the magnitude of threat to human health, alongside the benefits in setting a standard for human or environmental exposure. Or, Congress may permit cost considerations to be among other criteria an agency may consider. These statutes define how various considerations, such as cost and risk, are to be balanced in determining acceptable risk. A law may dictate *cost sensitive criteria,* which permits but does not necessarily require the agency to balance the benefits for a given regulatory standard (which may include health as well as monetary benefits) against the costs of its enforcement. Different laws provide varying formulas for assigning priorities to cost and benefit. "The Secretary [of Labor], in promulgating standards dealing with toxic materials or harmful physical agents under this subsection, shall set the standard which most adequately assures, to the extent feasible, on the basis of the best available evidence, that no employee will suffer material impairment of health or functional capacity . . . other considerations shall be . . . the feasibility of the standards, and experience gained under this and other health and safety laws." [Occupational Safety and Health Act (1970)] *Cost-benefit criteria* require agencies to balance the benefits against the economic costs in setting standards for exposure to a substance. "The Commission shall not promulgate a consumer product safety rule unless it finds . . . that the benefits expected from the rule bear a reasonable relationship to its costs; and . . . that the rule imposes the least burdensome requirement which prevents or adequately reduces the risk or injury for which the rule is being promulgated." [Consumer Product Safety Act (1972)]

A close reading of these guidelines reveals the enormous discretion customarily left to regulatory agencies in determining how to balance the various statutory criteria. It is often difficult to separate scientific from nonscientific issues; scientists usually become activists in standard setting as well as in determining the magnitude of risks on which the standards should be based. For instance, the Food and Drug Act's previous requirement that no food additive be permitted in the United States if it is "found to induce cancer when ingested by man or animal" raises scientific issues even as it attempts to serve as a criterion for regulators in setting policy. Over what period of time must the risk of cancer exist? Must substances be banned even if they are used in quantities so small that only extremely small risks may exist to humans? Are the cancers produced by a substance in animals the result of exposure to that substance alone?[42]

Limited by its lack of scientific expertise yet reluctant to leave agencies with too much discretion in determining acceptable risk, Congress often packs regulatory laws with so many criteria for risk determination—lest any important consideration be ignored—that regulatory decisions become enormously complicated. Consider, for instance, the criteria the EPA is ordered to use under TSCA when deciding whether the risks from exposure to a substance are "unreasonable":

> The type of effect (chronic or acute, reversible or irreversible); degree of risk; characteristics and number of humans, plants and animals, or ecosystems, at risk; amount of knowledge about the effects; available or alternative substances and their expected effects; magnitude of the social and economic costs and benefits of possible control actions; and appropriateness and effectiveness of TSCA as the legal instrument for controlling the risk.[43]

Agencies spend considerable time working out detailed internal regulations to translate these complexities into workable procedures. They may attempt to reach understandings concerning how criteria will be balanced, with interest groups active in the regulatory process. But agencies often face imperious deadlines for making regulatory decisions, fragmentary information relevant to many criteria for standard setting, and disputes between interest groups concerning the validity of information and the priorities for criteria in policy making. In the first years of a new regulatory program, an agency can expect virtually every major decision to be challenged through litigation, usually by an interest alleging the agency has failed to interpret properly its statutory responsibilities. An agency sometimes invites such litigation because it can work to its advantage. By interpreting the manner in which risk determinations should be made by agencies, judges often dissipate the fog of uncertainty about congressional intent and provide agencies with firm guidelines for future determinations.

Missing data and muddled laws often promote waffling when agencies struggle against such adversity to define acceptable risk. This is why one of EPA's encounters with TSCA's murky risk criteria seems like an adventure in Regulatory Wonderland. In 1991 the GAO asked the EPA why it had never used its authority under TSCA to require the testing of several chemicals whose toxicity was strongly suspected. The responsible EPA office replied that the chemicals did not pose the "significant risk to human health or the environment" that TSCA required for regulation. "In explaining why EPA has never used [its] authorities in the chemical testing program," commented the investigators, EPA stated that it ". . . uses a 'high threshold' of risk in assessing whether a chemical imposes significant or unreasonable risks. . . ." However, noted the GAO, "the EPA has never defined the meaning of 'significant' or 'unreasonable' for the purpose of implementing TSCA."[44] In light of TSCA's confounding definitions of acceptable risk, the EPA's behavior might be considered preordained.

Searching For Solutions: The "Bright Line"

In a belated effort to eliminate some of the difficulties involved in determining acceptable risk, Congress took an apparently sensible step by writing into the Clean Air Act Amendments of 1990 what has been called a "residual-risk bright line" for determining acceptable public exposure to air toxics. Essentially, the law required the EPA to assure that the increased lifetime cancer risk from exposure to an air toxic must not exceed one in a million (10^{-6}) for the affected population. Such a "bright line," apparently giving EPA a precise statutory definition of acceptable risk, seemed to add needed clarity to federal risk assessment and to provide a precedent for future regulation. Moreover, it satisfied the congressional urge to tighten control over EPA by limiting its discretion in risk management. However, it soon was obvious that the "bright line" left enormous discretion to EPA's risk assessors without simplifying their job very much. "A politically motivated risk assessor could, in many situations, easily manipulate his or her analysis to produce a desired outcome on *either* side of the line," observed a recent evaluation of EPA by the National Academy of Public Administration. "Even a more conscientious risk assessor with no interest in the impact of his or her results would make numerous decisions in the process that could change the final answers by several orders of magnitude," it concluded.[45] This perversity of administrative fortune has apparently stifled, at least momentarily, legislative ethusiasm for statutory "bright lines."

Political Bias

Agency formulas for determining acceptable risks also have proven to be highly sensitive to political pressures and to ideological biases. During the Carter years the White House directed OSHA to treat any suspected carcinogen as a proven hazard until tests proved otherwise—a stance well within OSHA's authority.[46] Moreover, a substance was deemed "suspect" if it induced either benign or malignant tumors in at least one laboratory study on animals. This approach, strongly biased toward regulation of workplace hazards, environmental protection, and strict control of suspected hazardous substances, fit comfortably into the activist regulatory bias of a liberal Democratic administration. The Reagan administration, however, rapidly changed these guidelines. It insisted that much more convincing proof would be required before a substance was considered even "suspect." OSHA abolished its list of suspected workplace carcinogens regularly published during the Carter years. And the levels of acceptable risk from substances were raised by factors of ten to one hundred over the earlier Carter criteria. Not surprisingly, these new guidelines were far more compatible with the Reagan administration's determination to place fewer substances under regulatory control and to decrease the compliance costs for business and other regulated interests. These changes, too, generally could be reconciled with OSHA's discretionary authority in determining acceptable risks from workplace exposure to hazardous substances.

The Disappearing Threshold

One of the most politically controversial aspects of determining acceptable risk remains the problem of the *disappearing threshold,* a largely unanticipated result of three tendencies among Congress and agencies concerned with environmental regulation. First, in writing and enforcing most environmental legislation during the 1970s, officials remained *risk averse* in dealing with potential hazards; risk reduction was preferred to risk tolerance. Second, Congress generally assumed that with many, or most, regulated substances there would be some threshold of exposure below which the risks to humans or the ecosystem were negligible. Congress certainly did not anticipate removing *all* traces of human or ecological hazards. Third, legislators, who were largely indifferent to regulatory costs compared with health criteria in setting regulatory standards, discouraged agencies from using cost-benefit analyses when determining acceptable risks.

Economics and technology now present regulation writers with some very difficult decisions as a result of these circumstances. Extremely sophisticated technologies enable scientists to detect hazardous substances in increasingly small concentrations, currently as small as parts per billion or trillion. It is usually impossible to assert scientifically that such low concentrations are wholly innocent of averse risk, however slight, to humans or the environment. Further, the cost of controlling hazardous substances often rises steeply as progressively higher standards are enforced; after reducing, for instance, 85 percent of a substance in a waterway, it may cost half as much or more to remove an additional 5 to 10 percent. In effect, the risk threshold once presumed by policy makers vanished; no measurable concentration of a substance apparently could be assumed innocent of potential harm to humans or the environment. To eliminate conclusively *any* probable risks from such substances, regulators would have to require the total elimination of the substance—an extraordinarily expensive undertaking. The threshold problem thus was created. Should a trade-off be made between the costs and benefits of risk prevention, and, if so, what criteria should govern the choice?

Critics assert that regulators err in this trade-off by insisting on extremely high standards for controlling risks out of all proportion to the benefits to society or the environment and without sensitivity to the economic burden imposed on regulated interests.[47] In critic Paul Johnson's terms, this is the "Custer Syndrome." Regulators "take action at any cost, do it as quickly as possible, and leave the thinking to afterwards."[48] This leaves the public with "unrealistic expectations" about the benefits, which in most cases will be extremely small if not undiscoverable when regulators insist on eliminating even minuscule risks from hazardous substances.[49] Advocates of strict risk management, however, usually respond that the full extent of risk is unknown or may be greater than currently estimated; they may dispute the accuracy of opposing data. Often, they are indignant at the suggestion that human lives may be endangered if the cost of protection is deemed excessive—an assertion, skillfully delivered, that implies officials are venal or inhumane for imperiling lives to save money for a regulated interest.

Elected officials are understandably wary in dealing with these publicly sensitive issues, especially when they may be cast as the villains by advocates of strict regulation. It is easy to make tolerance for even small risks appear to be a cruel gambling with the destinies of innocent people even though risk assessment deals in *probabilities,* not certainties, of accident, or death, or disease. The efforts of the Clinton administration to weaken the Delaney Clause in the Food and Drug Act illustrate the problem. The EPA, at the initiative of administrator Carol Browner, proposed relaxing the Delaney Clause's strict prohibition against any carcinogenic pesticide residue on food. Instead, the EPA proposed a new, but still rigorous, standard allowing pesticide residues whose health risks did not exceed the probability of one extra cancer death for every million persons—a proposal seemingly in accord with a 1989 recommendation by the National Academy of Sciences that the Delaney Clause's total ban on any pesticide residues was too rigid.[50] Nonetheless, environmental groups have opposed vigorously any modification of the Delaney Clause and Congress, intimidated by a possible public backlash, has refused to lift the existing ban on all carcinogenic residues.

Risk and Discrimination: The Problem of Environmental Justice

In October 1997, a jury in New Orleans awarded $3.4 billion in damages to 8,000 people who had been evacuated a decade previously from their community near a major train route after a tank car filled with the chemical butadiene had caught fire. The fact that most of the plaintiffs lived in a poor, underprivileged neighborhood, and thus were exposed to "environmental racism," appeared to have been a major consideration in the jury's generous damage award, even though their attorneys had only alluded to such racism during the trial. "No one said this is racism," explained one of the lawyers for the neighborhood, "but the facts were such that any commonsense appraisal would tell you that the poorer, underprivileged neighborhood was discriminated against."[51] It is testimony to the political potency of the environmental justice movement in the United States that a decade previously the idea of "environmental racism" was virtually unknown in public discourse or in the language of the courts, let alone as a cause for civil damage claims. By the end of the 1990s, issues of environmental justice—or "environmental equity"—were increasingly raised in so many different political and judicial venues that the language had become almost a staple in political discussions involving minorities and health risk.

The environmental justice movement has grown in size, organizational skill, and political influence throughout the 1990s. Its fundamental conviction—that cultural, racial, and ethnic minorities have been disproportionately exposed to health and safety risks throughout the United States—has inspired an aggressive campaign to identify and mobilize these minorities, to demand various forms of compensation for those afflicted by such discrimination, and to demand that governmental policy making be redesigned to weigh issues of environmental equity in environmental policy making. The movement has been powerfully aided by active support from numerous social action organizations affiliated with many of the nation's major religious denominations. Environmental justice has also generated a political gravity drawing minority advocates into close political orbit with organized environmentalism to which minorities had previously seemed largely indifferent. Environmental organizations, for their part, have aggressively seized upon environmental justice issues to attract minority support and to refute the accusation that they appeal overwhelmingly to a white, middle-class constituency.

This growing attention to problems of social equity in environmental regulation illustrates why the creation and solution of environmental risks is often inherently a political issue. In early 1994 President Clinton issued Executive Order 12898 instructing all federal agencies to develop strategies to assure that their programs "do not unfairly inflict environmental harm on the poor and minorities." The executive order, applicable to all federal agencies and to any program "that substantially affects human health or the environment," was the first comprehensive effort by the federal government to address a problem long implicit in environmental policy making and only reluctantly acknowledged by past administrations.[52] The EPA became one of the first federal agencies to recognize the importance of the environmental justice movement by creating its own Office of Environmental Justice as early as 1992.

No consensus exists in law or political debate over the meaning of "environmental justice" or "environmental equity." These terms are commonly used in situations where identifiable minorities have been exposed, deliberately or not, to disproportionate health or safety risks from a known hazard such as a chemical waste dump or an environment-polluting industrial site. Practically every definition of environmental justice or related terms abounds in ambiguities—what, for instance, is a "disproportionate health risk" and how is a "minority" defined? Robert D. Bullard, an environmental justice scholar and advocate, has attempted to clarify matters by suggesting at least three implications of environmental inequity:[53]

- *Procedural inequity*—The extent to which governing rules, regulations, and evaluation criteria are applied uniformly. Examples of procedural inequity are "stacking" boards and commissions with pro-business interests, holding hearings in remote locations to minimize public participation, and using English-only material to communicate to non-English-speaking communities.
  - *Geographical inequity*—A situation in which some neighborhoods, communities, and regions receive direct benefits, such as jobs and tax revenues, from industrial production while the costs, such as the burdens of waste disposal, are fixed elsewhere. Communities hosting waste-disposal facilities receive fewer economic benefits than communities generating waste.
  - *Social inequity*—When environmental decisions mirror the power arrangements of the larger society and reflect the still-existing racial bias in the United States. Institutional racism, for instance, influences the siting of noxious facilities, leaving many black communities in "sacrifice zones."

As these definitions demonstrate, advocates of environmental justice now use the term, or its close relations, to embrace an enormous diversity of political and economic practices far surpassing the human health and safety issues traditionally associated with "environmental risk." It has been left to the courts, legislators, advocacy groups, and scholars to render order from this definitional confusion as they struggle to translate such abstractions into law and political practice.

Fragmentary evidence accumulating for decades has suggested that minorities and the poor are disproportionately exposed to health risks from environmental pollutants. One study estimates that as many as

313,000 U.S. farm workers, the overwhelming majority of them non-white, may annually experience illness related to pesticide exposure. Other studies have indicated that African Americans and Hispanic Americans are more likely than white Americans to live in areas with potentially dangerous ambient air concentrations of ozone and carbon monoxide.[54] The economically disadvantaged may also be more likely than others to have a hazardous waste site for a neighbor. Several studies have suggested as much, including one Detroit survey, cited by sociologists Paul Mohai and Bunyan Bryant, indicating that "minority residents in the metropolitan area are four times more likely than white residents to live within a mile of a commercial hazardous waste facility."[55]

When it comes to the politics of risk, moreover, it appears that some Americans are more equal than others. Farm workers, for instance, are not protected from workplace hazards as are other workers under the Occupational Safety and Health Act and other major federal laws related to workplace dangers. Thus, for the disadvantaged, both exposure to risk and the availability of remedies are often politically determined through decisions by a wide variety of public institutions from local waste siting authorities to Congress. And it has been largely through political pressure that federal agencies have been forced to acknowledge the issue.

The most important and refractory problem in environmental equity, however, remains the lack of accurate information about population exposure to environmental risks. "Health or toxicity data for particular chemicals can be unavailable or inadequate," explains Rebecca A. Head, an environmental justice advocate and public health official. "Current health assessment models may also fail to be capable of using all the possible variables, and therefore can be unreliable in predicting and proving potential disease or injury due to environmental contamination. Risks or dangers associated with exposures to chemicals are especially problematic in communities housing multiple facilities that may be, albeit legally, emitting various chemicals into the air, water or soil. The chances are increased that residents will be exposed to many different chemicals simultaneously."[56] Especially when there is a possibility of population exposure to multiple environmental hazards—a situation quite common in minority communities—the appropriate scientific protocols for estimating individual or population exposure seldom exist, and almost never for regulatory decision making by government.

Overcoming these data deficiencies presents a formidable problem that public officials and scientific professionals have just begun to resolve. With the exception of lead exposure, very little reliable evidence still exists about the relationship of race or class to environmental health measures. Moreover, census information and other comprehensive social data seldom permit comparisons between economic or social groups and exposure to various environmental hazards. In addition, any estimates of selective exposure to environmental risk must take account of complex genetic, racial, and hereditary differences among populations. In short, the science base essential to establish convincing evidence of environmental inequities has yet to be constructed. Another formidable problem involves the appropriate strategies for identifying how risks may be distributed unfairly in environmental regulation and how this inequity can be solved. Over what period of time, for example, ought risk estimates be made? Which populations qualify as disadvantaged? To what extent should the ability of individuals to protect themselves from such risk be taken into account? What sort of environmental risks should be included? How can such issues be introduced early enough in the regulatory decision-making process to influence the outcomes?

The environmental justice movement now claims a salience on the agenda of national environmental policy unlikely to decline in the near future. For the nation's governments, one of the most daunting challenges is to find a way to effectively translate lofty goals like "environmental equity" or "environmental justice" into specific policy procedures and specific governmental actions. How does one bring environmental justice to the desktop and conference table of routine governmental regulation? It seems evident that a successful policy translation will require, at the least, the rapid development of a science base, which means acquiring and disseminating information about exposure of minority populations to specific environmental hazards and developing reliable methodologies for estimating individual and population risks from such exposure. Administrative law and procedure must be modified in detail and depth so that considerations of inequitable environmental risk can be considered in a timely and explicit manner in regulatory decision making. All this, in turn, will require resolute legislative and executive leadership and, eventually, active participation by the nation's judicial structures. Converting prescription into practice will be arduous, however, in light of the current discensus on appropriate metrics for measuring discrimination and equity and on the degree of difference among populations that constitutes inequity.

The Politicizing of Science

In policy conflict, one's data become a weapon, and science a bastion against one's critics. Indeed, torturing technical data to fit some partisan position has become an art form in policy debates. Environmental issues frequently place scientists in a highly charged political atmosphere in which impartiality and objectivity, among the most highly esteemed scientific virtues, are severely tested and sometimes fail.

Scientists are consulted by public officials in good part because the scientists' presumed objectivity, as well as technical expertise, makes them trustworthy advisers. But impartiality can be an early casualty in the highly partisan and polarizing policy conflict. Even if scientists maintain impartiality, they cannot prevent partisans of one or another policy from distorting technical information to gain an advantage. Scientists correctly suspect that their work will often be misrepresented in political debate and their credibility consequently diminished.

In any case, it is characteristic of environmental policy that scientific evidence and opinion frequently are divided for political reasons and, thus, expert disagreements will reinforce political conflicts. Especially when political conflict tends to polarize views and force division over issues, an expert can intentionally, or unwittingly, shade opinions to fit a favored position or manipulate materials until they fit a simplistic policy position. "Experts tend to behave like other people when they engage in a controversy," Allan Mazur, a sociologist and physicist himself, has observed. "Coalitions solidify and disagreements become polarized as conflict becomes more acrimonious."[57] Mazur further observed, for instance, that experts favoring nuclear power tend to support the notion that there exists a threshold of radiation exposure below which human risks are negligible; opponents of nuclear power plants, in contrast, favor a linear conception of risk that permits no such threshold.[58]

It would even seem as though there are Republican and Democratic theories of genetic chemistry. In the mid-1980s many Reagan administration officials and some experts sympathetic to the president's program to reduce environmental regulations were supporting the *epigenetic theory* of cell chemistry.[59] This theory asserts that many carcinogenic substances affect cell mechanisms other than the DNA strands with their genetically coded materials; such a theory could be interpreted to permit greater human exposure to known cancer-causing substances—and also less regulation of such substances—than previously had been federal policy. Under Administrator Anne Burford, the EPA did approve tolerance limits for several carcinogenic pesticides, including the potent pesticide permethren, on the basis of this epigenetic theory. Under the Carter administration, however, the *genotoxic theory* prevailed; this theory asserted that all carcinogens cause changes in genetic cell materials and hence must be considered dangerous. Although the genotoxic theory has been more generally accepted by experts, reputable scientists have supported the conflicting interpretation. One need not accuse either side of willful deceit in order to suggest that political and economic bias could, and probably does, play some part in convincing experts of the truth of a position.

Regulatory agencies, no less than individuals, are guilty of using scientific data selectively, sometimes with gross negligence. One of the worst examples became evident in the 1980s when it was revealed that the Atomic Energy Commission had suppressed deliberately and consistently for more than twenty years scientific evidence suggesting that radioactive fallout from nuclear weapons tests in Nevada may have endangered ranchers and others in its path during the 1950s.

All agencies at some time practice some type of data manipulation. One of the virtues in wide public exposure of regulatory proceedings is that opportunities exist for experts to expose and challenge such manipulation. The great potential in policy conflict for disrupting sound scientific inquiry and distorting data emphasizes the importance of permitting an open, prolonged, and comprehensive scientific review of major environmental policy decisions. Such a process does not ensure that any scientific consensus will emerge on strategic issues. But it does permit the widest latitude for scientific debate—for the uncovering and publicizing of information as well as for challenging and refining interpretations of data. It encourages among policy makers greater clarity about the full range and limits of the technical information confronting them. It invites a public airing of issues that experts otherwise might keep to themselves or confine to a small cadre of governmental and scientific insiders who become by virtue of their privileged information a powerful technocratic elite. It helps to discriminate between plausible and unrealistic policy options. If the politicizing of science in environmental issues is inevitable, it should at least be exploited to advantage when possible.

Gambling with the Future

The complex new problems of risk assessment in environmental regulation confirm that we live in a historically unique era of technocratic power. American science and industry, in common with those of other advanced industrial nations, now possess the capacity to alter in profound but often unpredictable ways the biochemical basis of future human life and thus to change future ecosystems radically. In its extreme form, represented by nuclear weapons, modern technology has the power to eradicate human society, if not humanity itself. But modern technologies also can alter the future ecosphere in a multitude of less dramatic but significant ways: through the deliberate redesign of genetic materials in human reproduction, through the depletion of irreplaceable energy resources such as petroleum or natural gas, through the multiplication of long-lived hazardous substances whose biological impacts on humans and the ecosystem may magnify through hundreds of years, and much more. We are practically the first generation in the world's history with the certain technical capacity to alter and even to destroy the fundamental biochemical and geophysical conditions for societies living centuries after ours. It is, as one social prophet noted, a power that people of the Middle Ages did not even credit to devils.

With this new technocratic power comes the ability to develop technologies, to manufacture new substances, and to deplete finite resources so that the benefits largely are distributed in the present and the risks for the most part displaced to the future. Future societies may inherit most of the burden to create the social, economic, and political institutions necessary for managing the risks inherent in this generational cost transfer. Such technical capacity can become an exercise of power undisciplined by responsibility for the consequences.

The status of nuclear wastes in many ways provides a paradigm for this problem. Because the wastes from civilian nuclear reactors currently cannot be recycled, as was assumed when the nuclear power industry began in the United States during the 1950s, the federal government now must find a safe and reliable way to dispose of the growing amount of nuclear wastes from these facilities.

Among the most dangerous of these substances are "high-level" wastes—those highly toxic to humans for long periods—found in the spent fuel rods from civilian reactors. Strontium-90 and cesium-137, for instance, must be isolated from human exposure for at least 600 years; other high-level wastes must be isolated for perhaps a thousand years. Equally dangerous and much more persistent are the transuranic wastes forming over long periods from the decay of the original materials in the spent fuel rods after they are removed from the reactors. Plutonium-239 remains dangerous to humans for at least 24,000 years, perhaps for as much as 500,000 years. This plutonium, notes one commentator generally sympathetic to the nuclear power industry, "will remain a source of radioactive emissions as far in the future as one can meaningfully contemplate." [60] Other transuranics include americum-241 (dangerous for more than 400 years) and iodine-129 (dangerous for perhaps 210,000 years).

Practically speaking, such figures mean that hazardous wastes must be prevented from invading the ecosystem for periods ranging from centuries to hundreds of millennia. Not only must they be securely isolated physically, but human institutions also must survive with sufficient continuity to ensure their responsible administration throughout these eons. Many other chemicals created in the past few decades, including widely used pesticides such as DDT, 2,3,5-T, and dieldrin are not biodegradable and may persist throughout the world ecosystem indefinitely. Though less dangerous than nuclear wastes, these and other substances also represent a displacement of risks to human health and to the ecosystem well into the future.

This transfer of risk raises fundamental ethical and social questions for government. Should public institutions be compelled in some formal and explicit way to exercise regard for the future impacts of decisions concerning environmental management today? And if so, how much regard? Should they be forced, if necessary, to consider not only the future ecological implications in developing dangerous technologies but also the ability of future societies to create institutions capable of controlling these technologies when deciding whether to develop them?

This issue is significant because governmental and economic institutions have a tendency to discount the future impacts of new technologies or newly developed chemicals when compared with the immediate impacts. In economic terms this is done in formal cost-benefit analysis by discounting future benefits and costs rather substantially. In political terms it amounts to adopting a strategy that favors taking environmental actions on the basis of short-term political advantage rather than long-term consequences. (Elected officials, especially, often treat as gospel the legendary advice of a former House Speaker to a new colleague: "Remember that when it comes time to vote, most folks want to know 'what have you done for me lately?'") It is particularly difficult for public officials to develop a sensitive regard for the distant future when there are no apparent political rewards for doing so. At some time the political cynic in practically all public officials whispers: "What has posterity recently done for you lately?"[61]

Conclusion

Scientific issues so permeate environmental problems that the scientist's substantial involvement in making environmental policy is essential. Science, however, has not proven to be an oracle in the environmental policy process. As we have seen, there are limits to the capacity of technical experts to resolve environmental problems and, sometimes, even to clarify them. These limitations arise from the frequent absence of essential technical data, or the ambiguity of available data, or disagreements among experts over the proper evaluation of scientific evidence relevant to environmental problems. Thus, expert opinions on environmental issues may run on a continuum from consensus to dissension; quite often differing opinions leave public officials without any clear and immediate policy options to adopt. Further, many environmental issues involve policy choices that are, as one commentator has remarked, "transcientific." These are issues in which matters such as the acceptability of risks from alternative policies are involved—questions for which the scientist can claim no special competence or superior understanding.

It is also apparent that policy partisans, public agencies, and others attempting to advance one policy or another often will attempt to use scientific evidence, or the scientist's own opinions, to legitimate their policy biases. This tactic often can amount to willful, or unwitting, misrepresentation of technical materials; it is also an almost irresistible temptation to someone in the policy process. Thus, major concerns in evaluating environmental policy should always be an alertness to the limits of scientific evidence in resolving policy issues and a sensitivity to the potential abuses of technical experts and evidence.

Often environmental policy must be formulated not only in the absence of definitive data concerning key issues but also with a likelihood that such data will not be available before a final decision must be made. In many cases, technical data that indisputably resolve scientific conflicts in environmental policy may never become available. Those who appeal for "more time to study the problem" or advise "waiting until more evidence is available" may only be attempting to prevent action as long as possible. It is among the most difficult, yet common, problems facing environmental policy makers that they must make prudent judgments concerning when "further study" will truly yield constructive new evidence and when it is only a pretext for prolonged inaction.

In the end science cannot relieve public officials and institutions from making many difficult and controversial environmental decisions. Nor are scientists and their work invulnerable to the pressures and prejudices of political life. Science can make essential and constructive contributions to environmental policy making by clarifying the impacts of policies, by identifying policy alternatives and evaluating their feasibility, and by suggesting new environmental issues for public consideration. There will always remain, however, a domain of choice for public officials that lies beyond the proper capacity of science to resolve, just as there are vast domains of scientific inquiry that ought to remain beyond the ability of politics to manipulate.

Notes

1. *New York Times*, Feb. 2, 1989.
2. Ibid.
3. *New York Times*, March 30, 1989.
4. Ibid.
5. Ibid.
6. *New York Times*, Feb. 2, 1989.
7. *New York Times*, Feb. 5, 1989.
8. *New York Times*, July 6, 1991.
9. Ibid.
10. *New York Times*, Feb. 25, 1989.

11. "Apple Juice: A Long Way from the Tree," *Consumer Reports* 54, no. 5 (May 1989): 293–296.
12. *New York Times,* Feb. 2, 1989.
13. National Academy of Public Administration, *Setting Priorities, Getting Results: A New Direction for EPA* (Washington, D.C.: National Academy of Public Administration, 1995), chap. 3.
14. Executive Order 12866—Regulatory Planning and Review, *Federal Register,* Oct. 4, 1993.
15. For a general discussion of the political and administrative setting of risk assessment, see Committee on Risk Assessment of Hazardous Air Pollutants, National Research Council, *Science and Judgment in Risk Assessment* (Washington, D.C.: National Academy Press, 1994), chap. 2
16. Roger Revelle, "The Scientist and the Politician," in *Science, Technology and National Policy,* ed. Thomas J. Kuehn and Alan L. Porter (Ithaca, N.Y.: Cornell University Press, 1981), 134.
17. General Accounting Office (GAO), "Superfund: Missed Statutory Deadlines Slow Progress in Environmental Programs," Report no. GAO/RCED 89-27 (Nov. 1988), chap. 2.
18. The epitome of this decision-making problem is explored in R. Dunlap, *DDT: Scientists, Citizens and Public Policy* (Princeton, N.J.: Princeton University Press, 1981), esp. chap. 8.
19. "Colleagues Say Frog Deformity Researchers Leaped Too Soon," *Washington Post,* November 3, 1997, A3.
20. GAO, "Pesticides: EPA's Formidable Task to Assess and Regulate Their Risks," Report no. GAO/RCED 86-125 (April 1986), 21–22.
21. GAO, "Hazardous Waste: Uncertainties of Existing Data," Report no. GAO/PEMD 87-11BR (Feb. 1987), 15–16.
22. GAO, "The Nation's Water: Key Unanswered Questions about the Quality of Rivers and Streams," Report no. GAO/PEMD 86-6 (Sept. 1986), 4.
23. GAO, "Coal and Nuclear Wastes—Both Potential Contributors to Environmental and Health Problems," Report no. EMD 81-132 (Sept. 21, 1981), 2.
24. See Council on Environmental Quality (CEQ), *Environmental Quality, 1979* (Washington, D.C.: CEQ, 1980), 194ff.
25. Ibid.
26. On the history of the controversy over dioxin, see John A. Moore, Renate D. Kimbrough, and Michael Gough, "The Dioxin TCDD: A Selective Study of Science and Policy Interaction," in *Keeping Pace with Science and Engineering: Case Studies in Environmental Regulation,* ed. Myron F. Ulman (Washington, D.C.: National Academy Press, 1993), 221–242.
27. Ibid.
28. *New York Times,* Aug. 15, 1991.
29. *New York Times,* Sept. 26, 1992.
30. *New York Times,* March 23, 1993.
31. Ibid.
32. On the general problems of animal experiments, see David D. Doniger, *The Law and Policy of Toxic Substances Control* (Baltimore, Md.: Johns Hopkins University Press, 1978), part I.
33. Animal data are cited in *New York Times,* June 25, 1983.
34. Ibid.
35. Doniger, *The Law and Policy of Toxic Substances Control,* 12.
36. Harvey Brooks, "The Resolution of Technically Intensive Public Policy Disputes," *Science, Technology and Human Values* 9, no. 1 (Winter 1984): 40. For estimates of discretionary judgments in risk assessment, see National Research Council, Commission on Life Sciences, Committee on the Institutional Means for Assessment of Risks to Public Health, *Risk Assessment in the Federal Government: Managing the Process* (Washington, D.C.: National Academy Press, 1983), chap. 1.

37. Frances M. Lynn, "The Interplay of Science and Values in Assessing and Regulating Environmental Risks," *Science, Technology and Human Values* 11, no. 2 (Spring 1986): 40–50.
38. Thomas M. Dietz and Robert W. Rycroft, *The Risk Professionals* (New York: Russell Sage Foundation, 1987), 111.
39. Dorothy Nelkin, ed., *Controversy: The Politics of Technical Decisions* (Beverly Hills, Calif.: Sage Publications, 1984), 17.
40. A comprehensive review of the various statutory standards for risk in federal law is found in John J. Cohrssen and Vincent T. Covello, *Risk Analysis: A Guide to Principles and Methods for Analyzing Health and Environmental Risks* (Washington, D.C.: CEQ, 1989), 14–15; see also Walter A. Rosenbaum, "Regulation at Risk: The Controversial Politics and Science of Comparative Risk Assessment," in Sheldon Kamieniecki, George A. Gonzalez, and Robert O. Vos, eds., *Flashpoints in Environmental Policymaking: Controversies in Achieving Sustainability* (Albany: State University of New York Press, 1997), 31–62.
41. This analysis is based on National Academy of Public Administration, *Setting Priorities, Getting Results*, chap. 3.
42. See William W. Lowrence, *Of Acceptable Risks* (Los Altos, Calif.: William Kaufmann, 1976).
43. CEQ, *Environmental Quality, 1979*, 218.
44. GAO, "EPA's Chemical Testing Program Has Not Resolved Safety Concerns," Report no. GAO/RCED 91-136 (June 1991), 14.
45. National Academy of Public Administration, *Setting Priorities, Getting Results*, 54.
46. *National Journal*, June 18, 1983.
47. A sampling of this literature may be found in the collection of articles by Peter Lewin, Gerald L. Sauer, Bernard L. Cohen, Richard N. Langlois, and Aaron Wildavsky in "Symposium on Pollution," *Cato Journal* (Spring 1982): 205ff.
48. Paul Johnson, "The Perils of Risk Avoidance," *Regulation* (May/June 1980): 17.
49. Ibid.
50. *New York Times*, Aug. 20, 1993.
51. *Wall Street Journal*, Oct. 29, 1997, B3.
52. From Executive Order 12898—Federal Actions to Address Environmental Justice in Minority Populations and Low-Income Populations, *Federal Register*, Feb. 11, 1994.
53. Robert D. Bullard, "Waste and Racism: A Stacked Deck?," *Forum for Applied Research and Public Policy* 8, no. 1 (Spring 1993) 29–35; on the general problems of defining environmental justice, see Evan J. Rinquist, "Environmental Justice: Normative Concerns and Empirical Evidence," in Norman J. Vig and Michael E. Kraft, eds., *Environmental Policy in the 1990s*, 3d ed. (Washington, D.C.: CQ Press, 1997), 231–254; and EPA, Office of Policy, Planning and Evaluation, *Environmental Equity: Reducing Risk for All Communities, Vol. 1: Workgroup Report to the Administrator* (Washington, D.C.: EPA, June 1992), 1.
54. Ivette Perfecto and Baldemar Valazquez, "Farm Workers: Among the Least Protected," *EPA Journal* 18, no. 1 (March/April 1992): 13–14; D. R. Wernette and L. A. Nieves, "Breathing Polluted Air," *EPA Journal* 18, no. 1 (March/April 1992): 16–17.
55. Paul Mohai and Bunyan Bryant, "Race, Poverty, and the Environment," *EPA Journal* 18, no. 1 (March/April 1992): 8.
56. Rebecca Head, "Health-Based Standards: What Role in Environmental Justice?," in *Environmental Justice: Issues, Policies and Solutions*, ed. Bunyan Bryant (Washington, D.C.: Island Press, 1995), 29.
57. Allan Mazur, *The Dynamics of Technical Controversy* (Washington, D.C.: Communications Press, 1981), 29.
58. Ibid., 27.
59. *National Journal*, June 18, 1983.
60. *New York Times*, May 12, 1983.
61. Quoting Sam Rayburn.

Suggested Readings

Bryant, Bunyan. *Environmental Justice: Issues, Policies, and Solutions*. Washington, D.C.: Island Press, 1995.

Davies, J. Clarence, ed. *Comparing Environmental Risks: Tools for Setting Governmental Priorities*. Washington, D.C.: Resources for the Future, 1996.

Kunreuther, Howard, and Paul Slovic, eds. "Challenges in Risk Assessment and Risk Management." *Annals of the American Academy of Political and Social Science* 545 (May 1966).

National Research Council. *Improving Risk Communication*. Washington, D.C.: National Academy Press, 1989.

National Research Council. *Science and Judgment in Risk Assessment*. Washington, D.C.: National Academy Press, 1994.

Chapter 5

More Choice: The Battle over Regulatory Economics

> . . . *Edison Electric Institute disputed the accuracy of a newsletter report that said that the utility trade association may have suppressed a study on the economic effects of greenhouse gas emissions reductions. On December 12, EEI requested the study from . . . IFC/Kaiser but then deep-sixed it "because it's not damaging enough," an unnamed source told [the publication]* Air Daily. *. . . IFC/Kaiser . . . concluded that the cost of electricity would rise by 4% to 9% if U.S. emissions were stabilized at 1990 levels by 2010. . . . In contrast, a study of similar scenarios done by . . . Charles River Associates for the auto industry said electricity prices would increase by 23% by 2010.*
>
> —Greenwire, November 19, 1997

Controversy over the economic rationality of environmental regulation has never ceased since the inception of Environmental Era I. Critics assert that both the process and objectives of environmental regulation are flawed by economic inefficiency, irrationality, and contradiction. Spokespersons for the business sector, state and local governments, and other regulated interests often join many economists in advocating fundamental changes in the criteria used in formulating environmental regulations and in the methods used to secure compliance with them.

Environmentalists and many economists, among others, believe that economic arguments are often inappropriate, if not deliberately deceptive, when used by critics to evaluate environmental policies. Nonetheless, environmentalists themselves have invoked benefit-cost analysis (BCA) while its promoters have also condemned it when it suited their purposes. Conflict over the economic implications of environmental policy is certain to continue. As regulatory costs and dissatisfaction over regulatory achievements mount, even the environmental movement, traditionally hostile to proposals for economic reform, has felt compelled to examine critically the economic basis of current environmental laws.

Controversy over economic reform has traditionally focused on two issues: the value of BCA as a major criterion in writing environmental regulations and the effectiveness of marketplace incentives rather than "command-and-control" methods for securing compliance with environmental standards. Increasingly, however, debate about the use of environmental economics in policy making has become a third important element in reform discussions.

The Benefit-Cost Debate

A common complaint about almost all environmental regulations written since 1970 is that the congressionally mandated procedures for setting environmental standards are too often insensitive to costs. "Cost-oblivious" laws, such as the Clean Air Act (CAA) or the Occupational Safety and Health Act (OSH Act), in which benefit-cost considerations are explicitly forbidden as regulatory criteria, are cited as examples of legislatively ordained disregard for the economic consequences of regulation. Other laws, such as the Resource Conservation and Recovery Act (RCRA), have been criticized for failing to require specifically that regulatory agencies consider costs among other factors in setting environmental standards. In the view of critics, this mandated indifference toward BCA breeds a carelessness about costs among regulators that inflicts economic penalties on regulated interests. Even in cases where Congress has permitted or required some kind of BCA in regulatory decision making, critics assert that too often agencies can ignore the results or treat them as a formality.[1]

A Long and Contentious History

Environmental regulation is a recent battle front in the conflict over BCA that resonates throughout American regulatory history. Every administration since John F. Kennedy's has attempted to promote sensitivity to economic costs and benefits in regulatory policy making by federal agencies through some institutional arrangement. In the latter 1970s, both White House and Congress began to pressure federal agencies through executive action and legislative mandates to give economic considerations greater attention in environmental regulation. Jimmy Carter, the most avowed environmentalist of all recent presidents, nonetheless established a White House review entity with the pugnacious acronym RARG (Regulatory Analysis Review Group) whose mission included reducing the cost of federal environmental regulations. The mildly controversial RARG, however, mostly annoyed environmentalists; what replaced it infuriated them.[2]

Ronald Reagan, whose administration was viewed by environmentalists with unanimous disfavor, initiated the most aggressive effort to promote BCA in environmental policy making with Executive Order 12291, issued practically the day he was inaugurated, requiring all federal agencies to prepare a Regulatory Impact Analysis (RIA) for any major new regulatory proposals and to demonstrate that the benefit for such proposals would exceed the anticipated costs. Executive Order 12291 vested responsibility for its implementation in the White House's Office of Management and Budget (OMB), which then created the first codified guidance for federal agencies on BCA preparation. Reagan's order unleashed a prolonged, bitter controversy between ideological supporters of Reagan's "regulatory reform" in Congress, the executive agencies, and the business community on one side and environmentalists, most congressional members, and other White House critics on the other. Proponents of the executive order believed it was long overdue, a sensible remedy to excessively numerous and expensive federal regulatory laws, a blow against increasingly costly governmental interference in economic life. Critics were convinced that Reagan's order was a covert attack on environmental regulation, virtually a subversion of congressionally mandated environmental programs, and the OMB's enforcement of it an illegal, if not unconstitutional, presidential encroachment on the regulatory process. Contention over Executive Order 12291 became a running theme during the Reagan years, dissipating only when the Bush administration found the contention too politically costly and quietly backed away from Reagan's aggressive enforcement policies.

The Clinton administration appeared to put the BCA controversy at least temporarily to rest when President Clinton issued Executive Order 12866 in September 1993, significantly relaxing requirements for the preparation and review of RIAs in federal agencies and greatly diminishing the OMB's role in the process, much to the satisfaction of environmentalists. Nonetheless, the new order still required federal agencies to prepare and review BCAs frequently, insisting that they remain a formal part of regulatory procedure. Thus, debates over the role of BCA in regulatory proposals continued.

Greater congressional interest in BCA also emerged during this period. One example of this occurred in 1990 when a Democratic-controlled Congress wrote into the Clean Air Act Amendments a requirement that the EPA conduct a BCA for the impact of all amendments to the Clean Air Act passed since 1970. The startling Republican victory in the 1994 congressional elections produced a Republican-controlled 104th Congress and a multitude of new Republican legislative proposals requiring not only that BCA be compulsory for all new federal regulations but that only proposed regulations with favorable BCAs be promulgated. Although these measures were (sometimes barely) defeated, the legislative mood was obvious to federal agencies: a Republican Congress would vigorously press BCA on regulatory agencies whenever possible and make economics a major consideration in regulatory policy debate.[3] Apparently, BCA in some form had come to stay in environmental regulation.

The Case for Benefit-Cost Analysis

A number of advantages are claimed for BCA. Economists assert that transparency is one of its attractions in the sense that "the results of a well-executed BCA analysis can be clearly linked to the assumptions, theory, methods and procedures used in it. This transparency can add to the accountability of public decisions by indicating where the decisions are at variance with the analysis."[4] Thus, an argument over the economic impact of a proposed environmental regulation in dispute would presumably be considerably clarified because a competent BCA would enable all sides to understand what went into the economic evaluation and to examine the validity of the various components of that valuation. Additionally, proponents believe that competent BCA can reveal where important information is lacking about costs and benefits from a policy—what has been called "ignorance revelation." Moreover, it is also argued, BCA enables policy makers to have a common metric for comparing policies and choosing among them.[5]

Proponents of BCA argue that at the very least it can point decision makers to the most economically desirable, or cost effective, policies for achieving a regulatory goal. "Even if one objects . . . to basing environmental policy on benefit-cost analysis," argued economist A. Myrick Freeman III, "it still makes good sense to be in favor of cost-effective environmental policies. Cost-effectiveness means controlling pollution to achieve the stated environmental quality standards at the lowest possible total cost."[6] Moreover, the proponents add, critics of BCA are really objecting to *incompetent* analysis, especially when deliberately created to produce a desired outcome. Competent BCA sometimes can identify policies that are both economically and environmentally wiser than those currently implemented. A case in point, Freeman argued, are the federally financed water resource developments such as dams, stream channelization, and flood control projects that were justified originally by questionable BCAs. Freeman noted that these analyses used techniques that systematically overstated the benefits of water resource development, understated the economic costs, and ignored environmental costs.

The result was construction of a number of projects that were economically wasteful and environmentally damaging and serious consideration of such misguided proposals as the one to build a dam in the Grand Canyon.[7]

When all the regulated sectors of the U.S. economy are considered, the critics reason, a huge inflationary diversion of capital from more economically desirable uses results. Critics frequently allege that excessive regulatory costs will drive some firms out of business or out of the country. Spokespersons for major national business associations, such as the Business Roundtable and the U.S. Chamber of Commerce, have alleged that excessive regulatory costs have depressed significantly the growth rate of the gross national product.

Few proponents of BCA argue, however, that it should be the sole criterion for regulatory strategies. Still, they believe that the routine use of the procedure would make regulators more sensitive to the cost of their regulatory decisions and more likely to select regulatory procedures with net benefits, or with the least cost among alternatives. Many also believe that BCA leads to a better quality of decision making. As economist Paul Johnson observed, "The value is that it injects rational calculation into a highly emotional subject. . . . It offers you a range of alternatives. Without stringent analysis, nobody knows whether costs imposed by regulatory programs are money well spent."[8] And, though seldom admitted, many advocates hope the publicity given to regulatory costs, especially when net benefits are lacking, will deter agencies from choosing such regulations.

The Case against Benefit-Cost Analysis

Environmentalists traditionally have opposed the routine use of BCA in setting environmental standards. Some still regard it a categorical evil, wholly inappropriate to the selection of environmental regulations. Others recognize that economic considerations may sometimes merit attention in writing environmental laws, but believe benefit-cost calculations are easily distorted to the advantage of regulated interests. Most environmentalists regard BCA as nothing less than a covert assault on environmental regulation whenever it is used. Environmentalists assert that BCA often distorts economic reality by exaggerating regulatory costs and underestimating benefits. Regulated interests, the argument continues, often deliberately magnify their compliance costs; it is difficult, in any case, to obtain accurate economic data from them. Further, regulated interests give little attention to the economic "learning curve," which often yields a substantial saving over the full period of regulation as they gain experience and expertise in controlling their pollutants. Benefits from regulation, in contrast, are often underestimated because they are not easily calculated. For instance, how are the health benefits from significantly cleaner air over the next several decades to be calculated? What value is to be placed on rivers, streams, and lakes made fishable and swimmable again? What is the dollars-and-cents value of an irreplaceable old-growth forest conserved for another generation?

Some benefits almost defy monetizing. For instance, an agency may consider regulatory alternatives involving different levels of risk to populations from exposure to hazardous or toxic substances. What is the appropriate value to be placed on a life saved? A variation of BCA sometimes advocated in such a situation is to compare the costs of regulation with estimates of the lives saved from the different strategies. Such a comparison implicitly requires regulators to decide how much an individual human life is worth. As a practical example, a study by the EPA on preventing acid precipitation suggested that stricter controls on air emissions from electric power plants in the Ohio River Valley would cost several hundred million dollars. It also would avert an estimated 54,000 additional pollution-related deaths by the year 2000. Comparing lives saved with dollars spent on pollution controls in this instance makes economic sense only if one assigns a dollar value to each life—an act sure to seem arbitrary, if not morally repugnant, to the political constituency.

Critics have noted, moreover, that BCA traditionally ignores equity considerations—an increasingly potent argument as the environmental justice movement expands. In a sense this is correct; common BCA lacks a social conscience because it is unconcerned with the social distribution of costs and benefits—with which groups are winners and losers in the distribution.[9] "It is often argued," explain economists Raymond J. Kopp, Alan J. Krupnick, and Michael Toman, "that [BCA] takes the existing distribution of income as given and does not consider the equity implications of the policies it seeks to evaluate. This criticism points to the anonymous manner in which the welfare changes of individuals are aggregated. . . ."[10] It is possible, however, to factor at least some equity considerations into BCA but it is uncommon and fraught with difficulties for regulatory agencies that must decide whose equities are to be considered and how to compare equity among different groups.

Perhaps the most persuasive reason for resisting BCA, in the environmentalist's view, is that reducing an environmental value such as clean air or water to a monetary figure makes it appear to be just another commodity that can be priced, bought, and sold. According to Stephen Kelman, "Many environmentalists fear that subjecting decisions about clean air or water to the cost-benefit tests that determine the general run of decisions removes those matters from the realm of specially valued things. . . . The very statement that something is not for sale enhances and protects the thing's value in a number of ways. . . . [It] is a way of showing that a thing is valued for its own sake, whereas selling a thing for money demonstrates that it was valued only instrumentally." [11] Environmentalists often believe they stand apart from regulated business through a profound ethical disagreement over the intrinsic worth of wild places, uncontaminated air and water, and other environmental amenities. This conviction of moral purpose imparts to the movement much of its passion and persistence. It also elevates arguments over BCA to the level of ethical principles, making compromise especially difficult.

Reality and Rhetoric

Until recently, BCA has proven more paper tiger than bulldog in regulatory affairs. Ronald Reagan's BCA initiative never achieved the epic impact its proponents wished because its implementation was badly flawed. Several major environmental programs, such as the CAA and the OSH Act, prohibited in the law BCA or severely limited its application in regulations implementing them (although the EPA spent $2 million preparing an unused BCA for an air-quality standard anyway).[12] Many other regulatory proposals escaped Executive Order 12291 because their impacts did not exceed $100 million. Agencies often prepared BCAs but, lacking confidence in the results, turned to other criteria in writing regulations. And agencies showed little consistency in how they prepared their analyses, notwithstanding OMB guidelines. Experience demonstrated the severe limitations and inherent biased implicit in data deficiencies. A GAO evaluation of the EPA's experience summarized the matter:

> EPA's benefit-cost analyses cannot provide exact answers to regulating complex environmental problems largely because of gaps in underlying scientific data. . . . This data gap is troublesome in estimating physical measures of the benefits of environmental regulation, such as improvements in water quality or better visibility. Problems also arise in calculating dollar values for these improvements . . . in estimating the costs of complying with environmental regulations. These data weaknesses . . . affect other federal agencies dealing with health and environmental regulations.[13]

None of this troubled the Reagan OMB. It processed more than 2,000 RIAs annually, accepting most RIAs accompanying regulatory proposals and, when possible, using them in arguments for revision or rejection of environmental regulations. It was here that Executive Order 12291 had its major impact on environmental laws. The OMB, together with Reagan-appointed officials in environmental regulatory agencies, exercised administrative discretion to apply these BCAs selectively to some proposals but not to others. BCA was seldom used when proposals were made to *deregulate* some aspect of the environment or some relevant private firm.[14] The Reagan administration's use of BCA, in the end, created a pervasive bias against environmental regulation that embittered environmentalists against RIAs and engendered deep suspicion of the OMB's role in regulatory review.

Federal agencies continue to struggle when attempting to estimate realistically the cost or benefits of the regulatory programs they implement. Whatever the reason—incompetence, inexperience, creative bookkeeping, or something else—regulatory cost estimates frequently prove inaccurate. The EPA's Superfund cost estimates have been unreliably low and the situation is no better for hazardous waste site remediation required by RCRA. "EPA does not know with certainty what it costs to oversee corrective actions," the GAO noted in 1993, and, with little experience in RCRA cleanups, EPA "cannot accurately predict the resource needs for overseeing future stabilization and final cleanup activities."[15] Often, EPA officials, like other regulatory officials, appear nonchalant about guidelines—or perhaps confounded by them—even when guidance is explicit.. For instance, the 1990 amendments to the Clean Air Act required the EPA to produce a BCA for any proposed regulations to implement the amendments. The Congress specifically required that the EPA describe the key economic assumptions, the extent to which benefits and costs were quantified, and the extent to which alternatives were considered in the BCA procedure When the GAO evaluated twenty-three of the RIAs written under these guidelines, it discovered considerable disparities. Eight of the RIAS did not identify such key economic assumptions as the value placed on human life. Analyses explicit about economic assumption were often silent about the reasons for those chosen. All of the RIAs assigned dollar values to the estimated costs of proposed regulations, but only eleven assigned dollar values to the benefits. "According to EPA officials," explained the report, "assigning dollar values to potential benefits is difficult because of the uncertainty of scientific data and the lack of market data on some of the effects."[16]

Regulatory officials, environmental or otherwise, still frequently discount their own agency analyses when making regulatory decisions. This is not necessarily administrative malfeasance—federal agencies are usually required only to consider the costs and benefits in the course of policy making—but the situation bespeaks considerable practical difficulty in using BCAs and substantial official uneasiness about the situation. Nonetheless, estimates about policy costs and benefits, some perhaps grievously flawed, continue to pack policy debates. One may wonder, at least, at the bland confidence with which the EPA reported in 1997 that amendments to the Clean Air Act since 1970 had cost at least $523 billion but had reduced bronchitis, asthma attacks, and heart disease among Americans, thereby "saving from $6 trillion to $49 trillion in medical costs alone." [17]

Some Lessons

Much can yet be learned from the experience of the last two decades. The blizzard of econometric data normally accompanying arguments over the cost of regulation should be at least initially suspect—on all sides. Willfully or not, regulated business will often overestimate the costs of regulation and proponents of regulation will often underestimate it. Also, as experience with the Reagan-Bush administrations illustrates, BCA is so vulnerable to partisan manipulation that it is often discounted by officials even when they are *allowed* to consider the economics of regulation. A former advisor to President Richard Nixon recalled, "In executive branch meetings, the EPA staff repeatedly seemed to minimize pollution costs, while other agencies weighed in with high costs to meet the identical pollution standard. Often, we halved the difference. . . ." [18] Many regulatory decisions made on the basis of political, administrative, or other considerations are sanctified later by economics for the sake of credibility. Sometimes, costs are inflated grossly not so much by individual regulations as by the multiplicity and unpredictability of regulatory procedures.

All of this should clarify at least a few aspects of the cost-benefit controversy. First, there is no substantial evidence that regulatory costs have become so excessive that BCA must be routinely imposed on *all* environmental regulation programs. Second, there are doubtless instances, perhaps a substantial number of them, in which BCA might suggest better solutions to environmental regulation than would otherwise be selected. For this reason, such analysis should not be excluded categorically from consideration unless Congress specifically mandates an exclusion. Third, it matters a great deal who does the calculating. All BCAs should be open to review and challenge during administrative deliberations. Fourth, Congress should indicate explicitly in the text of environmental legislation or in the accompanying legislative history how it expects regulatory agencies to weight economic criteria alongside other statutory guidelines to be observed in writing regulations to implement such legislation. Fifth, regulatory costs might be diminished significantly not by using BCA but by using economic incentives in securing compliance of regulated interests with environmental programs.

The Emerging Problem of Environmental Valuation

The BCA controversy illuminates an especially vexing problem inherent to most debates about environmental policy: how can environmental amenities be valued accurately if some metric must be devised? This issue drives to the core of traditional economic theory because it raises profound questions about the assumptions implicit in placing value on non-market goods, such as clean air or pristine wilderness. In recent years, this problem has stimulated considerable debate among economists and others concerned with environmental valuation, which in turn has led to several significant proposals for a radical change in the way environmental amenities are evaluated and, as a consequence, in how environmental policy making transpires.

Environmental Accounting.   Many economists, recognizing that the continuing development of environmental policy making increasingly confronts policy makers with problems of environmental valuation unaddressed by traditional economics, propose the development of "environmental accounting" as an alternative. In effect, environmental accounting attempts to broaden enormously the scope of environmental amenities to which society attaches significant value and to devise a metrics appropriate for comparing these values with other, usually monetary, values involved in policy evaluation. In this perspective, not only environmental amenities with obvious and immediate human benefit would be valued—clean air and water, for instance—but also habitats essential to the preservation or proliferation of species, ecological sites essential for biosphere preservation or improvement, environments of unusual beauty, flora and fauna of biological significance, or other aspects of the human environment important for *ecological* reasons. Identifying these distinctively valued ecological elements will be difficult and challenging but no less so than assigning an appropriate value to them.

Environmental accounting is especially difficult because it requires both economists and ecologists to work at the intellectual margins of their disciplines where theory and evidence are often tenuous—ecologists, for instance, may strongly suspect that the eradication of certain species will create economically long-term disruption of human environments without being able to prove it or to estimate the scope of the disturbance. Since many environmental amenities are neither bought nor sold in markets, economists would have to construct "shadow prices"—best estimates of real market value—by a tortuous, inevitably contentious logic. "Demand and supply curves must be constructed," explains economist Roefie Hueting. "The supply curve can, in principle, be constructed by estimating the costs of the measures necessary to prevent environmental damage. . . . However, constructing a complete demand curve is difficult because the intensity of individual preferences for environmental functions cannot be expressed in market behavior or translated into market terms. This is further complicated by the fact that the consequences of today's actions will often only be manifest in future damage." [19] Many economists assert, in rebuttal, that a procedure called "revealed preferences" is a reasonable substitute for a market in valuing environmental amenities. Economists Kopp, Krupnick, and Toman offer an example. "It would be wrong," they suggest, "to think of economic values as dollar-denominated values in one's brain to be downloaded when a person is asked the worth of a beautiful sunset; rather, such a value might be inferred from the things that one gives up to see the sunset (e.g., the cost of travel to the ocean). "To economists," they continue, "the importance of things (tangible or intangible) is revealed by what a person will give to obtain them. . . . If the thing given up was money, the value can be expressed in monetary units; otherwise, it is expressed in the natural units of the thing given." [20]

"Contingent Valuation." One profound consequence of environmentalism's political ascendancy in the United States has been to compel a sustained rethinking of traditional economic and ecological theories in order to come to terms with the problems of environmental valuation implicit in contemporary environmental regulation. One approach to environmental valuation currently proposed for federal policy makers is a methodology called "contingent valuation," meaning that a monetary value is to be assigned to an environmental amenity whose use, or destruction, would deprive others of its future availability. Contingent valuation could be used, for example, to estimate the monetary cost to the public created by haze over the Grand Canyon or widespread pollution of Alaskan waters caused by oil tanker spills, or by any other event that deprives the public of the passive value in an environmental amenity. In a typical case, a representative segment of the relevant public would be asked how much they would be willing to pay to avoid an oil spill, to prevent haze over a national park, or to preclude some other environmental problem. Through statistical procedures, a monetary value would then be assigned to an environmental amenity based on these public valuations. Alaska's state government used contingent valuation in the early 1990s to discover what value Americans who might never visit Prince William Sound would assign to preventing a catastrophic oil spill there— a strategy used to estimate the monetary damages for which the Exxon Corporation would be held liable for the devastating oil spill by the tanker *Exxon Valdez* in 1990. Based on an average response of $30 per person, Alaskan officials estimated that Americans would collectively pay $2.8 billion to avoid such a disaster.[21] In 1989 the federal courts, apparently influenced by an endorsement of contingent valuation by a panel of distinguished U.S. economists, ordered the Department of the Interior to take into account the losses to people not directly affected by environmental problems when estimating the cost of CAA and Superfund violations in facilities under its jurisdiction.

The first proposed guidelines for the use of contingent valuation in federal policy making, however, emerged from the National Oceanic and Atmospheric Administration in mid-1993.

Contingent valuation remains controversial among economists and other policy makers, as the Clinton administration's crabwise approach to the matter suggests. Many economists dismiss the methodology as "junk economics" because, they assert, the public cannot accurately assess the value in the passive use of an environmental amenity. The critics argue that the public is overly generous with hypothetical statements about personal outlays, tends to exaggerate the value of an amenity, and is often influenced by the wording of questions. To support these contentions, the critics cite studies showing enormous variability in public environmental valuations: saving an old-growth forest in the Pacific Northwest was valued between $119 to $359 billion; sparing the whooping crane from extinction between $51 and $715 billion.[22] Understandably, some of the most aggressive opponents of contingent valuation in federal policy making are corporations, such as Exxon, which feel at considerable financial risk. The Clinton administration has proposed that contingent valuation be discretionary in federal policy making and that, in any event, agencies using the procedure discount any contingent valuation by 50 percent for policy-making purposes. Whatever federal agency adopts the methodology can expect to defend it before a federal judge since it is certain to be legally challenged and, thus, unlikely to be implemented for several years.

"Environmental Risk" Instead.   An alternative approach to environmental valuation might be to substitute risk for dollars, thereby avoiding the problem of monetizing environmental amenities. Such an approach might, for instance, involve comparing the risks of losing an environmental amenity to those of preserving it, assuming that a satisfactory risk metric can be created. Or, in another variation the monetary benefits in altering an amenity might be compared to the risks in losing it. Suppose, for example, that federal regulators must decide whether to open a large portion of wilderness area, the habitat of a rare or endangered species, to oil and gas exploration. The benefits of exploration could be calculated in terms of the potential governmental royalties, new employment, regional economic development, corporate taxes, or other monetized considerations. These might be compared with the expected number of species endangered or lost, the extent of land made unusable for other purposes, the amount of air and water pollution generated, the special resources impacted (historic sites, national parks, recreation areas, etc.). These strategies require a comparison of dollars to risks, or risks to risks, each with its own difficulties. Nonetheless, environmental officials often do make such comparisons implicitly or informally in

arriving at regulatory decisions and formalizing the procedure would at least force the comparisons to become explicit and reviewable. Moreover, proponents of BCA or some variation in regulatory decision making argue that defensible, rational approaches can be created for ecological valuation with sufficient time and effort. Until that day arrives, however, all existing approaches to BCA in environmental decision making are likely to be contentious and, at best, greeted with profound suspicion among environmental interests.

Using the Marketplace Incentives

In 1979 the EPA moved sharply away from the traditional standards-and-enforcement approach to air pollution by introducing its "bubble policy" for controlling emissions from existing air pollution sources. The standards-and-enforcement strategy requires the federal government to create pollution standards, define acceptable pollution levels, prescribe the required control technologies for each type of polluter, license and monitor pollution sources, and identify and punish violators of pollution laws. The "bubble" policy substituted economic incentives for legal prescriptions in an effort to secure compliance with environmental regulation. During the 1980s, the EPA continued to experiment on a very limited scale with other market-based approaches to enforcing portions of the CAA. The 1990 amendments to the CAA enormously expanded the scope of regulatory policy reform through Title IV's "emissions trading" approach to regulating sulfur oxide emissions, an important precursor of acid deposition.

Title IV's innovative approach, long recommended by many economists, required the EPA to allocate to each major coal-fired electric utility an allowance for each ton of emission permitted and to limit emissions to the total of allowances issued. Other detailed provisions provide for the creation of additional allowances to permit economic growth without exceeding acceptable national limits on sulfur oxide emissions. These allowances can be bought, sold, and traded among the holders, or purchased by others (including environmentalists who might wish to retire them from use). In theory, a market will be created for sulfur oxide emissions that will allocate pollution control costs with the greatest economic efficiency while assuring that pollution limits will be achieved. Title IV represents the most ambitious national effort to reform environmental regulation by substituting market-based approaches for command-and-control techniques.[23] The legislation culminates a decade of increasing dissatisfaction with command-and-control regulation and, if even moderately successful, will undoubtedly hasten market-based reforms in other domains of environmental regulation. Properly used, marketplace incentives may prove a practical means to reduce the costs of regulation and overcome many problems inherent in traditional regulatory styles.

Economic Alternatives to Command-and-Control

The traditional command-and-control approach to environmental regulation (which is fully described in Chapter 6) has much to recommend it, but also serious flaws in the opinion of most economists and many other policy experts.[24] Until recently, Congress and most state, federal, and local regulatory officials have been reluctant to try more innovative, market-based policies as alternatives or supplements to the traditional method. This reticence arose from lack of legal or administrative experience with incentive systems, from the environmental movement's intense dislike for market approaches, and from the deeply entrenched command-and-control culture among pollution control specialists and administrators. Soaring regulatory costs and mounting dissatisfaction with the pace of environmental cleanup—to say nothing of the administrative entanglements—have gradually created a more receptive attitude toward market approaches to environmental management even among many of its traditional detractors.

What's Wrong With Command-and-Control?   Critics believe that almost three decades' experience with command-and-control regulation has demonstrated its severe deficiencies. First, they assert, it offers regulated interests few economic incentives to comply rapidly and efficiently with mandated pollution standards. In the economist's perspective, standards-and-enforcement lacks an appeal to the economic self-interest of the regulated. Even severe penalties for noncompliance with the law often fail to motivate polluters to meet required pollution control deadlines. Penalties are often unassessed or severely weakened by negotiation with regulatory agencies. Some firms find it more profitable to pay penalties and to continue polluting in violation of law than to assume the far steeper costs of compliance. Additionally, polluters have no economic incentive to reduce their emissions below the regulatory requirements.

Second, traditional regulatory approaches require the federal government to specify the appropriate technologies and methods for their use in practically every instance in which pollutants are technologically controlled. Highly complicated, exquisitely detailed specifications that make poor scientific or economic sense for particular industries or firms can result. One reason is that neither Congress nor administrators may have sufficient scientific training or experience to make correct judgments about the appropriate technologies for pollution abatement in a specific firm or industry. Also, regulators sometimes lack sufficient information about the economics of firms or industries to know what technologies are economically efficient—that is, which achieve the desired control standards least expensively. In general, according to economists Allen V. Kneese and Charles L. Schultze:

> Problems such as environmental control ... involve extremely complicated economic and social relationships. Policies that may appear straightforward—for example, requiring everyone to reduce pollution by the technologically feasible limit—will often have ramifications or side effects that are quite different from those intended. Second, given the complexity of these relationships, relying on a central regulatory bureaucracy to carry out social policy simply will not work: there are too many actors, too much technical knowledge, too many different circumstances to be grasped by a regulatory agency.[25]

Examples of costly mistakes in specifying technological controls are not hard to find. Instances occurred in the writing of regulations to implement the Surface Mining Control and Reclamation Act of 1977:

> International Inc., a General Electric subsidiary, complained that the EPA and the Office of Surface Mining in the Interior Department required that all runoff from areas disturbed by surface mining must pass through a sedimentation pond although other management practices, such as the use of straw dikes and vegetative cover, would achieve substantially the same results. The company had to build at its Trapper Mine near Craig, Colorado, a $335,000 sedimentation pond when alternative methods could have achieved the same results at 10 percent of the cost.[26]

The Conoco Company complained that Consolidated Coal, its subsidiary, unnecessarily spent $160 million annually to meet engineering standards imposed on surface mines by the federal government. The National Academy of Sciences, speaking through its National Research Council, had recommended a different, less expensive, and apparently equally effective approach.[27]

Third, proponents assert that incentive approaches can be simply and economically administered. "Incentive-based systems are administratively simple", notes the National Academy of Public Administration (NAPA), " because . . . they require much of the regulatory energy to be expended up front in the design state of the regulatory program. If the design is correct, less burdensome administration may be facilitated. Further, once the program is in place, regulators can rely on the energies of the private sector to drive pollution downward."[28] The alternative seems to require bureaucratic legions toiling endlessly in the regulatory vineyards. "Command-and-control regulation," notes the NAPA, "may impose a never-ending requirement on regulators to develop new and more stringent industry-specific regulations on smaller and smaller discharge points." [29]

Finally, proponents point out that a market incentive approach is easier for the public to understand, and presumably easier to approve. Economic incentives focus upon a pollution reduction goal which the public would presumably find much more comprehensible—-hence, easier for government to defend politically—than technology specifications with all the mystifying technical disputation about its appropriateness and efficiency.

Bubbles, Nets, and Offsets: Emissions Trading at the EPA.   Between 1970 and 1990, the EPA approved various emissions trading strategies that created on a very limited scale marketplace incentives for interests regulated by the CAA to control their pollutants.[30] In 1974, the EPA allowed firms creating a new emissions source within a plant to reduce emissions from another source in the same plant so that net emissions did not significantly increase (a procedure called netting). In 1976, the Agency approved emissions trading through "offsets." A new pollution source—a coal-fired electric utility, for instance—could locate in a "nonattainment area" (a region not meeting national air-quality standards) only if it could offset its new pollution emissions by reducing emissions from other sources already in the area, such as those from another power plant. It could also buy pollution reductions by other firms in the area to offset its own net pollution.

In 1980, the EPA introduced "bubbling," its most ambitious form of emissions trading prior to 1990. This policy assumed "that an imaginary enclosure, or bubble, is placed over an industrial plant. From this enclosure, or bubble, a maximum allowable level of emissions is permitted. A firm in this bubble would be free to use more cost-effective pollution controls than are usually allowed." [31] For example, a firm with three smokestacks emitting pollution might find it least costly to cut back severely on the emissions from one stack while leaving the others only slightly controlled. If the total emissions leaving the imaginary bubble over the plant did not violate air-quality standards, the firm would be free to decide how best to comply with the law. Advocates of the approach assumed that the result would be a substantial cost saving for the firm and quicker compliance with pollution standards because the firm would be free to choose the solution best suiting its economic self-interest. With bubbling the EPA also allowed "emissions banking," which permitted a regulated firm to earn "credits" for keeping pollutants below the required level. Firms could apply these credits against their own future emission-control requirements, sell them to other firms, or save them.

The results have been inconclusive since air pollutants have been netted, offset, bubbled, and banked. Estimates suggest that the aggregate cost savings for firms have been modest. By the mid-1980s, the 132 federal and state sanctioned "bubbles" had saved firms an estimated $435 million, netting about $4 billion, both relatively small sums when compared to the total compliance costs for firms regulated by the CAA.[32] Some experts believe that the savings from emissions trading have been exaggerated by the private sector. Others argue that the rules have not been vigorously enforced. In any case, few firms seized the opportunity to start emissions trading. Then came Title IV of the 1990 amendments to the CAA initially permitting 111 of the nation's biggest fossil-fuel-fired electric utilities to create what could potentially be a huge market for emissions trading. Title IV also allows smaller utilities to join the "big dirties"—the most polluting industries—within a few additional years, thereby expanding the prospective marketplace in emissions. Title IV creates by far the most significant test of market-based regulation since the inception of Environmental Era I. And Title IV's acceptance by influential spokespersons for mainstream environmentalism—albeit with fingers crossed—betrays a recognition that market-based reform is probably inevitable, and perhaps overdue.

The Gamble on Emissions Trading

The most innovative provision of the 1990 amendments of the CAA is the emissions trading scheme created by Title IV. Critics of command-and-control regulation, including most economists, regard Title IV as a welcome effort to substitute more economically efficient market-based incentives for the older approach to pollution management. While a few major environmental organizations, led by the Environmental Defense Fund, consider the new approach a valuable experiment, many more regard it as trafficking with the devil. However, all sides are watching the implementation of Title IV with keen interest. Its fate will become a powerful argument for or against the proliferation of future market-based regulatory schemes.

One very important aspect of Title IV is its intent to limit sulfur oxide emissions from the most polluting utilities and especially from Midwestern utilities considered responsible for much of the acid precipitation affecting the Northeast and southern Canada. Eventually, more than 2,200 utilities will be entitled to enter the market in emissions trading. While the details of the emissions trading scheme prescribed in Title IV are extraordinarily complex, the main purpose is relatively simple: to create a cap on the total amount of sulfur oxide emissions annually produced by utilities, to progressively lower that cap, and to encourage the trading of emissions permits in the most economically efficient manner. To this end, all regulated utilities may buy, sell, bank, or otherwise use their emission permits as a currency in trade. One interesting feature of this arrangement is the possibility that environmental organizations might also be able to purchase emissions permits and retire them, or bank them, thereby reducing the total emissions available to the utilities subject to the emissions limits.

By late 1993, the Chicago Board of Trade had created a national emissions-trading market for Title IV and some trading had occurred there, and in California, between a few utilities. Several important issues were evident immediately. First, environmental groups in the Northeast expressed a concern that Midwestern utilities will purchase permits from other areas and stockpile them, thus permitting themselves to continue emissions at unacceptably high levels. Proponents of Title IV, however, believe that other utilities will not have emission permits enough to sell to the advantage of the Midwestern facilities. A second concern among environmentalists is that some of the big dirties will abandon plans to replace existing plants with new, less polluting facilities and will, instead, stockpile emission permits for older, dirtier facilities. Midwest utilities and their proponents, in contrast, have been concerned that the emissions limits will inhibit economic growth in the economically depressed Ohio River Valley and adjacent areas. Utilities elsewhere have been concerned also with the effect of emissions levels on economic growth. Most utilities remain apprehensive about the impact of the new scheme on their own market share and economic future.

Most economists believe it is too early to pass judgment on the impact of emissions trading but many assert that significant cost savings have already been demonstrated. Economist Robert N. Stavins, an expert on emissions trading and Title IV, believes there have been other, less tangible but equally important benefits as well. The Title IV experience has demonstrated to both sides of the debate that emissions trading can be implemented without a multitude of lawsuits, argues Stavins, and proves as well that the system can be administered with relative simplicity. Stavins suggests that environmentalists should take the credit for a valuable lesson learned from experience with Title IV. The program, he notes, "has brought home the importance of monitoring and enforcement provisions. In 1990, as their 'price' for supporting an allowance trading system, environmental advocates insisted on continuous emissions monitoring . . . a feature that some analysts now consider to be a major achievement of the act.[33] At the same time, many economists and other experts on emissions trading have warned against using the limited experience with Title IV as a justification for prescribing a similar approach to controlling global greenhouse gases. While Congress may be tempted to take this one-size-fits-all approach to controlling air pollution emissions internationally, most experts feel much more domestic experience with emissions trading is still necessary.

Conclusion

To most Americans, the nation's environmental troubles are epitomized by polluted air, fouled water, dangerously unregulated hazardous and toxic wastes, and a multitude of other ecological derangements. This chapter illuminates a less obvious dimension of the environmental crisis that is equally dangerous in its ecological implications: the economic problems to implementing environmental policy effectively. In many critical respects, the institutions and policies the nation now depends on to reverse its ecological degradation are failing, sometimes badly. Equally as imperative as new technological solutions to ecological ills are new economic and institutional solutions. Finding these solutions will require critical, difficult debate within the environmental movement and among public policy makers at all governmental levels concerned with ecological restoration.

These problems are especially refractory because they often originate in the fundamental constitutional design of the political system, or in deeply rooted political traditions. Among these is an historic dependence on traditional policy approaches to environmental problems, particularly the standards-and-enforcement method of regulation and the single-media approach to controlling specific pollutants. While other approaches often seem more appropriate, and in some cases have been tried experimentally, they are strongly resisted by a multitude of institutional, professional, and economic interests with a stake in the status quo. Often, the environmental movement itself has been excessively conservative in resisting policy innovation.

Among the significant economic problems arising from environmental regulation, none is more often debated than the high cost of environmental regulation. As costs continually rise well above expectations, the need to find cost-effective, cost-saving approaches to policy making grows more apparent. While cost-benefit analysis is sometimes a useful strategy for reducing regulatory costs, its serious political and economic deficiencies suggest that other approaches, involving more economic incentives for pollution abatement in the private sector, are likely to be more broadly effective. None of the problems now associated with regulatory incapacity are likely to be solved easily or quickly.

Notes

1. The arguments for considering costs in environmental regulation are usefully summarized in Allen V. Kneese and Charles L. Schultze, *Pollution, Prices and Public Policy* (Washington, D.C.: Brookings Institution, 1975). See also A. Myrick Freeman III, "Economics, Incentives, and Environmental Regulation," in *Environmental Policy in the 1990s,* 2d ed., ed. Norman J. Vig and Michael E. Kraft (Washington, D.C.: CQ Press, 1997), 189–208.

2. On the history of BCA, see Richard A. Liroff, "Cost-Benefit Analysis in Federal Environmental Programs," in *Cost-Benefit Analysis and Environmental Regulations: Politics, Ethics and Methods,* ed. Daniel Swartzman, Richard A. Liroff, and Kevin G. Croke (Washington, D.C.: Conservation Foundation, 1982), 35–52; Richard N. L. Andrews, "Cost-Benefit Analysis as Regulatory Reform," in *Cost-Benefit Analysis and Environmental Regulations,* ed. Swartzman, Liroff, and Croke, 107–136; and Norman J. Vig, "Presidential Leadership and the Environment: From Reagan to Clinton," in *Environmental Policy in the 1990s,* ed. Vig and Kraft, 98–118.

3. For a summary of the issues involved, see Walter A. Rosenbaum, "Regulation At Risk: The Controversial Politics and Science of Comparative Risk Assessment," in *Flashpoints in Environmental Policymaking: Controversies in Achieving Sustainability,* ed. Sheldon Kamieniecki, George A. Gonzalez, and Robert O. Vos (Albany: State University of New York Press, 1997), 31–62.

4. Raymond J. Kopp, Alan J. Krupnick, and Michael Toman, "Cost-Benefit Analysis and Regulatory Reform: An Assessment of the Science and Art," Discussion Paper No. 97-19 (Washington, D.C.: Resources for the Future, 1997), 14.

5. Ibid.

6. Freeman, "Economics, Incentives and Environmental Regulation," 150, 153.

7. Ibid.

8. Paul Johnson, "The Perils of Risk Avoidance," *Regulation* (May/June 1980): 17.

9. Kopp, Krupnick, and Toman, "Cost-Benefit Analysis and Regulatory Reform."

10. Ibid.

11. Stephen Kelman, "Cost-Benefit Analysis: An Ethical Critique," *Regulation* (Jan./Feb. 1981): 39.

12. Government Accounting Office (GAO), "Cost-Benefit Analysis Can Be Useful in Assessing Regulations, Despite Limitations," Report no. GAO/RCED 84-62 (April 1984), iii.

13. Ibid.

14. On the history of the OMB's use of BCA under the Reagan administration, see W. Norton Grubb, Dale Whittington, and Michael Humphries, "The Ambiguities of Cost-Benefit Analysis: An Evaluation of Regulatory Impact Analysis under Executive Order 12,291," in *Environmental Policy under Reagan's Executive Order,* ed. V. Kerry Smith (Chapel Hill: University of North Carolina Press, 1984), 121–166; GAO, "Cost-Benefit Analysis Can Be Useful in Assessing Regulations, Despite Limitations," 7; Edward Paul Fuchs, *Presidents, Managers and Regulation* (Englewood Cliffs, N.J.: Prentice-Hall, 1988), 124ff; and Joseph Cooper and William F. West, "Presidential Power and Republican Government: The Theory and Practice of OMB Review," *Journal of Politics* 50, no. 4 (Nov. 1988): 864–895.

15. GAO, "Much Work Remains To Accelerate Facility Cleanups," Report no. GAO/RCED 93-15 (January 1993), 17.

16. GAO, "Improving EPA's Regulatory Impact Analyses," Report no. GAO/RCED 97-38 (1997), 2.

17. Traci Watson, "Clean Air: EPA Report Hails Law As Success," *USA Today,* Oct. 21, 1997.

18. John C. Whitaker, "Earth Day Recollections: What It Was Like When the Movement Took Off," *EPA Journal* 14, no. 6 (July/Aug. 1988): 11.

19. Roefie Hueting, "Correcting National Income for Environmental Losses: A Practical Solution for a Theoretical Dilemma," in *Ecological Economics,* ed. Rajaram Krishan, Jonathan M. Harris, and Neva R. Goodwin (Washington, D.C.: Island Press, 1995), 248.

20. Kopp, Krupnick, and Toman, "Cost-Benefit Analysis and Regulatory Reform," 30.

21. *New York Times,* Sept. 6, 1993.

22. Ibid.

23. For a comprehensive analysis of the 1990 Clean Air Act Amendments, see Gary C. Bryner, *Blue Skies, Green Politics: The Clean Air Act of 1990 and Its Implementation,* 2d ed. (Washington, D.C.: CQ Press, 1995), especially chaps. 3 and 4.

24. Thomas G. Ingersoll and Bradley R. Brockbank, "The Role of Economic Incentives in Environmental Policy," in *Controversies in Environmental Policy,* ed. Sheldon Kamieniecki, Robert O'Brien, and Michael Clarke (Albany: State University of New York Press, 1986), 210–222.
25. Kneese and Schultze, *Pollution, Prices and Public Policy,* 116.
26. *National Journal,* May 30, 1981, 971–973.
27. Ibid.
28. National Academy of Public Administration, *The Environment Goes to Market* (Washington, D.C.: National Academy of Public Administration, 1994), 12.
29. Ibid.
30. Robert W. Hahn and Gordon L. Hester, "EPA's Market for Bads," *Regulation* (Dec. 1987): 48–53.
31. Ibid.
32. Ibid.
33. Robert N. Stavins, "What Can We Learn From the Grand Policy Experiment?: Positive and Normative Lessons From SO2 Allowance Trading," *Journal of Economic Perspectives* 12, no. 2 (1998).

Suggested Readings

Anderson, Terry, and Donald Leal. *Free Market Environmentalism.* Boulder, Colo.: Westview Press, 1991.
Krishman, Rajaram, Jonathan M. Harris, and Neva R. Goodwin, eds. *A Survey of Ecological Economics.* Washington, D.C.: Island Press, 1995.
National Academy of Public Administration. *The Environment Goes to Market: The Implementation of Economic Incentives for Pollution Control.* Washington, D.C.: National Academy of Public Administration, 1994.
Schultz, Charles L. *The Public Use of Private Interest.* Washington, D.C.: Brookings Institution, 1977.

Chapter 6

"Command and Control" in Action: Air and Water Pollution Regulation

The eight Northeastern states that petitioned the U.S. EPA to order emissions reductions at 40 Midwest power plants will sue the agency for failing to respond. . . . [Says] New York Attorney General Dennis Vacco: "The EPA has been fiddling while New Yorkers burn."
—Greenwire, Oct. 16, 1997

Texas officials on 12/10 unveiled an initiative to reduce pollution in 140 rivers, lakes and streams in the state, in response to a U.S. EPA mandate directing states to enforce portions of the Clean Water Act dealing with surface water quality. Under the plan, environmental officials will identify the amount of pollution each watershed can tolerate while state and local agencies will implement new controls. . . . Of the state's 386 watersheds, 140 are not in compliance with state standards.
—Houston Chronicle, Dec. 11, 1997

Clean air and clean water are powerful public images. Leaders of the environmental movement regard the Clean Air Act (CAA) of 1970 and the Federal Water Pollution Control Act Amendments (FWPCAA) of 1972 as foundations of the first environmental era. Public opinion polls show that Americans universally recognize the nation's degraded air and waters as major ecological problems. And so clean air and water acquire political chic. Politicians so routinely assure constituents of their unceasing regard for clean air and clean water that both have become clichés instead of realities.

After almost thirty years of sustained effort by federal, state, and local governments to eliminate air and water pollution and an estimated public expenditure during the past decade of more than a half trillion dollars, the nation's air and water remain seriously polluted. Some dramatic

178

achievements, many lesser but impressive gains, and a multitude of marginal improvements comprise the veneer that brightens reports about implementation of the CAA and FWPCAA with a cosmetic success. But air and water quality remain seriously degraded throughout much of the United States. In the late 1990s more than 46 million Americans, mostly urbanites, live in counties where pollution levels exceed at least one national air quality standard.[1] The water quality in almost two-thirds of the nation's river miles has never been assessed because of deficient state monitoring resources.[2] The water quality in approximately one third of the nation's surveyed lakes, estuaries, and streams is still considered by the EPA to be significantly impaired.[3]

Why not truly impressive results from so massive a national investment? Many difficulties arise from inexperience in the implementation of wholly new regulatory programs. To many observers, as noted in the discussion of market approaches to regulation in Chapter 5, the problem is the policy itself, the "command-and-control" logic so firmly embedded in the two earliest, and most important, national pollution laws of the environmental era. Other difficulties result from new or unexpected scientific discoveries that complicate pollution control. But all of these difficulties are compounded by a failure of political will: a reluctance to invest the enormous resources, and to make the politically difficult decisions, essential to deal effectively with air and water pollution on a national scale. These and other significant influences shaping current air and water pollution regulation will become apparent as this chapter examines the implementation of the CAA and the FWPCAA during the past two decades. It will be helpful to begin by describing briefly the "standards-and-enforcement" regulatory framework used in the CAA and the FWPCAA, with particular attention to the administrative and political consequences of the laws.

Command and Control

Like all other regulatory programs affecting the U.S. environment, the CAA and FWPCAA are based on the "command-and-control" approach to regulation, also called "standards and enforcement." The structure and philosophy of this approach create many of the characteristic processes and problems associated with governmental management of the environment. Regulatory horror stories abound, convincing believers that a better approach lies in less direct governmental involvement and more economic incentives to encourage pollution abatement. In fact, both approaches have virtues and liabilities.[4] Command and control can best be understood as a set of five phases through which pollution policy evolves: goals, criteria, quality standards, emission standards, and enforcement.

Goals

In theory, the first step in pollution abatement begins with a determination by Congress of the ultimate objectives to be accomplished through pollution regulation. In practice, these goals are often broadly and vaguely worded. Sometimes, as when Congress decides to "press technology" by setting pollution standards that it hopes will force industry to develop control technologies not currently available, the goals are deliberately made extremely ambitious as an incentive for vigorous regulatory measures by regulated interests. The principal goals of the CAA are, for example, to protect public health and safety. Vague goals are not as important in defining the operational character of a regulatory program as are the more detailed specifications for the setting of pollution standards, emission controls, and enforcement—the real cutting edges of regulation. Statements of goals, however, may be very politically significant as signals to the interests involved in regulation concerning which pollutants and sources will be given priority and how vigorously Congress intends to implement programs. The goal of the CAA of establishing national air-quality standards for major pollutants, for instance, was an unmistakable signal that Congress would tolerate no longer the continual delays in controlling air pollution caused by past legislative willingness to let the states create their own air-quality standards. It was also evidence that regulated interests had lost their once dominant position in the formation of air pollution policy.

Criteria

Criteria are the technical data, commonly provided by research scientists, indicating what pollutants are associated with environmental damage and how such pollutants, in varying combinations, affect the environment. Criteria are essential to give public officials some idea of what pollutant levels they must achieve to ensure various standards of air and water quality. If regulators intend to protect public health from the effects of air pollution, they must know what levels of pollution—sulfur oxides, for instance—create public health risks. In a similar vein, restoring game fish to a dying lake requires information about the levels of organic waste such fish can tolerate. Criteria must be established for each regulated pollutant, and sometimes for combinations of pollutants.

Obtaining criteria frequently is difficult because data on the environmental effects of many pollutants still may be fragmentary or absent. Even when data are available, there is often as much art as science in specifying relationships between specific levels of a pollutant and its environmental effects because precise correlations may not be obtainable from the information. The reliability of criteria data also may vary depending on whether they are obtained from animal studies, epidemiological statistics, or human studies. Criteria are likely to be controversial, especially to those convinced that a set of data works to their disadvantage. Given the limitations in criteria data, regulatory agencies often have had to set pollution standards with information that was open to scientific criticism but was still the best available.

Quality Standards

Goals and criteria are preludes to the critical business of establishing air- and water-quality standards—the maximum levels of various pollutants to be permitted in air, soil, workplaces, or other locations. As a practical matter, defining standards amounts to declaring what the public, acting through governmental regulators, will consider to be "pollution." An adequate set of quality standards should specify what contaminants will be regulated and what variation in levels and combinations will be accepted in different pollutant categories.

Creating quality standards—in effect, another way of defining acceptable risk—is ultimately a political decision. Criteria documents rarely provide public officials with a single number that defines unambiguously what specific concentration of a pollutant produces precisely what effects. A rather broad range of possible figures associated more or less closely with predictable effects is available; which one is accepted may be the result of prolonged struggle and negotiation among interests involved in regulation. This battle over numbers is a matter of economics as much as science or philosophy. The difference between two possible pollution standards, only a few units apart, may seem trivial to a lay person. But the higher standard may involve millions or billions of additional dollars in pollution control technologies for the regulated interests and possibly many additional years before standards are achieved. Sometimes Congress establishes a standard based on a number's political "sex appeal." The original requirements in the CAA that automobile emissions of hydrocarbons and carbon monoxide be reduced by 90 percent of the 1970 levels no later than 1975 were largely accepted because the 90 percent figure sounded strict and spurred the auto industry into action. In practical terms the figure might have been set at 88 percent or 85 percent, or some other number in this range, with about the same results. Air-quality standards created by the EPA for the major "criteria" pollutants—pollutants that the CAA specifically designates for regulation because of their well-known, pervasive threat to public health—are identified in Table 6-1.

Table 6-1   *National Ambient Air Quality Standards*

Pollutant	Standard value[a]		Standard type[b]
Carbon Monoxide (CO)			
8-hour average	9 ppm	10 mg/m³	Primary
1-hour average	35 ppm	40 mg/m³	Primary
Nitrogen Dioxide (NO₂)			
Annual arithmetic mean	0.053 ppm	100 µg/m³	Primary and secondary
Ozone (O₃)			
1-hour average	0.12 ppm	235 µg/m³	Primary and secondary
Lead (Pb)			
Quarterly average		1.5 µg/m³	Primary and secondary
Particulate <10 micrometers (PM–10)			
Annual arithmetic mean		50 µg/m³	Primary and secondary
24-hour average		150 µg/m³	Primary and secondary
Sulfur Dioxide (SO₂)			
Annual arithmetic mean	0.03 ppm	80 µg/m³	Primary
24-hour average	0.14 ppm	365 µg/m³	Primary
3-hour average	0.50 ppm	1,300 µg/m³	Secondary

Source: Environmental Protection Agency, Office of Air Quality Planning and Standards, *http://www.epa.gov/airs/criteria.html.*

[a] Units of measure for the standards are parts per million (ppm), milligrams per cubic meter of air (mg/m³), and micrograms per cubic meter of air (µg/m³).

[b] The Clean Air Act established two types of national air quality standards: *primary standards* set limits to protect public health, including the health of "sensitive" populations such as asthmatics, children, and the elderly; *secondary standards* set limits to protect public welfare, including protection against decreased visibility and damage to animals, crops, vegetation, and buildings.

Emission Standards

Standards for clean air or water are only aspirations unless emission standards exist to prescribe the acceptable pollutant discharges from important sources of air or water contamination. If emission standards are to be effective, they must indicate clearly the acceptable emission levels from all important pollution sources and should be related to the pollution control standards established by policy makers.

Congress has used two different methods of determining how emission standards should be set. In regulating existing air pollution sources under the CAA, Congress requires that emissions be limited to the extent necessary to meet the relevant air-quality standards; determining what emission controls are necessary depends on where the quality standards are set. In controlling new air pollution sources, and most water polluters, the emission controls are based on the available technologies. This technology-based approach sets the emission levels largely according to the performance of available technologies.

There is a very direct and critical relationship between air-quality standards and emission controls. For example, once the EPA declares national ambient air-quality standards, each state is required in its State Implementation Plan (SIP) to calculate the total emissions of that pollutant within an airshed and then to assign emission controls to each source of that pollutant sufficient to ensure that total emissions will meet air-quality standards. In effect, this calls for the states to decide how much of the total pollution "load" within an airshed is the responsibility of each polluter and how much emission control the polluter must achieve. This has become a bitterly controversial process. Experts often have difficulty in determining precisely how much of a pollution load within a given body of water or air can be attributed to a specific source; this compounds the problem of assigning responsibility for pollution abatement equitably among a large number of polluters.[5] Regulated interests, aware of the relationship between air-quality standards and emission controls, will attack both in an effort to avoid or relax their assigned emission controls. Regulated industries also chronically complain that insufficient attention is given to the cost of emission controls when government regulators prescribe the acceptable technology. Polluters often balk at installing specific control technologies prescribed by governmental regulators. The scrubber wars between electric utilities and regulatory authorities, for instance, continued for more than two decades. Alleging that the scrubbers—complex and expensive technologies that remove toxic gases from power plant air emissions—prescribed by the government are inefficient and unreliable, coal-fired utilities fiercely resisted installing the scrubbers until compelled to do so. The battle ended only when the 1990 amendments to the CAA permitted other control alternatives.

The backlash against emission controls often falls on state government officials who, under existing federal law, usually are responsible for setting specific emission levels, prescribing the proper technologies, and enforcing emission restraints on specific sources. This is accomplished largely through issuing a permit to individual dischargers specifying the permissible emission levels and technological controls for their facilities. Despite several decades of experience and substantial financial assistance from the federal government, some state regulatory authorities remain understaffed and undertrained. In the latter 1990s, however, most state regulatory agencies had become highly professional to the point where failures in state environmental regulation could no longer be routinely attributed to incompetence. The political and economic influence of regulated interests, nonetheless, is often far more formidable in state capitals than in Washington, D.C., and state regulators often feel especially vulnerable to these local pressures.

Enforcement

A great diversity of enforcement procedures might be used to ensure that pollution standards are achieved; adequate enforcement must carry enough force to command the respect of those subject to regulation. Satisfactory enforcement schemes have several characteristics: they enable public officials to act with reasonable speed—very rapidly in the case of emergencies—to curb pollution; they carry sufficient penalties to encourage compliance; and they do not enable officials to evade a responsibility to act against violations when action is essential. It is desirable that officials have a range of enforcement options that might extend from gentle prodding to secure compliance at one end all the way to litigation and criminal penalties for severe, chronic, or reckless violations at the other. In reality, when it comes to enforcement, administrative authority is often the power to "make a deal." Armed with a flexible variety of enforcement options, administrators are in a position to bargain with polluters in noncompliance with the law, selecting those enforcement options they believe will best achieve their purposes. This bargaining, a common occurrence in environmental regulation, illustrates how political pressure and administrative discretion concurrently shape environmental policy; enforcement will be examined in greater detail shortly. In the end an effective pollution abatement program largely depends on voluntary compliance by regulated interests. No regulatory agency has enough personnel, money, and time to engage in continual litigation or other actions to force compliance with pollution standards. Furthermore, litigation usually remains among the slowest, most inflexible, and inefficient means of achieving environmental protection. Administrative agencies prefer to negotiate and maneuver to avoid litigation as a primary regulatory device whenever possible.

The Political Anatomy of Regulation

The standards-and-enforcement approach to regulation creates a number of characteristic political processes and issues regardless of which specific pollution program is involved. The technicality of pollution regulation frequently creates a language and style of action that conceals (sometimes deliberately) the extent to which political forces are operating behind the facade of regulatory procedures. Nonetheless, regulation is fundamentally a political enterprise.

Opportunities for Political Influence

Political influence and conflict occur wherever administrative discretion exists in the regulatory process, just as they develop in any other aspect of bureaucracy. There are several characteristic points at which such administrative discretion ordinarily is found in pollution regulation.

When Words, Phrases, or Policy Objectives Are Unclear.   Congress may deliberately shift responsibility to administrators for settling disputes between interests in conflict over how a law should be phrased. Tossing this political hot potato to administrators ensures that partisans for all sides of an issue with something to gain or lose by the law's interpretation will scramble to influence whatever officials or bureaucracies resolve such obscurities. Sometimes this lack of legislative clarity results less from deliberation than from congressional confusion or ignorance. In any case, regulators usually find themselves caught between competing group pressures to interpret statutes or regulations in different ways. Such pressures, in fact, should be considered routine in the regulatory process.

When Technical Standards Must Be Created or Revised.   Existing legislation regulating air pollution, water pollution, and hazardous substances ordinarily requires the EPA to define the standards and prescribe the appropriate control technologies necessary to meet mandated standards; often regulatory agencies also are required by such legislation to review periodically and, if appropriate, revise such standards or technology requirements. Legitimate disagreement often exists, as noted in the previous chapter, over the technical and economic justification for most regulatory standards. In the presence of expert dissension about such issues, a large measure of discretion rests with regulatory agencies for resolving such disputes. This discretion, and the conflict it invites, will reappear when regulatory standards are reviewed. In fact, virtually all major technical determinations by regulatory agencies are politicized by the activity of pressure groups, Congress, competing governmental agencies, and other interests seeking to shape discretionary decisions to their respective advantage.

When Compliance Deadlines Are Flexible.   Pollution legislation may bristle with explicit compliance deadlines, but administrators almost always have authority to extend them. Legislation is particularly generous in granting administrators authority to extend compliance deadlines when, in their opinion, economic hardship or other inequities may result from strict enforcement. Thus the CAA instructs the EPA to set emission standards for new air pollution sources by considering, among other things, "the degree of emission limitation achievable through the application of the best system of emission reduction which (taking into account the cost of achieving such reduction) the administrator determines has been adequately demonstrated." Such a fistful of discretionary authority in effect permits the EPA to extend compliance deadlines for specific air pollution sources by increasing the time allowed to search for pollution controls meeting these multiple criteria. In many cases a compliance deadline also may be relaxed if an agency determines that it is beyond the technical ability of a polluter to install the proper controls in the required time. Agencies sometimes can achieve "backdoor" extension of compliance deadlines by deliberately delaying the establishment of a standard long enough to permit the regulated interests to make adjustments to the anticipated standard. The EPA, for instance, waited until 1976—more than two and a half years after vinyl chloride was identified as a human carcinogen—before setting an exposure standard for that substance. The reason, the Agency explained, was to avoid creating "unacceptably severe economic consequences" for the vinyl chloride manufacturers and users through an earlier standard establishing a more rapid deadline for controlling the chemical's emissions.[6]

When Enforcement Is Discretionary.   Few provisions in current pollution legislation compel federal officials to stop a polluting activity. Most often enforcement actions are discretionary, as in section 111 of the CAA, which instructs the EPA administrator to regulate any pollutant from a stationary source when, in the judgment of the administrator, it may cause or contribute to "air pollution which may reasonably be anticipated to endanger public health or welfare." Even when enforcement action is initiated, officials are usually given optional methods for securing compliance.

Beyond Public View

It is worth noting that implementing most environmental regulatory programs does not routinely involve the public, or public opinion, in the process. Unlike the White House and Congress, the federal bureaucracy is neither highly visible nor readily understood by the public; regulation operates, in the words of Francis Rourke, behind an "opaque exterior"[7] that the public seldom cares to penetrate. A 1981 public opinion poll that indicated 31 percent of the public knew "nothing at all about the Clean Air Act" and another 39 percent "knew a little" at a time when the Act was a topic of major congressional debate typifies public attention to most regulatory matters.[8] This dearth of dependable public interest means that the constellation of political forces and actors involved in regulatory politics ordinarily is confined to organized interests, governmental officials, scientists, technicians, and other "insiders." Given the complexity and technicality of environmental issues, this situation is not surprising. But it emphasizes the extent to which regulatory politics tends to involve a process highly specialized and commonly closed to public involvement.

The Enforcement Problem

The intermingling of administrative discretion and political pressure in regulatory policy making is evident in the enforcement of environmental law. Typically, air and water pollution laws are enforced through state or local agencies with considerable discretion to decide what level of emission control will be required of an air or water polluter and when emission controls must be achieved. These become conditions for the permit that all air and water polluting firms must obtain from state, federal, and local authorities to operate. In air pollution regulation, for instance, this discretion can arise from the regulator's authority under the CAA to decide which emission controls are technically and economically feasible and to issue "variances" that temporarily waive emission control deadlines or technology specifications.[9] Regulators seek voluntary compliance. They want to avoid penalties as a means of ensuring compliance if possible because they know that resort to administrative or judicial tribunals likely will involve a protracted, inflexible process with no assurances that the polluter will be compelled to control emissions speedily and efficiently at the conclusion. In fact polluters often provoke such action, hoping to avoid emission controls indefinitely by exploiting the complexities of the administrative or judicial procedures involved.

Regulated firms commonly balk at a regulatory agency's initial specification of acceptable control technologies and deadline dates for compliance with emission standards. The usual solution is bargaining between regulator and regulated, particularly when regulatory agencies confront an economically and politically influential firm, or group of firms, capable of creating political pressures on the regulatory agency to reach some accommodation over required control technologies or compliance deadlines. Regulatory agencies typically will make some concession to firms concerning required control technologies or compliance deadlines. One form of these concessions is the frequently used variance that allows a firm some delay in achieving emission controls otherwise required under the law. A firm commonly is able to negotiate a variance permitting it to discharge on an interim basis at its existing emission levels and to obtain several additional variances that can delay significantly achievement of required emission controls.

Agencies also heavily depend on firms to monitor and to report their own pollution emissions, in part because of the sheer volume of regulated entities. Under the CAA, for instance, more than 3,400 major sources and 45,600 minor sources of waste water discharge must be controlled. The CAA Amendments of 1990 increased the regulated sources to more than 35,000 major and 350,000 minor facilities.[10]

Most regulatory agencies still lack the personnel and other resources to inspect routinely and monitor all emission controls within their jurisdictions. Voluntary compliance is almost a necessity in regulation. Quite often, as Paul B. Downing and James N. Kimball noted in their careful review of enforcement studies, regulatory agencies accept the firm's own reports of its behavior under all but exceptional circumstances:

> We find that the typical agency does not inspect frequently. Furthermore, those inspections which do occur are usually pre-announced. Thus we find that the probability of being found in violation is virtually zero. There are two exceptions to this conclusion. One would be cases where a third party reports a violation. . . . The other occurs when a source self-reports a violation. Our case study did indicate that many violations were reported by the regulated companies." [11]

While administrative discretion and political pressure clearly do limit the vigor and strictness in enforcement of environmental regulations, these constraints are sometimes inevitable and may even be prudent. Often the use of administrative discretion to "make a deal" over pollution allows a regulatory agency to achieve more pollution abatement than would be the case if it insisted on extremely stringent emission standards in full and immediate compliance with the law. This is true particularly when the regulated firm is either unable to comply fully and immediately with a strict interpretation of the law or willing to fight indefinitely in the courts or administrative hearing rooms to prevent any regulation. Many regulatory agencies, limited by staff and funding inadequate for their mandated responsibilities, have no practical alternative to relying on voluntary compliance and accommodation. Finally, regulatory agencies often confront regulated interests—including other governmental agencies subject to pollution control—too politically or economically powerful to be compelled to comply fully and immediately with the law. While this should be no excuse for exemption from full compliance with environmental regulation, it is often an immutable political reality with which regulatory agencies must make peace. In such circumstances agencies may logically conclude that it is better to bargain with the regulated interests in the hope of achieving some limited goals than to adopt what may well become an ultimately futile strategy of insisting on stringent compliance with the law in spite of massive resistance from the polluter.

Discretion in the enforcement of pollution regulation, however inevitable, also means that discretion at times will be abused. Discretion sometimes leads agencies to yield needlessly and negligently to political pressures preventing enforcement of essential pollution controls. It is unfortunate that these are among the unavoidable risks inherent in the exercise of discretionary authority without which environmental administration would be impossible.

The Nation's Air Quality

Since the inception of Era I, the federal government has continually monitored a variety of environmental indicators and has published current assessments of environmental quality using these indicators. These data provide a useful baseline for observing change in national environmental quality since major federal environmental programs began in the early 1970s and an essential standard for judging the impact of the Clean Air Act and other federal legislation. Standards for pollutants regulated by the Clean Air Act are called "National Ambient Air Quality Standards" (NAAQS) and, once established, must be enforced by all state and local government agencies. However, the states may enact more stringent standards for airsheds in their jurisdiction.

"Progress Has Been Made"

Overall, national air quality has undoubtedly improved—in a few instances, dramatically—since the Clean Air Act's enactment in 1970. Between 1970 and 1990 the CAA regulated fourteen air pollutants, whose health effects are described in Table 6-2.

The most important of these are the criteria pollutants—carbon monoxide, nitrogen oxides, volatile organic compounds, particulate matter, sulfur dioxide and lead. Reduction in the emission of these six pollutants between 1970 and 1995 has been, in most cases, significant and in one instance dramatic, as Table 6-3 indicates. Airborne lead, especially hazardous to children, has been virtually eliminated through the abolition of leaded automobile fuels. Sulfur oxide emissions decreased by more than 40 percent and large airborne particulates by almost 80 percent during the same period. America's urban environment has significantly improved. In Los Angeles, claimant to the most polluted urban air in 1960, the air quality in 1996 was the best on record. The data understate the significance of these achievements because they do not estimate what pollution emissions would have been in the absence of regulation, during a period when the U.S. population increased by 70 percent and vehicle miles traveled by 116 percent. Improvements in air quality have been especially significant since the mid-1980s as the cumulative effect of earlier regulation began to appear. The near-term achievements evident in Table 6-3, which compares both air emissions and air concentrations of the criteria pollutants between 1987 and 1996, seems to vindicate the EPA's verdict that air quality in the last several decades has demonstrated "great improvement."

Table 6-2   Health Effects of Regulated Pollutants

Pollutant	Health concerns
Criteria pollutants	
Ozone	Respiratory tract problems, such as difficult breathing and reduced lung function; asthma; eye irritation; nasal congestion; reduced resistance to infection; premature aging of lung tissue
Particulate matter	Eye and throat irritation; bronchitis; lung damage; impaired vision
Carbon monoxide	Impaired ability of blood to carry oxygen; effects on cardiovascular, nervous, and pulmonary systems
Sulfur dioxide	Respiratory tract problems; permanent harm to lung tissue
Lead	Retardation and brain damage, especially in children
Nitrogen dioxide	Respiratory illness and lung damage
Hazardous air pollutants	
Asbestos	A variety of lung diseases, particularly lung cancer
Beryllium	Primary lung disease; effects on liver, spleen, kidneys, and lymph glands
Mercury	Effects on several areas of the brain, as well as the kidneys and bowels
Vinyl chloride	Lung and liver cancer
Arsenic	Cancer
Radionuclides	Cancer
Benzene	Leukemia
Coke oven emissions	Respiratory cancer

Source: Environmental Protection Agency, *Environmental Progress and Challenges: EPA Update* (Washington, D.C.: Environmental Protection Agency, 1988), 13.

But Much Remains To Be Done

Despite improvement, the nation's air still remains seriously degraded in several respects. First, ground-level ozone (03), a primary component of urban smog, remains a pervasive problem. This low-level ozone poses significant human health risks and produces over $1 billion in agricultural crop damage annually. Table 6-3 reveals that low-level (or tropo-

Table 6-3 Percentage Change in National Air Quality Concentrations and Emissions, 1987–1996

	Air quality concentration % change 1987–1996	Emissions % change 1987–1996
Carbon Monoxide (CO)	−37	−18
Lead (Pb)	−75	−50
Nitrogen Dioxide (NO₂)	−10	+3 (NO₂)
Ozone (O₃)	−15	−18 (VOC)
Particulate < 10 micrometers (PM = 10)$^\alpha$	−25	−12[b]
Sulfur Dioxide (SO₂)	−37	−14

Source: Adapted from Environmental Protection Agency, Office of Air Quality Planning and Standards, *National Air Quality and Emission Trends Report, 1996: Executive Summary* (Washington, D.C.: Environmental Protection Agency, 1997), 1.

[a] Based on 1988 to 1996 data.

[b] Includes only directly emitted particles. Secondary PM = 10 formed from SO_x, NO_x, and other gases comprise a significant fraction of ambient PM = 10.

spheric) ozone has been only slightly reduced in recent years. Currently, more than 100.8 million Americans, mostly urbanites, live in areas that are not in compliance with the ozone standard. Second, only slight gains have been made in the reduction of nitrogen dioxide, a precursor of acid precipitation and a "greenhouse" gas, while concentrations of airborne particulates—a major component of smog—have increased in the 1990s. Third, emissions of greenhouse gases, especially sulfur and nitrogen oxides, still exceed the levels now considered essential to mitigate or to avert a global climate warming—a matter of growing international concern to be fully discussed in Chapter 10. Finally, air toxics have yet to be adequately regulated. The CAA Amendments of 1990 required the EPA to regulate 188 air toxics, including well-known health threats such as dioxins, benzene, arsenic, beryllium, mercury, and vinyl chloride. Presently, EPA has established standards for forty-seven of these pollutants.

Improved air quality, like other environmental gains in recent decades, is fragile, highly vulnerable to technological change, economic cycles, and other social impacts. A case in point is the rapidly growing consumer demand for light trucks, minivans, pick-ups, and other sports vehicles. Sports vehicles, the fastest growing segment of the domestic automotive market, emit more smog-producing pollutants than conventional cars. The EPA estimates that light trucks will be the fastest growing source of greenhouse gases in the next decade, exceeding the combined emissions of all domestic industrial sources.

Equally important, sports vehicles paralyze the political will. Federal officials, aware of the vehicles' popularity, are loath to propose more stringent emission controls for this environmentally hazardous technology. Light truck regulation, especially, has become a "third rail" political issue. "Detroit is giving people what they want," noted one observer. "Americans—even ones who fancy themselves as environmentalists—have fallen in love with trucks." [12]

The Clean Air Act of 1970 and Its Amendments

The CAA of 1970, together with its important 1977 and 1990 amendments, constitutes one of the longest, most complex, and most technically detailed regulatory programs ever enacted on a federal level. The CAA creates a standards-and-enforcement program in which the federal government establishes national air-quality standards for major pollutants, the states assume primary responsibility for implementing the program within federal guidelines, and the two levels of government share enforcement responsibilities. In broad outline, the act mandates the following programs:

1. *National Air-Quality Standards.* The Act directed the EPA to determine the maximum permissible ambient air concentrations for pollutants it found to be harmful to human health or the environment. The EPA was instructed to establish such standards for at least seven pollutants: carbon monoxide, hydrocarbons, lead, nitrogen oxide, particulates, ozone, and sulfur oxides. The Agency was to set two types of National Ambient Air Quality Standards (NAAQSs) without considering the cost of compliance:

   a. *Primary Standards.* These were supposed to protect human health with an adequate margin of safety for particularly vulnerable segments of the population, such as the elderly and infants. Originally all air quality control regions in the United States were required to meet primary standards by 1982; this deadline was extended several times and still remains unenforced.

   b. *Secondary Standards.* These were intended to maintain visibility and to protect buildings, crops, and water. No deadline was mandated for compliance with secondary standards. The EPA is required by the 1977 CAA to review all criteria for ambient air quality every five years after 1981.

2. *Stationary Source Regulations.* The EPA was to set maximum emission standards for new sources (plants and factories) called New Source Performance Standards (NSPSs). In doing this, the following procedures were to be followed:

a. Standards were to be set on an industry-by-industry basis; the states then were to enforce the standards.

b. In setting NSPSs, the EPA was required to take into account the costs, energy requirements, and environmental effects of its guidelines.

c. For existing sources (those dischargers active at the time the Act was passed), the EPA was to issue control-technique guidelines for the states' use.

3. *State Implementation Plans.* Each state was required to create a SIP indicating how it would achieve federal standards and guidelines to implement the Act fully by 1982. The SIPs, which the EPA was to approve no later than 1979, were to contain information relating to several important elements:

a. The nation was divided into 247 Air Quality Control Regions (AQCRs) for which states were made responsible. The regions were classified as "attainment" or "nonattainment" regions for each of the regulated pollutants.

b. States were also made responsible for enforcing special air-quality standards in areas with especially clean air called Prevention of Significant Deterioration (PSD) regions.

c. States were required to order existing factories in nonattainment areas to retrofit their plants with control technologies representing "reasonably available control technology." Companies wanting to expand or build new plants in nonattainment areas had to install control equipment that limited pollutants to the least amount emitted by any similar factory anywhere in the United States. This technology was to be specified by the states without regard to the cost.

d. New factories in nonattainment areas also were required to purchase "offsets" from existing air polluters. This involved purchasing new pollution equipment for an existing polluter or paying an existing polluter to eliminate some of its pollution to the extent that the offset equalled the pollution the new source was expected to emit after it installed its own control technology.

e. States in nonattainment areas were given until 1987 to meet carbon monoxide and ozone standards if the state required an annual automobile inspection and maintenance on catalytic converters on newer automobiles. In 1987 Congress extended the deadline for compliance in nonattainment areas to 1988.

f. In PSD areas, all new stationary emission sources were required to install the best available control technology.

4. *Mobile Source Emission Standards (for automobiles and trucks).* Title II of the Act created a detailed but flexible timetable for achieving auto and truck emission controls.

a. For autos there was to be a 90 percent reduction in hydrocarbon and carbon monoxide emissions by 1975 and a 90 percent reduction in nitrogen oxide emissions by 1976, when measured against 1970 emission levels.

b. The administrator of the EPA was authorized to grant extensions of these deadlines for approximately one year. Considerable extensions were granted by the EPA and others authorized by Congress:

i. In 1973, the EPA granted a one-year extension of the 1975 deadline for hydrocarbons and carbon monoxide emissions and a one-year extension of the nitrogen oxide deadline.

ii. In 1974, Congress granted an additional one-year extension for all emission deadlines.

iii. In 1975, the EPA granted another one-year deadline extension for enforcement of hydrocarbon and carbon monoxide standards.

iv. In 1977, compliance deadlines for all emissions were extended for two more years, to be followed by stricter standards for hydrocarbons and carbon monoxide in 1980 and further tightening of the hydrocarbon standard in 1981, together with higher nitrogen oxide standards.

v. Since 1982, Congress repeatedly has waived compliance deadlines for auto emission controls; the new deadlines extended to the early 1990s.

By 1990, the original CAA and its massive 1977 amendments apparently had achieved significant reductions in several ambient air pollutants, particularly suspended particulates, lead, and carbon monoxide, as Table 6-3 indicated. With the exception of lead, however, reductions in other pollutants still seemed unsatisfactorily slow and urban air pollution—especially concentrations of nitrogen oxide, ozone, and volatile organic compounds—continued to be a major concern. After almost a decade of bitter impasse arising from the Reagan administration's opposition to amending the CAA, the Bush administration cooperated with environmentalists and a congressional majority to rewrite comprehensively the 1970 legislation by passing the CAA Amendments of 1990, the most important, and imaginative, regulatory reform in more than a decade.

The Clean Air Act Amendments of 1990

The new amendments are a curious melange of hammer clauses, multitudinous deadlines, and other tread-worn approaches combined with a timely sensitivity to emerging problems and an aggressive new approach

Table 6-4   *Areas Classified as "Extreme Ozone" and "Serious Carbon Monoxide" Nonattainment Areas Under the 1990 Amendments to the Clean Air Act*

Baltimore, Md.
Houston, Texas; Galveston, Texas; Brazoria, Texas
Milwaukee, Wis.
Philadelphia, Pa.; Wilmington, Del./Trenton, N.J.
Ventura County, Calif.
Chicago, Ill.
Los Angeles, Calif.
N.Y./N.J./Conn. metro area
The Mohave Desert, Calif.

Source: Pro-Act, *Approaches for Clean Air: Geographical or Regional Approach to Air Pollution,* http://www.afcee.brooks.af.mil/pro_act/main/fact/fact/caa7_96/07_96_2.HTM.

to global climate protection based on an innovative market-inspired scheme for emissions trading. This mix of tradition, invention, and desperation represents what may be the last, best hope of fortifying the original CAA sufficiently to achieve its purpose. The 1990 amendments added to the original Act two new titles concerning acid precipitation and ozone protection and substantially amended most of the remaining provisions while keeping the basic command-and-control approach of the original legislation.[13] The major features are outlined in the sections that follow.

Title I: Nonattainment Areas.   The amendments established a new classification of areas failing to meet national air-quality standards for ozone, carbon monoxide, and particulates and created deadlines from three to twenty years for attainment of these standards. They also created a graded set of regulatory requirements for each area, depending on the severity of the pollution. An example of the new regulatory regime is found in Table 6-4, which identifies areas required to meet two regulatory standards depending on their degree of ozone and carbon monoxide pollution. Unlike the original Act, which required only that cities make "reasonable further progress" in meeting air-quality standards, the new amendments set specific air-quality goals and deadlines.

Title II: Mobile Sources.   The new amendments set more than ninety new emission standards for autos and trucks. The most important emission requirements are outlined.

• Tailpipe emissions of hydrocarbons were to be reduced by 35 percent and nitrogen oxides were to be reduced by 60 percent for all new cars by the 1996 model year.
• Beginning in 1998, all new cars were required to have pollution control devices with a ten-year, 100,000-mile warranty.

• Auto manufacturers were required to produce a fleet of experimental cars available in Southern California by 1996 meeting emission standards more stringent than the 1996 levels already required by the amendments.

• Petroleum companies were required to produce cleaner-burning fuel to be used in the most polluted areas by 1992 and in all areas with ozone problems by 1996.

Title III: Hazardous Air Pollutants.   The amendments required that emission limits be established for all major sources of hazardous or toxic air pollutants and specified 189 chemicals to be regulated immediately. They established a multitude of specific deadlines by which the EPA was ordered to list categories of industrial processes that emit dangerous air pollutants, to establish health-based standards for each hazardous chemical emission, and to assure that sources of hazardous emission have established safety controls at their facilities.

Title IV: Control of Acid Deposition.   The amendments created a new emissions trading program for sulfur oxides, a major precursor of acid precipitation. Under this new approach, the EPA was "to allocate to each major coal-fired power plant an allowance for each ton of emission permitted; sources cannot release emissions beyond the number of allowances they are given. Allowances may be traded, bought, or sold among allowance holders. . . . The EPA [was] required to create an additional pool of allowances to permit construction of new sources or expansion of existing ones." [14] Title IV required that national sulfur oxide emissions be reduced by half: a reduction of 10 million tons annually from the 1980 levels, to be achieved by the year 2000. The 110 largest sulfur oxide sources in the utility industry were required to meet stricter emission standards. In addition, emissions of nitrogen oxides were to be reduced by 2 million tons annually when compared to 1980 levels through more traditional regulatory methods.

Title VI: Stratospheric Ozone Protection.   Title VI listed specific ozone-depleting chemicals and created a schedule for phasing out their production or use. It also pledged the United States to an accelerated phase-out of ozone-depleting chemicals that exceeds the schedule to which the United States agreed in the 1989 Montreal Protocol on Substances that Deplete the Ozone Layer.

Emissions Trading

The emission trading section of the 1990 amendments created, as noted earlier, the most innovative reform in air pollution control since the original CAA was written in 1970. Because the sulfur dioxide (SO_2)

trading program in Title IV did not become fully operative until the end of 1995, evaluations are still tentative. Economist Robert N. Stavins, like many policy specialists carefully tracking Title IV's effects, believes the trading program has already proven successful. "The SO_2 allowance trading program," he concludes, "has performed successfully in two fundamental areas: targeted emissions-reductions have been achieved, indeed exceeded; and total abatement costs have been significantly less than what they would have been in the absence of the trading provisions"—a cost savings over the alternative command-and-control approach which Stavins estimates could be as high as $1 billion annually.[15] Environmental organizations are generally ambivalent toward Title IV. Many now concede its potential value. But there is the usual worry about regulated utilities eventually finding a way to exceed their allowable emissions. Also, some environmental organizations fear that the technical details of the trading program will permit utilities in the Ohio River valley to remain a pollution "hot spot." Almost all environmental organizations, in any case, believe that very limited experience with Title IV does not justify a one-size-fits-all congressional approach to new regulation in which emissions trading is treated like a sovereign cure for any future regulatory ill.

Pressing Technology: Does It Work with Urban Air Pollution?

The EPA, Congress, and numerous state regulatory officials have been threatening and cajoling the nation's cities to clean their air for more than two decades. The CAA Amendments of 1990 represented the biggest of the regulatory "big sticks" yet applied to the nation's cities. Enforcement failure and delay are often cited as explanations why urban air pollution remains so intractable. Other major reasons are inadequate control technologies and overly restricted regulatory objectives. It seems evident now that attaining the urban goals of the CAA will require much greater reliance on many newer, more innovative strategies than "pressing technology," the principal approach in the original CAA and still important to the 1990 amendments. The clean fuels provisions of the 1990 amendments (Title II), for example, require domestic petroleum producers to provide "reformulated" gasoline in communities with extremely high levels of carbon monoxide and to provide "alternative" cleaner-burning gasoline in other areas. But creation of the newer fuels involves significant trade-offs, even if they are produced. These fuels, Gary Bryner noted, "result in reduced carbon monoxide emissions and higher octane levels, but may result in increased emissions of volatile organic compounds, nitrogen oxides, and toxic chemicals. They also reduce fuel economy and are more expensive to produce."[16] Whether these trade-offs, and the economic impacts on the petroleum industry, are politically acceptable remains a question. Meanwhile, the urban problem of air pollution persists.

Combative Federalism: The Smog Wars

Regulating urban smog has been difficult because so many varied sources contribute to its creation. Large stationary sources, such as fossil-fuel fired utilities, factories, mineral smelters, and chemical manufacturers, are major contributors. But thousands of small sources, most previously unregulated and many until recently unrecognized—including paint manufacturers, dry cleaners, and gasoline stations—collectively make a major contribution. The automobile stubbornly remains a chronic polluter despite the advent of efficient emission-control technologies. One reason is that pre-1970 vehicles, the worst auto polluters because they lack emission controls, are not being replaced as quickly as predicted. And at least one-fourth of the new car pollution-control devices are "disabled" (in the EPA's illusive phrase)—that is, deliberately destroyed.[17] Additionally, an ever-growing fleet of new, highly polluting light trucks and other sports vehicles continues to capture a large proportion of the domestic new vehicle market. Many state and local governments also have failed to enforce their own SIPs, especially requirements for annual auto emission inspections, proposals to limit auto access to urban areas, and other arrangements publicly annoying and costly to business. Even the best available technologies may be insufficient to control adequately all important emissions. The newest Detroit emission controls now remove 96 percent of the pollutants emitted before controls were instituted in 1972.[18] Many experts believe existing auto emission controls have reached "the knife edge of technological feasibility" and further emission reductions are unlikely unless a great many states require motorists to switch from conventional to new, more expensive reformulated fuels.

In a forceful, politically risky move to reduce urban air pollution further, the EPA in 1997 promulgated new ambient air-quality standards for ozone and particulates (soot), two primary causes of smog, but only after a ferocious political fight that laid bare the tensions between state and federal governments inherent in regulatory federalism. EPA's review of these standards had been long overdue according to the requirements of the CAA and was compelled only through a lawsuit sponsored by the American Lung Association. The new standards, finally proposed in early 1996, were considerably tougher than the existing ones. The full impact cannot be fully known until late 1998, but experts predicted that the new regulations would increase the number of counties (virtually all urban) out of compliance with particulate standards from 41 to 150 and those violating the ozone standard from 106 to 280—in short, a huge increase in the population and political weight of the counties affected. Massive opposition from organized business quickly developed. "[I]ndustry and business interests, led by the National Association of Manufacturers and the American Petroleum Institute, have urged that the . . . standards not be tightened," observed the Congressional Reference Service, "claiming excessive costs, lack of significant demonstrable benefits, loss of competitiveness, and technical infeasibility. An industry-business Air Quality Standards Coalition has been formed to contest the stronger rules, and has picked up support from the small business community, farm groups, and the U.S. Conference of Mayors. At the same time, health and environmental stakeholders have either supported the proposals or proposed tightening them further." [19] The EPA defended its decision by citing the strong support from its own scientific advisory panels and by asserting that the new rules would avert 15,000 premature deaths, 350,000 cases of aggravated asthma, and 1 million cases of decreased lung function in children.

Congress—the second front in all political battles between the states—was immediately embroiled in the affair. Eleven different congressional committees collectively held more than a month of hearings on the revised standards. More than 250 senators and representatives wrote to EPA and congressional committees about the matter. Congressional alignments generally reflected the ongoing battle over smog between the Northeastern and Midwestern states. Northeastern states believed the new regulations would diminish cross-border air pollution originating in the Midwest and compel Midwestern utilities to assume more responsibility for reducing those emissions. The Midwestern states, generally in compliance with existing air quality standards, anticipated having to enact economically costly, politically distasteful new air emission controls, especially upon utilities, some of which would have to reduce existing emissions by 85 percent. The Clinton administration wavered for months in the political heat despite outspoken support for the proposals by EPA Administrator Carol Browner; the president's own congressional party was divided deeply on the matter. Finally, in July 1997, President Clinton approved the regulations, to the surprise of many environmentalists convinced the president would never accept the political risks. Several months later, even as the EPA proposed stringent new emissions controls on utilities to implement the new air-quality standards, the Northeastern states renewed the geographic struggle. Asserting that the EPA's newly proposed emission controls would take too long to implement, they sued the EPA for failing to order emission reductions in forty Midwest power plants in accord with other provisions of the CAA.

Litigation, however, is unlikely to end such a tooth-and-claw sectional brawl because the conflict feeds upon deeply nested political tensions in the federalist system: sectional competition for political and economic power, conflicts over interpretation of the Constitution's federalist language, corporate conflicts over state market regulation, and more. Still, the contention is a virtual primer on American environmental regulation. It involves both separated federal institutions and state governments, pluralistic private and public interests, congressional advocacy of state and regional viewpoints, scientific contention about environmental standards, judicial intervention in regulation, the resort to litigation as a political weapon, and much more that is fundamental to U.S. environmental policy making. In broadest perspective, it is politics American-style.

Science and Regulatory Change: Particulates and Airborne Toxins

Regulation strives for predictability, consistency in interpreting and applying the law, and stability in established norms for decision making. Science breeds discovery, embraces change, promotes experimentation, and challenges tradition. Science is troublesome to regulatory order. The CAA currently regulates both airborne particulates and toxics. But the continuing enrichment of the scientific base for regulation over the past twenty years is forcing a change in understanding which substances should be regulated and what levels can be tolerated. New scientific evidence poses difficult new regulatory choices in both instances.

New Discoveries About Particulates.   In 1971, the EPA issued air-quality standards for particulates without distinction regarding size. Particulates—extremely small solid particles of matter found in the air and produced by dust, smoke, fuel combustion, agriculture, and forest cultivation, among other sources—have been known for many decades to pose health hazards. Initially, however, the EPA's standards on particulates assumed that size was not a significant factor in the health risks posed. By 1987, accumulating scientific research had demonstrated conclusively that small particulates, those smaller than 10 microns (one micron equals 1/25,000 inch), are especially hazardous to humans because they can be inhaled into lung tissue, unlike larger particulates that are caught in the air passages to the lungs.[20] These smaller particulates are commonly found in cigarette smoke, diesel engine emissions, windblown dust, and many other sources. They are also dangerous because they can carry carcinogenic chemicals into the lungs. In 1987, the EPA issued new air-quality standards for small particulates. However, existing emission controls for particulates were not designed specifically to control small particulates, and many sources of small particulates were not regulated at all.

About 250 AQCRs failed the new ambient air-quality standards for fine particulates. In the West, a major problem was windblown dust not easily controlled by any existing technology. The EPA established tailpipe standards for emissions from diesel trucks and buses, beginning with model year 1988, that became increasingly stringent for models beginning in 1991. But monitoring data about the origin and distribution of fine particulates were inadequate and states were slow to identify the magnitude of their problems and the sources to be regulated. Control technologies for stationary sources of small particulates were not well tested, and the control costs not accurately known. In effect, small particulates had become a separate emission-control problem and the states spent much of the 1990s acquiring a capability to regulate them. The EPA's most recent particulate standards, enacted concurrently with the 1997 revised smog rules, created new regulations specifically for particulates smaller than 2.5 microns because scientific research had demonstrated that these posed a distinctive human health risk. Automobile manufacturers and fossil-fuel burning facilities were predictably concerned about the additional compliance costs to meet the proposed standard. And they were angered by this regulatory "ratcheting"—the appearance of progressively more stringent new regulatory rules to which they must comply—creating the third different particulate standard in a decade. Proponents of the new standards argued that they were protecting the elderly, children, and people with chronic lung disease from a new, scientifically verified health risks. For regulated interests, the real problem seemed to be the potent, economically disruptive impact of regulatory science on environmental management.

Regulation at a Crawl: Airborne Toxics.   Section 112 of the CAA authorized the EPA to establish emission standards for airborne toxic or hazardous substances, defined in the law as any substance that causes or contributes to "an increase in mortality or an increase in serious irreversible or incapacitating illness." More than 320 toxic chemical substances are emitted into the air annually. By the time the 1990 amendments to the CAA were passed, the EPA had evaluated about thirty of these toxics but only eight were regulated: arsenic, asbestos, benzene, beryllium, coke oven emissions, mercury, radionuclides, and vinyl chloride. The federal government had identified at least sixty airborne chemicals as known carcinogens, including acrylonitrile, butadiene, cadmium, and carbon tetrachloride. Other toxics are known to cause birth defects or neurological disease.

Officials from the EPA had complained that the CAA's provisions affecting airborne toxics were so cumbersome and expensive, and so vulnerable to legal challenge, that the Agency had been unable to add more substances to the regulated list.[21] Regulation was indeed slow and expensive. The EPA had to take the initiative in assembling the list of prospective chemicals to be examined, in gathering the appropriate scientific data and reviewing it, and in determining which among hundreds of chemicals merited more detailed study. The Agency had then to identify the sources of chemicals on its "short list," obtain data if possible from these sources about the character and volume of their chemical releases, and visit at least some emission sites to verify their estimated releases. If the EPA decided to regulate a substance under Section 114, the federal government bore the burden of proof in demonstrating that the risks of exposure to that substance were sufficient to merit regulation if the decision were challenged legally. This obligation encouraged an extremely cautious approach to decision making, made even more deliberate by the frequent inadequacies and gaps in scientific data on the health effects of many suspected chemicals. And it was an expensive business. In the mid-1980s, for example, the EPA's ten on-site emission tests for chromium—just one phase of its evaluation—cost between $300,000 and $400,000.[22]

The 1990 amendments to the CAA, reflecting congressional frustration with EPA's erratic regulation, attempted to drive the EPA with the legislative lash and hammer. In addition to requiring the EPA to regulate 188 listed air toxics, Title III also required the Agency to list categories of industrial processes in chemical plants, oil refineries, steel plants, and other facilities emitting toxic pollutants, and to issue standards for each process by a specified deadline, using minimum criteria specified in the law itself. Many of the deadlines in Title III were among the fifty-five major rules the EPA was ordered to create within two years of the amendments' passage. Additional deadlines were created for a second round of health-related standards within eight years after the law's passage, and other programs and deadlines are mandated through the middle of the twenty-first century. By 1998, the EPA had issued standards for forty-seven air toxics, still leaving 140 to be regulated. In light of the practical difficulties involved and the anti-regulatory congressional mood following the 1994 elections, the EPA's achievement was remarkable. EPA predicted that the forty-seven standards already written would reduce the nation's total toxic emissions from stationary sources by 35 percent.[23] But the list of toxics awaiting regulation is long and the congressional mood volatile. The more difficult toxics remain on the agenda. Whether the EPA will be able to continue implementing the CAA's air toxics provisions at the same credible pace past the year 2000 is unclear.

In many respects, the most potent attack on air toxics may be mounted not from Title III but from the Superfund Amendments and Reauthorization Act of 1986 (SARA). The national survey of chemical emissions now required annually by SARA, the *Toxics Release Inventory (TRI),* has contributed valuable information about the character and dispersion of toxic substances nationally and the resulting publicity has created considerable political pressure on pollution sources to control their toxic emissions. Nonetheless, the variety and distribution of emission sources pose serious problems because many are not easily or economically controlled. Although the chemical industry is the single greatest source of these emissions, other sources include manufacturing plants, dry cleaning and paint removal processes, sewage treatment plants, hazardous waste processing and disposal facilities, smelters, and metal refining industries. Data are especially scarce on the long-term effects of low-level exposure to hazardous chemicals because most current information is obtained from industrial workers.

A highly productive cause of regulatory delay continues to be the opposition of chemical manufacturers and commercial users to regulation. Since the scientific base for estimates of risk from exposure to these substances is often meager, legal and administrative challenges even to the designation of a proven carcinogen can postpone regulation for years. The determined resistance of the asbestos industry turned control efforts into a regulatory trench war that lasted many years. The asbestos manufacturers agreed to virtually nothing, rejecting among other things a proposal that the federal government inform the public about the potential harm that might afflict children spending much time in school buildings containing asbestos insulation.[24]

Urban smog, airborne toxics, and small particulates are a few among many ambient air problems challenging the nation's ability to realize the ambitious goals set by the CAA more than twenty years ago. These problems test the nation's technological skill and economic resiliency. They will challenge the political determination of its officials and the public's commitment to the environmental protection the majority professes to support. These problems are also reminders of how incrementally slow has been the implementation and how modest have been the achievements of the CAA. The nation's experience with water pollution has been much the same.

Regulating Water Quality

The nation's aquatic inheritance is not just water but different water systems, each essential to modern U.S. society and each currently threatened, or already severely polluted, by different combinations of pollutants.

Surface Water

The nation's surface waters—streams, rivers, lakes, and the sea—are the nation's most visible water resource. Almost 99 percent of the population lives within fifty miles of a publicly owned lake. Streams, rivers, and lakes account for a very high proportion of all recreational activities, commercial fishing grounds, and industrial water resources. Because surface waters are so intensively used and so highly visible, their rapidly accelerating degradation became the most immediate cause for congressional action in the 1960s and 1970s; arresting water pollution and restoring the nation's once high water quality became a focal point for environmental legislation. Most of the fragmentary data available on national water quality during the past three decades come from monitoring surface-water conditions.

Throughout the late 1970s and 1980s, the Council on Environmental Quality (CEQ) and the EPA reported an ambiguous verdict on the nation's surface water. Throughout the 1980s, the CEQ and the EPA could report only that there had been "little or no change in water quality nationally." [25]

This might seem impressive considering the enormous volume of pollutants that might have been expected with growing population and economic activity over more than a decade. But the EPA's conclusion ignored more than 10,000 U.S. lakes considered to have serious pollution problems. And federal agencies such as the EPA and the CEQ base their surface water quality indexes on only six pollutants, excluding such important sources of water degradation as heavy metals, synthetic organic compounds, and dissolved solids.

Even in the late 1990s, estimates of surface-water quality continue to be ambiguous and uncertain, largely because comprehensive, reliable monitoring data remain unavailable. In general, surface-water quality seems, despite some spectacular achievements, to have remained in about the same condition since the late 1980s. In late 1996, EPA's national water quality report to Congress concluded darkly: "Based on the latest information to EPA by States, Tribes, and other jurisdictions with water quality responsibilities, about 40% of the Nation's surveyed rivers, lakes, and estuaries are not clean enough for basic uses such as fishing or swimming. The results are consistent with data last reported in 1992 and show that more work is needed if waters are to be made clean and healthy in all communities." [26] It is often difficult, in any case, to know what significance to impute to such statistics because EPA assessments cover only about a third of all U.S. surface water area. Figure 6-1 illustrates the scope of the missing information based on the most recent comprehensive data available to EPA.

The states' haphazard water quality monitoring continues to create massive information deficiencies that frustrate accurate national assessment. The U.S. General Accounting Office (GAO) verdict still stands. After struggling with the information, it admitted defeat and left Congress adrift in the data:

Figure 6-1   Percent and Quality of Waterbodies Assessed, 1995

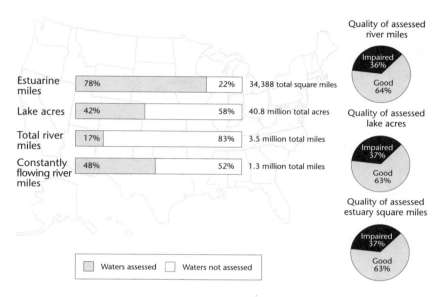

Source: Environmental Protection Agency, Office of Water, *Environmental Indicators of Water Quality in the United States* (Washington, D.C.: Environmental Protection Agency, 1996), 14.

> GAO was not able to draw definitive, generalizable conclusions ... because evaluating changes in the nation's rivers and streams is inherently difficult, the empirical data produced by the studies sparse, and the methodological problems reduce the usefulness of the findings. Therefore, little conclusive information is available to the Congress to use in policy debates on the nation's water quality.[27]

In the absence of any "definitive, generalizable conclusions," presumably the side mounting the most persuasive figures will win the debate over water quality.

The leading causes of surface water pollution, summarized in Figure 6-2, can be readily identified. By far the largest contributors to this pollution are agricultural runoff, urban runoff, and other so-called "nonpoint" sources, the most technologically and politically formidable pollutants yet to be controlled.

The Federal Water Pollution Control Amendments

The federal government's major water pollution regulatory program is embodied in the Federal Water Pollution Control Act Amendments of

Figure 6-2　Leading Stressors Causing Water Quality Impairment

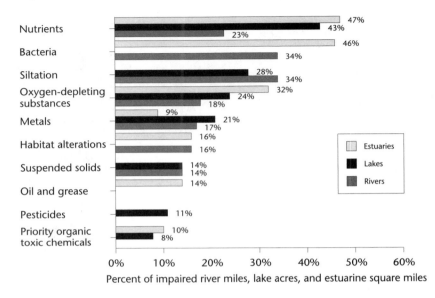

Percent of impaired river miles, lake acres, and estuarine square miles

Source: Environmental Protection Agency, Office of Water, *Environmental Indicators of Water Quality in the United States* (Washington, D.C.: Environmental Protection Agency, 1996), 14.

Note: This graph shows the percentage of river miles, lake acres, and estuarine square miles that are affected by a particular stressor. The affected waters include only those that have been assessed by states and tribes and identified as impaired (see Figure 6-1).

1972 and concerns primarily surface-water quality. The 1972 legislation amended the earlier Water Pollution Control Act of 1948. The 1972 amendments completely changed the substance of the earlier legislation and established the regulatory framework prevailing ever since. This 1972 legislation was greatly strengthened by new amendments passed in 1987 as the Water Quality Act. In more than 120 pages of fine print, the FWPCAA mandates the following regulatory program for the nation's surface waters:

1. *Goals.* The amendments established two broad goals whose achievement, if possible, assumed an unprecedented regulatory structure and unusually rapid technological innovation:

    a. "the discharge of pollutants into navigable waters of the United States be eliminated by 1985"

b. "wherever attainable, an interim goal of water quality which provides for the protection and propagation of fish, shellfish and wildlife and provides for recreation in and on the water be achieved by 1 July 1983"

2. *Regulatory Provisions for Existing Dischargers.* The legislation required that all direct dischargers into navigable waterways satisfy two different standards, one relating to water quality, the other to effluent limits. The water-quality standards, established by the states according to guidelines by the EPA, were to identify the use for a body of water into which a polluter was discharging (such as recreation, fishing, boating, waste disposal, irrigation, and so forth) and to establish limits on discharges in order to ensure that use. Effluent standards, established by the EPA, were to identify what technologies any discharger had to use to control its effluents. In meeting these dual requirements, the polluter was required to achieve whichever standard was the more strict. A different set of standards was established for publicly owned waste treatment facilities.

a. *Effluent limits for existing nonmunicipal sources.* Except for city waste treatment plants, all existing dischargers were required to have technological controls, prescribed by the EPA, which were to meet the following criteria:

i. the "best practicable control technology currently available" by 1 July 1979

ii. the "best available technology economically achievable" by July 1983

b. *Effluent limits for municipal treatment plants.* All treatment plants in existence on July 1, 1977, were required to have "secondary-treatment" levels. All facilities, regardless of age, were required to have "the best practicable treatment technology" by 1 July 1983.

c. *Effluent limits for new nonmunicipal sources.* All new sources of discharge, except municipal treatment plants, were required to use control technologies based on "the best available demonstrated control technology, operating methods or other alternatives."

d. *Toxic effluent standards.* The EPA was required to establish special standards for any discharge determined to be toxic.

3. *Regulatory Provisions for Indirect Dischargers.* Many pollutants, including chemical toxics, are released into municipal waste-water systems by industrial and commercial sources and later enter waterways through city sewage treatment plants that are unable to eliminate them. The law required the EPA to establish "pre-treatment" standards, which were to prevent the discharge of any pollutant through a public sewer that "interferes with, passes through or otherwise is incompatible with such works." The purpose of this provision was to compel

such "indirect dischargers" to treat their effluent before it reached the city system.

4. *Federal and State Enforcement.* The EPA was authorized to delegate responsibility for enforcing most regulatory provisions to qualified states that would issue permits to all polluters specifying the conditions for their effluent discharges.

5. *Waste Treatment Grants.* The Act authorized the expenditure of $18 billion between 1973 and 1975 to assist local communities in building necessary waste-water treatment facilities. The federal government assumed 75 percent of the capital cost for constructing the facilities.

6. *Nonpoint Pollution Regulation.* Amendments added in 1987 require each state to have a plan approved by the EPA for controlling pollution from nonpoint sources. Such plans must include "best management practices" but states are permitted to decide whether to require owners and managers to use such practices or to make them voluntary.

The 1972 legislation was written by a Congress unchastened by the political, economic, and technological obstacles to pressing technology in pollution regulation. The legislation, as originally written, was the purest example of "technology forcing" in the federal regulatory code. The use of effluent standards in addition to water-quality standards for dischargers was based on the premise that "all pollution was undesirable and should be reduced to the maximum extent that technology will permit."[28] Compliance deadlines were almost imperiously ordained for the total elimination of water pollution in a decade. The administrative and technical complexities of making the legislation work seemed surmountable. The original legislation serves as an enduring monument to the American politician's belief in the possibilities of social engineering and to the political muscle of the environmental movement in the early 1970s.

Even the most ardent of the legislation's advocates, however, recognized that the rigorous compliance deadlines for effluent treatment and waste-water facility construction would not be attained. They were convinced that pressing technology ultimately worked—eliminating all pollutants from the nation's waters hardly seemed impossible to a people who would launch a satellite carrying their language a billion light years into space. Acknowledging the likelihood of short-term failures, the legislation's advocates were nonetheless convinced that only by pressing technology relentlessly for rapid compliance with regulations could they sustain the sense of urgency and bring sufficient weight of federal authority to bear on polluters to obtain their long-term objectives.

The Political Setting

The political struggle over implementation of the FWPCAA has been shaped by several factors. First, the implementation of the legislation is federalized. The 1972 amendments made concessions to the states that Congress had been unwilling to make in the CAA of 1970 and that environmentalists generally opposed. The 1972 amendments permitted the states to decide on the designated use for a body of water. In general, state regulatory agencies are more vulnerable than Washington, D.C., to pressure from local water polluters to designate uses for bodies of water that will permit moderate to heavy pollution. This propensity of local regulatory agencies to accommodate regulated interests extends, as well, to enforcement of designated water uses and the associated emission controls. Regulated interests often are likely to press vigorously for a major state role in the administration and enforcement of water-quality standards, believing that this works to their advantage more than implementation through the EPA's regional and national offices. State enforcement of pollution controls on major dischargers has improved significantly in the 1990s but many violators still go undetected or unpunished. In the mid-1990s, the GAO calculated that as many as one in every six of the nation's major dischargers regularly violated their permits, but the EPA estimated the number might be twice that amount.

Thirty-five states have assumed major implementation responsibilities, such as issuing and enforcing permits for effluent dischargers, initiating requests for federal grants to build new local waste treatment facilities, and supervising the administration of the grant programs in their jurisdictions. The states thus exercise considerable influence on program implementation directly through their own participation—and the pursuit of their own interests in the program—and through their congressional delegations, which remain ever vigilant in protecting the interests of the folks back home. Moreover, conflict arising from differing state and federal viewpoints on program implementation becomes interjected immediately into the daily administrative implementation of the law. Control standards vary greatly among the states for the same pollutant, often provoking states with strict standards to a complain that more lenient ones enjoy an unfair advantage in the competition for new business. Among six major states, for instance, the same five toxic pollutants were treated very differently: ". . . in some states, the permitting authorities consistently established numeric limits on the discharges, while in other states, the authorities consistently required monitoring. In some states, no controls were imposed. In addition, the numeric discharge limits for specific pollutants differed from state to state and even within the same state for facilities of similar capacity." [29]

The political character of the program also depends on the enormous administrative discretion left to the EPA in prescribing the multitude of different technologies that must be used by effluent dischargers to meet the many different standards established in the law. At the time the Clean Water Act was amended in 1972, for instance, about 20,000 industrial dischargers were pouring pollutants into more than 2,500 municipal waste treatment facilities. The EPA was charged with identifying the pretreatment standards to be used by each major class of industrial discharger. This might eventually require standards for several hundred different classes and modified standards for subclasses. The final standards issued by the EPA in 1976 for industries producing "canned and preserved fruits and vegetables" alone contained specifications for fifty-one different subcategories. Administrators also are limited by the state of the art in treatment technologies and by dependence on the regulated interests for information concerning the character of the discharger's production processes and technical capacities. We already have noted that administrative discretion invites political pressure and conflict. The technical determinations required in setting effluent standards also invite controversy and litigation.

Finally, the program's implementation continually has been affected by the active, if not always welcome, intervention of the White House, Congress, and the federal courts in the program's development. Federal and state regulatory agencies have had to conduct the program in a highly political environment, in which all major actions have been subject to continual scrutiny, debate, and assessment by elective public officials and judges. This is hardly surprising for a program involving so many billions of dollars and so many politically and economically sensitive interests. But, as we shall observe, the economic and environmental costs of such politicized administration are high.

The Nonpoint Pollution Problem

The most common source of surface-water pollution has remained virtually uncontrolled in every state since the 1972 passage of the FWP-CAA. Nonpoint pollution—pollution arising from diffuse, multiple sources rather than from a pipe or other "point" source—is estimated to be the major cause of pollution in 65 percent of the stream miles not meeting state standards for their designated use.[30] Overall, more than one-third of the stream miles in the United States appear to be affected by nonpoint pollution. Nonpoint pollution also affects groundwater quality. Earlier we noted that nonpoint pollution is the leading cause of water quality impairment in the late 1990s. Figure 6-3, which indicates the proportion of nitrogen in major streams across the United States

Figure 6-3   Estimated Share of Nitrogen Delivered to Streams by Point and Nonpoint Sources

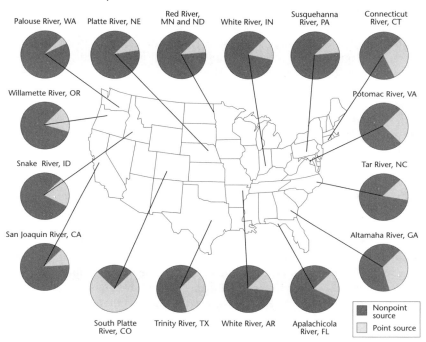

Source: Environmental Protection Agency, *Environmental Indicators of Water Quality in the United States* (Washington, D.C.: Environmental Protection Agency, 1996), 19.

originating from nonpoint sources, illustrates the geographic breadth of nonpoint pollution. This pollution is especially troublesome for several reasons. It is not easily controlled technically or economically. Many different sources require many different control strategies. The largest source of nonpoint pollution is agriculture: crop lands, pasture, and range lands together pollute about one-third of the nation's stream miles with metabolic wastes from animals, sediment, fertilizers, pesticides, dissolved solids, and other materials.

Agricultural nonpoint pollution and urban storm water runoff are the major causes for the eutrophication of lakes, whereby dissolved organic substances create such a high level of oxygen demand in the waters that higher forms of plants and animals die from oxygen deprivation. Eutrophication eventually leaves most lakes lifeless.

Reducing agricultural pollution requires a number of difficult strategies because technological solutions are rarely available. Most often, production practices must be altered. Farmers might be encouraged, or required, to reduce the volume of fertilizer, pesticides, and other chemicals used in crop production. Animal populations might be limited or dispersed. New crop and land management techniques might reduce soil runoff. In many instances, land-use planning might be used to prevent, or reduce, agricultural activities. But powerful agricultural groups and members of Congress for whom they are a major constituency believe such strategies will have adverse economic impacts and have opposed most measures intended to reduce agricultural runoff by most of these methods. Many state governments, fearful of damaging a major component of the state economy, are reluctant to do more than encourage farmers to voluntarily seek ways to limit their pollution runoff.

Attempts to manage other major nonpoint pollution sources will set regulators on a collision course with the commercial timber industry, the commercial and residential construction industry, meat packers and shippers, coal mining firms, and a multitude of trades and professions associated with each. Because technological controls are seldom available to manage these pollution sources, the alternatives are usually costly and difficult to implement. Regulators understandably prefer to avoid as long as possible the political bloodletting likely to arise when nonpoint source controls must be implemented. That day will be forced on them if the nation's surface waters are ever to meet state water-quality standards.

Results: Is "Significant" Really Significant?

The nation did not eliminate all pollution discharges into its waters by 1985, nor did it make even most waterways "fishable and swimmable" by mid-1983, as the FWPCAA intended. The combined impacts of the multibillion-dollar Construction Grants Program and the national permit system for pollution dischargers have prevented the further degradation of many surface waters, reduced pollution in others, and undoubtedly saved some high-quality waters from degradation. But evidence of a major, long-term improvement in the overall quality of the nation's surface waters is, as earlier noted, quite elusive. Considering the nation's population growth and economic expansion of the past two decades, the stability of water quality must be considered an achievement of sorts—it could have been much worse. But the quality of the nation's surface water is apparently not greatly improved and the goals of the FWPCAA still seem decades from achievement.

The EPA has tried to salvage optimism from this ambiguity with frequent references to "significant headway" and other vague expressions in assessments of surface water quality.[31] But the states and the EPA base their water-quality indexes largely on measurement of only six indicators: biochemical oxygen demand, dissolved oxygen, fecal coliform bacteria, total lead, total mercury, and total phosphorus. These indexes exclude such important sources of water degradation as heavy metals, synthetic organic compounds, and dissolved solids. Moreover, a large proportion of water pollution sources for which the states issue permits are expected to monitor their own pollution emissions and, in about two-thirds of the states, no attempt has yet been made to identify unregulated facilities that have not reported themselves to state officials.[32]

There is no convincing evidence that massive governmental spending on municipal waste-water treatment plants has significantly improved the nation's waters. Since 1960, the nation's governments have spent more than $113 billion to construct or upgrade these facilities.[33] This governmental largess has certainly produced high-quality treatment plants in abundance. Since 1970, more than 8,000 projects in 5,000 municipalities have been undertaken. Today almost three-quarters of all municipal facilities achieve at least secondary treatment for their wastes and the proportion of the nation served by these high-quality plants has risen from 42 to 56 percent.[34] But more high-technology treatment plants do not necessarily mean better water quality. The amount of pollutants dumped into the nation's surface waters from municipalities has decreased, but it is unclear how much this decrease has improved water quality.[35] Monitoring data and other information essential to assessing the impact of the construction grants on surface water quality are inadequate. Existing information is often inconsistent. And so things will remain as long as the dull but essential task of data collection remains politically unattractive and underfunded.

Groundwater

During the 1980s, the nation's groundwater became a major concern. Lying below the earth's upper porous surface and a lower layer of impermeable rock, groundwater percolates through the upper layer and collects until it eventually saturates subsurface soil and rock. Much of this water flows slowly to the sea through permeable layers of sand or gravel called aquifers. These aquifers sustain the life and vitality of communities throughout much of the United States. Groundwater is as essential as surface water to the nation's existence and far more abundant: the annual flow of groundwater is fifty times the volume of surface flows, and most lies within one-half mile of the earth's surface. Almost 50 percent of the U.S. population and 95 percent of its rural residents depend on groundwater for domestic uses. More than 40 percent of all agricultural irrigation originates from groundwater. Because groundwater filters slowly through many levels of fine soil as it percolates downward and

Table 6-5 Major Sources of Groundwater Contamination Reported by States

Source	Number of states reporting source[a]	Number of states reporting as primary source[b]
Septic tanks	46	9
Underground storage tanks	43	13
Agricultural activities	41	6
On-site landfills	34	5
Surface impoundments	33	2
Municipal landfills	32	1
Abandoned waste sites	29	3
Oil and gas brine pits	22	2
Saltwater intrusion	19	4
Other landfills	18	0
Road salting	16	1
Land application of sludge	12	0
Regulated waste sites	12	1
Mining activities	11	1
Underground injection wells	9	0
Construction activities	2	0

Source: Environmental Protection Agency, *Environmental Progress and Challenges: EPA's Update* (Washington, D.C.: Environmental Protection Agency, Aug. 1988), 48.

[a] Based on a total of fifty-two states and territories that reported groundwater contamination sources in their 1986 305(b) submittals to the EPA.

[b] Some states did not indicate a primary source.

flows onward through the aquifers, it traditionally has been virtually free of harmful pollutants. Today, however, groundwater is seriously degraded in many geographic areas of the United States.

Almost every state has one or more sources of serious groundwater contamination. Table 6-5 lists the most common sources and the number of states reporting these as a significant problem. Estimates of contamination are crude because reliable data are scarce. The U.S. Geological Survey first reported the good news in 1978 that the nation's underground water condition was "generally good," with only 1 to 3 percent of the total contaminated with specific sources; then it delivered the bad news: "available data, especially data about the occurrence of synthetic organic and toxic substances, generally are inadequate to determine the full extent of groundwater contamination in the nation's aquifers or to define trends in groundwater quality." [36]

Because of the complexity of groundwater systems and the expense of monitoring, the EPA has said, "we may never have a complete picture of the nature and extent of the problem." [37] But the EPA has identified an enormous number of actual or potential sources of groundwater contamination:

- about 13,000 hazardous waste sites are now potential candidates for the Superfund National Priority List (an inventory of the most dangerous sites)
- millions of septic systems
- more than 180,000 surface impoundments, such as pits, ponds, and lagoons
- an estimated 500 hazardous waste land disposal facilities and about 16,000 municipal and other landfills
- millions of underground storage tanks
- thousands of underground injection wells
- millions of tons of pesticides and fertilizers spread on the ground, mostly in rural areas

Many Programs, Many Governments, Many Agencies. The 1977 discovery of massive groundwater contamination caused by the abandoned hazardous waste site at New York's Love Canal became the nation's first groundwater crisis. Groundwater contamination has been a crisis-driven issue, thrust on governmental agendas by waves of public apprehension following revelations of widespread groundwater contamination from hazardous waste dumps, agricultural chemicals, and industrial and governmental chemical accidents. Improved monitoring has also added urgency to the groundwater issue by revealing previously unknown chemical contamination (although often in only trace amounts). But monitoring has only begun and the quality of most underground waters remains unknown.

Traditionally, groundwater management has been considered a state and local governmental responsibility. Although the federal government has no comprehensive groundwater management program, approximately forty-five different federal programs affect groundwater in some manner.[38] The primary federal responsibility for implementing many of the major programs affecting groundwater rests with the EPA. In addition to the FWPCAA, other important legislation affecting groundwater quality include the Marine Protection, Research and Sanctuaries Act (1972); the Safe Drinking Water Act (1974) and its 1986 amendments; the Resource Conservation and Recovery Act (1976); and the Superfund legislation (1980) together with its 1984 amendments. However, many other agencies and programs are also involved. The mélange of federal agencies and programs involved in groundwater management assures incoherence, inconsistency, and competing authority in the federal government's approach to groundwater problems.

The states' considerable responsibility for groundwater management has been acquired through federal legislation and their own initiative. Forty-one states currently have their own groundwater quality standards, although little consistency exists among them. The number of groundwater contaminants currently regulated varies from 14 in one state to 190 in another. In addition, almost all of the states have assumed responsibility for implementing federal drinking water standards established under the Safe Drinking Water Act.

Controlling subsurface pollution is troublesome because groundwater filters very slowly as it flows. An aquifer may move no more than ten to one hundred feet annually. In any case, many toxic contaminants are not captured or neutralized by filtering. Moreover, the extent of groundwater pollution may be impossible to estimate adequately because the pollution plume radiating outward through an aquifer from a pollution source can take a number of unpredictable directions. Often, plumes will contaminate millions or billions of gallons of water.

Many sources of groundwater contamination, however, are still being identified. The nation's estimated 1.2 million abandoned oil and gas wells, of which perhaps 200,000 are not properly plugged, are examples. Abandoned wells, often drilled to a depth of more than one mile, can contaminate groundwater with brine, four times more saline than seawater, containing heavy metals, radioactivity, and other possible toxics. In Texas, perhaps 40,000 to 50,000 abandoned wells may pose pollution problems and an estimated 386,000 wells have never been registered. Said one Texas Health official, "We've found leaking wells from the old days that were rock-plugged, bucket-plugged, tree-stump plugged and even one plugged with nothing more than a glass jug." In Louisiana, almost 1,500 unplugged wells are uncontrolled because money is lacking.[39]

Continuing Chemical Contamination. The many substances known or suspected to contaminate groundwater defy concise enumeration. One survey indicated that the states collectively have set standards for approximately 35 inorganic compounds, 39 volatile organic compounds, 125 nonvolatile organic compounds, and 56 pesticides, among other substances.[40] These represent only a small portion of the chemicals used in the U.S. economy and found in groundwater. These contaminants originate from many sources. The states are only beginning to regulate many of these sources, such as underground storage tanks, underground injection wells, and abandoned waste sites. Although most states have at least some standards for groundwater quality, it is unclear how well they are enforced. "It is very difficult to know precisely how the states' standards were used," concluded a 1988 GAO survey. "At best, we could identify only the principal areas where they were used. . . . However, how the states actually implemented these objectives in state programs and how well the objectives were met is completely unknown at the present time."[41] Among groundwater contaminants, chemicals remain especially difficult to regulate because of their great number and wide diffusion in the ecosystem. Most states set standards for and monitor only a fraction of the chemicals likely to be present in groundwater. Almost all states identify toxics as a major source of water-quality problems. These toxics can originate in thousands of abandoned and poorly regulated hazardous waste sites, from agricultural activity, underground injection wells, municipal landfill, and sludges. Sludges—the semisolid wastes produced in many air and water pollution control activities— often contain many hazardous or toxic chemicals. Municipal waste treatment plants in the United States annually produce more than 7.7 million dry metric tons of hazardous sludge and this figure is expected to double by the year 2000. The dangerous chemicals removed from water as sludge frequently infiltrate the ecosystem again when they migrate to surface and underground water. Many states as yet have no regulatory program to manage this cross-media pollution migration.[42]

During the 1990s, federal and state regulators have made three chemical groundwater contaminants a priority: neutrients, pesticides and leaking underground storage tanks (LUSTs). Neutrients, such as nitrates, are found most often in groundwater affected by agricultural production, including both crops and livestock. Recent estimates indicate that nitrate concentrations exceeding federal standards around found in about 12 percent of domestic water supply well; trace amounts, not considered dangerous, are more often found in wells near agriculture activity.[43] Nitrate infiltration is not now considered a major national problem but pesticides and LUSTs are more troublesome. In the last decade, at least 143 pesticides and 21 of their transformation products have been detected in the groundwater of 43 states. In most cases, these pesticide concentrations do not exceed state water-quality standards for agricultural areas. However, pesticides may be a more serious problem in non-agricultural areas, particularly around golf courses, commercial and residential areas, rights-of-way, timber production and processing areas, and public gardens. A major concern is the very limited information available about the health effects associated with exposure to most pesticides, even in trace amounts. Federal groundwater standards, called "maximum contaminant limits" (MCLs), have yet to be established for most of these pesticides. Existing MCLs are often based on very incomplete information. The U.S. Geological Survey cautions: ". . . existing criteria may be revised as more is learned about the toxicity of these compounds. . . . MCLs and other criteria are currently based on individual pesticides and do not account for possible cumulative effects if several different pesticides are present in the same well. Finally, many pesticides and most transformation products have not been widely sampled for in ground water and very little sampling has been done in urban and suburban areas, where pesticide use is often high."[44]

Governmental concern about LUSTs has grown steadily through the 1990s with the increasing number of discovered sites. Five to six million tanks, most used for retail gasoline or petroleum storage, are buried throughout the United States. Of the 1.7 million tanks currently regulated, at least 300,000 are known to be leaking.[45] These leaks contaminate the groundwater, damage sewer lines and buried cables, poison crops, and ignite fires and explosions. More than 80 percent of the tanks currently in use, constructed of bare steel, are easily corroded and should be replaced with safer containers. Unfortunately, many of these tanks have been abandoned and long forgotten. Often located under active or abandoned gasoline stations, airports, large trucking firms, farms, golf courses, and manufacturing plants, many leaking sites may never be discovered. Federal law requires the states to insure that all currently operated tanks meet stringent new containment standards by the end of 1998 but most states have been overwhelmed by the magnitude of the regulatory task, especially since new sites are continually discovered. A recent estimate suggests that perhaps half the high-risk sites are not being adequately controlled.[46]

Drinking Water

One need look no further than the kitchen sink for one emerging groundwater concern. All ecosystems are intricately and subtly interrelated. The negligent dumping of contaminants into surface water and groundwater eventually follows a circle of causality, delivering the danger back to its source. So it is in the United States. More than 80 percent of the nation's community water systems depend on groundwater for domestic use and the remainder use surface water. Recognizing that community drinking water was threatened by the rising volume of pollutants entering surface and groundwater, Congress passed in 1974 the Safe Drinking Water Act (SDWA), amended in 1986, to ensure that public water supplies achieved minimum health standards. In 1977 the EPA, following the Act's mandate, began to set National Primary Drinking Water Standards that established maximum levels in drinking water for microbiological contaminants, turbidity, and chemical agents. Currently, standards exist for approximately thirty substances. Standard-setting is badly lagging at the EPA, however. In another demonstration of congressional overcontrol, the 1986 amendments to the SDWA required the EPA to adopt standards for 61 more contaminants by mid-1989, create 25 more standards from a new list by 1991, and set standards for 25 additional chemicals every three years thereafter. Once standards are established, the states are given primary responsibility for enforcing them, and other provisions of the Act, on more than 79,000 public water systems. Since the 1986 amendments were written, the number of regulated contaminants has expanded to 72 and is expected to reach 100 by the end of the 1990s.

Evidence is growing that a great many states lack the financial, technical, and staff resources to enforce even the SDWA's minimum standards and that very many small and large water systems are virtually ignored. "Severe resource constraints have made it increasingly difficult for many states to effectively carry out the monitoring, enforcement, and other mandatory elements of EPA's drinking water program," the GAO reported in 1993, and the situation ". . . promises to deteriorate further, as the program requirements continue to expand and states' resources remain constrained." [47] Unfortunately, faltering regulation is the counterpoint to growing evidence that the nation's water systems, including some of the largest, are still infiltrated by dangerous concentrations of chemical and biological contaminants, many for which no standards exist and, as a consequence, no regulatory controls exist. The EPA has listed among the major problems:

- In the period 1975–1985, between 1,500 and 3,000 water supplies exceeded the EPA standards for inorganic substances, particularly fluoride and nitrates.
- Major problems with toxic organic substances were reported in some wells in almost every state west of the Mississippi River.
- Overall, more than 600 contaminants have been detected in the nation's drinking water systems.
- Nearly all of the nation's 58,000 community water systems, serving more than 219 million consumers, will have been affected by one or more new regulations on drinking water contaminants. [48]

Injection wells, used to dispose of hazardous and solid wastes by flushing them into deep aquifers, appear to be a major source of drinking water contamination. More than 253,000 active or abandoned injection wells exist in the United States. About half of the liquid hazardous waste generated in the United States is pumped into these injection wells, the largest portion from oil and gas production and refining facilities. While liquid hazardous wastes are subject to federal regulation, no detailed national standards exist for solid waste eliminated through injection wells. Rural water supplies seem especially vulnerable to contamination from injection wells and abandoned hazardous waste sites. A 1984 EPA assessment of rural water quality reported unsafe levels of cadmium in about one-sixth of the nation's rural wells, mercury concentrations above safe levels in about one-quarter of the wells, and lead at dangerous levels in one-tenth of these wells.

Conclusion

Air and water are the primary issues on the environmental agenda; they are the first, most essential, most politically visible, and most important tasks of environmental restoration and regulation. The condition of the nation's air and water has been examined in considerable detail to emphasize the daunting scope and complexity of the challenge of ecological restoration and to illustrate how short a distance the United States has traveled toward that goal in the three decades and two eras since environmentalism emerged as a major political force in the country.

This chapter illustrates that difficulties in cleaning up the nation's air and water cannot be blamed solely on political incompetence, policy deficiencies, administrative failures, or scientific bungling. Rather, scientific and technological development continually poses new challenges to regulation by creating new chemicals, and new technologies, with unanticipated environmental effects. Further, scientific research continually redefines and elaborates the nature of environmental degradation and its consequences—as shown in the study of airborne particulates and toxics, for instance—forcing continual rethinking and change in regulatory strategies. And even so unexciting and obscure an activity as environmental monitoring leads to new definitions of environmental degradation, as the study of groundwater contamination reveals. The United States, as with all other nations now committed to environmental restoration, must suffer a learning curve: it must acquire experience in a policy domain with which no government on earth was involved a scant few decades ago. Those who govern can learn, but it takes time.

This review of the nation's current air and water pollution control programs is a sobering reminder that it will take a very long time, and require an enormous amount of money, scientific resources, and administrative skill, to give us back the healthful air and water we once had and hope to have again. So formidable a goal will not be easily realized. It may not happen in the lifetime of any American living today.

Notes

1. Environmental Protection Agency (EPA), Office of Air Quality Planning and Standards, *National Air Quality and Emissions Trends Report, 1996: Executive Summary* (Washington, D.C.: EPA, 1998), 3.
2. Council on Environmental Quality (CEQ), *Environmental Quality, 1996* (Washington, D.C.: CEQ, 1997), 454.
3. EPA, Office of Water, *Water Quality Conditions in the United States: Quality Inventory Report to Congress* (Washington, D.C.: EPA, 1997), 6.
4. National Academy of Public Administration, *The Environment Goes To Market* (Washington, D.C.: National Academy of Public Administration, 1994), chap. 1; Paul R. Portney, ed., *Current Issues in U.S. Environmental Policy*, (Baltimore, Md.: Johns Hopkins University Press, 1978), especially chap. 1; and Erica L. Dolgin and Thomas

G. P. Guilbert, eds., *Federal Environmental Law* (St. Paul, Minn.: West Publishing, 1974), especially Robert Zener, "The Federal Law of Water Pollution Control," 682-791, and Thomas Jorling, "The Federal Law of Air Pollution Control," 1058-1148.
5. On the problem generally, see Allen V. Kneese and Charles L. Schulze, *Pollution, Prices and Public Policy* (Washington, D.C.: Brookings Institution, 1975), chap. 2.
6. David D. Doniger, *The Law and Policy of Toxic Substances Control* (Baltimore, Md.: Johns Hopkins University Press, 1978), 67.
7. Francis E. Rourke, *Bureaucracy, Politics, and Public Policy* (Boston: Little, Brown, 1969), 103.
8. *Public Opinion* (Feb./March 1982): 36.
9. Paul B. Downing and James N. Kimball, "Enforcing Pollution Laws in the U.S.," *Policy Studies Journal* 11, no. 1 (Sept. 1982): 55-65.
10. General Accounting Office (GAO), "EPA Cannot Ensure the Accuracy of Self-Reported Compliance Monitoring Data," Report no. GAO/RCED 93-21 (March 1993), 4; and GAO, "Air Pollution: Difficulties in Implementing a National Air Permit Program," Report no. GAO/RCED 93-59 (Feb. 1993), 2.
11. Downing and Kimball, "Enforcing Pollution Laws in the U.S."
12. Keith Bradsher, *New York Times,* Nov. 30, 1997.
13. These summaries are adapted from Gary C. Bryner, *Blue Skies, Green Politics: The Clean Air Act of 1990 and Its Implementation,* 2d ed. (Washington, D.C.: CQ Press, 1995), chap. 4.
14. Ibid., 126.
15. Robert N. Stavins, "What Can We Learn From the Grand Policy Experiment?: Positive and Normative Lessons From SO2 Allowance Trading," *Journal of Economic Perspectives* 12, no. 2 (1998).
16. Bryner, *Blue Skies, Green Politics,* chap4.
17. *New York Times,* August 27, 1985.
18. *New York Times,* March 29, 1989.
19. James E. McCarthy, "Clean Air Act Issues," Issue Brief 97007 (Washington, D.C.: Congressional Research Service, October 8, 1997).
20. EPA, Office of Air and Radiation, *1995 National Air Quality Trends Brochure: Particulate Matter (PM-10)* (Washington, D.C.: EPA, 1997).
21. David M. O'Brien, *What Process Is Due?* (New York: Russell Sage Foundation, 1987); and *New York Times,* March 23, 1989.
22. GAO, "Chemical Data: EPA's Collection Practices and Procedures on Chemicals," Report no. GAO/RCED 86-63 (Feb. 1986), 6.
23. Lawrence Mosher, "Time Bomb," *National Journal,* May 1, 1982, 778.
24. Ibid.
25. CEQ, *Environmental Quality, 1981* (Washington, D.C.: CEQ, 1982), 52. See also EPA, *Environmental Progress and Challenges: EPA's Update* (Washington, D.C.: EPA, August 1988), 70.
26. EPA, Office of Water, *Water Quality Conditions in the United States: Water Quality Inventory Report to Congress: A Profile from the 1994 National Water Quality Inventory Report to Congress* (Washington, D.C.: EPA, 1996).
27. GAO, "The Nation's Waters: Key Unanswered Questions about the Quality of Rivers and Streams," Report no. GAO/PEMD 86-6 (Sept. 1986), 3.
28. Zener, "The Federal Law of Water Pollution Control," 694.
29. GAO, "Drinking Water Quality," Report no. GAO/RCED 97-123 (1997), 3-4.
30. EPA, *Environmental Progress and Challenges,* 49.
31. Ibid.
32. GAO, "The Nation's Water," 63. See also GAO, "EPA Cannot Insure the Accuracy of Self-Reported Compliance Monitoring Data," Report no. GAO/RCED 93-21 (March 1993), 3.
33. GAO, "The Nation's Water," 87.
34. EPA, *Environmental Progress and Challenges,* 46.
35. Conservation Foundation, *State of the Environment: A View Toward the Nineties* (Washington, D.C.: Conservation Foundation, 1987), 105.

36. CEQ, *Environmental Quality, 1979* (Washington, D.C.: CEQ, 1980), chap. 2.
37. EPA, *Environmental Progress and Challenges,* 52.
38. GAO, "Groundwater Quality: State Activities to Guard against Contaminants," Report no. GAO/PEMD 88-5 (Feb. 1988), 13.
39. *New York Times,* April 2, 1992.
40. GAO, "Groundwater Quality," 38-39.
41. Ibid., 95.
42. GAO, "Water Pollution: Serious Problems Confront Emerging Municipal Management Program," Report no. GAO/RCED 90-57 (March 1990), 3.
43. U.S. Geological Survey, "Nutrients in the Nation's Waters-Too Much of a Good Thing?" USGS Circular 1136 (Washington, D.C.: U.S. Geological Survey, 1996).
44. U.S. Geological Survey, "Pesticides in Ground Water," USGS Fact Sheet FS-255-95 (Washington, D.C.: U.S. Geological Survey, 1995).
45. EPA, *Securing Our Legacy* (Washington, D.C.: EPA, 1988); and EPA, *Environmental Progress and Challenges,* 102-103.
46. EPA, Office of Underground Storage Tanks, *The UST Corrective Action Program* (Washington, D.C.: EPA, 1997).
47. GAO, "Drinking Water Program: States Face Increased Difficulties in Meeting Basic Requirements," Report no. GAO/RCED 93-144 (June 1993), 3.
48. EPA, *Environmental Progress and Challenges,* 52-53. See also GAO, "Drinking Water: Noncompliance Undermines EPA Drinking Water Program," Report no. GAO/RCED 90-127 (June 1990), 62-63.

Suggested Readings

Bryner, Gary C. *Blue Skies, Green Politics: The Clean Air Act of 1990 and Its Implementation.* 2d ed. Washington, D.C.: CQ Press, 1995.
Cohen, Stephen, and Sheldon Kamieniecki. *Environmental Regulation Through Strategic Planning.* Boulder, Colo.: Westview Press, 1991.
Portney, Paul R., ed. *Public Policies for Environmental Protection.* Washington, D.C.: Resources for the Future, 1990.

Chapter 7

A Regulatory Thicket:
Toxic and Hazardous Substances

> *Outdated birth control pills, 96,000 drums of chemicals, hospital wastes including extracted tumors and tapeworms, carcinogenic solvents, toxic metals, radioactive substances, dioxin, 28 million pounds of contaminated soil and ash, phosgene nerve gas, 500 pounds of TNT, nitroglycerin, and picric acid.*
>
> —Partial inventory of Chemical Control Company's Elizabeth, New Jersey, site shortly before it exploded on April 21, 1980

If, by a perverse whim, legal historians should choose a Top Ten in Toxic Litigation, a place surely will be reserved for the small community of Glen Avon, California. There, in early 1993, a legal spectacle began that demanded superlatives. "It's got to be among the top five civil cases in the history of American jurisprudence," one defense lawyer burbled as the proceedings began. Indeed, everything seemed dramatically oversized, like a production from some Hollywood of Hazardous Waste.[1] After eight years of planning and screening 2,000 jurors, the trial itself began with 4,000 plaintiffs (all Glen Avon residents), 13 defendants, including the state of California and such major corporations as Rockwell International, Northrop, McDonnell Douglas, and Montrose Chemicals, and injury claims exceeding $800 million. At issue was liability for injuries alleged to have been inflicted on Glen Avon residents from exposure to more than 200 chemicals in 34 million gallons of waste dumped into the Stringfellow Canyon between 1956 and 1972.

By the time the trial began, Glen Avon residents had already received more than $50 million in damages from 100 companies that had used the site for dumping, but $22 million had already been spent to initiate the new trail. The 30 lawyers and 24 jurors would eventually review more than 300,000 pages of court documents, and 13,000 defense and 3,600 plaintiff exhibits for the initial proceeding. The trial, held in installments, will stretch indefinitely into the future. The first trial, involving 17 plaintiffs, ended on September 17, 1993, when the jury found the state of California responsible for allowing toxic releases from the Stringfellow site but awarded the plaintiffs only $159,000 of the $3.1 million they had claimed in damages. The second trial, which began in September 1994, involved plaintiffs claiming much more serious injuries. And the trials will continue until all the 3,800 civil suits now pending over the Stringfellow disposal pit are concluded.[2] The Stringfellow Canyon site is considered to be among the worst on the Superfund National Priority List (NPL), an inventory of the nation's most dangerous hazardous waste dumps. Even so, many legal experts believe that the Stringfellow litigation is but a signpost along an upward road to even more expansive and expensive future litigation as hazardous waste regulations multiply and government seeks ever more aggressively to satisfy public apprehension about hazardous and toxic substances.

An ironic counterpoint to this growing litigation with its burgeoning liability awards has been the mounting disagreement among scientific experts about the actual extent of public risk from exposure to manufactured, stored, and abandoned chemical substances. Indeed, in no other area of environmental regulation has scientific uncertainty about the extent of risk and identity of hazardous substances been greater or more public.

Regulating the nation's hazardous and toxic substances, and the thousands of dangerous waste products that they eventually produce, is proving continually more difficult, costly, and time consuming. After almost three decades of massive public investment in a multitude of regulatory programs aimed at almost every aspect of hazardous waste, accomplishments have seldom satisfied either program proponents or critics— although the EPA enforces thirteen major laws affecting hazardous substance use and disposal in the United States. Most of these laws are burdened by the daunting variety of materials to be regulated, by inadequate data on the distribution and effect of these substances on humans and the environment, by political and administrative impediments to implementation, and by widespread public criticism and distrust. These chronic problems debilitate the nation's waste management laws so gravely that their continuation threatens to create a crisis of regulatory capacity before the end of the decade.

An Ambiguous Inheritance

The environmentalist's hell is a firmament of compacted pesticide awash in toxic sludge. Environmentalists are not alone in attributing to chemicals a special malevolence. Most Americans apparently believe that the air, water, and earth are suffused with real or potential toxic menaces. The Roper Organization polled a sample of Americans in 1990 concerning what environmental risks they considered "very serious" and discovered that hazardous waste and industrial chemicals dominated public apprehensions. The public's top four environmental risks were: (1) active hazardous waste sites; (2) abandoned hazardous waste sites; (3) water pollution from industrial waste; and (4) worker exposure to toxic chemicals.[3]

Americans are often misinformed about the extent of environmental risks and frequently exaggerate the danger from materials listed high on the Roper Poll. But widespread media coverage of hazardous chemical spills, newly discovered abandoned toxic waste sites, and other real or alleged crises involving dangerous substances have forced attention on hazardous and toxic substances and imparted a sense of urgency to resolving the problems. Moreover, mounting evidence about the pervasiveness of potentially dangerous chemicals throughout the United States and uncertainty about the risks they pose to society and the environment increase public apprehension and provoke demands that the government do something to control public exposure to these substances. Hazardous and toxic substances have progressed rapidly from secondary importance in the environmental agenda at the start of Era I to primary importance in Era II.

Chemicals

Most hazardous and toxic substances are an inheritance of the worldwide chemical revolution following World War II. The creation of synthetic chemicals continued at such a prolific pace after 1945 that by the mid-1960s the American Chemical Society had registered more than 4 million chemicals, an increasing proportion of which were synthetics created by American chemists since 1945. Today, more than 70,000 of these chemicals are used daily in U.S. commerce and industry. About 500 to 1,000 new chemicals are created annually. Currently, the EPA has more than 10,000 new chemicals pending review, as required by the Toxic Substances Control Act (TSCA) of 1976.[4]

About 98 percent of chemical substances used commercially in the United States are considered harmless to humans and the ecosystem. Less than 7 percent of approximately 1,000 new chemicals proposed for manufacture and reviewed by the EPA have aroused concern among the Agency's scientific review panels.[5] However, about 120,000 establishments in the United States create and distribute chemicals; the industry's growing capacity to produce and distribute still more new substances increases. As new chemicals proliferate and the long-term risks associated with older chemicals are better understood, the need to protect humans and the environment from the relatively small but enormously diverse set of hazardous or toxic substances grows more imperative.

Toxic and Hazardous Chemicals

While many chemicals have been tested to determine their hazardousness—it is often relatively easy to decide if a chemical is corrosive, or ignitable, or otherwise clearly dangerous when handled or abandoned in the environment—few have been tested rigorously to determine their risk to human or environmental health ("toxicity"). Testing is particularly difficult and expensive when the long-term effects of a chemical are being investigated. Studies may require decades.

Cancer is the gravest and most widely feared of all toxic impacts from hazardous substances. In the late 1990s, perhaps 1,500 to 2,000 of all chemical substances, a small proportion of all suspected carcinogenic chemicals produced in the United States, had been tested sufficiently to determine their carcinogenicity. Among those tested, more than 800 showed substantial evidence of carcinogenicity.[6] The substances, or industrial processes, most strongly linked to human cancer are identified in Table 7-1.

The list of chemicals convincingly associated with acute or chronic human cancer is slowly growing. However, convincing scientific evidence that *environmental* pollutants are causing widespread cancer is still largely unavailable. For example, the National Cancer Institute and the Centers for Disease Control and Prevention reported a lack of confirmed evidence that such pollutants were associated with cancer epidemics. The Institute estimated that perhaps 1 to 3 percent of all annual U.S. cancer death resulted from exposure to environmental pollution.[7] The elusiveness of data, in turn, seems to the critics of current regulation like a confirmation that existing toxics legislation is scientifically, as well as economically, flawed.

Currently, more than twenty-four federal laws and a dozen federal agencies are concerned with regulating the manufacture, distribution, and disposal of carcinogenic substances. Their work is seriously impeded not only by disagreement over the health risks posed by chemicals under their jurisdiction but also by a lack of accurate, current information about the variety and composition of the many chemicals within their jurisdiction.

Pesticides are a very large component of hazardous and toxic waste. More than 50,000 pesticides currently are registered for use in the United States. In the late 1990s, the United States was producing more than 1.2 billion pounds of pesticides annually, with more than 600 active

Table 7-1   *Chemicals or Industrial Processes Associated with Cancer Induction in Humans*

Chemical or industrial process	Main type of exposure[a]	Target organs in humans	Main source of exposure[b]
Aflatoxins	Environmental, occupational[c]	Liver	Oral, inhalation[c]
4-Aminobiphenyl	Occupational	Bladder	Inhalation, skin, oral
Arsenic compounds	Occupational, medicinal, environmental	Skin, lung, liver[c]	Inhalation, skin, oral
Asbestos	Occupational	Lung, pleural cavity, G.I. tract	Inhalation, oral
Auramine manufacturing	Occupational	Bladder	Inhalation, skin, oral
Benzene	Occupational	Hemopoietic system	Inhalation, skin
Benzidine	Occupational	Bladder	Inhalation, skin, oral
Bis(chloromethyl)-ether	Occupational	Lung	Inhalation
Cadmium-using industries (possibly cadmium oxides)	Occupational	Prostate, lung	Inhalation, oral
Chloramphenicol	Medicinal	Hemopoietic system	Oral, injection
Chloromethyl ether[d]	Occupational	Lung	Inhalation
Chromate-producing industries	Occupational	Lung, nasal cavities[c]	Inhalation
Cyclophosphamide	Medicinal	Bladder	Oral, injection
Diethylstilbestrol (DES)	Medicinal	Uterus, vagina	Oral
Hematite mining	Occupational	Lung	Inhalation
lsopropyl oil	Occupational	Nasal cavity, larynx	Inhalation
Melphalan	Medicinal	Hemopoietic system	Oral, injection
Mustard gas	Occupational	Lung, Larynx	Inhalation
2-Naphthylamine	Occupational	Bladder	Inhalation, skin, oral
Nickel refining	Occupational	Nasal cavity, lung	Inhalation
N.N-bis(2-chloroethyl)-2-naphthylamine (chlornaphazine)	Medicinal	Bladder	Oral
Oxymetholone	Medicinal	Liver	Oral
Phenacetin	Medicinal	Kidney	Oral
Phenytoin	Medicinal	Lymphoreticular tissues	Oral, injection
Soot, tars, and oils	Occupational, environmental	Lung, skin, scrotum	Inhalation, skin
Vinyl chloride	Occupational	Liver, brain[c], lung[c]	Inhalation, skin

Source: Council on Environmental Quality, *Environmental Quality, 1979* (Washington, D.C.: Government Printing Office, 1980), 199–200.

[a] The main types mentioned are those by which the association has been demonstrated.

[b] The main routes given may not be the only ones by which such effects could occur.

[c] Denotes indicative evidence.

[d] Possibly associated with bis(chloromethyl)-ether.

ingredients.[8] Pesticides are so widely and routinely used in U.S. agriculture that many farmers believe productivity cannot be sustained without them.

Common foods are treated with dozens of possible carcinogens used widely in commercial agriculture; for example, there are twenty-five used for corn, twenty-four for apples, twenty-three for tomatoes, and twenty-one for peaches.[9] Consider the chemical bath in which the dinner table onion was likely raised:

Fungicides: bravo, 2 pints per acre, seven to ten times a year; manex or maneb, 1 to 3 pounds per acre, seven to ten times a year; ridomil, 1.5 to 2 pounds per acre, once a year
Insecticides: parathion, 0.5 pint per acre, or guthion, 1 to 1.5 pounds per acre, two or three times a season; lorsban, placed in furrow at planting and sprayed twice to control onion maggots
Herbicide: goal, 0.25 ounces per acre, one application a season
Sprout inhibitor: maleic hydrazide, 2 pounds per acre before harvest to prevent onions from sprouting before they reach market.[10]

By the late 1990s, the EPA had prohibited or restricted the manufacture of more than 500 commercial chemicals, including many proven carcinogens such as dioxin, asbestos, polychlorinated biphenyls (PCBs), and the pesticide DDT. Even if a substance is restricted or prohibited, the EPA often lacks the resources to implement controls quickly. Although the EPA estimates that more than half a million office buildings, apartment houses, stores, and other public or commercial buildings presently contain potentially dangerous loose asbestos, the Agency decided as early as 1988 to take no action because the federal government, the states, and the private sector lacked the money and personnel to remove safely the deteriorating asbestos.[11]

Chemical Testing

Chemical testing of any sort is time consuming and costly, but when the long-term effects of a chemical are investigated, studies may require decades. Moreover, substances currently suspected of toxic effects often have not existed long enough for long-term impacts to be apparent. Today's middle-aged, American blue-collar workers may be the first generation of U.S. laborers to reveal the chronic effects of workplace exposure to chemicals introduced in American industry during World War II. If testing deals with chronic effects of exposure to small quantities of chemicals—doses as small as parts per billion or trillion—difficulties in identifying the presence of the substance and the rate of exposure among affected populations may be formidable. Thus, a major problem in regulating dangerous substances has been to obtain the essential test data on which determinations of risk depend.

Pesticides illustrate the test burden confronting EPA. Most of the 50,000 pesticide products used in the United States since 1947 were registered before their long-term effects were understood. Amendments in 1972 to the existing federal insecticide, fungicide, and rodenticide legislation require the EPA to reevaluate all existing pesticides in light of new information about their effects on humans and the environment. More than 3 billion pounds of pesticide are used annually in the United States. These contain about 600 active ingredients that must be reviewed by the EPA. The EPA has prohibited, or limited severely, the use of many pesticides, including DDT, aldrin, dieldrin, toxaphene, and ethylene dibromide, and, as a result, levels of persistent pesticides in human fatty tissue have declined from about 8 parts per million (ppm) in 1970 to slightly more than 2 ppm in the mid-1980s. However, the EPA is decades behind in reviewing all the active ingredients and the pesticide compounds made from these ingredients.

Airborne Toxics

In the 1990s airborne toxics received major federal attention for the first time, adding an additional large category of substances to the EPA's regulatory responsibilities. The Superfund Amendments and Reauthorization Act of 1986 (SARA) required the EPA to create the first national inventory of toxic releases into the environment from industries in the United States. Almost all of these chemicals are among the 188 specifically destined for regulation under the Clean Air Act Amendments of 1990. The latest *Toxic Release Inventory* (TRI), issued by the EPA in mid-1997, disclosed discharges totaling 1.7 billion pounds in 1995— about 77 pounds per person in the United States.[12] These discharges included:

- 1.2 billion pounds of air emissions
- 302 million pounds of surface water emissions to streams, rivers, and lakes
- 150 million pounds of underground waste injections
- 266 million pounds of direct land releases

One encouraging aspect of the 1995 report is the significant decrease in the total volume of toxic releases: between 1988 (the first reporting year) and 1995, the volume decreased by 47 percent (see Figure 7-1). However, the TRI greatly underestimates the total volume of toxic

Figure 7-1   Distribution of TRI Releases, 1988–1995

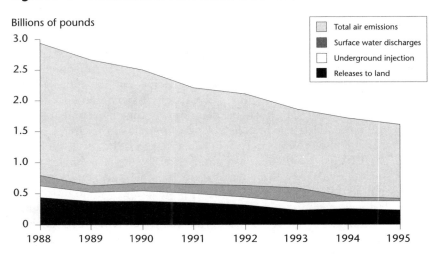

Billions of pounds

Legend:
- Total air emissions
- Surface water discharges
- Underground injection
- Releases to land

Source: Environmental Protection Agency, Office of Pollution Prevention and Toxics, *1995 Toxics Release Inventory, Chapter 5: Year-to-Year Comparisons of TRI Data* (Washington, D.C.: Environmental Protection Agency, 1997), 119.

Note: Does not include delisted chemicals; chemicals added in 1990, 1991, 1994, and 1995; and aluminum oxide, ammonia, hydrochloric acid, and sulfuric acid.

releases because it excludes facilities with fewer than ten employees, all manufacturing and processing plants discharging less than 25,000 pounds of a listed chemical, and such important non-manufacturing industries as mining and electric utilities. Nonetheless, the TRI has demonstrated the enormous scale of the toxic release problem that affects every state and territory (see Table 7-2). The TRI has also become an especially effective psychological weapon for environmentalists because the average American now can readily identify the nature and source of toxic releases at home or work.

Abandoned Wastes

Two decades ago, the discovery of a huge abandoned toxic waste site near Niagara, New York, made the site—called Love Canal—a national synonym for chemical contamination. The debacle of Love Canal rapidly escalated into a national media event dramatizing to Americans the apparent danger of abandoned toxic wastes throughout the United States. A flood tide of further media revelations about abandoned chemical wastes throughout America followed, together with intense environmentalist lobbying and growing public pressure for congressional response. In the crisis-driven style characteristic of the 1970s, Congress reacted by passing in 1980 the Comprehensive Environmental Response, Compensation, and Liability Act (CERCLA), popularly called the "Superfund," which included an appropriation of $1.6 billion to clean up the nation's worst abandoned hazardous and toxic waste sites. By the latter 1990s, however, it was evident that the magnitude of the abandoned waste problem and the cost to clean up the worst abandoned waste sites far exceeded original expectations. Moreover, Superfund's implementation proceeds glacially. By 1997, 500 of the nation's worst 1,275 waste sites (the National Priority List) identified by the EPA had been cleaned up substantially. But the EPA expects to add about 100 additional sites to this priority list annually until the total reaches approximately 2,100 by the year 2000.[13] Superfund, plagued from its inception by mammoth cost overruns, technical complexities, political squabbles, and endless litigation, now lumbers toward an uncertain future amid growing debate over its necessity and effectiveness.

Most of the waste annually produced in the United States is not dangerous if it is properly disposed. But a ton (literally) of hazardous waste is created annually for every American in the United States. Among the more than 14,000 regulated producers of waste, the overwhelming majority are chemical manufacturers or allied industries that produce almost 80 percent of the nation's hazardous waste. Other significant sources include mining and milling, municipal household and commercial waste, and the processing of radioactive materials. America's chemical junkyards are increasing in volume by an estimated 3 to 10 percent annually. Superfund regulations required the EPA to identify the total number of dangerous abandoned waste sites currently in the United States; the EPA has estimated that there are at least 58,000 such sites, but many experts believe the actual number of sites may exceed this estimate by at least 20,000.[14] In 1982, as required by Superfund, the EPA released its first National Priority List of the nation's most dangerous waste dumps. By 1995, the list of actual and proposed "priority sites" had grown to 1,270, distributed across the United States as indicated in Table 7-3.

Contributing to the abandoned waste problem is the deep burial or underground injection method commonly used to dispose of many hazardous substances. More than half the nation's liquid waste is flushed into deep underground cavities, or water systems, where it is presumed to disperse too deeply to contaminate water or soil used by humans. However, such disposal is seldom carefully monitored or regulated. Experts suspect that many hazardous materials buried in this way will

Table 7-2 TRI Releases by State or Territory, 1995

State or territory	Facilities (N)	Total air emissions (lbs.)	Surface water discharges (lbs.)	Underground injection (lbs.)	Releases to land (lbs.)	Total releases (lbs.)
Alabama	520	91,867,818	3,589,626	16	7,307,586	102,765,046
Alaska	10	5,405,584	1,070,617	193	483,911	6,960,305
American Samoa	1	5,300	0	0	0	5,300
Arizona	187	7,306,986	4,829	14	28,520,806	35,832,635
Arkansas	387	29,792,097	916,093	2,637,068	1,336,719	34,681,977
California	1,478	36,819,632	2,641,665	478,974	2,786,805	42,727,076
Colorado	182	4,159,933	294,179	0	121,314	4,575,426
Connecticut	329	7,179,523	1,489,456	0	95,110	8,764,089
Delaware	71	4,209,960	286,148	0	14,327	4,510,435
District of Columbia	3	10,460	255	0	19,000	29,715
Florida	528	32,028,305	821,305	25,343,332	25,779,920	83,972,862
Georgia	718	47,606,516	6,345,066	0	1,572,312	55,523,894
Guam	1	0	3,100	0	0	3,100
Hawaii	16	443,607	1,510	24,306	545	469,968
Idaho	60	4,689,903	1,390,186	0	2,107,947	8,188,036
Illinois	1,334	70,935,342	5,779,855	365	23,037,696	99,753,258
Indiana	1,008	70,573,627	2,357,535	3,398	6,843,418	79,777,978
Iowa	410	29,600,556	3,783,443	0	1,381,081	34,765,080
Kansas	279	19,450,900	394,121	1,674,129	1,297,174	22,816,324
Kentucky	418	40,703,729	432,680	0	788,794	41,925,203
Louisiana	314	84,841,485	28,268,576	54,494,533	4,654,598	172,259,192
Maine	92	9,242,209	610,781	0	314,865	10,167,855
Maryland	194	8,868,815	1,881,350	0	2,571,728	13,321,893
Massachusetts	509	7,996,222	116,200	0	28,631	8,141,053
Michigan	903	62,996,379	653,999	7,566,827	4,046,748	75,263,953
Minnesota	493	21,559,433	375,055	0	525,136	22,459,624
Mississippi	322	44,048,247	8,373,840	82,251	4,250,916	56,755,254

Missouri	568	31,778,685	3,282,973	0	14,585,208	49,646,866
Montana	27	4,374,595	96,659	0	39,420,586	43,891,840
Nebraska	164	10,014,706	283,104	0	660,179	10,957,989
Nevada	36	1,349,667	0	0	2,209,741	3,559,408
New Hampshire	99	2,472,394	79,718	0	10,960	2,563,072
New Jersey	607	12,728,407	1,632,366	5	284,578	14,645,356
New Mexico	37	1,892,903	1,153	0	16,812,196	18,706,252
New York	723	30,045,576	5,334,499	5	1,192,979	36,573,059
North Carolina	874	65,805,573	2,622,401	5	17,732,509	86,160,483
North Dakota	35	2,538,973	21,589	0	1,275	2,561,837
Ohio	1,623	73,749,306	3,433,797	14,469,938	30,217,526	121,870,567
Oklahoma	270	23,563,664	718,224	10,238	661,337	24,953,463
Oregon	261	18,949,703	597,554	0	1,647,454	21,194,711
Pennsylvania	1,213	47,232,633	5,487,942	0	1,539,478	54,260,053
Puerto Rico	163	9,397,960	22,262	0	4,456	9,424,678
Rhode Island	145	2,734,284	48,475	0	40	2,782,799
South Carolina	494	51,850,487	1,747,320	0	741,224	54,339,031
South Dakota	72	1,911,132	1,487	0	387	1,913,006
Tennessee	633	103,130,070	1,549,615	1,174,570	5,328,644	111,182,899
Texas	1,193	128,694,945	23,413,945	118,850,176	12,973,077	283,932,143
Utah	148	69,215,983	16,236	0	7,089,515	76,321,734
Vermont	38	547,459	2,712	0	2,674	552,845
Virgin islands	2	1,403,451	30,876	0	2,461	1,436,788
Virginia	447	50,856,146	872,506	0	1,184,680	52,913,332
Washington	286	24,025,989	2,367,757	0	57,224	26,450,970
West Virginia	139	18,393,929	8,665,922	1,000	296,542	27,357,393
Wisconsin	858	28,534,060	2,094,078	5	549,601	31,177,744
Wyoming	29	2,786,865	8,984	8,168,366	38,347	11,002,562
Total	21,951	1,562,322,113	136,315,624	234,979,709	275,131,965	2,208,749,411

Source: Environmental Protection Agency, Office of Pollution Prevention and Toxics, *1995 Toxics Release Inventory, Chapter 4: TRI Releases and Transfers* (Washington, D.C.: Environmental Protection Agency, 1997), 24.

Table 7-3   Hazardous Waste Sites on the National Priority List,
by State or Territory, 1995

State or territory	Total sites	Rank	Percent distribution	Federal	Non-federal
Alabama	13	30	1.02	3	10
Alaska	8	42	0.63	6	2
Arizona	10	38	0.79	3	7
Arkansas	12	32	0.94	0	12
California	96	3	7.56	23	73
Colorado	18	21	1.42	3	15
Connecticut	15	27	1.18	1	14
Delaware	19	20	1.50	1	18
District of Columbia	0	NA	0.00	0	0
Florida	55	6	4.33	5	50
Georgia	14	28	1.10	2	12
Guam	2	NA	NA	1	1
Hawaii	4	45	0.31	3	1
Idaho	10	38	0.79	2	8
Illinois	38	9	2.99	4	34
Indiana	33	12	2.60	0	33
Iowa	17	23	1.34	1	16
Kansas	13	30	1.02	2	11
Kentucky	20	19	1.57	1	19
Louisiana	17	23	1.34	1	16
Maine	12	32	0.94	3	9
Maryland	14	28	1.10	5	9
Massachusetts	30	13	2.36	8	22
Michigan	78	5	6.14	1	77
Minnesota	37	11	2.91	3	34
Mississippi	4	45	0.31	0	4
Missouri	22	18	1.73	3	19
Montana	9	41	0.71	0	9
Nebraska	10	38	0.79	1	9
Nevada	1	50	0.08	0	1
New Hampshire	17	23	1.34	1	16

migrate through subsurface water flows until they contaminate drinking water wells, aquifers used for irrigation, lakes, rivers, or soil. For these reasons, the National Academy of Science has recommended that the federal government promote incineration, chemical processing, or other more modern procedures for waste disposal.

The Rush to Regulate

Considering all the difficulties involved in regulating toxic and hazardous substances, Congress and environmentalists expected too much of science by requiring in the Toxic Substances Control Act of 1976 that all new chemicals be screened before marketing to determine their toxi-

Table 7-3   Continued

State or territory	Total sites	Rank	Percent distribution	Federal	Non-federal
New Jersey	107	1	8.43	6	101
New Mexico	11	36	0.87	2	9
New York	80	4	6.30	4	76
North Carolina	23	17	1.81	2	21
North Dakota	2	49	0.16	0	2
Ohio	38	9	2.99	5	33
Oklahoma	11	36	0.87	1	10
Oregon	12	32	0.94	2	10
Pennsylvania	103	2	8.11	6	97
Puerto Rico	9	NA	NA	1	8
Rhode Island	12	32	0.94	2	10
South Carolina	25	15	1.97	2	23
South Dakota	4	45	0.31	1	3
Tennessee	18	21	1.42	4	14
Texas	27	14	2.13	4	23
Utah	16	26	1.26	4	12
Vermont	8	42	0.63	0	8
Virgin Islands	2	NA	NA	0	2
Virginia	24	16	1.89	6	18
Washington	52	7	4.09	17	35
West Virginia	7	44	0.55	2	5
Wisconsin	41	8	3.23	0	41
Wyoming	3	48	0.24	1	2
Total	1,283	NA	NA	159	1,124
United States	1,270	NA	100.0	157	1,113

Source: U.S. Department of Commerce, Bureau of the Census, *Statistical Abstract of the United States, 1996* (Washington, D.C.: Government Printing Office, 1996), 238.

Note: NA = not applicable. Includes both proposed and final sites listed on the National Priorities List for the Superfund program as authorized by the Comprehensive Environmental Response, Compensation, and Liability Act of 1980 and the Superfund Amendments and Reauthorization Act of 1986.

city. It is difficult, perhaps impossible, to know in advance how a chemical will be used, in what quantities, and where, even though manufacturers are required to provide an estimate in their "Premanufacture Notice" to the EPA.[15]

The Risk Problem

The risk assessment problems discussed in Chapter 4 abound with toxic and hazardous chemical regulation, as illustrated by the continuing controversy over the effects of toxic chemicals on the neighborhood adjacent to the Love Canal dump site. In late 1982, the EPA released the results of a massive inquiry it had made, along with the U.S. Public

Health Service, into the health effects of the Love Canal site. Contrary to earlier studies by the state of New York, the EPA asserted that it had found the neighborhood near Love Canal no less safe for residents than any other part of Niagara Falls, New York. The evidence seemed formidable. More than 6,000 samples of human and environmental materials near the site were collected and subjected to 150,000 analytical measurements to determine what contaminants they contained. This evidence suggested that only a ring of houses a block from the waste site or closer had been affected significantly. But the study was challenged immediately because 90 percent of the samples were free of *any* chemicals. This, asserted experts, could mean either an absence of chemicals or insufficient sensitivity among the measuring procedures. Although the assistant secretary for health and the deputy EPA administrator for New York testified to congressional committees that they were confident the undetected chemicals could not be present in more than minute quantities, the Environmental Defense Fund's own scientific expert asserted that so much variance existed in the competence of the many laboratories conducting the tests and so many sources of error could exist in some tests that chemicals could indeed have been present. Officials at the National Bureau of Standards also questioned the sensitivity of the test procedures. Less than a year later, the federal Centers for Disease Control released their own study of former Love Canal area residents, indicating that they were no more likely to suffer chromosome damage than residents elsewhere in Niagara Falls. Even if such damage were present, noted the study, it was impossible to know if it was linked to the later occurrence of illnesses.[16]

Uncertainties about risk must almost be assumed to be a constant in regulating hazardous substances, and as a consequence, errors of judgment leading to excessively strict regulation or perhaps to dangerously negligent control of chemical substances are probably inevitable. In general, Congress and the regulatory agencies implementing congressional hazardous waste programs have been risk-averse, preferring to err, if err they must, in the direction of stricter control and more willingness to accept pessimistic estimates of risk from toxic substances. Beginning with the later years of the Carter administration, however, federal agencies have moved toward greater attention to costs and regulatory complexity in setting standards of exposure and control.

Costs and Complexity

It is doubtful that either friend or foe of the federal regulatory programs enacted in the mid-1970s realistically understood the enormous expense that would be involved in the new hazardous substance legislation. New regulatory agencies would have to be created, or existing ones expanded. An inventory of many thousands of chemicals would have to be created, existing literature on the health effects of chemicals searched, new research initiated, new regulations promulgated, litigation involving the legality of new regulatory standards conducted, and so forth. Only as regulatory agencies began the first tentative steps in assembling data on the human and environmental effects of chemical substances did the vast vacuum of relevant information become obvious. A major reason for the protracted delays in implementing the new laws has been the tedious but essential work of building a foundation of necessary technical data on which regulatory standards could be erected. The collective costs to the 14,000 regulated chemical manufacturers will add billions of dollars to the regulatory total.

A small sample of direct and indirect costs associated with recent hazardous substance legislation can only suggest the scale on which such regulatory programs must operate:

> The average priority abandoned waste site cleaned up by the EPA under Superfund legislation has cost $2.1 million and will cost far more in the future; the aggregate expense for eliminating all the nation's worst abandoned waste sites is expected to be many times the initial Superfund authorization of $1.6 billion.[17]

> The EPA's regulations for disposal of hazardous waste on land sites exceeded 500 pages in the *Federal Register*. EPA officials say the costs of compliance for the affected industries will exceed $1 billion yearly.[18]

When massive costs are projected against the fragmentary scientific data on the effects of many chemicals and the often tenuous evidence relating to chronic impacts from extremely low levels of exposure, arguments over the acceptability of the costs in light of the benefits inevitably arise. Critics of federal environmental programs have asserted that most impose not only unacceptable costs for the regulation of acknowledged hazards but also staggering costs for the stringent control of substances with unproven effects. Some critics, including leaders in the Reagan and Bush administrations, argued that costs and benefits should become a routinely important—though not necessarily the most important—factor in determining whether a substance should be regulated.

Criticism of regulatory costs often feeds on the disparity between the timing and character of the costs and the timing and character of the benefits from regulation. The costs tend to be tangible, immediate, and massive: dollars must be spent, agencies created, rules promulgated, and other expensive actions initiated. In contrast, years or decades may pass before any apparent benefits accrue. The benefits may be intangibles—

deaths and illnesses prevented, public costs of future regulation avoided, or public safety enhanced—that tend to be discounted by those who must pay for regulation in the present. Examples exist that show how the future benefits of regulation can be enormous. The number of U.S. deaths from exposure as much as forty years ago to asbestos will grow to between 8,000 and 10,000 annually by the century's end. More than 100,000 claims outstanding against major asbestos manufacturers in the late 1990s must be settled. The current value of these future claims has been estimated conservatively at $40 billion.[19]

An Emerging Controversy: Endocrine Disruptors

The list of worrisome chemicals enlarged in the latter 1990s when scientific and governmental attention suddenly turned to a potentially huge inventory of chemicals called "endocrine disruptors." Scientific research has suggested that certain externally produced chemicals, especially many human-made synthetic compounds, may sometimes mimic naturally produced hormones in humans and animals and may interfere, perhaps disastrously, with the normal functioning of the endocrine system. Many of these disruptors, according to some scientific theories, gain their potency from the bioaccumulation of extremely small doses in human and animal tissue over long periods of time. The possible human health effects could include cancers of the reproductive system, reduced sperm counts in males, abnormalities of fetal development leading to learning and behavioral disorders, and many other pathologies associated with hormonal malfunctions. Among animals, some scientists believe that disruptors have been responsible for sexual abnormalities and deformities in gulls, terns, eagles, and fish.[20]

If endocrine disruptors exist, apprehension seems prudent. "The number of substances which have been suggested as possibly contributing to perturbation of the endocrine system . . . is vast," explains one careful study of the issue. "Man-made or generated substances include broad classes of chlorinated and non-chlorinated compounds and heavy metals widely used in industrial and household products such as paints, detergents, lubricants, cosmetics, textiles, pesticides, and plastics, as well as byproducts of sewage treatment and waste incineration and other forms of combustion. Many pharmaceutical products, including contraceptives, have hormonal activity. There are also large amounts of plant hormones (mainly phytoestrogens) commonly ingested in human (and animal) diets—especially vegetarian products. . . ."[21] In short, something to unnerve everybody. Yet the disruptor issue emerges from a fog of enormous uncertainty and scientific controversy. The effect of disruptors on humans and animals, the identity of truly dangerous substances, the results of long- and short-term exposures, the relative dangers to adults and fetuses, and much more are largely unknown. Scientists themselves disagree about the danger. "Even though sound scientific evidence can be found on both sides . . . simple cause and effect data are not available," explains one expert review of the evidence. "But even without certain scientific evidence, the potential health, social and economic effects are forcing government, organizations and the general public to take notice." [22]

The public history of endocrine disruptors is the very model of how environmental issues acquire political clout. Expert meetings held in the United States in 1991 and 1993 first called major scientific attention to the possible danger of endocrine disruptors. However, the issue's political momentum began to mount when the BBC broadcast in 1993 a documentary, "Assault on the Male," which suggested that human and animal reproductive problems might both arise from endocrine disruptors. The issue rose to national attention with the publication in 1996 of *Our Stolen Future,* written by a team of America scientific interpreters, who vividly described the menace presumably posed by disruptors:

> Hormone-disrupting chemicals are not classical poisons or typical carcinogens. They play by different rules. They defy the linear logic of current testing protocols built on the assumption that higher doses do more damage. For this reason, contrary to our long-held assumptions, screening chemicals for cancer risk has not always protected us from other kinds of harm. Some hormonally active chemicals appear to pose little if any risk of cancer . . . such chemicals are typically not poisons in the normal sense. Until we recognize this, we will be looking in the wrong places, asking the wrong questions. . . .[23]

This aura of mystery, dread, and imminence proved to be a powerful political catalyst, creating further media attention, provoking public concern, and compelling a response from governmental officials. In 1996, Congress reacted by amending several major federal environmental and public health laws to require that EPA within three years create a screening program to determine whether endocrine disruptors existed and, if they do, take appropriate measures to control adverse health effects. EPA, in turn, appointed a scientific advisory committee on endocrine disruptors in 1996 and its work is currently proceeding.

Chemical Threat or Chemiphobia?

Endocrine disruptors raise anew the recurring controversy about whether the public and its governments have become chemiphobic—exaggerating the health risks posed by chemicals and intolerant of even reasonable risks. The controversy grows with the relentless increase in the cost and complexity of regulation. One issue is the actual danger from abandoned hazardous waste sites. A 1992 report of the National Research Council, for instance, declared that toxic waste cleanup is still impeded by difficulty in discriminating between dumps that pose significant health hazards and those that do not. In particular, the report noted "a striking lack of scientific data" about how people are affected by exposure to low levels of chemicals leaking into air or water."[24] Thus, while experts agree that the public should be concerned about health risks associated with exposure to chemical substances and chemical wastes, they cannot easily determine *which* kinds of exposure and *how much* exposure are unacceptably risky. A related issue is that the elimination of *all* risk from exposure to hazardous or toxic substances is often impossible or unacceptably expensive, yet federal regulations such as the Superfund legislation do not clearly define how much cleanup is enough. The problem, two informed critics observed, is "how clean is 'clean,'" and the solution is not apparent. Marc Landy and Mary Hague comment:

> In principle, one would want to clean until [an abandoned hazardous waste] site is called perfectly "safe." However . . . there is no scientifically identifiable point at which an "unsafe" site becomes "safe." No matter how much cleanup has been performed at a site, it can always be argued that more cleanup would reduce risk even further.[25]

A second issue involves political chemistry. When public fear about hazardous substances blends with official eagerness to appear tough on pollution, the resulting "risk averse" political climate often spawns hasty, severe regulatory policies. The political synergy between public fear and governmental overreaction often results, as we have previously observed, in targeting for greatest attention those pollutants exciting the greatest public apprehension rather than those posing the most scientifically documented health risks. Risk-averse regulation can result in a regulatory intolerance for even minimal health risks, mistaken environmental priorities, and excessive regulatory costs.

Finally, regulatory costs have been especially controversial in hazardous and toxic substance regulation because of the very rapid and severe escalation in the number of regulations and the growing recognition that future regulations will cost enormously more. Federal regulations released in 1991, for instance, require all municipal landfills to be built with plastic and clay liners, liquid collectors, and treatment systems to prevent leaking toxic waste. This has raised the cost of opening a new municipal waste dump to more than $10 million and forced most of the country's existing 6,500 landfills to close. However, future landfill costs may be far greater as the variety of waste-dump toxics and their health risks are better documented.[26]

To many critics, all these problems are proof of "chemiphobia" impelling governmental regulators to appease public opinion through excessively harsh chemical controls at enormous economic, scientific, and political cost to the nation. To many conservative critics, these regulations are too often "animated by a quasi-religious mind-set that combines an aversion to even minimal risks with a strong preference for governmental intervention in markets and a fierce hostility toward corporations."[27] Even the many experts who disagree with these conclusions often recognize, as subsequent discussion will reveal, that toxic and hazardous substance regulation is the most difficult, least satisfactory domain of contemporary environmental policy making.

Federal Law: Regulation from the Cradle to the Grave?

Among the two dozen federal laws relating to hazardous or toxic substances, three passed in the 1970s define the fundamental framework for regulating the disposal of these substances: the Toxic Substances Control Act of 1976, the Resource Conservation and Recovery Act of 1976 (RCRA), and the Comprehensive Environmental Response, Compensation, and Liability Act of 1980 (more commonly known as Superfund). These laws represent a congressional effort to create a comprehensive regulatory regime for all chemical substances from initial development to final disposal—the cradle-to-grave control that seemed essential to achieving for the first time responsible public management of chemical products. Few laws, even by the standard of recent environmental legislation, mandate a more complex and technically formidable administrative process than do these programs. A brief review of the major provisions will suggest the immense regulatory tasks involved.

TSCA: Regulating Chemical Manufacture and Distribution

The major purpose of TSCA and its important 1986 amendments (the Asbestos Hazard Emergency Response Act) is to regulate the creation, manufacture, and distribution of chemical substances so that those hazardous to humans and the environment can be identified early and then controlled properly before they become fugitive throughout the ecosystem. TSCA and its amendments require the EPA to achieve five broad objectives:

1. *Gather Information.* The EPA is required to issue rules asking chemical manufacturers and processors to submit to the administrator information about their use of important chemicals. The information is to include the chemical's name, its formula, uses, estimates of production

levels, description of byproducts, data on adverse health and environmental effects, and the number of workers exposed to the chemical. In achieving these goals the administrator also is to:

    a. publish a list of all existing chemicals

    b. see that all persons manufacturing, processing, or distributing chemicals in commerce keep records on adverse health reactions, submit to EPA required health and safety studies, and report to EPA information suggesting that a chemical represents a previously undetected significant risk to health or the environment

2. *Screen New Chemicals.* Manufacturers of new chemicals are to notify the EPA at least ninety days before producing the chemical commercially. Information similar to that required for existing chemicals is required for new chemicals also. The EPA is allowed to suspend temporarily the manufacture of any new chemical in the absence of adequate information as required under the law and to suspend permanently a new chemical if it finds a "reasonable basis to conclude that the chemical presents or will present an unreasonable risk of injury to health or the environment."

3. *Test Chemicals.* The EPA is given the authority to require manufacturers or processors of potentially harmful chemicals to test them. An Interagency Testing Committee, composed of representatives from eight federal agencies, was created to recommend to the EPA priorities for chemical testing. As many as fifty chemicals are allowed to be recommended for testing within one year.

4. *Control Chemicals.* The EPA is required to take action against chemical substances or mixtures for which a reasonable basis exists to conclude that the manufacture, processing, distribution, use, or disposal presents an unreasonable risk of injury to health or the environment. Permitted actions range from a labeling requirement to a complete ban. The control requirements are not to "place an undue burden on industry," yet at the same time they are to provide an adequate margin of protection against unreasonable risk. TSCA specifically required regulation and eventual elimination of PCBs.

5. *Control Asbestos.* The EPA is required to develop a strategy for implementing the congressional mandate that all schools be inspected for asbestos-containing material, and develop and implement plans to control the threat of any asbestos discovered.

RCRA: Regulating Solid Waste

The major purposes of RCRA and its 1980 and 1984 amendments are to control solid waste management practices that could endanger public health or the environment and to promote resource conservation and recovery. Solid wastes are defined in the Act to include waste solids, sludges, liquids, and contained gases—all forms in which discarded hazardous or toxic substances might be found. In addition to providing federal assistance to state and local governments in developing comprehensive solid waste management programs, RCRA also mandates the following:

1. *Criteria for Environmentally Safe Disposal Sites.* The EPA is required to issue regulations defining the minimum criteria for solid waste disposal sites considered environmentally safe. It is also required to publish an inventory of all U.S. facilities failing to meet these criteria.

2. *Regulating Hazardous Waste.* The EPA is required to develop criteria for identifying hazardous waste, to publish the characteristics of hazardous wastes and lists of particular hazardous wastes, and to create a "manifest system" that tracks hazardous wastes from their points of origin to their final disposal sites. The EPA also is to create a permit system that would require all individuals or industries generating hazardous waste to obtain a permit before managing such waste. Permits would be issued only to waste managers meeting the safe disposal criteria created by the EPA.

3. *Resource Recovery and Waste Reduction.* The Act requires the Commerce Department to promote commercialization of waste recovery, to encourage markets for recovered wastes, and to promote waste recovery technologies and research into waste conservation.

4. *State Implementation.* The Act provides for state implementation of regulations affecting solid waste management and disposal if state programs meet federal standards. The EPA will enforce these provisions in states that do not, or cannot, comply with federal regulations for the program's enforcement.

5. *Mandated Deadlines and Waste-by-Waste Review.* The 1984 amendments create deadlines for the EPA to set standards for disposal of specific wastes or congressionally mandated standards will be applied. The EPA is also ordered to evaluate nineteen specific substances, and deadlines are established for the Agency to regulate new kinds of waste disposal activity.

The 1984 amendments—bristling with mandated deadlines and meticulously detailed instructions—bespeak a profound congressional distrust of the EPA's commitment to enforcing RCRA during the first Reagan administration. The amendments were conceived in an atmosphere strident with congressional censure of the EPA. Sen. George J. Mitchell (D-Maine) captured the mood of the majority:

[S]trong congressional expression of disapproval of EPA's slow and timid implementation of the existing law is necessary, as well as a clear congressional direction mandating certain bold, preventive actions by EPA which will not be taken otherwise. . . . The Agency has missed deadlines, proposed inadequate regulations, and even exacerbated the hazardous waste problem by suspending certain regulations.[28]

Congress was determined to drive the EPA hard. So Congress instructed the EPA in exquisite detail concerning how to implement virtually every aspect of RCRA, from the allowable permeability of liners for surface impoundments to the concentrations at which many different chemical wastes must be banned from land disposal. Twenty-nine different deadlines for specific program activities were listed: a ban on land disposal of bulk liquid in landfills within six months, new regulations for small quantity waste generators within seventeen months, interim construction standards for underground storage tanks within four months, and so forth.[29]

Superfund

When the first Superfund legislation was enacted, the nation's abandoned and uncontrolled hazardous waste dumps were largely an uncharted wasteland. The nation's governments knew little about the location or composition of many waste sites, some abandoned longer than memory of their existence. The law seldom clearly placed financial responsibility for the management or removal of these wastes with their creators; liability for damage or injury to individuals or communities from such wastes often was difficult, or impossible, to assign or to enforce. Often, procedures for cleaning up waste sites were unknown, or local officials were ignorant of them. The financial burden on state and local governments to control or remove these wastes seemed overwhelming. Because a comprehensive, collaborative program among the nation's governments seemed essential, Congress attempted to address these and other major abandoned waste problems through four major Superfund programs:

1. *Information Gathering and Analysis.* Owners of hazardous waste sites were required to notify the EPA by June 1981 about the character of buried wastes. Using this information, the EPA would create a list of national sites.

2. *Federal Response to Emergencies.* The Act authorized the EPA to respond to hazardous substance emergencies and to clean up leaking chemical dump sites if the responsible parties failed to take appropriate action or could not be located.

3. *The Hazardous Substance Response Fund.* The Act created an initial trust fund of $1.6 billion to finance the removal, cleanup, or remedy of hazardous waste sites. About 86 percent of the fund was to be financed from a tax on manufacturers of petrochemical feedstocks and organic chemicals and on crude oil importers. The remainder was to come from general federal revenues.

4. *Liability for Cleanup.* The Act placed liability for cleaning up waste sites and for other restitution on those responsible for release of the hazardous substances.

By the mid-1980s, it was obvious that the number of abandoned sites needing immediate cleanup and the costs had been grossly underestimated. The 1984 chemical disaster at Bhopal, India, had drawn congressional attention to our own national lack of community planning for chemical emergencies. And Congress was increasingly critical of the slow pace of Superfund site cleanups. In 1986, Congress passed the Superfund Amendments and Reauthorization Act, which changed the original legislation significantly.

1. *Greatly Increased Spending.* The new amendments authorize an additional $8.5 billion for NPL site cleanups and an additional $500 million specifically to clean up pollution created by abandoned underground liquid storage tanks.

2. *New Cleanup Standards.* The standards mandated for all sites are to be permanent remedies to the maximum extent practicable, using the best available technologies. State standards for cleanup are to be followed when they are more stringent than federal standards. The public living near sites are to be informed about all phases of the process and involved in these activities.

3. *The Emergency Planning and Community Right-to-Know Act.* Title III of SARA authorizes communities to get detailed information about chemicals made by, stored in, and emitted from local businesses. It requires the formation of state and local planning committees to draw up a chemical emergency response plan for every community in the nation.

As much as feasible, the intent of Congress was to make the creators of hazardous waste sites bear as much financial responsibility as possible for ensuring the safety of the sites. With Superfund, Congress finished its attempt to craft within less than a decade the first truly comprehensive federal regulation of virtually all hazardous or toxic materials in the United States. With TSCA, RCRA, and Superfund, Congress in effect ordered the federal government, in collaboration with state and local authorities, to become the primary manager of all dangerous chemical substances currently used or planned for production.

The Regulatory Thicket

All these regulatory programs, each a morass of administrative and technical complexity, were passed in less than four years. The EPA and other responsible governmental agencies were confronted with an avalanche of new regulatory mandates, bristling with insistent compliance deadlines, for which they were expected to be rapidly prepared. It is doubtful that the agencies could have discharged satisfactorily these responsibilities under the most benign circumstances. From their inception, all the programs were afflicted in varying degrees by technical, administrative, and political problems impeding their development. By the late 1990s, most of these programs were running years behind statutory deadlines, mandated or not. The nation is still at serious risk from the hazardous and toxic waste problems Congress intended to remedy with TSCA, RCRA, and Superfund. Serious doubt exists that the programs will ever achieve their legislative objectives without radical reformulation.

Regulatory Achievements: Significant But Few

There have been a few conspicuous successes. Federal regulations have largely eliminated the manufacture of PCBs, chemicals used primarily in commercial electrical equipment such as capacitors and transformers. Of the billion pounds produced in the United States between 1929 and 1976 (when PCB production was halted), less than 300 million pounds are still used in millions of electrical devices.[30] High levels of PCBs in human tissue declined from 12 percent of the population in 1979 to virtually 0 percent in the late 1980s. Trace amounts, once found in as many as 62 percent of the U.S. population, declined to approximately 9 percent by the late 1980s.[31]

In conjunction with the Federal Insecticide, Fungicide, and Rodenticide Act, the newer regulatory programs have largely eliminated all domestic uses of the pesticides DDT, aldrin, dieldrin, toxaphene, and ethylene dibromide and most domestic uses of chlordane and heptachlor, all known carcinogens. Asbestos is slowly being eliminated from domestic commerce and industry. U.S. production of asbestos has dropped by more than half since 1976 and practically all industrial and commercial uses are being eliminated. In 1978, the EPA banned the use of chlorofluorocarbons from domestic aerosol cans, an important first step in controlling the destruction of the atmospheric ozone layer. The elimination or reduction of these substances removes some of the most dangerous and widespread chemicals in the United States, yet these represent only a tiny portion of the chemicals known, or strongly suspected, of posing grave risks to humans or the environment.

TSCA and RCRA: Administrative Overload

TSCA and RCRA abound in delays and complications. Many of these problems arise from the volume and complexity of work thrust on the EPA within a few years. The numerous failures in program implementation also testify to the difficulty in obtaining technical data, to protracted scientific disputes over regulatory decisions, to lack of resources and experience in program management, and to past political interference that plunged the EPA into demoralizing and acrimonious disputes with Congress.

One formidable problem is that each new law requires the EPA to assume the initiative for creating and interpreting a vast volume of integrated technical information. Obtaining the data often requires that chemical manufacturers, processors, consumers, and waste depositors provide timely, accurate information—information they previously guarded jealously. With this heavy burden of initiative, the Agency would have been hard pressed to meet all its program obligations under TSCA and RCRA with even the most benevolent funding and generous personnel levels. The Reagan administration's sharp budget reductions in the early 1980s severely impaired the EPA's regulatory performance even after modest improvements occurred in the late 1980s. For instance, Sections 8(a) and (b) of TSCA required the EPA to create an inventory of chemicals manufactured or imported into the United States from 1975 to 1977. By 1985, the inventory included more than 63,000 chemicals. But the EPA had no resources to verify the accuracy of the information provided. The inventory had not been updated by the end of the Reagan administration even though many chemicals listed were no longer produced, the production volume and location may have changed, and many new chemicals should have been added.[32]

The required testing of potentially harmful chemicals has been an exercise in frustration. Consider, for instance, the Agency's attempt to create test rules for a whole category of chemicals. Some chemical groups are quite small, but others are voluminous: the aryl phosphates include about 300 existing chemicals with more continually being manufactured. The chemical industry complained that testing by broad categories would involve very high costs, would stigmatize many "innocent" chemicals along with dangerous ones in the same group, and would prevent introduction of new chemicals until all existing chemicals in a category

Table 7-4   *Quantity of RCRA Hazardous Waste Generated and Number of Hazardous Waste Generators, by State or Territory, 1995*

State or territory	\<Hazardous Waste Quantity\> Rank	Tons generated	%	\<Large Quantity Generators\> Rank	N	%
Alabama	16	1,286,262	0.5	23	278	1.4
Alaska	51	3,438	0.0	42	65	0.3
Arizona	40	66,865	0.0	27	199	1.0
Arkansas	33	274,158	0.1	26	204	1.0
California	3	17,029,474	6.1	2	1,635	8.2
Colorado	36	169,554	0.1	31	156	0.8
Connecticut	30	310,825	0.1	18	395	2.0
Delaware	41	66,021	0.0	43	64	0.3
District of Columbia	54	764	0.0	49	18	0.1
Florida	22	558,122	0.2	17	414	2.1
Georgia	25	459,543	0.2	16	430	2.2
Guam	55	299	0.0	53	13	0.1
Hawaii	21	592,900	0.2	45	53	0.3
Idaho	17	1,209,841	0.4	46	52	0.3
Illinois	5	13,892,416	5.0	5	1,151	5.8
Indiana	12	1,733,196	0.6	10	606	3.0
Iowa	48	11,507	0.0	37	108	0.5
Kansas	13	1,722,483	0.6	25	212	1.1
Kentucky	18	1,149,881	0.4	14	440	2.2
Louisiana	4	15,469,654	5.5	21	359	1.8
Maine	45	19,459	0.0	33	144	0.7
Maryland	26	442,826	0.2	28	189	0.9
Massachusetts	20	606,282	0.2	12	472	2.4
Michigan	6	12,459,834	4.5	9	707	3.6
Minnesota	31	293,489	0.1	22	285	1.4
Mississippi	14	1,579,260	0.6	32	152	0.8
Missouri	42	62,070	0.0	29	181	0.9
Montana	50	7,640	0.0	47	51	0.3
Navajo Nation	56	195	0.0	54	11	0.1
Nebraska	38	89,878	0.0	43	64	0.3

are tested. Small wonder that the EPA explained its delay in establishing chemical testing guidelines by citing "gross underestimation of the number and complexity of the issues and time spent in resolving one-time issues."[33]

Another example of failed implementation relates to TSCA's requirements for PCB regulation. The EPA has issued regulations requiring all facilities having PCBs to properly mark, store, record, and dispose or destroy most items containing PCBs within a year after removal and storage. TSCA required the removal from service of perhaps a million electrical capacitors by late 1988 and thousands of PCB transformers by late 1990. The EPA has estimated that between 700,000 to 750,000 PCB

Table 7-4   *Continued*

State or territory	Hazardous Waste Quantity			Large Quantity Generators		
	Rank	Tons generated	%	Rank	N	%
Nevada	49	8,348	0.0	39	78	0.4
New Hampshire	43	26,009	0.0	34	130	0.7
New Jersey	27	437,202	0.2	7	1,049	5.3
New Mexico	35	204,494	0.1	48	44	0.2
New York	9	2,557,088	0.9	1	1,878	9.4
North Carolina	32	286,339	0.1	11	587	2.9
North Dakota	23	520,226	0.2	51	16	0.1
Ohio	11	1,774,939	0.6	3	1,354	6.8
Oklahoma	24	511,918	0.2	30	168	0.8
Oregon	39	68,187	0.0	24	220	1.1
Pennsylvania	15	1,523,362	0.5	6	1,110	5.6
Puerto Rico	19	893,006	0.3	41	68	0.3
Rhode Island	44	25,428	0.0	36	112	0.6
South Carolina	34	261,015	0.1	19	371	1.9
South Dakota	53	780	0.0	51	16	0.1
Tennessee	2	38,686,622	13.9	13	467	2.3
Texas	1	145,073,442	52.0	4	1,297	6.5
Trust Territories	46	12,154	0.0	55	3	0.0
Utah	28	418,523	0.1	38	98	0.5
Vermont	47	11,811	0.0	40	75	0.4
Virgin Islands	52	3,329	0.0	56	1	0.0
Virginia	37	98,678	0.0	19	371	1.9
Washington	8	3,250,971	1.2	8	721	3.6
West Virginia	7	8,489,828	3.0	35	117	0.6
Wisconsin	29	404,659	0.1	15	432	2.2
Wyoming	10	1,972,177	0.7	50	17	0.1
Total		279,088,670	100.0		19,908	100.0

Source: Environmental Protection Agency.

Note: Columns may not sum due to rounding.

storage sites exist—but the Agency cannot find most of them. "Because [EPA's site] lists are limited and out of date," reports the GAO, "EPA still does not know which facilities have PCBs. As a result, EPA has continued to inspect non-PCB facilities, while facilities with PCBs have gone without inspection."[34] RCRA's plodding progress defies the multitude of mandatory program deadlines intended to speed its implementation. For example, Congress had mandated deadlines for five major studies of large-volume waste producers. In late 1987, two of the studies had been issued, one on time and the other six years late. Both needed more information. The remaining studies were three to four years behind and the EPA did not complete them until 1990.[35] RCRA required the EPA to determine which wastes are hazardous and need regulation to protect human health and the environment. Over a thousand waste materials are likely to qualify for the list. By the late 1990s, the EPA had added few new wastes to that list. By 1998 the Agency was able to provide a rough estimate of the volume and location of regulated wastes. As Table 7-4 illustrates, every state shares some responsibility for the problem.

It is becoming evident, moreover, that the number of potential waste storage and treatment facilities in the United States requiring corrective actions under RCRA is likely to exceed vastly the initial estimates. The EPA has estimated that perhaps 3,700 waste treatment and storage facilities will require cleanup under RCRA rules, but by early 1998 only about 8 percent (301 sites) had completed the required cleanup while more than half had yet to initiate the necessary cleanup program.[36] Moreover, the current list of 20,000 facilities subject to RCRA inspections is likely to grow as more facilities are discovered. If the estimates are accurate, the size and scope of the cleanup program would be as large as the expected Superfund cleanup and may cost more than $22.7 billion. The cleanup of all sites may not be completed until the year 2025.

The impediments to the RCRA program are common to most federal regulatory efforts: cost and complexity, foot-dragging by regulated waste managers, insufficient money for needed oversight, and wrangling about cleanup terms. "The agency, the states, and companies often disagree on how cleanup should be pursued," explains the GAO. "These disagreements prolong the cleanup process because more time is needed [to define] the cleanup terms, and companies must sometimes meet the duplicate requirements of both federal and state regulators."[37]

Superfund: "The Largest, Most Complicated, and Most Disliked"

The Superfund program has been a consensus choice as the most controversial, expensive, and problematic of all the environmental era's showcase legislation—a legislative *Titanic* that only the most ardent environmentalists still believe is viable with minor repairs. Superfund statistics have often read like a regulatory requiem. Since Superfund's enactment in 1980, 1,600 abandoned hazardous waste dumps have been registered on the NPL of the most dangerous sites. Another 11,500 sites are considered potential additions. About 500 of these sites had been substantially cleaned up by early 1998.

A Slow and Costly Start.   Total Superfund costs will greatly exceed the $15.2 billion that Congress has so far authorized and the $26.4 billion that the EPA estimated in the early 1990s would be necessary to complete the program. Completed cleanups have averaged about $2.1 million each, but the EPA predicted in mid-1993 that future site costs will average about $26 million.[38] About 20 to 33 percent of each Superfund site expenditure has been absorbed in litigation and negotiation, which has become a growth industry for the legal profession. One estimate suggests that approximately 20,000 lawyers are now engaged in Superfund litigation.[39]

The reasons for Superfund's plodding pace and bloated costs are clear. The enormous legal costs generated by Superfund are largely the result of the complexities involved in establishing liability for abandoned hazardous waste dumps and the difficulty in recovering damages from private parties. In 1984, for instance, the EPA placed the Helen Kramer Landfill in Mantua, New Jersey, high on the NPL and awarded $55.7 million for the cleanup contract. In order to recover these costs through liability claims, the federal government subsequently sued 25 private firms and the state of New Jersey sued the same firms and 25 additional ones. A few of these 50 defendants sued 239 other parties who they claimed were actually responsible for these wastes, including the city of Philadelphia and other municipalities. And most of these litigants have sued their insurance companies.[40] The litigation was still active in the late 1990s. So far, the EPA has been able to recover only a small fraction of cleanup expenses from parties alleged to be liable for the costs.

A further inducement to delay and expense has been controversy between regulatory officials and communities affected by Superfund over the appropriate amount of cleanup required to make sites safe. Since the Superfund legislation and its implementing regulations do not clearly establish cleanup criteria, Superfund officials have been under considerable community pressure to insist on the most stringent and costly standards for site restoration. When officials and communities disagree about the matter, litigation often results even before cleanup begins. In addition, the list of prospective Superfund sites continues to grow.

An Improving Record.   In late 1997, the EPA celebrated the completion of the five hundredth NPL cleanup, which administrator Carol Browner noted was symbolic "of the progress we are making."[41] EPA officials, increasingly testy at continued criticism of Superfund, now point to significant improvements in the speed and economy of site cleanups, particularly since Browner's appointment in 1993. In early 1998, EPA officials were aggressively promoting the program's accomplishments, including:

- More NPL sites had been cleaned up since 1994 than in all prior years of the program.
- Over 82 percent of all the NPL sites currently listed were undergoing cleanup construction or had completed cleanup.

• Responsible parties had performed more than 75 percent of the long-term cleanups, thus saving taxpayers $12 billion.[42]

Superfund administrators expect continuing improvement and dismiss much current criticism as outdated. Thus, when a recent federal study complained about program sluggishness and inefficiency, the Agency quickly fired back. "EPA said that its reforms have brought relevant stakeholders into the process earlier, increased the number of small parties who are protected from liability," noted the report, "adopted liability allocations worked out by the relevant parties, and reduced the time required for and the costs associated with Superfund cleanups."[43] Additionally, EPA could note a significant reduction in the administrative and legal costs of site management and increased spending on actual site cleanups.

The Beat Goes On.   The unquestionable improvements in the Superfund program have not pacified program critics, especially congressional Republicans who seldom ever found much to like about Superfund. Less partisan experts and even many Superfund proponents, however, also believe further reforms are imperative. Among the most important, in the opinion of a great many, is the development of a reliable method for ranking all Superfund sites according to human and environmental health risks and allocating cleanup dollars on the basis of risk priorities. Many believe EPA needs to recover a much larger share of the site cleanup costs from private parties. Also, many assert that EPA and the states need to reduce the time required to add a qualifying site to the NPL list.

Congress and the White House have been under increasing pressure from insurance companies, private industry, state and local governments—indeed, practically all parties potentially liable to Superfund cleanup claims—to radically simplify the process by which liability for site cleanup is established and to create a cleanup standard that does not require total elimination of all risk from site wastes. These, and many other reforms, have been repeatedly proposed in Congress since 1996, and many observers believe that Congress will finally pass a a major Superfund reform measure before the turn of the century.

The NIMBY Problem

He appears most often as a white-collar professional or executive, articulate, well educated, politically sophisticated. She is often a housewife, an executive, or a professional. They personify the members of a growing citizen resistance movement known as NIMBYism ("Not in My Backyard").[44] NIMBYism is all too familiar to federal, state, and local officials attempting to implement state programs for permitting hazardous waste sites as required by RCRA, or trying to plan for the designation or cleanup of a Superfund site. NIMBYism poses a formidable obstacle to waste site management under RCRA and Superfund. It is the environmental movement's problem, too. NIMBYism is a dissonance within the environmental ethic—a disturbing contradiction between the movement's commitment to participatory democracy and its insistence on rapid, effective environmental regulation.

NIMBYism thrives because of numerous, and still increasing, state and federal laws that empower citizen activism in the implementation of many different environmental laws and regulations. Currently, twenty-one states have legislation in which citizens are given some role in the writing, implementation, and enforcement of environmental laws. Sixteen states require the appropriate agencies to prepare environmental impact statements for their activities and mandate public notice and involvement in the process.[45]

Federal law provides many opportunities for citizen participation in environmental regulation. Major environmental laws, such as the Clean Air Act, Clean Water Act (CWA), RCRA, and Superfund grant citizens "standing" to sue federal agencies to compel their enforcement of environmental regulations. The Surface Mining Control and Reclamation Act (1977), the 1984 RCRA amendments, and the CWA amendments of 1972, among many others, require the responsible federal and state agencies to involve the public in writing and implementing regulations. Several federal environmental laws also permit citizens, or citizen organizations, to sue private firms for failure to comply with the terms of their pollution discharge permits and to recover the costs involved in the suits. Public notice and hearings are routinely required of environmental agencies before major regulations are promulgated or permits are issued for pollution discharges or hazardous waste sites. Behind these generous provisions for citizen participation, Michael Greve noted, is congressional distrust, a "reflexive suspicion that the executive, if left to itself, would systematically underenforce the law."[46]

These statutory provisions have set in motion political forces powerfully abetting NIMBYism. One is the rapid proliferation of national and state organizations specifically committed to educating Americans about hazardous waste and to helping local communities organize politically to deal with local hazardous waste problems. Among the earliest and most visible national organizations is the Citizen's Clearinghouse for Hazardous Waste, created in 1981 by Lois Gibbs, a housewife whose experiences with the Love Canal waste crisis of 1978 convinced her of a need to educate other communities about hazardous waste. There also has been an explosion of ad hoc state and local groups that have organized to deal with specific hazardous waste issues, ranging from the closing of city waste dumps to state policy for hazardous waste transportation.

Many existing state and national environmental organizations now give major attention to hazardous waste issues and provide technical assistance and education for concerned citizens. These groups believe they are ultimately contributing to better implementation of RCRA and Superfund by ensuring greater citizen understanding and acceptance of waste policy decisions made by government officials. Often, however, this activism arouses or emboldens citizen opposition to permits for local hazardous waste sites. Public officials and waste producers commonly complain that organized citizen groups too often agitate rather than educate in community waste issues.

Public resistance to hazardous waste site permits and management plans under RCRA or Superfund is a serious and unsolved political problem afflicting both programs. Coupled with litigation, the many political and administrative strategies available to citizen groups determined to prevent permits for local hazardous waste dumps can delay program implementation for years or decades. Richard Andrews, for instance, studied 179 attempts to site hazardous waste facilities across the United States between 1980 and 1986 and reported that 25 percent were rejected, 53 percent were still pending, and only 22 percent had been sited.[47] Public opposition was a significant factor in almost all delays or rejections of site permits. During the first year of Pennsylvania's hazardous waste site permit program, more than 75 percent of the state's proposed permits were challenged by organized groups. More than a third of these protests were led by municipal officials or other governmental officers.[48] Equally important, almost half of these protests led to permit rejection, withdrawal, or delay.

State governments are not innocent of NIMBYism. Almost any hazardous waste proposal can arouse it. When the Department of Energy in the mid-1980s evaluated several states as potential permanent repositories for high-level nuclear waste, state officials crowded public hearings to object. Michael Kraft observed that a public hearing was "a perfect forum for elected officials and the general public to give vent to fears and concerns, and to denounce decisionmaking on the siting question. The public hearing procedure . . . facilitated the classic NIMBY response to siting unwanted facilities that impose localized costs and risks while offering diffuse national benefits."[49] In a 1989 variation, Alabama announced it would no longer accept hazardous waste from twenty-two other states and the District of Columbia. These states would have to find some other place for the 700,000 tons of hazardous materials they had been trucking annually to Alabama.[50]

Many administrative strategies have been tried but none seems to dispel NIMBYism. States that financially compensate local governments and citizens for risks and other problems entailed in accepting a hazardous waste site are no more successful in gaining public approval for the siting than states using only scientific criteria for site selection. Evidence suggests that most citizens who oppose a hazardous waste site will not change their minds under any circumstances.[51] Opponents may occasionally be converted if they are convinced that the local community will have continuing, accurate information about the site status and continuing control over the site's management. But converts are few. Opponents to hazardous waste sites are numerous, vocal, and unyielding. Moreover, they are apt to win their fights.

NIMBYism will continue to be tough, stubborn, and durable, its ranks crowded with well educated, socially active, organizationally experienced people. NIMBYism is rarely routed by better information, more qualified experts, improved risk communication techniques, and other palliative actions premised on the assumption that the public will be more reasonable about hazardous facility siting if it is better educated about the issues. All this belies the widespread belief among scientific experts and risk professionals that NIMBYism is rooted in the public's scientific illiteracy.[52]

Why is "better" risk communication not enough? Because NIMBYs usually distrust the *source* of governmental risk information: public officials and their scientific spokespersons. In addition, critics of governmental hazardous waste management often have their *own* experts and information sources. The conflicting sides, Harvey Brooks noted, tend to become "noncommunicating publics that each rely on different sources and talk to different experts. Thus, many public policy discussions become dialogues of the deaf. . . ."[53] Often, the true wellsprings of public anxiety about waste siting are uncomprehended by technical experts: people worry about "potentially catastrophic effects, lack of familiarity and understanding, involuntariness, scientific uncertainty, lack of personal control by the individuals exposed, risks to future generations," and more.[54]

Critics often hold environmentalists responsible for NIMBYism. They assert that the environmentalist rhetoric favored by NIMBYs is little more than deceptive but respectable packaging for middle-class selfishness. In reality, argue the critics, most NIMBYs want somebody else to bear whatever risks are associated with hazardous waste sites while they continue to benefit from the products and economic activities that produce the waste. Even if NIMBYism is well intentioned, critics also note, it fails to solve waste problems. Eventually, waste has to go someplace. It is unfortunate, the critics conclude, that the waste often ends at whatever sites are the least well defended politically, not at the most appropriate places.

Whatever its merits, the certain continuation of NIMBYism poses difficult problems for environmental regulation. Is it possible to secure informed public consent to the siting and management of hazardous waste facilities? If no public involvement techniques or risk communication procedures can produce public consensus or acquiescence to hazardous waste site planning under RCRA and Superfund, must solutions be imposed by judicial, administrative, or political means? Is there danger that continuing promotion of public involvement in making these decisions will enshrine procedural democracy at the expense of social equity—in effect, will citizen participation gradually result in selectively exposing the least economically and politically advantaged publics to the most risks from hazardous waste? How much responsibility for the worst impacts of NIMBYism rests with the environmental movement? These questions can only grow in importance as the hazardous waste problem magnifies into the next century.

Conclusion

In no other major area of environmental policy is progress measured in such small increments as the regulation of toxic and hazardous wastes. The slow pace at which TSCA, RCRA, and Superfund have been implemented so far has produced a quality of regulation so tenuous and variable that a serious question often exists whether regulation in any significant sense has yet been achieved. Hazardous waste in abandoned or deliberately uncontrolled landfills numbering in the thousands have yet to be properly controlled. Federal and state governments have yet to approve and implement on the appropriate scale the required strategies to ameliorate hazardous waste problems. The risks already associated with hazardous substances, and the many others to become apparent with continuing research into the next century, are unlikely to diminish within the decade without a massive and continuing federal commitment of resources to implement the programs as intended by Congress—a commitment of resources and will on a scale lacking so far.

Even with sufficient resources, the implementation of TSCA, RCRA, and Superfund is likely to be slow because these laws raise technical, legal, and political problems on an order seldom matched in other environmental policy domains. First, no other environmental programs attempt to regulate so many discrete, pervasive substances; we have observed that the hazardous substances that may lie within the ambit of these laws number in the tens of thousands. Second, regulation is delayed by the need to acquire technical information never previously obtained by government, to conduct research on the hazardousness of new chemicals, or to secure from corporations highly guarded trade secrets. Third, almost every major regulatory action intended to limit the production, distribution, or disposal of chemical substances deemed toxic or hazardous by government is open to technical controversy, litigation, and other challenges concerning the degree of risk associated with such substances and their suitability for regulation under the laws. Fourth, opponents of regulatory actions under TSCA, RCRA, and Superfund have been able to use to good advantage all the opportunities provided by requirements for administrative due process and the federalized structure of regulation to challenge administrative acts politically and judicially. Fifth, in many instances the states responsible for implementing the programs have been slow to provide from their own resources the means necessary to ensure proper implementation. None of these problems are unique to hazardous substance regulation, but few other environmental policies raise all these problems so persistently and acutely.

In a broader perspective, the enormous difficulties in controlling hazardous substances once they are released into the ecosystem, together with the problems of controlling their disposal, emphasize the crucial role that production controls must play in hazardous substance management. Indeed, it may be that the human and environmental risks from hazardous chemicals may never be satisfactorily constrained once these substances are let loose in the environment. American technology development has proceeded largely with an implicit confidence that whatever human or environmental risks may be engendered in the process can be adequately contained by the same genius that inspired technology's development—a faith, in effect, that science always will cure what ills it creates. The risk to humans and the environment from now pervasive chemical substances created within the past half century ought to prompt some thoughtful reservation about the efficacy of technological solutions to technological problems. Toxic and hazardous substances pose for the nation a formidable technological challenge: how to reckon the human and environmental costs of technology development while technologies are yet evolving and, then, how to prudently control dangerous technologies without depriving the nation of their benefits.

Notes

1. *New York Times,* Feb. 5, 1993.
2. *New York Times,* Sept. 17, 1993.
3. The Roper Organization, "Environmental Protection in the 1990s: What the Public Wants," (Presentation to the U.S. Environmental Protection Agency, June 1991). See also *New York Times,* May 22, 1989.
4. Environmental Protection Agency (EPA), *Environmental Progress and Challenges: EPA's Update* (Washington, D.C.: EPA, August 1988), 126. See also Government

Accounting Office (GAO), "Toxic Substances: Status of EPA's Reviews of Chemicals under the Chemical Testing Program, " Report no. GAO/RCED 92-31FS (Oct. 1991).

5. Conservation Foundation, *State of the Environment: A View Toward the Nineties* (Washington, D.C.: Conservation Foundation, 1987), 136; and Council on Environmental Quality (CEQ), *Environmental Quality, 1981* (Washington, D.C.: CEQ, 1982), 11.

6. CEQ, *Environmental Quality, 1981,* 115.

7. *New York Times,* March 26, 1993.

8. U.S. Department of Commerce, Bureau of the Census, *Statistical Abstract of the United States, 1989* (Washington, D.C.: Government Printing Office, 1989), 203.

9. *New York Times,* April 16, 1989.

10. Ibid.

11. *New York Times,* Feb. 29, 1988.

12. EPA, Office of Pollution Prevention and Toxics, *1995 Toxics Release Inventory: Chapter 5: Year-to-Year Comparisons of TRI Data* (Washington, D.C.: EPA, 1997), 118.

13. GAO, "Superfund: Cleanups Nearing Completion Indicate Future Challenges," Report no. GAO/RCED 93-188 (Sept. 1993), 12–13. See also CEQ, *Environmental Quality, 1992* (Washington, D.C.: Government Printing Office, 1993), 127–130.

14. GAO, "Superfund: Estimates of Number of Future Sites Vary," Report no. GAO/RCED 95-18 (Nov. 1994), 14. See also CEQ, *Environmental Quality, 1992,* 127.

15. Joseph G. Morone and Edward J. Woodhouse, *Averting Catastrophe* (Berkeley: University of California Press, 1986), 34–35.

16. *New York Times,* Aug. 10, 1982.

17. GAO, "Superfund," 1, 47.

18. *New York Times,* July 14, 1982.

19. Estimates by Paul MacAvoy, *New York Times,* Feb. 14, 1982. See also Library of Congress, Congressional Reference Service, *Six Case Studies of Compensation for Toxic Substances Pollution* (Report to the Committee on Environment and Public Works, U.S. Senate, No. 96-13, Washington, D.C., 1980).

20. Center for Bioenvironmental Research, Tulane and Xavier Universities, *Environmental Estrogens: What Does The Evidence Mean?* (New Orleans, La.: Center for Bioenvironmental Research, 1996); Center for the Study of Environmental Endocrine Disruptors, *Significant Government Policy Developments* (Washington, D.C.: Center for the Study of Environmental Endocrine Disruptors, 1996); and Center for the Study of Environmental Endocrine Disruptors, *Effects: State of Science Paper* (Washington, D.C.: Center for the Study of Environmental Endocrine Disruptors, 1995).

21. Center for the Study of Environmental Endocrine Disruptors, "Effects."

22. Center for the Study of Environmental Endocrine Disruptors, *Policy Developments.*

23. T. Colborn, D. Dumanoski, and J. P. Meyers, *Our Stolen Future: Are We Threatening Our Fertility, Intelligence and Survival?* (New York: Penguin Books, 1996).

24. *New York Times,* Oct. 22, 1992.

25. Marc Landy and Mary Hague, "The Coalition for Waste: Private Interests and Superfund," in *Environmental Politics: Public Costs, Private Rewards,* ed. Michael S. Greve and Fred L. Smith (New York: Praeger, 1992), 70.

26. *NewYork Times,* Jan. 6, 1992.

27. Michael S. Greve, "Introduction," in *Environmental Politics,* ed. Greve and Smith, 5–6.

28. Quoted in Christopher Harris, William L. Want, and Morris A. Ward, *Hazardous Waste: Confronting the Challenge* (New York: Quorum Books, 1987), 87.

29. Ibid., 90–91.

30. CEQ, *Environmental Quality, 1986* (Washington, D.C.: CEQ, 1987), Table 9-6.

31. GAO, "Toxic Substances: EPA Has Made Limited Progress in Identifying PCB Users," Report no. GAO/RCED 88-127 (April 1988), 3; and CEQ, *Environmental Quality, 1986,* Table 9-9.

32. GAO, "Chemical Data: EPA's Data Collection Practices and Procedures on Chemicals," Report no. GAO/RCED 86-63 (Feb. 1986), 24.

33. Ibid., 219.

34. GAO, "Toxic Substances," 7–8.

35. Ibid.

36. GAO, "RCRA Corrective Action Program," Report no. GAO/RCED 97-3 (1997).

37. Ibid., 2.

38. *New York Times,* Jan. 29, 1994. See also GAO, "Superfund," 47.

39. Landy and Hague, "The Coalition for Waste." On the general problems with Superfund, see, for example, Steven Cohen and Sheldon Kamieniecki, *Environmental Regulation Through Strategic Planning* (Boulder, Colo.: Westview Press, 1991); and Daniel Mazmanian and David Morell, *Beyond Superfailure: America's Toxics Policy for the 1990s* (Boulder, Colo.: Westview Press, 1992).

40. *New York Times,* June 5, 1991.

41. Marc Jaffee, "Browner Touts 500th Site To Come Off Superfund List," *Philadelphia Inquirer,* Dec.11, 1997.

42. EPA, Office of Emergency and Remedial Response, "Superfund Facts: The Program At Work" (1997) (*http://www.epa.gov/superfund/oerr/watsnew/facts5_7.htm*).

43. GAO, "Duration of the Superfund Process," Report no. GAO/RCED 97-20 (1997), 15.

44. On the sources and impact of NIMBYism generally, see Luther J. Carter, *Nuclear Imperatives and Public Trust: Dealing with Radioactive Waste* (Washington, D.C.: Resources for the Future, 1987); Clarence Davies, Vincent T. Covello, and Frederick W. Allen, eds., *Risk Communication* (Washington, D.C.: Conservation Foundation, 1987); Roger E. Kasperson, "Six Propositions on Public Participation and Their Relevance for Risk Communication," *Risk Analysis* 6, no. 3 (Sept. 1986): 275–281; and Patrick G. Marshall, "Not in My Backyard," *CQ Editorial Reports,* June 1989, 311.

45. Michael S. Greve, "Environmentalism and Bounty Hunting," *Public Interest* 97 (Fall 1989): 15–29.

46. Ibid., 24.

47. Ibid.

48. Walter A. Rosenbaum, "The Politics of Public Participation in Hazardous Waste Management," in *The Politics of Hazardous Waste Management,* ed. James P. Lester and Ann O'M. Bowman (Durham, N.C.: Duke University Press, 1983), 191–192.

49. Michael E. Kraft, "Managing Technological Risks in a Democratic Polity: Citizen Participation and Nuclear Waste Disposal" (Paper presented at the national conference of the American Society for Public Administration, Boston, 1987).

50. *New York Times,* Aug. 31, 1989.

51. William Lyons, Michael R. Fitzgerald, and Amy McCabe, "Public Opinion and Hazardous Waste," *Forum for Applied Research and Public Policy* 2, no. 3 (Fall 1987): 89–97. See also Michael E. Kraft, "Risk Perception and the Politics of Citizen Participation: The Case Radioactive Waste Management," in *Advances in Risk Analysis,* Vol. 9, ed. Lorraine Abbott (New York: Plenum, 1990).

52. Thomas M. Dietz and Robert W. Rycroft, *The Risk Professionals* (New York: Russell Sage Foundation, 1987), 60.

53. Harvey Brooks, "The Resolution of Technically Intensive Public Policy Disputes," *Science, Technology and Human Values* 9, no. 1 (Winter 1984): 48.

54. Kraft, "Risk Perception and the Politics of Citizen Participation," 7.

Suggested Readings

Davis, Charles E. *The Politics of Hazardous Waste.* Englewood Cliffs, N.J.: Prentice-Hall, 1993.

Hird, John A. *Superfund: The Political Economy of Environmental Risk.* Baltimore, Md.: Johns Hopkins University Press, 1994.

Kamieniecki, Sheldon, and Janie Steckenrider. "Two Faces of Equity in Superfund Imple-
mentation." In *Flashpoints in Environmental Policymaking: Controversies in Achiev-
ing Sustainability*. Ed. Sheldon Kamieniecki, George A. Gonzales, and Robert O. Vos.
Albany: State University of New York Press, 1997.
Mazmanian, Daniel, and David Morell. *Beyond Superfailure: America's Toxics Policy for
the 1990s*. Boulder, Colo.: Westview Press, 1990.
Rabe, Barry G. *Beyond NIMBY: Hazardous Waste Siting in Canada and the United States*.
Washington, D.C.: Brookings Institution, 1994.

Chapter 8

Black Gold and Nuclear Dreams:
The Politics of Energy

There is no technical tooth fairy that is going to come along and solve these problems.

—Department of Energy official
commenting on cleanup problems
at nuclear weapons facilities

No nation was endowed with a greater bounty of natural resources than the United States. The sinews of the American economy have been forged from a seemingly inexhaustible inheritance of all the natural resources essential for national prosperity: abundant water, fertile soil, forests reaching beyond the horizon, a benign climate, and below the soil metal ores, gold, silver, coal, petroleum, and natural gas. The United States was given more than abundance: it was given an extravagance of resources. Only in this century have Americans belatedly come to recognize that much of this inheritance could soon approach exhaustion or irreversible degradation. At the heart of the politics of natural resources is the struggle to determine how the remaining resources will be used and who will make such decisions. That these resources are finite, fragile, or unique adds passion and urgency to the struggle. The American environment will be affected profoundly by the outcome.

This chapter concerns energy, one of the nation's greatest natural endowments. Energy policy is environmental policy. Most forms of energy production on which the United States depends create significant, often adverse environmental impacts. Any change in the amount, variety, or duration of U.S. energy production or consumption will produce corresponding alterations in environmental quality.

Energy Consumption

The United States has a ravenous energy appetite. Collectively, Americans consume about one-fourth of the world's energy production; on average, one American uses more energy in a year than a European, a South American, and an Asian *combined*.[1] Many of the nation's major pollution problems are caused directly by current methods of producing and consuming this energy. Consider the environmental impact of fossil fuels. About 86 percent of all energy currently consumed in the United States comes from petroleum, natural gas, and coal.[2] The ecological consequences of this combustion are enumerated:

- Transportation and other fossil fuel combustion annually produce 34 percent of the volatile organic compounds, 78 percent of the carbon monoxide, 85 percent of the sulfur oxides, and 95 percent of the nitrogen oxides emitted into the air.[3]
- The land area disturbed by coal surface mining in the United States by the latter 1990s had reached more than 5.7 million acres, an area equal in size to the state of New Hampshire. Of this total, more than 3 million acres remained "unclaimed," creating an abandoned, sterile wasteland.
- During the 1990s, an average of more than 9,000 large spills of hazardous substances, mostly petroleum, were reported in U.S. waters yearly. More than one million gallons of petroleum and chemicals were spilled annually during the decade.[4]

So intimate is the association between energy and environmental quality—a link revealed again by the emerging problems of global climate warming and acid precipitation—that the nation's environmental agenda for the next decade will become energy policy by another name. The environmental movement has always recognized the interdependence of energy and environmental policy. When leaders of the nation's major environmental organizations presented President Bush with their agenda for environmental policies in the 1990s, energy conservation ranked in priority only behind global warming and ozone destruction.[5]

Until 1990, the average American's interest in energy matters had been fading as fast as memories of the 1970s "energy crisis." Then came Iraq's invasion of Kuwait in August. Domestic gasoline prices climbed sharply, stock values vacillated, and rising apprehension about economic turbulence in the wake of the invasion was compounded with anxiety about U.S. security. Again, Americans were compelled to recognize how dependent they had become on Middle Eastern petroleum and, thus, how gravely their military and economic future could be affected by the volatile politics of the Persian Gulf. The dispatch of U.S. troops to the Middle East to counter the Iraqi invasion was a grim reminder that the nation's tenuous Middle Eastern oil lifeline could even lead to a war for control of the world's remaining petroleum reserves.

During the 1990s, environmentalists joined many national security experts in warning that the United States was poised between the energy crisis it had momentarily averted in the 1970s and its certain return, hastened by the nation's failure to learn from its earlier energy troubles. That first energy crisis, lasting from 1973 to 1978, was triggered by a sudden, brief Arab embargo on petroleum exported to the United States. Americans were forced for the first time to recognize their dangerous dependence on imported petroleum. Briefly, it appeared as if the United States might face a worldwide petroleum shortage so severe that the country might be compelled to accelerate rapidly, at severe ecological risk, the mining of its huge coal reserves and the construction of more nuclear utilities. But new domestic energy regulations and the Arab cartel's failure to maintain its export controls solved the first energy crisis. By 1990, the United States had lapsed back into the patterns of energy consumption and energy policies that had invited the first energy crisis. The 1990 Iraqi invasion momentarily reawakened the specters of economic dislocation, national insecurity, energy shortages, and a new raid on nonpetroleum energy resources familiar little more than a decade ago. By the late 1990s, however, Americans had apparently relapsed into their rising, and untroubled, dependence upon imported petroleum.

Imported Oil and Fossil Fuels: A Perilous Combination

The American energy economy today can be sustained only by huge infusions of fossil fuel, especially in the form of imported oil. One major cause of environmental stress is continued dependence on nonrenewable fossil fuels: 86 percent of current domestic energy consumption originates in fossil fuels. U.S. dependence on imported oil declined sharply in the years immediately following the second oil shock created by Iran's sudden 1978 cutback in U.S. petroleum exports, and it seemed for a few years that the United States had learned the lesson of the oil embargoes. But imports rose again and by 1996 the nation was importing 46 percent of its annual petroleum consumption—more than the 38.8 percent imported when the first Arab embargo hit.[6] Moreover, an increasing proportion of this imported oil—currently about one barrel in five consumed in the United States—originates in an Arab nation. At the same time, U.S. oil production is slowly dwindling. In 1997, U.S. production was at its lowest level since 1954 and was not ever expected to increase.[7]

This resurgent addiction to imported oil occurs amid considerable uncertainty about the duration of global petroleum reserves. Many experts believe world petroleum consumption may be outpacing world production, largely because of the continuing decline in U.S. and Russian oil production and the anticipated growth of oil consumption in Eastern Europe and Southeast Asia. However, other experts believe that proven world petroleum reserves will continue to increase at least through the 1990s, thereby keeping the cost of petroleum relatively low for a few more years and discouraging energy conservation among the world's major consumers. The economic and political assumptions undergirding all predictions of future world energy supply are at best informed speculation, often easily confounded by unanticipated events. Given these uncertainties, and the enormous ecological, economic, and security risks entailed in continuing heavy dependence on imported oil, the United States has reason to consider imported oil a major problem.

A Fading Public Concern

Public consumption of imported oil is vigorous, but public concern about the consequences is not. By 1985, energy had vanished from the list of important national concerns produced by the major polls. Public apprehension about energy supply and consumption that was awakened by the energy shocks of the 1970s was hurried to extinction by the Reagan administration's rapid dismantling of the energy conservation and regulatory programs enacted in the late 1970s, and by the return of ample world petroleum supplies and lower petroleum prices. The Reagan administration pressed for more energy production, not energy conservation, and preached the need for more confidence in the marketplace and less governmental regulation. In 1988, the federal government cut by 70 percent the press run of a booklet listing gas mileage for all new automobiles. It was a last rite for the energy crisis.

By the early 1990s, attention to energy conservation and efficiency was everywhere retreating. National energy efficiency, measured by the ratio of energy used for each dollar of gross national product (GNP), had increased by 24 percent from 1976 to 1986, but it remained unchanged in 1987 and declined after 1988.[8] There was another portent of changing times: "muscle cars" were back. By the mid-1990s, Ford Motor Company was installing the once-banished V-8 engine in almost half of its new Mustangs. The Japanese auto manufacturers were adding to their U.S. lines high-performance, big-horsepower models. Many Americans at the end of the 1990s were not driving an energy guzzler but were living in one. Developers were no longer promoting energy-efficient homes. Many no longer built them.

A Decade of Indifference

The Reagan administration largely ended the federal government's promotion of energy efficiency and conservation with congressional and public approval. Auto efficiency standards mandated by Congress in 1975 had raised new U.S. cars from an average 14.2 miles per gallon in 1974 to 28.5 miles per gallon in 1988 before the Reagan administration's decision to end the mandatory standards at the 1986 level halted efficiency gains. Raising the national speed limit from 55 to 65 miles per hour on interstate highways in 1985 added an estimated half-million barrels of oil to daily U.S. consumption.[9] Federal funding for research and development promoting renewable energy technologies collapsed to 18 percent of 1980 levels and federal tax credits for residential and commercial use of wind and solar technologies were permitted to expire. Given these circumstances, it is not surprising that construction of power plants running on renewable energy such as wind or solar energy began to drop steeply in the late 1980s, leaving the United States capable today of generating only about 7 percent of its electric power demand from all renewable sources, including hydropower.

The Reagan administration also accelerated the deregulation of price controls on petroleum and natural gas, hastened the demise of an ill-conceived attempt to create a national synthetic fuels industry, attempted to secure a huge increase in the amount of public lands leased for energy exploration, and ceaselessly campaigned for a revival of the moribund commercial nuclear power industry. The times were auspicious for this kind of retrenchment to traditional American energy habits: world petroleum supplies were abundant, prices low. The Arab oil cartel seemed impotent and irresolute. All this inhibited domestic price inflation and encouraged a steady, healthy growth in GNP throughout the 1980s. Neither Congress nor the public, perhaps recalling the unpleasant 1970s, was disposed to challenge the return of national oblivion about energy conservation. Nor did the Bush administration seem interested in disturbing the reverie. Thus, Bill Clinton entered the White House in 1992 after a decade of public and governmental disinterest in national energy conservation or planning.

By an environmental accounting, however, the national energy condition by the late 1990s was disturbing. The United States had no coherent energy plan to deal with the continuing, and perhaps accelerating, depletion of global petroleum reserves, including its own. It possessed only a small and faltering renewable energy sector that lacked the technology, trained professionals, and supporting infrastructure to respond quickly and effectively to any sudden need for renewable energy in the event of another severe shortfall in petroleum supply. It continued to rely on fossil fuels, particularly petroleum and coal, which were fraught with severe ecological consequences that it was committed to mitigating. And the commercial nuclear power industry, the nation's most technologically and economically advanced alternative to fossil fuels, remained economically stagnant and environmentally menacing, its ecological threat magnified by repeated failures to solve its technological problems.

The intricate interdependence of these energy problems and their ecological implications can be better appreciated by examining three major national energy issues of the 1990s in greater depth. Conventional nuclear power and coal, both important energy sectors, pose significant ecological risks likely to continue as long as the United States builds its energy future on a foundation of fossil fuel. And the sudden emergence of a new nuclear issue—the staggering financial and technical task of cleaning up the nation's military nuclear weapons facilities—threatens to create costs so massive and work so protracted that it will be the most expensive federal environmental program through most of the next century.

Nuclear Twilight or Second Dawn?

In the late 1990s, statistics about commercial nuclear power read like the industry's obituary. For almost two decades, the Nuclear Dream—the vision of almost unlimited, cheap electricity generated from nuclear reactors by the hundreds—has been dying. The commercial nuclear power industry has been failing under a burden of economic and technological misfortunes, an increasingly hostile political climate, inept public relations, persistent environmental risks, and regulatory pressures that have been mounting since the early 1970s. Predictions of the industry's imminent demise have been common.

The nuclear industry still hopes to revive itself through what might be called the "other Greenhouse Effect." Buoyed by a tenuous hope that global warming and acid precipitation would dispel its gathering misfortunes, the industry began in the early 1990s to promote itself as the most desirable economic and environmental alternative to fossil fuel for electric power generation. Environmentalists largely reject this assertion, citing the industry's continuing ecological risks and unresolved technological difficulties. Nonetheless, governmental and private consideration of the nuclear option has been revived. But proponents of nuclear power have massive difficulties to overcome before the technology can again be considered a plausible national energy option.

The Peaceful Atom and Its Problems

Peaceful atomic power began with the Eisenhower administration's determination to demonstrate to the world that the United States was concerned with more than the military uses of nuclear power and to prevent the global spread of nuclear materials. The nation's electric power industry was uninterested in commercial nuclear power until the federal government promised to subsidize the initial research and development, to assume the costs and responsibilities for mining and refining the required nuclear fuels, and to share the patents it had monopolized. The federal government also threatened to compete directly with the utilities by developing the technology itself if the industry refused. Once the industry agreed to the bargain, the regulation and management of the new technology were invested in the Atomic Energy Commission (AEC), which already had been created to regulate existing civilian uses of atomic energy, and in the Joint Committee on Atomic Energy, a new congressional watchdog for the commission.[10]

Soon the two federal entities joined the emerging nuclear power industry and the scientific community involved in the nuclear enterprise to form a powerful, politically autonomous subgovernment whose control of nuclear policy was largely uncontested for almost two decades. The industry prospered from benevolent regulation, huge infusions of federal subsidies reaching between $12 and $15 billion by the mid-1980s, public and political favor, and unique governmental concessions never given its competitors, such as the Price-Anderson Act (1957) limiting a nuclear utility's insurance liability to $540 million for any single reactor accident, thus ensuring that the industry would obtain the necessary insurance coverage. Until the 1970s, all but a handful of scientists, economists, and public officials associated with the new technology seemed, in the words of economists Irvin Bupp and Jean-Claude Derian, so "intoxicated" by the enterprise that they largely ignored grave technical and economic problems already apparent to a few critical observers.[11] When problems could not be ignored they usually were hidden from public view; when critics arose they were discredited by Washington's aggressive defense of the industry.

The Nuclear Dream seemed most resplendent in 1975: 56 commercial reactors had been built, another 69 were under construction, and 111 more were planned. Never again would the nuclear power industry be so robust. The near catastrophic reactor meltdown at Three Mile Island, near Harrisburg, Pennsylvania, in March 1979 became the most politically damaging episode in the program's brief history, forcing national attention on an industry already in serious trouble. Grave technical and economic problems had been evident even in the early 1970s. The accident at Three Mile Island, however, was a catalytic political event, powerfully altering public consciousness about nuclear power and strengthening the credibility of the industry's critics. Moreover, the industry's grave economic, technical, and environmental problems continued to worsen as the 1980s progressed. The May 1986 core meltdown at the

Chernobyl nuclear power plant in the Soviet Ukraine was one more catastrophe in a series of baleful events hastening the extinction of the Nuclear Dream. As the twentieth century ended, the domestic industry was almost moribund.

The Nuclear Industry Today

In 1997 there were 110 operating nuclear reactors licensed to U.S. electrical utilities. Most reactors are located along the East Coast, in the Southeast, and in the Midwest (see Figure 8-1). These reactors currently generate about 22 percent of peak summer electric power production. Under current schedules, half the present reactors will end their legal operating lives between the years 2005 and 2015; the remainder will shut down before the year 2075. In short, commercial nuclear power will disappear within another generation. The major reason is that U.S. utilities have not ordered a new reactor since 1979, while simultaneously cutting back sharply on planned construction.

Despite notable improvements in the industry's safety procedures and technology development since Three Mile Island, its troubles remain substantially unrelieved. The malaise is compounded by economic and technical difficulties, unsolved waste management problems, and a volatile regulatory climate.

Economic Ills.   The cost of constructing and maintaining commercial nuclear power plants has climbed so steeply within the past decade that investment capital is scarce and costly. Many operating facilities are producing power at a unit cost far exceeding original projections. Facilities completed in the late 1990s in general will be 500 to 1,000 percent over budget.[12] New Hampshire's bitterly contested Seabrook No. 1 facility, finally granted an operating license in 1990 after a fifteen-year battle with opponents, was originally expected to cost $900 million. At startup in 1990, the costs had exceeded $5.8 billion. When Detroit Edison's Enrico Fermi II plant began generation in 1988, it was $4 billion over its original budget.[13] Discounting inflation, the real cost for constructing the nuclear facility had risen from $1,135 per kilowatt of power in 1980 to $4,590 by 1989.[14]

Among the major reasons for this cost escalation are several involving public safety and environmental protection. The time required to secure the many governmental licenses that ensure the facility will meet safety and environmental standards has been continually lengthening. Currently, surmounting these regulatory hurdles requires four to eight years and may involve almost a hundred different federal, state, and local governmental permits. Industry officials also complain about the costs imposed during plant construction through regulatory "ratcheting" by

Figure 8-1 Commercial Nuclear Power Reactors in the United States, December 31, 1995

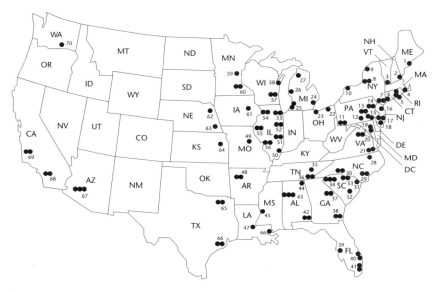

Site key

1 - Maine Yankee	19 - Calvert Cliffs 1 2	37 - Alvin W. Vogtle 1 2	55 - Quad Cities 1 2
2 - Seabrook 1	20 - North Anna 1 2	38 - Edwin I. Hatch 1 2	56 - LaSalle 1 2
3 - Vermont Yankee	21 - Surry 1 2	39 - Crystal River 3	57 - Point Beach 1 2
4 - Pilgrim 1	22 - Perry 1	40 - St. Lucie 1 2	58 - Kewaunee
5 - Millstone 1 2 3	23 - Davis-Besse 1	41 - Turkey Point 3 4	59 - Monticello
6 - Haddam Neck	24 - Enrico Fermi 2	42 - Joseph M. Farley 1 2	60 - Prairie Island 1 2
7 - Indian Point 2 3	25 - Donald C. Cook 1 2	43 - Browns Ferry 1 2 3	61 - Duane Arnold 1
8 - Nine Mile Point 1 2	26 - Palisades 1	44 - Bellefonte*	62 - Ft. Calhoun 1
9 - James A. FitzPatrick	27 - Big Rock Point	45 - Grand Gulf 1	63 - Cooper
10 - Robert Emmett Ginna 1	28 - Shearon Harris 1	46 - Waterford 3	64 - Wolf Creek
11 - Beaver Valley 1 2	29 - Brunswick 1 2	47 - River Bend 1	65 - Comanche Peak 1 2
12 - Three Mile Island 1	30 - Wm. B. McGuire 1 2	48 - Arkansas 1 2	66 - South Texas 1 2
13 - Limerick 1 2	31 - H.B. Robinson 2	49 - Callaway 1	67 - Palo Verde 1 2 3
14 - Susquehanna 1 2	32 - Virgil C. Summer 1	50 - Clinton 1	68 - San Onofre 2 3
15 - Peach Bottom 2 3	33 - Catawba 1 2	51 - Braidwood 1 2	69 - Diablo Canyon 1 2
16 - Oyster Creek 1	34 - Oconee 1 2 3	52 - Dresden 2 3	70 - WNP 1
17 - Salem 1 2	35 - Watts Bar 1	53 - Zion 1 2	
18 - Hope Creek 1	36 - Sequoyah 1 2	54 - Byron 1 2	

Source: U.S. Department of Energy, Office of Scientific and Technical Information, *Nuclear Reactors Built, Being Built, or Planned* (Washington, D.C.: Government Printing Office, 1997), 22.

Note: There are 110 nuclear power reactors licensed to operate in the United States. There are no commercial reactors in Alaska or Hawaii.

* Construction deferred/halted.

the Nuclear Regulatory Commission (NRC)—its habit of requiring facilities to make new safety modifications or other expensive design changes retroactively. Additional costs have been imposed on many utilities by protracted litigation involving environmental groups and others challenging various aspects of plant design and safety. These costs have reduced the market competitiveness of nuclear-generated electricity in comparison to fossil fuel-fired plants. With the prospect that the federal government will deregulate the electric utility market before the century's end, the nuclear future looks ever grimmer. A portent of that future occurred in early 1998 when Chicago's Commonwealth Edison closed its Zion nuclear power plant permanently—the costliest commercial nuclear shutdown in U.S. history.[15] The industry's economic ills cannot be blamed wholly on regulators and environmental critics. Operating plants seldom perform at design levels. The average facility has been "down" about one-third of its total operating time because of routine maintenance. Many plants suffer from overcapacity as a result of unanticipated levels of new electric power demand. Serious, expensive technical problems continue to beset the industry.

Technical Problems.   Proponents of nuclear power correctly argue that its safety record, notwithstanding the accident at Three Mile Island, is excellent and that critics have exaggerated its technical problems. However, continuing revelations of technical difficulties suggest serious deficiencies in the basic design and operation of the plants, and frequent carelessness or incompetence in plant management. Whatever their "real" significance, these problems have worked against the industry politically. Continuing admissions of safety risks and technical difficulties at a time of growing public apprehension about nuclear power inspire the opposition.

Several technical problems have been especially damaging to the industry. Materials and design standards for many plants currently operating or under construction have failed essential safety requirements. Reactor parts, for instance, have aged much faster than anticipated. Steam generators meant to last a plant's lifetime—approximately fifty years—are wearing out much sooner; this is a particularly serious problem in New York, Florida, Virginia, Wisconsin, and South Carolina.[16] Mistakes have been made in plant specifications or construction. Pipes have cracked and "wasted" (the walls becoming thinner) from extended exposure to radiation. In 1988, the General Accounting Office (GAO) recommended a mandatory inspection of all plants for pipe deterioration after finding that nearly a third of the plants it surveyed had the problem. The NRC betrayed its own misgivings about plant safety in 1979 when it repudiated its 1974 estimate, contained in the so-called "Rassmussen Report," that a potential catastrophic reactor accident would occur only once in 10 million years of reactor operation—as probable as a single meteorite striking someone on earth. The NRC failed at the time to provide an alternative safety estimate.

Finally, continuing revelations of plant mismanagement, administrative bungling, and secrecy raise serious questions about the competence of plant managers and technicians. The industry must contend with such disclosures as the following:

- In 1987, the NRC shut down Philadelphia Electric's Peach Bottom plant, the first time a nuclear power plant had been closed for a nonmechanical reason. Operations were suspended when it was discovered that plant technicians, who came to work in jeans and T-shirts, passed much of their time with magazines, video games, and rubber band fights, and took turns sleeping at night, although sometimes everyone on the shift was asleep.[17]
- In 1989, NRC records showed that four of five U.S. nuclear utilities had failed to complete sweeping safety changes required after the accident at Three Mile Island in 1979. Only 24 of 112 licensed reactors had installed all 149 changes.[18]
- In 1997 the NRC fined Berlin, Conneticut-based Northeast Utilities $2.1 million for safety violations, "the largest fine ever imposed" by the agency, and said "some of the utility's actions could lead to criminal prosecution. NU was forced to shut down all three nuclear reactors at the Millstone nuclear power plant in Waterford, CT, because of safety concerns. Among the more than 50 infractions . . . were the failure to properly identify, correct and prevent major problems and the failure to operate the plant according to its license design requirements."[19]

Industry officials insist that critics have distorted and misrepresented the safety record of commercial nuclear utilities by seizing on these disclosures as if they characterized the entire industry. Indeed, many utilities have a virtually uninterrupted record of safe operations and skilled management. Still, after more than thirty years of operation, the industry continues to experience serious design, management, and engineering failures. The risk of a major plant accident is not insignificant and several near disasters have occurred. Moreover, the industry has not solved its grave waste disposal and emergency management problems.

The Waste Nobody Wants.   No problem has proven more politically troublesome to the nuclear power industry and its federal regulators than where, and how, to dispose of the enormous, highly toxic, and mounting volume of nuclear wastes in the United States. The problem, never anticipated when commercial nuclear power was first promoted, has been especially difficult because reactor wastes incite great public fear and chronic conflict among federal, state, and local officials concerning where to put them.

This nuclear waste originates from uranium mining, civilian nuclear power plants, military nuclear weapons programs, hospitals, educational institutions, and research centers. Current controversy involves four categories of waste:

High-level wastes. Highly radioactive liquids created through the reprocessing of reactor fuels. These wastes are generated by both civilian and military reactor programs. Currently, more than 100 million gallons of high-level wastes are stored in temporary containment facilities in the states of Idaho, New York, South Carolina, and Washington.

Transuranic wastes. Some of the elements in these radioactive by-products of reactor fuel and military waste processing remain dangerous for extraordinarily long periods. Plutonium-239, with a half-life of 24,000 years, and americum-243, with a 7,300-year half-life, are among the transuranics. Other more exotic transuranic elements have a half-life exceeding 200,000 years.

Spent nuclear fuel. About 32,000 metric tons of spent fuel, mostly from civilian reactors, are stored temporarily in "cooling ponds" at reactor sites. By the year 2000, as more nuclear plants become operational, this spent fuel is expected to increase to 42,000 metric tons.

Low-level wastes. Any material contaminated by radiation and emitting low levels of radioactivity itself belongs in this category. This includes workers' clothing, tools, equipment, and other items associated with nuclear reactors or nuclear materials. Low-level wastes currently are stored at repositories in Nevada, New York, and South Carolina.

Figure 8-2 shows where the wastes from commercial reactors and military activities are currently stored. In the early years of nuclear power promotion, it was assumed that spent fuel from civilian and military plants would be reprocessed: the fissionable materials, primarily plutonium, would be recovered for use again as reactor fuel and the remaining high-level waste eventually would be contained and isolated at appropriate disposal sites. In the planners' early view, the high-level and transuranic wastes remaining after reprocessing posed a largely technical and readily solvable problem of finding the appropriate containment materials and geographic location for permanent storage. They did not anticipate the failure of civilian reprocessing and the resulting volume of nuclear waste. They did not foresee the necessity to store military wastes for decades longer than the containment structures were designed to last. They did not anticipate the political repercussions in trying to find a place to put the waste.

Figure 8-2   Location of Spent Nuclear Fuel and High-Level Waste, 1996

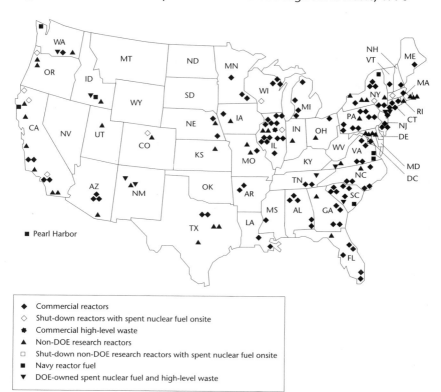

■ Pearl Harbor

◆   Commercial reactors
◇   Shut-down reactors with spent nuclear fuel onsite
✳   Commercial high-level waste
▲   Non-DOE research reactors
☐   Shut-down non-DOE research reactors with spent nuclear fuel onsite
■   Navy reactor fuel
▼   DOE-owned spent nuclear fuel and high-level waste

Source: U.S. Department of Energy, *Spent Fuel Storage Requirements, 1993–2040* (Washington, D.C.: Government Printing Office, 1996).

Existing and planned commercial facilities were designed to store temporarily no more than three years' worth of accumulated spent fuel in cooling ponds until the fuel assemblies were reprocessed. Since the early 1970s, however, virtually all spent fuel has been stored in these cooling ponds. Space and time are now running out. The United States continues to reprocess its spent military fuel, thereby generating most of the high-level liquid wastes accumulating at military nuclear reservations. Until 1982, the federal government had no comprehensive plan for the permanent storage of these nuclear wastes. The federal government and the states quarreled for more than a decade over how a permanent waste depository would be designed and which states would be depository sites—nobody wanted it.[20] Idaho and South Carolina, already accommodating large volumes of high- and low-level wastes from other states, were increasingly reluctant to accept more. In 1976, California ordered a moratorium on the construction of commercial nuclear facilities until Washington, D.C., could certify that a permanent repository for their spent fuel existed. The nuclear waste issue was approaching crisis.

   The States Play Nuclear "Keep Away."   In 1982 Congress finally passed the Nuclear Waste Policy Act (NWPA), which was intended to create a process for designating and constructing the first permanent repositories for nuclear waste. The act appeared to end a decade of nasty legislative infighting during which each state scrambled to write language into the law assuring it would not be a candidate for the repository. The legislation assigned the site selection task to the Department of Energy (DOE) and created what appeared to be a meticulously detailed, impartial, and open process by which all possible sites would be thoroughly studied and reduced to a few from which the president would eventually select two, one east and one west of the Mississippi River. The president was to designate the first site by March 31, 1987, and the second by July 1, 1989. To demonstrate its confidence in the process, the DOE agreed to begin accepting high-level commercial wastes sometime in 1998.

   Following procedures required by the NWPA, the DOE in 1985 nominated three permanent sites to the president from which he was to select one: Texas (Deaf Smith County), Washington (the Hanford nuclear military reservation), and Yucca Mountain, Nevada (near the Nevada atomic test site). Every stage of the designation process, however, had been accompanied by political fireworks. Republican senators and representatives from each designated state complained to the White House that the designation of their state would penalize the party at the polls in 1986 and 1988. The political leadership of both parties in all three states complained bitterly that their states had been improperly designated and attempted to overturn the designation in the courts. Environmental groups in each state went to court, challenging the designations on technical and procedural grounds. And Congress anticipated another rancorous round when the president was scheduled to select the second repository site from another set of states in 1989.

   Rather than abide the continuing controversy, Congress found a simpler solution to the designation problem. In December 1987, the Congress suddenly renounced the procedures it had ordered in the NWPA and summarily designated Nevada to be the first permanent waste site. As a consolation, Nevada was assured up to $20 million annually to manage the job. Nevada legislators were outraged. It "will turn our state into a federal colony," accused Republican representative Barbara F. Vucanovich.[21] "Instead of leadership and principle, it's a gang-rape mentality," added a spokesperson for Richard Bryan,

Nevada's governor. The man who arranged it all thought otherwise. "If I were a Nevadan living in the real world, I would be happy with this bill," asserted Sen. J. Bennett Johnston (D-La.). "I would bet that in a very few years, Nevada will deem this one of their most treasured industries." Throughout the 1990s, however, Nevada continued to resist development of the Yucca Mountain facility with every political resource it had available.

This trench warfare slowed the facility's construction to a crawl but Congress in 1997 left little doubt that Nevada was still the nation's most eligible nuclear waste bin. Both House and Senate passed legislation, over the state's vehement objections, that would create a "temporary" repository near the Yucca Mountain site for the high-level nuclear waste still awaiting the completion of the permanent Nevada site.[22] In the keep-away politics of nuclear waste, the most weakly defended constituency was still "it."

Repository Problems

"It's fair to say we've solved the nuclear waste problem with this legislation," Senator Johnston assured his colleagues with premature optimism after they awarded the waste to Nevada. But after more than two years of preliminary work and an expenditure of $500 million at the Nevada site, the DOE announced in 1989 that it was abandoning its initial repository plan because it lacked confidence in the technical quality of the proposal.[23] The DOE predicted that the repository would be delayed until at least the year 2010, even though it was committed to accepting high-level wastes from commercial reactors by 1998 and the commercial utilities had already paid $3 billion in taxes to use the repository. However, by 1998 it was evident that the DOE would not be ready to receive the wastes at even a temporary repository and the availability of a permanent repository remained equally speculative. "A realistic date for having a permanent repository operational keeps receding farther into the future. . . ," concluded the GAO.[24]

Meanwhile reports on the DOE's nuclear waste management projects have been unrelieved bad news since the late 1980s. In mid-1989, the DOE announced that it was delaying the opening of its Waste Isolation Pilot Project (WIPP) near Carlsbad, New Mexico. The WIPP, begun in the late 1970s, was intended to store the plutonium wastes generated at the Rocky Flats nuclear military facility near Denver, where space for the liquid wastes was fast disappearing. The underground repository had been scheduled to receive its first shipments in 1992 but the DOE's scientific advisors urged a delay of two or three years because the DOE needed to complete technical diagrams of twenty-one systems already built into the structure, including the electrical, radiation control, and fire protection systems.[25]

The WIPP's delay adds another chapter to the already protracted, acrimonious debate about the safety of that facility, and raises doubts that the WIPP will ever be used. Thus, the nation still lacks a permanent repository for either its civilian or military nuclear wastes. Waste storage capacity at civilian utility sites continues to dwindle. At the same time, military waste-containment structures are deteriorating dangerously at places such as the Hanford, Washington, military reservation, where 440,000 cubic yards of high-, low-, and extremely long-lived nuclear waste are stored, some since 1943, awaiting permanent deposition.[26] This is not, however, the whole of the national nuclear waste problem. The controversy attending reactor waste deflects public attention from the emerging problem of disposing of nuclear facilities themselves after they have outlived their usefulness.

Decommissioning Problems

Once civilian or military nuclear facilities have finished their useful lives, the NRC and the DOE require that the owners "decommission" their facility by removing from the site the radioactive materials, including land, groundwater, buildings, contents, and equipment, and by reducing residual radioactivity to a level permitting the property to be used for any other purpose.[27] Since a commercial reactor's life span is expected to be fifty years, an increasing number of the nation's reactors will have to be decommissioned beginning in the 1990s. However, no utility has yet decommissioned a large plant and none expect to do so until a permanent high-level waste depository is available. Instead, the utilities plan to partially decommission their facilities and to put them in "safe storage" while awaiting the completion of a permanent repository.

In fact, little is known about how large facilities can be taken apart and rendered safe. Few of the nation's utilities have done much practical planning for decommissioning their own plants. No reliable estimates are available for decommissioning costs, which have been calculated to range from tens of millions to $3 billion for each facility.[28] The NRC currently requires utilities to set aside $105 million to $135 million for decommissioning, but many experts believe these estimates are too low. Utilities are also required to have decommissioning plans, cost estimates, or written certification that they will meet NRC's cost estimates. Still, no utility has yet created a decommissioning fund, assessed its rate payers for the costs, or filed a decommissioning plan with the NRC in the absence of a permanent high-level waste repository.

The DOE's responsibility for decommissioning the nation's military reactors presents even more formidable problems. Investigations of the nation's military nuclear facility management in the late 1980s revealed appalling negligence in waste storage and management, leaks of dangerous radioactive materials for decades into the surrounding environment and civilian settlements, and deceit and secrecy in managing information about the lethal dangers created both on- and off-site from waste mismanagement. This legacy of a half-century's negligence leaves the DOE with a conservatively estimated cost of $230 billion to decontaminate and decommission its nuclear facilities.[29] Many experts believe the costs will climb much higher, so intolerably high that the sites will be, as some plant engineers privately predict, "national sacrifice zones" never adequately decontaminated.[30]

Waste management and nuclear plant decommissioning problems will trouble Americans for centuries and remain a reminder of the technological optimism and mission fixation that inspired Washington's approach to nuclear technology development. Indeed, the politics of civilian nuclear power development has been as important in shaping the economic, ecological, and technological character of the industry as its science. So it will continue to be. The future of commercial nuclear power will be determined, in good part, by how the Congress, the White House, and the NRC respond to its present ills and challenges. The battle for the nuclear future is still being fought in these political arenas.

The Nuclear Regulatory Commission in the Middle

The NRC works in the vortex of controversy over commercial nuclear power regulation. Critics of the nuclear power industry almost ritually indict the NRC for its regulatory failures. But even its friends recognize a problem. It was an NRC commissioner newly appointed by President Reagan, a pronuclear spokesperson for a pronuclear administration, who publicly complained shortly after assuming office about the "surprising lack of professionalism in the construction and preparation . . . of nuclear facilities" and "lapses of many kinds—in design analysis resulting in built-in design errors, in poor construction practices, in falsified documents. . . ."[31] The NRC's regulatory deficiencies arise, in large part, from the political circumstances of its origin and the outlook of its professional staff. The NRC was created in 1974 when Congress abolished the AEC and vested that agency's regulatory authority in the new NRC. The new agency could not readily dissolve the strong, congenial professional and institutional relationships linking former AEC staff to the nuclear power industry, nor could it eliminate the impulse to promote and protect the industry that was so deeply rooted in the AEC's history. The NRC remains unapologetic about its commitment to nuclear power. "People who serve on this commission and on its staff do believe in the nuclear industry," retorted one to a critic.[32] Successive NRC commissioners and their staffs often tried to regulate without prejudice and sometimes succeeded, but institutional history and professional experience often—the critics say *usually*—prevailed against regulatory rigor.

In the aftermath of Three Mile Island, the NRC has made an effort to be a more aggressive and foresighted regulator and its relationship to the industry has become more complex. The NRC required a multitude of changes in plant management that cost utilities an average of $50 million. It has been quicker and harsher in assessing regulatory penalties, but the commission is still cited for serious regulatory lapses. For example, a GAO study of five nuclear facilities between 1986 and 1987 disclosed that "despite records of chronic safety violations, NRC did not close them. With only one exception, a safety incident occurred that made continued operation impossible or the utilities shut them down when the problems grew severe." Regarding plant safety standards it noted that the "NRC may take from several months to 10 or more years to resolve . . . generic issues, including those NRC believes pose the highest safety risk." [33] A GAO investigation of the NRC's supervision for the decommissioning of eight small reactors in 1987 found that the "NRC fully or partially released two sites for unrestricted use where contamination at one was up to 4 times, and at the other up to 320 times higher than NRC's guidelines allowed. . . . Also, for five licenses that buried waste, NRC does not know the types and amounts of radioactive waste that have been buried at four of the sites." [34]

Defenders of the NRC assert that many of its regulatory lapses result from understaffing and underfunding, and that the regulatory changes required by the NRC often take years for utilities to accomplish. Some observers argue that the NRC must be doing its job reasonably well because it is also a frequent target of criticism from the nuclear power industry itself. One certainty is that the NRC operates in a radically different political environment from that prior to the accident at Three Mile Island. Relentless public exposure, politically potent and organized critics from the scientific and environmental community, fading congressional enthusiasm for nuclear power, and technical controversy over nuclear power's safety and economic prospects all produce a politically volatile regulatory climate in which the NRC must expect to operate in the 1990s. The transcendent political question for the NRC in the next decade, however, is whether it will be presiding over the death of the Nuclear Dream.

Stubborn Hope: Breakthrough Technology, the White House, and the Greenhouse

If the nuclear power industry has cause for optimism about the future, it lies in the development of a new generation of safer reactors, in renewed White House promotion of nuclear power, and in nuclear power's revival as an alternative to fossil fuels, which are thought responsible for climate warming.

Spokespersons for the industry assert that the lessons learned from almost four decades of experience with commercial nuclear power are being applied in the design of a new generation of smaller, safer reactors free from the technical and economic ills of the present ones.[35] The Advanced Light Water Reactor presently at design stage is alleged to be ten times safer than current reactors in severe accident prevention. Two other promising technologies, the Modular Gas Temperature Gas Cooled Reactor, sometimes called the pebble-bed reactor, and the Liquid Metal Reactor, are also at design stage. The nuclear industry asserts that this new generation of reactors, while smaller than present ones, could be used in combination (as "modules") to produce as much power as needed much more safely and economically in future power plants. Moreover, the industry now supports the adoption of a standard design for all future commercial reactors instead of the multiple designs now in use. This strategy would facilitate the rapid development and application of safety standards for the whole industry.

The commercialization of this new generation of reactors will require a huge investment in research and development. The nuclear power industry, unable to raise capital on this scale in light of its presently bleak prospects, looks to the federal government for help. The Reagan administration strongly supported the industry but left its future largely to market forces. The Bush administration declared its belief in the "nuclear option" and committed to support research and development for the industry.[36] In late 1989, for instance, the DOE awarded the General Electric Company and Westinghouse Electric Corporation about $50 million each to plan more efficient and reliable commercial reactors at a time when the DOE was not aggressively promoting other energy technologies.[37] Congress, equally reluctant to preclude the "nuclear option," helped to keep the industry alive by renewing the Price-Anderson Act, which limits the insurance liability of utility operators, now to a maximum of $7 billion for any single commercial reactor accident. This new liability limit is still much smaller than a nuclear utility would ordinarily expect to pay in liability for an accident without the Price-Anderson Act.

Proponents of nuclear power also argue that the United States must continue commercial reactor development lest it become too dependent for electric power production on uncertain supplies of increasingly scarce and costly petroleum or on coal with all its environmental risks. With the resurgent growth in demand for new electric power in the 1990s, proponents of nuclear power assert, the United States can no longer count on the large unused power-generating capacity the nation enjoyed in the 1980s.

Advocates for continued reactor development also argue that should an alternative for fossil fuels be needed in the future, the nation cannot afford to have only the present flawed reactor technologies available. After reviewing the considerable uncertainties over future availability of fossil fuels and other energy alternatives, science policy specialists Joseph G. Morone and Edward J. Woodhouse concluded that the nuclear option still makes sense.

> We cannot predict what energy the nation and world will want or need, nor what options will be available to meet the demands. . . . It is conceivable that there will be enough options to render nuclear power unnecessary in many nations, but equally conceivable that there will not be. And if such difficulties as the greenhouse effect do force a shift away from coal, and financially feasible energy alternatives are not available, much of the world may be backed into a corner: either rapidly construct a new generation of giant light water reactors, feared by a substantial portion of the population, or face the economic and other consequences of extremely tight energy supplies.[38]

The nuclear industry has been quick to seize on national apprehension over climate warming to boost its failing fortunes. Trade associations have paid handsomely for media advertising portraying nuclear power as an attractive alternative to increased fossil fuel combustion with its climate warming threat. While most environmentalists argue that energy conservation and rapid development of renewable energy sources are better solutions to the Greenhouse problem, many politicians, scientists, and economists are giving nuclear power a hard second look. Eight pounds of enriched uranium can produce the energy equivalent of 6,000 tons of oil or 8,000 tons of coal. A large reactor can generate enough power for 1.5 million households. Nuclear technology can be beguiling in an era of climate warming consciousness if its technological risks can be reduced and a more congenial political climate created for the nuclear option. Both the mainland Chinese and the Taiwanese governments are currently promoting nuclear power aggressively as the most politically attractive response to climate warming. The Chinese government in late 1997 announced plans to order thirty new nuclear reactors for electric power generation. The Nuclear Dream is not yet dead.

The Cold War's Wasteland:
Nuclear Weapons Facilities

On the threshold of the twenty-first century, it appears that the largest environmental program in U.S. history will be the environmental restoration of military facilities, especially the numerous sites now administered by the DOE in which military nuclear weapons research, production, and testing have been conducted for almost a half-century. The luckless DOE had inherited the weapons facilities from the AEC when the Commission was abolished in 1974. However, private corporations continued to operate the facilities under contract to the DOE, which was assumed to be exercising regulatory oversight. Some of the resulting environmental problems were accidents or mistakes, perhaps inevitable. But contractors and their federal watchdogs alike too often behaved as if regulations were irrelevant. The legacy is environmental damage on a scale inviting disbelief.

Carelessness, incompetence, and willful evasion of regulations compounded with criminal negligence afflicted the weapons program from its inception, tainting public and private participants alike. Most of these acts were concealed by a wall of military secrecy until the 1970s. By the early 1990s, however, the wall was thoroughly breached. In 1992, for example, the federal government admitted a shared responsibility with its contractors for environmental crimes at the Rocky Flats, Colorado, weapons facility. One contractor, Rockwell International, admitted guilt for ten crimes, including five felonies, and paid an $18.5 million fine. The DOE itself admitted that during the 1980s it had deliberately resisted any effort by the EPA or state environmental agencies to make its weapons facilities comply with environmental laws.[39] The DOE's evasions were inspired, in good part, by fear of multiple lawsuits from state governments, facility employees, and other private interests if Washington, D.C., admitted liability for environmental negligence or crimes. The suits came anyway.

"The Toughest, Most Dangerous Work in the World"

Site restoration now involves seventeen major locations in twelve states and more than fifty smaller sites—in all, more than 122 facilities in thirty states and the Marshall Islands. DOE estimates suggest that cleanup of all sites—if the appropriate technologies can be created—will take at least seventy-five years and require at least $230 billion, or more than the Mercury, Gemini, and Apollo space programs combined, and could exceed $300 billion. Alone, the nuclear weapons cleanup would become the largest public works program in U.S. history. If it is extended to the more than 11,000 other military facilities where various kinds of "mixed" hazardous waste, including radioactive waste, currently exist, the total cost of environmental restoration of national military facilities could exceed a half-trillion dollars and require the better part of a century. However, cost and time estimates are educated guesses, the bottom line of which has been steadily increasing since the late 1980s.

Secretary of Energy Hazel O'Leary's description of the cleanup as the "toughest, most dangerous work in the world" seems appropriate in light of DOE's own grim appraisal of its task:

> Many facilities are old and deteriorating and present serious threats to those who work in and around them. The complex is regulated under a mix of internal and external regulatory and advisory bodies that administer a maze of laws, regulations, directives, orders, and guidance. The result is intense frustration through DOE's workforce, serious overlaps and gaps in regulatory requirements, and a failure to address hazards according to their relative risks, costs and benefits.[40]

The Wastes

The radioactive and chemical wastes now contaminating the DOE facilities have been accumulating for more than forty years. Some of the most dangerous wastes, such as liquid radioactive chemicals at the Hanford, Washington, site and the Rocky Flats, Colorado, facility near Denver, have been stored since the early 1940s in badly deteriorating containment tanks designed to last less than twenty years. Only after the Bush administration initiated an aggressive investigation did the extent of the environmental contamination begin to appear. As the investigation widened under the Clinton administration, it became clear that accurate estimates about the extent of chemical contamination remaining on the sites and migrating off-site were difficult. The DOE has estimated that at least 500 "waste streams," or flows of waste from weapons sites, exist together with at least 500,000 cubic meters of "mixed" (radioactive and chemical) wastes.[41] Many of the liquid and solid chemical wastes, particularly "high-level" and "transuranic" substances, can be dangerous to humans and the environment for 100,000 years or more.

Damage estimates are problematic because accurate records at the weapons sites are elusive—in some cases, for instance, monitoring of waste streams moving off military reservations created in the 1940s was not initiated until the early 1990s. The DOE may be only partially responsible for these conditions but it bears most of the legal and administrative liability for site restoration and becomes the lightning rod in the political turbulence sure to arise. The DOE must characterize the wastes involved, stabilize any dangerous waste containment struc-

Figure 8-3　Historical and Projected Cumulative Volumes of Untreated High-Level Waste in Storage

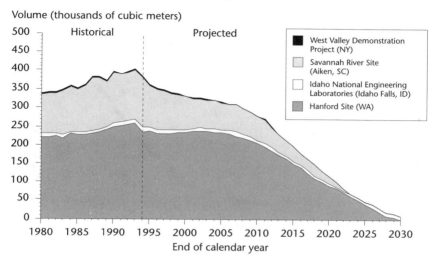

Volume (thousands of cubic meters)

Legend:
- West Valley Demonstration Project (NY)
- Savannah River Site (Aiken, SC)
- Idaho National Engineering Laboratories (Idaho Falls, ID)
- Hanford Site (WA)

End of calendar year

Source: U.S. Department of Energy, *Spent Fuel Storage Requirements 1993–2040* (Washington, D.C.: Government Printing Office, 1996), 38.

tures, remove all nuclear and hazardous materials from the sites, and sequester them in safe repositories. Many of the highly dangerous radioactive liquid and solid wastes are not well understood. The technologies for managing many wastes do not yet exist. Safe and permanent repositories for the most dangerous wastes do not yet exist. Site cleanup will also require prolonged collaboration with a multitude of other agencies including the Department of Defense, the EPA, the Department of the Interior, and all the state governments whose jurisdictions are affected by site work. Figure 8-3 depicts the past and projected magnitude of the high-level wastes accumulating at the four major DOE nuclear facilities. Figure 8-4 shows the projected growth in new containment canisters at these sites.

The DOE, with desperate optimism, describes its task as the "vigorous challenge of cleaning up and safely containing waste for a thousand years. Scientific, environmental, and technical professionals must work closely with managers, educators, lawyers, innovators, and communicators to find the best solutions for cleaning up the environment and safely managing waste now and in the future. DOE's cleanup goal is one of the

Figure 8-4   Projected Cumulative Number of High-Level Waste Canisters

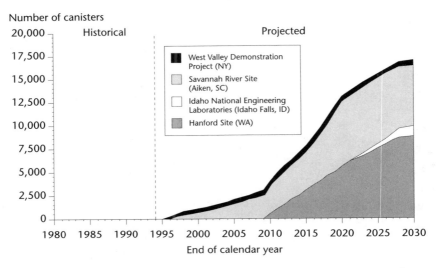

Source: U.S. Department of Energy, Spent Fuel Storage Requirements 1993–2040 (Washington, D.C.: Government Printing Office, 1996), 38.

most difficult and vital tasks of our time."[42] A brief examination of conditions at the most thoroughly investigated site, the Hanford Military Reservation near Richland, Washington, suggests how intimidating the challenge will be.

Billion Dollar Burps and Cleanup Careers

The Hanford Military Reservation is almost half the size of Rhode Island. Its highly radioactive military wastes dating from the early days of World War II will become the costliest, most complex, most technically challenging restoration facing the DOE. The most dangerous of Hanford's wastes are 7 million gallons of highly corrosive liquid radioactive materials stored in 117 tanks designed almost forty years ago to last for no more than several decades. It is known that at least 1 million gallons of these materials have leaked from sixty-six of the tanks during the past forty years, most into subsurface soil and groundwater. Much of this waste has migrated to major surface waters including the Columbia River. Federal investigation has revealed a long history of administrative and technical bungling by the prime contractor, Westinghouse, most of it concealed with bureaucratic obfuscation. In 1968, for instance, a major safety lapse involving an overheating and partial fuel melting at a nuclear weapons assembly plant was reported as "an improbable mechanical failure." [43] DOE reports indicated that at least sixteen times since 1987 workers at the facility were exposed to toxic gas leaking from the liquid containment tanks, and some workers suffered permanent lung damage. Cleanup at the site is expected to cost between $30 and $50 billion. "People's careers are going to be over before this is done," remarked a spokesperson for Westinghouse.[44]

The witches' brew of problems posed by Hanford can be appreciated by considering Tank 101-SY, one of the most dangerous of the numerous liquid waste containments dating from the 1940s. Tank 101-SY holds 1.14 million gallons of extremely unstable, high-level radioactive waste stored so long that its chemistry and behavior are no longer well understood. The tank is known to contain potentially explosive concentrations of hydrogen gas that must be "burped" from the containment every hundred days. Videotapes made inside the tank in 1991 revealed what looked like "a partly cooled lava inside a volcano, seething and lurching as it burps noxious and explosive gases . . . produced by chemical and nuclear reactions. . . . The shifting wastes splash the walls and bend metal parts . . . a narrator describes 'rollover events' in which the tank agitates itself." [45]

The state of Washington, suspicious of both the DOE and its Hanford contractors, has insisted on site inspection by its own regulators. At Tank 101-SY, an inspector in early 1992 found "three separate leak-detection systems, all inoperable: a sump pit that would detect liquids but was already flooded with water, an instrument for measuring radiation that was broken, and a liquid detector that was supposed to be suspended just above the floor between the inner and outer walls of the tank, but instead was hanging two and a half feet up, so it would not detect anything until wastes reached that level." [46] The federal government has been sued by the state of Washington, Westinghouse employees, environmental organizations, and private citizens for environmental contamination alleged to have been created throughout the Hanford site's history. Cleanup will require close collaboration not only with state and local interests but with the EPA, because wastes on- and off-site are subject to regulation under almost all major environmental laws, including the Clean Air Act, the Toxic Substances Control Act, the Resource Conservation and Recovery Act, the Clean Water Act, and Superfund legislation. In the mid-1990s, however, the DOE had just begun to identify the nature and location of the wastes to which these various regulations apply.

Hanford is the DOE's worst problem but the complexities of site restoration are alike at most of the DOE weapons sites. Many experts believe that full restoration of all the DOE sites will be technically and economically impossible, forcing Congress or the DOE to practice administrative triage by selecting the priority sites (a responsibility the DOE fervently wishes to avoid, so nasty would be the congressional infighting).

A Perverse Economic Boon

If there is any political good news at the DOE sites, it is that restoration should be an economic windfall for communities and counties surrounding the facilities. DOE site cleanups will likely be a national growth industry. In Richland, Washington, and the neighboring cities of Pasco and Kenniwick, a real estate boom has been under way since 1991 and employment at the Hanford site is expected to exceed the largest work force during the site's operating years. The cleanup has doubled the work force required to manage sites such as Tank 101-SY. Spending for environmental cleanup in two other states meant no net loss of income for areas surrounding the weapons sites. The DOE's Savannah River Site, presently employing 24,000 persons, is South Carolina's largest employer, the work force of which is expected to grow.[47] The economics of the DOE's cleanup has also complicated its restoration job, for site cleanup has become a coveted local expenditure that attracts considerable congressional attention, generating a minefield of political pressures and calculations to which the DOE must respond in making any important site decisions.

Black Gold

Every American president from Richard Nixon to Ronald Reagan tried to dam the flow of imported oil into the United States with a wall of coal. Coal is the nation's most plentiful fossil fuel. With reserves sufficient for 250 years at current consumption rates, it is inevitable that federal energy planners should repeatedly attempt to substitute abundant domestic coal for expensive, insecure imported oil. Economic and environmental problems, however, continue to inhibit a massive national conversion to coal combustion. The Reagan administration, convinced that excessive environmental regulation impeded coal consumption, was determined to have more coal and less environmental regulation. Reagan's successor, however, could not afford to regard coal so cordially. Most of the highly publicized environmental problems confronting the Bush administration had "coal" written all over them: acid precipitation, climate warming, and more than one hundred major American cities with severe smog problems. Nonetheless, coal will remain for many decades a major fossil fuel and a continuing environmental problem.

The Saudi Arabia of Coal

Coal represents about 90 percent of the remaining U.S. hydrocarbon reserves. The coal industry liked to remind Americans during the energy crisis of the 1970s that the nation had the equivalent of Saudi petroleum reserves in coal. This coal rests in three geologic reserves: Appalachia's wooded hills and hollows sprawling across parts of seven southeastern states, the Midwestern plains, and the western plains and grasslands.

In the late 1990s, coal provided about 22 percent of U.S. energy consumption. Electric utilities, the prime coal consumers, generate more than half their power from coal-fired boilers and have been increasing their coal consumption. Although U.S. coal production stays at record levels, the industry has been afflicted since the 1950s with declining employment, chronic labor violence, and boom-or-bust economic cycles. The industry's economic fortunes are closely tied to the electric power and metallurgical industries, which consume, respectively, 85 and 13 percent of annual coal production. Because more than eight of every ten tons of mined coal are transported by rail, many railroads have become heavily dependent on coal production for revenue.

Every administration from Richard Nixon to Ronald Reagan proposed massive new coal consumption to diminish U.S. dependence on imported petroleum. The Nixon and Ford administrations' largely fanciful "Project Independence" promised that the United States could become almost independent of imported petroleum by 1980 through reliance on coal and conservation. President Carter, ignoring the chimera of "energy independence," still proposed in his 1977 energy plan to diminish U.S. dependence on petroleum through a 66 percent increase in domestic coal combustion within a decade and the creation of a massive new synthetic fuels industry based on coal feedstocks. The Reagan administration announced its intention to sell new coal mining leases in western public lands containing 5 billion tons of coal as a means of encouraging more production. The coal industry, sensing a possible reversal of its fortunes, was quick to proclaim coal the "great black hope of America" and to shift its political weight behind new White House coal initiatives.

There were several plausible reasons for coal's continuing attraction to energy planners despite related economic and environmental problems. According to some estimates, accelerated coal combustion might displace as much as 2.5 million barrels of imported petroleum consumed by the United States daily. A coal boom might bring 100,000 new workers to Appalachia, reviving its stagnant economy, and perhaps 50,000 more workers to the West; coal-related income in the West and Great Plains might rise by $850 million to $1 billion. Large "mine-mouth" electric generating plants, located adjacent to coal seams to reduce transportation costs, could provide dependable, secure electric power for the growing West and Midwest. The Carter energy plan might have increased railroad coal loadings by 350 percent between 1978 and 1985. Coal was secure energy, unmenaced by Middle Eastern politics and unpredictable world petroleum markets. Coal could glitter as gold if only the new coal boom could be made environmentally and economically tolerable.

Can Surface Mining Be Regulated?

The most significant adverse environmental impacts associated with coal use are created by surface mining and combustion. Many of the problems associated with coal combustion have been examined in Chapter 6 on air pollution. The regulation of surface mining has been no less contentious.

Surface Mining. Virtually all coal mined west of the Mississippi River and half the coal produced in Appalachia is surface mined. Surface mining rapidly has replaced underground mining because it is cheaper, more efficient, more profitable, and less labor intensive. Unless rigorously regulated, however, surface mining is environmentally catastrophic. More than 1.5 million acres of American land have been disturbed by coal surface mining; more than a million of these acres remain a wrecked and ravaged waste, long abandoned by its destroyers. More than 1,000 additional acres are disturbed each week by surface mining, and more than thirty states have been scarred by unreclaimed surface mines.

In Appalachia surface miners roamed the hills virtually uncontrolled for decades; the evidence is written in thousands of sterile acres, acidified streams and rivers, decapitated hills, and slopes scarred by abandoned mine highwalls. In western prairies and grasslands, unregulated surface mining left thousands of barren, furrowed acres buried under spoil banks so hostile to revegetation they seemed like moonscapes to observers. After decades of resistance, the mining industry has come to recognize the necessity for the environmental regulation of surface mining, but vigorous controversy continues over the manner of this regulation and its effectiveness.

The Surface Mining Control and Reclamation Act. President Carter, fulfilling a promise made during his election campaign, signed the Surface Mining Control and Reclamation Act of 1977 (SMCRA) and thereby created the first federal surface mining regulatory program. The Act, strongly promoted by environmentalists against fierce resistance from the mining industry and two vetoes by President Gerald R. Ford, was intended to control the environmental ravages of surface mining by restoring surface-mined land to productivity whenever possible. The major features include:

1. Environmental performance standards with which all surface miners were to comply in order to operate. Standards were to be established to regulate the removal, storage, and redistribution of topsoil; siting and erosion control; drainage and protection of water quality; and many other matters affecting environmental quality.

2. Requirements that mined land be returned, insofar as possible, to its original contours and to a use equal or superior to that before mining commenced.

3. Special performance and reclamation standards for mining on alluvial valley floors in arid and semiarid areas, on prime farmland, and on steep slopes.

4. Enforcement of the Act through a mining permit program administered jointly by the federal government and the states, according to federal regulations.

5. Protection of land unsuitable for mining from any mine activity.

6. Creation of a special fund, financed from a tax on existing surface mining, to reclaim "orphan" mine sites.

7. Creation of an agency, currently the Office of Surface Mining Reclamation and Enforcement (OSMRE) within the Department of the Interior (DOI), to enforce the Act.

The Reagan Onslaught.   Few federal regulations were more directly and consistently attacked by the Reagan administration than those arising from SMCRA. To the Reagan reformers, the Act epitomized the excesses of federal authority, the red tape, confusion, and inflated costs inflicted on industry and the states by federal environmental laws. Under secretary of the DOI James G. Watt, pervasive alterations in the name of "regulatory relief" were made in the administrative structure set up to enforce SMCRA. The attack fell squarely on the OSMRE, and on the regulations it wrote. OSMRE's field offices were drastically reduced, its full-time staff inspectors diminished by half. Estimates suggest that Watt's office may have rewritten more than 90 percent of the regulations originally formulated by the DOI under President Carter.[48]

The Reagan administration charged into an already heated controversy when it promised to grant the states increased discretion in enforcing SMCRA. While conflict between the federal government and the states over their respective authority is inevitable in regulatory federalism, surface mine regulation has been especially contentious. SMCRA encouraged the states to accept responsibility for its implementation—called "primacy"—and appeared to grant them discretion in applying its provisions to their mining industries. By the early 1980s, twenty-four of the twenty-seven states affected by SMCRA had accepted primacy. But many states soon complained that OSMRE's regulations were too strict and its willingness to give the states discretion in applying the regulations was too limited. Congress was, in fact, responsible for much of the problem. SMCRA had been written to give the states maximum opportunity to take responsibility in procedural matters such as processing permits. But Congress was also alarmed at surface mining's ecological devastation and determined to strike hard at eastern mining companies especially. It wrote SMCRA's stringent regulatory standards in great length and fine detail to ensure that OSMRE would start with a strong program. The Carter administration ensured that OSMRE would be a tough, aggressive regulator by deliberately recruiting an environmentalist staff.

The states initially greeted the promise of more discretion with enthusiasm because it implied that they would have greater opportunity to ease the regulatory burden on local mining companies. But the Reagan administration also reduced federal financial and technical support at the same time that it increased the administrative burden for SMCRA's enforcement. Many states, suffering the fiscal effects of prolonged revenue shortfalls, lacked the money and personnel to compensate for this diminished federal assistance. Thus, "regulatory reform" for many states meant more responsibility and less enforcement for SMCRA. It appeared to many primacy states by the end of Reagan's first term that their ability to enforce SMCRA was becoming dangerously compromised and their enthusiasm for regulatory relief waned.

By the beginning of Reagan's second term, OSMRE was approaching impotence, its personnel disorganized and demoralized. With six acting directors in its first eight years, its programs lacked continuity and credibility. OSMRE had become a constant target of congressional criticism. Environmentalists increasingly resorted to litigation to compel OSMRE to assume its statutory responsibilities for enforcing the law. Evidence of deliberate program subversion became abundant. With James Watt's abrupt departure from the DOI, the administration attempted to restore some credibility to OSMRE. Donald Hodel, Watt's successor, responded to judicial orders and congressional criticism by eliminating some of the most blatant examples of program subversion. Personnel policies were modified to restore some continuity and confidence among program administrators. A modest increase in personnel and funding was achieved in the latter Reagan years and OSMRE appeared less frequently in headlines and federal court dockets. OSMRE promised more constructive assistance to the primacy states in enforcing their programs.

A Slow and Uncertain Recovery.   Despite improvements after 1985, SMCRA remains a troubled and debilitated program. A succession of directors continues through OSMRE's revolving door. The amount of improvement in program administration remains questionable. It seems apparent, at least, that OSMRE cannot or will not exercise dependable, vigorous administrative oversight over state enforcement programs. In 1986, for instance, the GAO concluded after studying program enforcement in four of the most important primacy states that they "generally do not accept evidence of violations observed by federal inspectors during oversight inspections which could be used to cite [violations] by [mine] operators."[49] A year later, the GAO studied three additional states and discovered that one collected fines on one-tenth of the violations it discovered and another collected on less than one-third of the violations.[50] Still, some observers believe that the controversies surrounding SMCRA have had constructive results, including greater sensitivity in Washington, D.C., to the needs of the states and greater economic efficiency through more flexibility in program regulations. One important test of surface mine regulations is whether they result in an environmentally safer mining industry and a significant restoration of the many thousand orphan mine sites across the United States. An answer is elusive, partially because the restoration of surface mine sites is difficult under the best of circumstances.

The Restoration Gamble

Obscured in the controversy over SMCRA's enforcement has been an issue even more important to the future of surface mining: is restoration of mined lands in the manner contemplated by the Act achievable? Technical studies suggest that the capacity of mining companies to restore mined land to conditions equal or superior to their original condition is likely to be site specific—that is, dependent on the particular biological and geological character of each mining site. Western mining sites are often ecologically fragile; relatively limited varieties of sustainable vegetation and scarce rainfall make ecological regeneration of the land difficult. With only limited experience in the restoration of western mine sites, most experts are reluctant to predict that mine sites can be restored to ecological vitality even with good intentions, generous funding, and high-quality technical resources.

The prospects for restoration are less forbidding in Appalachia, where an abundance of precipitation, richer soil, and a greater diversity of native flora and fauna are available. Nonetheless, many experts believe that disruption of subsurface hydrology and the drainage of acids and salts from the mines' spoil heaps may not be controlled easily even when surface revegetation is achieved. Restoration remains a gamble with nature. If restoration proves difficult, confronting public officials with the prospect that a major portion of all surface-mined land may remain virtually sterile for centuries, a further national controversy may erupt over continuing surface mining.

More than a decade of experience with SMCRA leaves only fragmentary evidence of its success. After studying SMCRA's enforcement among many primacy states, for instance, political scientist Uday Desai concluded that the consequences have been mixed, at best. Environmentally safe conditions apparently were being maintained at active mine sites in Montana, Pennsylvania, and Wyoming. But in Kentucky, a major mining state, the law appeared to have had only a "marginal" impact, and in West Virginia, another important coal state, it "had not been thoroughly and rigorously enforced in many areas." [51] The conclusion suggests how far SMCRA's enforcement has yet to go in achieving its purpose:

> It is not possible to make an unqualified overall national assessment, but the evidence . . . indicates that, in most (but by no means all) cases, surface coal mining is being carried out in environmentally less destructive ways than before the Act. However, accomplishment of its ultimate objective has fallen far short of the expectations of many. In addition, there has been a serious deterioration of the situation on the ground in some states such as Kentucky. [52]

The nation's coal production was never higher, nor its future more uncertain, than in the 1990s. New amendments to the Clean Air Act require that national sulfur oxide and nitrogen oxide emissions be reduced, respectively, by about 50 percent and 10 percent—a policy likely to bring economic recession to Appalachia's troubled coal fields. Increasing emission control costs will create strong incentives for utilities to seek alternative fuel sources when possible. Policies to mitigate global climate warming all contemplate major reductions in U.S. fossil fuel combustion—another assault on Old King Coal. One tenuous hope for the coal industry lies in the commercialization of experimental "clean coal" technologies, such as fluidized bed combustion, which could reduce coal's sulfur content before combustion. The commercial prospects for these technologies remain unproven, and the industry's future precarious. Only coal mining's ecological devastation is assured. It will be the inheritance of unborn generations, a legacy written in Appalachia's scarred hills and acidified streams, in sterile mine waste plowed into moonscapes across the western plains and deserts.

Conclusion

Coal combustion and civilian nuclear power are two examples of the implicit and inevitable association between environmental quality and patterns of energy development. The United States is currently following a path of energy development that can make vast, and possibly irreversible, changes in the nation's environment. Continuing coal use perpetuates surface mining, along with all its environmental risks, across Appalachia and the West. Industrial and utility coal combustion can intensify problems of air pollution, acid precipitation, and possibly the Greenhouse Effect through the decade. Even if civilian nuclear power should fail to develop beyond facilities currently operating or under construction, the risks of accidents and the institutional difficulties in managing nuclear waste and decommissioning plants will remain significant well into the next decade at least. It should be evident that serious technical, administrative, and political difficulties exist in the enforcement of legislation intended to protect the nation from the most environmentally malignant impacts of these technologies.

Equally important are the environmental implications of current energy policy for the future. First, the United States today has no explicit, comprehensive program of energy conservation, nor does it have any governmental commitment to promoting the development and proliferation of energy-conserving technologies beyond what may be accomplished through the deregulation of energy prices. This implies that energy development throughout the remainder of the decade is likely to place growing stress on environmental quality and nonrenewable resources such as fossil fuels.

Second, the continuing U.S. dependence on nonrenewable energy resources, along with the adverse environmental impacts often associated with these resources, is slowly but resolutely moving the United States into a position where it may have to contemplate a severe energy-environment trade-off should a new energy crisis emerge. Public opinion polls have long suggested that environmental quality is most politically vulnerable to an energy crisis. Should the public and its officials feel they must choose between more energy or continuing environmental protection, there seems to exist a strong disposition to opt for energy development. Continued reliance on environmentally threatening energy sources leaves U.S. policy makers with few options but environmentally dangerous ones in the face of another energy crisis.

Third, it should be apparent from discussions of coal and nuclear power development that many of the environmental risks associated with these energy sources are created or exacerbated by failure of institutional management or design. Stated somewhat differently, the problems of decommissioning reactors or finding a safe and publicly acceptable repository for nuclear waste illustrate the failure of policy makers to anticipate the institutional arrangements essential to ensuring the safety of energy technologies. An essential aspect in planning the future development of energy technologies through government, whether it be synfuels technologies, nuclear fusion, or something else, should be careful and prolonged consideration of the institutional arrangements essential to ensure the technologies' safety—a sort of institutional risk assessment that raises tough and realistic questions about the impact of technologies on governmental institutions and their capacities to manage such technologies in an environmentally sound way.

Notes

1. U.S. Department of Commerce, Bureau of the Census, *Statistical Abstract of the United States, 1989* (Washington, D.C.: Government Printing Office, 1990), 563.
2. U.S. Department of Commerce, Bureau of the Census, *Statistical Abstract of the United States, 1997* (Washington, D.C.: Government Printing Office, 1998), 584.
3. Council on Environmental Quality (CEQ), *Environmental Quality , 1992* (Washington, D.C.: Government Printing Office, 1993), 331.
4. U.S. Department of Commerce, *Statistical Abstract, 1997, 273.*
5. Kennedy P. Maize, ed., *Blueprint for the Environment: Advice to the President-Elect from America's Environmental Community* (Salt Lake City, Utah: Howe Brothers, 1989).
6. U.S. Department of Commerce, *Statistical Abstract of the United States, 1993* (Washington, D.C.: Government Printing Office, 1994), 704.
7. CEQ, *Environmental Quality, 1996* (Washington, D.C.: Government Printing Office, 1997).
8. U.S. Department of Energy (DOE), Energy Information Administration, *Annual Energy Review, 1993* (Washington, D.C.: Government Printing Office, 1994), 199.
9. On energy policy during the Reagan years generally, see Franklin Tugwell, *The Energy Crisis and the American Political Economy* (Palo Alto, Calif.: Stanford University Press, 1988), chaps. 7, 8, and 9; and Richard H. K. Vietor, *Energy Policy in America Since 1945: A Study of Business-Government Relations* (New York: Cambridge University Press, 1984).
10. On the history of U.S. commercial nuclear power see Irvin C. Bupp and Jean-Claude Derian, *The Failed Promise of Nuclear Power* (New York: Basic Books, 1978); and Steven L. Del Sesto, *Science, Politics and Controversy: Civilian Nuclear Power in the United States, 1946–1974* (Boulder, Colo.: Westview Press, 1979).
11. Bupp and Derian, *The Failed Promise,* chap. 5.
12. Christopher Flavin, *Nuclear Power: The Market Test* (Washington, D.C.: Worldwatch Institute, 1983), 27.
13. *New York Times,* Jan. 14, 1988.
14. *New York Times,* Jan. 1, 1990.
15. *Wall Street Journal,* Jan. 16, 1998.
16. *New York Times,* June 22, 1989
17. *New York Times,* March 27, 1988.
18. *New York Times,* March 27, 1989.
19. "Nuclear Safety: Northeast Utilities Hit With Record Fine," Greenwire, December 11, 1997.
20. Walter A. Rosenbaum, "Nuclear Wastes and Federalism: The Institutional Impacts of Technology Development," in *Western Public Lands: The Management of Natural Resources in a Time of Declining Federalism,* ed. John G. Frances and Richard Ganzel (Totowa, N.J.: Rowman and Allanheld Publishers, 1984). See also Luther J. Carter, *Nuclear Imperatives and Public Trust* (Washington, D.C.: Resources for the Future, 1987), chaps. 4 and 5; and Edward J. Woodhouse, "The Politics of Nuclear Waste Management," in *Too Hot to Handle? Social and Policy Issues in the Management of Radioactive Waste,* ed. Charles A. Walker, Leroy C. Gould, and Edward J. Woodhouse (New Haven, Conn.: Yale University Press, 1983), 151–183.

21. Quoted in "Nevada to Get Nuclear Waste, Everyone Else 'Off the Hook,' " *Congressional Quarterly Weekly Report,* Dec. 19, 1987, 3136–3137.
22. "Nuclear Waste: House Approves Temporary Storage Bill," Greenwire, April 16, 1997.
23. *New York Times,* Nov. 29, 1989.
24. General Accounting Office (GAO), "Nuclear Waste: Yucca Mountain Project Behind Schedule and Facing Major Scientific Uncertainties," Report no. GAO/RCED 93-124 (May 1993), 4.
25. *New York Times,* June 13, 1989. See also GAO, "Nuclear Waste: Storage Issues at DOE's Waste Isolation Pilot Plant in New Mexico," Report no. GAO/RCED 90-1 (Dec. 1989).
26. *New York Times,* Dec. 15, 1989. See also GAO, "Nuclear Energy: Environmental Issues at DOE's Nuclear Defense Facilities," Report no. GAO/RCED 86-192 (Sept. 1986), 2–4.
27. GAO, "Nuclear Regulation: NRC's Decommissioning Procedures and Criteria Need to Be Strengthened," Report no. GAO/RCED 89-119 (May 1989), 2–3. On decommissioning problems generally, see Cynthia Pollock, *Decommissioning: Nuclear Power's Missing Link* (Washington, D.C.: Worldwatch Institute, 1986).
28. Pollock, *Decommissioning,* 25–33.
29. DOE, *Estimating the Cold War: The 1995 Baseline Environmental Management Report* (Washington, D.C.: Government Printing Office, 1996).
30. *New York Times,* Oct. 31, 1988.
31. Quoted in *New York Times,* Dec. 12, 1981.
32. Quoted in *New York Times,* Jan. 21, 1985.
33. GAO, "Nuclear Regulation: Efforts to Ensure Nuclear Power Plant Safety Can Be Strengthened," Report no. GAO/RCED 87-141 (Aug. 1987), 2–3.
34. GAO, "Nuclear Regulation: NRC's Decommissioning Procedures," 2–3.
35. Richard E. Balzhiser, "Future Consequences of Nuclear Nonpolicy," in *Energy: Production, Consumption and Consequences,* ed. John L. Helm (Washington, D.C.: National Academy Press, 1990), 184–204. See also Christopher Flavin, *Reassessing Nuclear Power: The Fallout from Chernobyl* (Washington, D.C.: Worldwatch Institute, 1987), 62–74.
36. Kirk Victor, "The Nuclear Turn-on," *National Journal,* Sept. 9, 1989, 2196–2200.
37. *New York Times,* Nov. 26, 1989.
38. Morone and Woodhouse, *The Demise of Nuclear Energy?* 147.
39. *New York Times,* March 27, 1993.
40. Lawnie H. Taylor, Sr., *Ten Year Cleanup of U.S. Department of Energy Waste Sites: The Changing Roles of Technology Development in an Era of Privatization* (Washington, D.C.: Department of Energy, 1996), chap. 1.
41. DOE, Office of Environmental Restoration and Waste Management, *Fact Sheets: Environmental Restoration and Management* (Washington, D.C.: Government Printing Office, 1991), 21.
42. Ibid., 2.
43. *New York Times,* Jan. 25, 1992. See also GAO, "Nuclear Waste: Problems and Delays with Characterizing Hanford's Single-Shell Tank Waste," Report no. GAO/RCED 91-118 (April 1991).
44. *New York Times,* June 21, 1993.
45. *New York Times,* Dec. 24, 1992.
46. Quoted in *New York Times,* June 21, 1993.
47. *New York Times,* Aug. 17, 1990; Aug. 5, 1993.
48. Changes in OSMRE regulations during this period are discussed in Conservation Foundation, *State of the Environment, 1982* (Washington, D.C.: Conservation Foundation, 1984), 303–410. Estimates of the number of regulations rewritten are found in *New York Times,* Nov. 5, 1983.
49. GAO, "Surface Mining: Interior Department and States Could Improve Inspection Programs," Report no. GAO/RCED 87-40 (Dec. 1986), 3. See also Richard Miller, "Implementing a Program of Cooperative Federalism in Surface Mining Policy," *Pol-*

icy Studies Review 9, no. 1 (Autumn 1989): 79–87; and Richard Harris, "Federal-State Relations in the Implementation of Surface Mining Policy," *Policy Studies Review* 9, no. 1 (Autumn 1989): 69–78.
50. GAO, "Surface Mining: States Not Assessing and Collecting Monetary Penalties," Report no. GAO/RCED 87-129 (June 1987), 3.
51. Uday Desai, "Assessing the Impacts of the Surface Mining Control and Reclamation Act," *Policy Studies Review* 9, no. 1 (Autumn 1989): 104–105.
52. Ibid., 105.

Suggested Readings

Bupp, Irvin C., and Jean-Claude Derian. *The Failed Promise of Nuclear Power*. New York: Basic Books, 1978.

Hamlett, Patrick W. *Understanding Technological Politics: A Decision-Making Approach*. Englewood Cliffs, N.J.: Prentice-Hall, 1992.

Morone, Joseph G., and Edward J. Woodhouse. *Averting Catastrophe: Strategies for Regulating Risk Technologies.* Berkeley: University of California Press, 1986.

Tugwell, Franklin. *The Energy Crisis and the American Political Economy*. Palo Alto, Calif.: Stanford University Press, 1988.

U.S. Office of Technology Assessment. *Complex Cleanup: The Environmental Legacy of Nuclear Weapons Production*. Washington, D.C.: Office of Technology Assessment, 1991.

Chapter 9

Our 700 Million Acres:
The Battle for Public Lands

> *Sales of "predator friendly" wool that "comes from operations where nonlethal means of predator control are used" are on the rise, reports the* New York Times. *Llamas, guard dogs and burros that scare off predators are among the handful of creatures that a growing number of "environmentally minded western ranchers hope will replace lethal means of coyote control.". . . Demand for the green-marketed wool, which can cost up to [a] $1.50 more per pound than conventional wool, "has grown substantially in the past year." The Nature Conservancy recently agreed to feature the green-marketed wool in its catalogue. . . .*
>
> —Greenwire, December 13, 1997

In 1976, the bicentennial year of the Republic, the government of the United States officially ended after almost two centuries its policy of conveying public lands to private control. During that time more than 1.1 billion acres of land, an expanse larger than western Europe, had been surrendered to the states, farmers and trappers, railroads, veterans, loggers and miners, canal builders—to any interest with the political strength to make a persuasive claim to Congress. American land shaped American character more decisively than any other aspect of the nation's environment. Though vastly reduced, the public domain remains an enormous physical expanse embracing within its continental sprawl, often accidentally, some of the nation's most economically and ecologically significant resources, a biological and physical reserve still largely unexploited. The struggle to determine how this last great legacy shall be used constitutes, in large part, the substance of the political struggle over public lands.

Once most of the land of this country was public domain. Over the past two centuries the federal government has owned almost four of every five acres on the continental United States. This land, held in trust for the people of the nation, is governed by Congress, in whom the Constitution vests the power to "dispose and make all needful Rules and Regulations respecting the Territory or other Property belonging to the United States." [1] Until the turn of this century, Congress had been concerned primarily with rapidly divesting itself of the lands, turning them over to the states or to private interests in huge grants at bargain-basement prices. Only belatedly did Congress, powerfully pressured by the new American conservation movement, awaken to the necessity of preserving the remaining natural resources on the public domain before they were wholly lost. By this time most of the remaining public lands lay west of the Mississippi River; much was wilderness too remote and inaccessible to be easily exploited or grasslands and rangelands seemingly devoid of economic attraction.

The Public Domain

Today the federal government owns approximately 650 million acres of land, about 29 percent of the total U.S. land area. Many western states are largely public domain: more than half of Alaska, Idaho, Nevada, Oregon, Utah, and Wyoming are federally owned; public lands constitute more than a third of Arizona, California, Colorado, and New Mexico (see Table 9-1, p. 300). Much of this land, originally ceded to the western states when they joined the Union, was rejected as useless for timbering, grazing, or farming; some was held in trust for Native American tribes by the federal government. Only later, well into the twentieth century, did exploration reveal that vast energy and mineral resources might reside under the tribal reservations, wilderness, timber, and grasslands remaining in the public domain. The economic value of public lands was increased greatly in 1953 when the United States joined other nations in redefining the limits of national authority over offshore waters. Prior to 1953, the traditional standard had limited national sovereignty to 3 miles offshore. In 1953, Congress passed the Outer Continental Shelf Act (Pub. L. 82-212) despite the vigorous opposition of coastal states such as Florida and California, declaring federal government ownership of continental shelf (OCS) lands extending as far as 200 miles offshore. The legislation, ratifying an international treaty negotiated by the State Department, ended a longstanding dispute between the federal and state governments over control of offshore energy resources by immediately vesting in the federal government control over almost all of the 1.1 billion acres of submerged continental shelf land. By accident and design that third of the nation, together with its spacious offshore lands, now controlled by the federal government, has become a public trust of potentially huge economic value.

An Unanticipated Bounty

The actual magnitude of mineral, timber, and energy reserves on the public domain remains uncertain; many areas, including much of the gigantic Alaskan wilderness, have yet to be fully inventoried. Estimates of resources on more accessible lands also can be controversial. However, commonly cited figures suggest the reasons why public lands have assumed such importance to major economic interests in the United States:

• About 30 percent of the nation's remaining oil and gas reserves, 40 percent of its coal reserves, and 80 percent of its shale oil may be on public domain.
• About 60 percent of low-sulfur U.S. coal resides on federal lands west of the Mississippi River.
• About 56 percent of undiscovered U.S. petroleum reserves and 47 percent of natural gas reserves are estimated to reside on federal OCS lands.
• About 30 percent of the nation's forests remain untimbered on federal wilderness land or national forest areas.[2]

Beyond those resources on which a price can be placed, the public domain contains both incalculable natural treasures whose worth has become evident to generations—Yosemite, Yellowstone, the Grand Canyon, and the other national parks—and nameless wild and free places, the wilderness that the naturalist Aldo Leopold has called "the raw material out of which man has hammered the artifact called civilization" and to which, he reminds us, we need often return, in fact and imagination, as to a sanctuary.[3] Indeed, much of what remains undisturbed on the American earth, still available to this generation in something like its original condition, can be found only in federal wilderness areas. Whether wilderness is or should be a thing beyond price and beyond exploitation remains among the most bitterly controversial of all environmental issues.

Diversity Within the Public Domain

The public domain has been divided by Congress into different units committed to different uses and administered by different executive agencies. The most important of these uses are the following:

U.S. National Wilderness Preservation System. Created by Congress in 1964, the National Wilderness Preservation System currently includes 79.8 million acres of land, including more than 50 million acres of

Table 9-1   Total and Federally Owned Land, by State, 1993

State	Total (1,000 acres)	Not owned by federal government (1,000 acres)	Owned by federal government[a] Acres (1,000)	Percent
AK	365,482	117,483	247,999	67.9
AL	32,678	31,599	1,079	3.3
AR	33,599	30,840	2,759	8.2
AZ	72,688	38,374	34,314	47.2
CA	100,207	54,997	45,210	45.1
CO	66,486	42,400	24,086	36.2
CT	3,135	3,127	8	0.3
DC	39	30	9	24.1
DE	1,266	1,237	29	2.3
FL	34,721	31,745	2,977	8.6
GA	37,295	35,799	1,497	4.0
HI	4,106	3,455	650	15.8
IA	35,860	35,524	336	0.9
ID	52,933	20,328	32,605	61.6
IL	33,795	34,833	962	2.7
IN	23,158	22,695	464	2.0
KS	52,511	52,087	424	0.8
KY	25,512	24,432	1,080	4.2
MA	5,035	4,938	97	1.9
MD	6,319	6,131	188	3.0
ME	19,848	19,684	163	0.8
MI	36,492	31,900	4,592	12.6
MN	51,206	45,828	5,377	10.5
MO	44,248	42,159	2,089	4.7
MS	30,223	28,919	1,304	4.3
MT	93,271	67,204	26,067	27.9
NC	31,403	29,397	2,005	6.4
ND	44,452	42,566	1,887	4.2
NE	49,032	48,321	711	1.4

Alaskan wilderness added in 1979. By legislative mandate wilderness lands are to be set aside forever as undeveloped areas.

National Park System. Created more than a century ago with the designation of Yellowstone National Park, the system currently constitutes 38 parks and 257 national monuments, historic sites, recreational areas, near-wilderness, seashores, and lake shores, altogether embracing more than 83 million acres. Closed to mining, timbering, grazing, and most other economic uses, the system is to be available to the public for recreational purposes.

National Wildlife Refuge System. The system currently includes almost 92 million acres, two-thirds in Alaska but also distributed among all fifty states. The 413 refuges are to provide habitat to migratory water-

Table 9-1   *Continued*

State	Total (1,000 acres)	Not owned by federal government (1,000 acres)	Owned by federal government[a] Acres (1,000)	Percent
NH	5,769	5,034	733	12.7
NJ	4,813	4,651	162	3.4
NM	77,766	51,513	26,253	33.8
NV	70,264	11,969	58,295	83.0
NY	30,681	30,469	212	0.7
OH	26,222	25,883	339	1.3
OK	44,088	43,371	716	1.6
OR	61,599	29,300	32,298	52.4
PA	28,804	28,173	631	2.2
RI	677	672	5	0.7
SC	19,374	18,630	744	3.8
SD	48,882	48,076	2,805	5.7
TN	26,728	25,708	1,019	3.8
TX	168,218	165,941	2,277	1.4
UT	52,697	19,935	32,762	62.2
VA	25,496	23,683	1,813	7.1
VT	5,937	5,579	358	6.0
WA	42,694	30,603	12,091	28.3
WI	35,011	31,474	3,537	10.1
WV	15,411	14,388	1,022	6.6
WY	62,343	31,888	30,455	48.9
Total	2,271,343	1,621,021	650,322	28.6

Source: U.S. Department of Commerce, Bureau of the Census, *Statistical Abstract of the United States, 1996* (Washington, D.C.: Government Printing Office, 1997), Table 364.

Note: As of end of fiscal year.

[a] Excludes trust properties.

fowl and mammals, fish and waterfowl hatcheries, research stations, and related facilities.

National Forests. Since 1897 Congress has reserved large forested areas of the public domain and has authorized the purchase of additional timberlands to create a forest reserve, to furnish continuous timber supplies for the nation, and to protect mountain watersheds. Forest lands are to be managed by a "multiple-use" formula that requires a balance of recreation, timber, grazing, and conservation activities. Currently exceeding 187 million acres, national forests are found principally in the far west, the Southeast, and Alaska.

National Rangelands. The largest portion of the public domain, located primarily in the West and Alaska, is made up of grassland and prairie land, desert, scrub forest, and other open space collectively known as "rangelands." Although often barren, a substantial portion of the 328 million acres of rangeland is suitable for grazing; permits are issued to ranchers for this purpose by federal agencies.[4]

Such a classification implies an orderly definition of the uses for the public domain and a supporting political consensus that do not exist. Behind the facade of congressionally assigned uses stretches a political terrain strewn with conflicts of historical proportions over which lands shall be placed in different categories, which uses shall prevail among competing demands on the land, how much economic exploitation should be permitted in the public domain, and how large the public domain should be.

Since 1970, two national public land policies have provoked the most significant of these conflicts: the congressionally mandated practices of multiple use, or balanced use, for much of the public domain and the creation of vast "wilderness areas" in the public domain to be protected forever from human development. In this chapter we shall examine the ecological and political context in which multiple-use and wilderness conflicts arise and the participants who are drawn into the struggles. These conflicts characteristically pit federal resource management agencies, state and local governments, commodity producers and users, and environmentalists against each other over issues that long predate the modern environmental era.

Conflicts over Multiple Use

Disputes over multiple use of the public domain customarily evolve in roughly similar political settings. Conflict focuses on land administered by one of the federal resource agencies, usually the Department of the Interior's (DOI) Bureau of Land Management (BLM) or the Agriculture Department's Forest Service, charged with the stewardship of millions of acres of the public domain under a multiple-use mandate.

Struggling to interpret an ambiguous congressional mandate for land management, the agency will commonly find among the parties in conflict over its interpretation of multiple use the states within whose jurisdictions the land resides, the various private economic interests with a stake in the decision, congressional committees with jurisdiction over the agency's programs, and perhaps the White House. Especially within the past two decades, environmental interests have been important and predictable participants. Sometimes the issues are resolved—that is, if they are resolved—only by congressional reformulation of land-use policy.

The Land-Use Agencies

Management of the public domain is vested principally in four federal agencies whose collective jurisdiction, more than a million square miles, exceeds the size of Mexico. The Forest Service, the National Park Service, the BLM, and the Fish and Wildlife Service control more than 690 million acres—about 90 percent of all the land currently in the public domain. The Forest Service and the BLM control by far the largest portion of this collective jurisdiction. Unlike the National Park Service and the Fish and Wildlife Service, Congress requires that the BLM and the Forest Service administer their huge public trusts under the doctrine of multiple use. The two agencies come to this task with strikingly different political histories and territorial responsibilities.

The Forest Service. Created as part of the Agriculture Department in 1905, the Forest Service is one of the proudest and most enduring monuments to America's first important conservation movement. Founded by Gifford Pinchot, one of the nation's greatest conservationists, the Service has a long and distinguished history of forest management. Widely recognized and publicly respected, the Service has been adept at cultivating a favorable public image—who is not familiar with Smokey the Bear and other Service symbols of forest preservation?—and vigorous congressional support. The Service's jurisdiction covers most of the land, including some grasslands, within the U.S. Forest System. With more than 39,000 employees and a budget exceeding $3.1 billion, the Forest Service historically has possessed a strong sense of mission and high professional standards. "While the Forest Service has frequently been at the center of political maelstroms," political scientist Paul Culhane wrote, "it has also been regarded as one of the most professional, best managed agencies in the federal government."[5] Operating through a highly decentralized system of forest administration, local forest rangers are vested with great discretion in interpreting how multiple-use principles will apply to specific forests within their jurisdiction.

The Bureau of Land Management. The BLM manages more than 300 million acres of public domain and leases another 200 million acres in national forests and private lands, but remains obscure outside the West. The BLM's massive presence throughout the West is suggested by Figure 9-1, which identifies the proportion of state lands currently managed by the BLM and suggests, as well, why western political interests have been so deeply implicated in the BLM's political history. The Bureau has struggled to establish standards of professionalism and conservation that would free it from its own long history of indifference to conservation values and from unflattering comparisons with the Forest Service.

Figure 9-1 Percentage of State Acreage Managed by the U.S. Bureau of Land Management

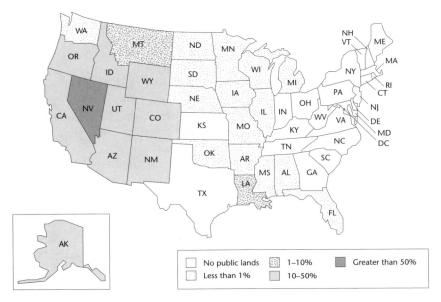

Source: U.S. Department of the Interior, Bureau of Land Management, *Annual Report, 1996* (Washington, D.C.: Government Printing Office, 1997), 80.

The BLM was created in 1946 when President Harry S. Truman combined the DOI's old Grazing Service and General Land Office to form the new Bureau with the largest land jurisdiction of any federal agency. Starting with responsibility for managing federal grasslands and grazing lands, the Bureau gradually added to its jurisdiction other lands with mineral resources and, more recently, 78 million acres of Alaskan lands, including many large wilderness areas. The BLM has inherited a great diversity of lands with different dominant uses: the Alaskan wilderness; more than 2.5 million acres of prime Douglas timber in western Oregon; 146.9 million acres of grazing lands. The BLM also is responsible for arranging the leases for mineral exploration on all public domain lands and the OCS.

Lacking the prestige of the Forest Service and burdened with a long history of deference to the ranching and mining interests that form a major portion of its constituency, the BLM has struggled to create greater professionalism, more sensitivity to conservation, and more aggressive enforcement of land-use regulations within its jurisdiction.

Throughout its history it also has suffered chronic understaffing and underfunding—its budget and staff are less than a third of that of the Forest Service despite its greater jurisdiction. And the BLM has never enjoyed the relative insulation from top departmental management that the Forest Service has experienced. This, to many environmentalists, is one of its chronic problems. According to resource expert James Baker, "The multiple-use concept suffers at the BLM because management decisions are influenced by top policy personnel appointed by the administration in power, who inherently focus on one single use, such as mining, and ignore or give short shrift to such other legitimate uses as wildlife and recreation."[6]

The BLM and the Forest Service work in a political milieu whose character is shaped by the ambiguous, and sometimes inconsistent, requirements of multiple-use land management; by pressures from the private interests seeking access to resources on land within agency jurisdictions; by conflicts with environmentalists over the appropriate balance between environmental protection and resource use—both of which the agencies are expected to promote; by frequent conflicts between the president and Congress over their respective authority over the agencies; and by state governments, particularly in the West, determined to press on the agencies, Congress, and the White House the states' claims for preference in policy making. All these conflicts were exacerbated in the 1980s by the determination of the White House to force major changes in existing understandings about such issues and in the 1990s by the growing political strength of the "wise use" movement in opposition to environmentalist pressures on federal land management agencies.

An Ambiguous Mandate

In carrying out their assigned tasks, managers in these agencies often must walk an administrative tightrope fashioned from the inconsistencies and vagaries of their legislatively defined missions. Three different federal statutes charge the BLM and Forest Service to administer the lands in their trust by multiple-use principles. The most elaborate definition of the doctrine, ripe with the ambiguities that create so many problems in its implementation, is found in section 531 of the Multiple Use–Sustained Yield Act (1960):

> "Multiple use" means: the management of all the various renewable surface resources of the national forest so that they are utilized in the combination that will best meet the needs of the American people; making the most judicious use of the land for some or all of these resources or related services over areas large enough to provide sufficient latitude for periodic

adjustments in use to conform to changing needs and conditions; that some land will be used for less than all of the resources; and harmonious and coordinated management of the various resources, each with the other, without impairment of the productivity of the land, with consideration being given to the relative values of the various resources, and not necessarily the combination of uses that will give the greatest dollar return or the greatest unit output.[7]

The intent of this complicated mandate is to make sure that in land management "any use should be carried out to minimize interference with other uses of the same area and, if possible, to complement those other uses."[8] But it provides to agency managers scant information concerning how these differing values are to be defined and balanced when differing claims on land use must be resolved. Since almost 60 percent of all public lands are held by federal agencies under some form of multiple-use law, such problems are commonplace and conflict over their resolution predictable. The BLM, for instance, has wrestled for years with managing desert areas east and north of Los Angeles to the satisfaction of both conservationists and vehicle racing enthusiasts. Each year the BLM processes more than one hundred applications for motorcycle races, some annual events with as many as 3,000 competitors. Conservationists have argued that the races permanently scar the land, alter the native ecological balances, and create noise and other disruptions for other recreationists.[9] In trying to reduce the impact of such racing, the BLM must determine the proper balance between recreation and conservation values in terms of these specific desert lands; any decision becomes controversial.

The agencies frequently discover that multiple use also leads to a conflicting mandate. The Forest Service is expected to protect the national forests from excessive timbering but at the same time to assist state and private forest owners in obtaining access to federal forests. Wildlife refuges are supposed to protect and preserve the ecologically viable habitat for endangered species but also to provide grazing, hunting, and perhaps mining opportunities to private interests.

But the multiple-use doctrine also gives both agencies, and particularly the local resource managers who must often translate the doctrine into operational terms, a means of managing the conflicting interest pressures on the land. Multiple use requires a balancing of uses, and concern for a variety of claims, without ensuring any one dominance—a formula that leaves resource managers with the opportunity to balance and negotiate among interests claiming use of public resources. It also promises constant pressure on the agencies to create or alter interpretations of multiple use by whatever interests feel existing interpretations discriminate against their claims on the land.

State and Regional Interests

State governments, particularly in the West, historically have been deeply concerned with federal land-use policies and for more than a century have pressed Washington, D.C., for greater control over public lands within their boundaries. Since the public domain constitutes so large a portion of many western states, decisions made at the federal level affecting land use can have an enormous economic, political, and social impact on the western governments. The states have a direct economic stake in multiple-use management. Approximately 20 percent of Forest Service receipts for timber sales are returned to local governments in lieu of property taxes on federal lands. More than a third of the BLM's annual receipts for mining royalties and other uses of its land is returned to the states. There are also large political concerns. In general, the western states have long believed that they have been denied a properly important voice in decisions affecting their lands; they often perceive themselves to be governed by a remote and unresponsive bureaucracy insensitive to their special concerns. In particular, the western states want a louder voice in determining grazing rights, in setting conditions for mineral exploration, in establishing timbering quotas, and in deciding how revenues from resource use on the public domain will be allocated. Many states, such as Utah, have insisted that the federal government ought to divest itself of much land within the state borders, turning the land and all its resources over to the states. By the 1980s the western determination to assert greater state and regional control over federal lands had assumed a political identity as the "Sagebrush Rebellion."

Conflict between Washington, D.C., and the states over land use was exacerbated by the energy crisis of the 1970s. Even before the 1973 oil embargo, the states had fought bitterly and unsuccessfully with Washington, D.C., to control the energy resources immediately off their shores in the OCS. By the late 1970s many western political leaders shared Colorado governor Richard D. Lamm's "growing feeling of regional paranoia" because they suspected the western lands might be reduced to an "energy colony" through exploitation by the more populous, politically powerful, and energy-hungry states in the Northeast and Sun Belt. Animating this fear is a realization that conditions for coal, oil, and natural gas exploration in the West are largely determined in Washington, D.C. At the same time, western states want to know that they will receive a substantial royalty for any mineral resources extracted from federal lands within their jurisdiction. In the opinion of many northeastern states, the royalties have become too substantial. These states, as major consumers of western coal, have complained of excessive severance taxes. By the mid-1990s the severance taxes going to western states for coal and other energy resources will exceed $4 billion annually. One spokesperson for northeastern and midwestern states feared that the western energy states were becoming "a United Arab Emirates of Western states which will have all the resources."[10] As long as the federal government continues to push aggressively for greater energy exploration and production on public lands, the states will continue to press with equal determination for greater influence, if not control, over decisions about such activities within their own borders.

State and regional interests, in short, constitute one of the organizational givens in the policy arena in which federal land-use decisions are fashioned. They represent the continual problem of reconciling national land-use needs and policies with local considerations, of balancing one set of public interests against another.

Private Resource Users

Interests using resources on the public domain, or ambitious to be among the elect, are important participants in the process of making public land-use policy. Each of the major federal land-use agencies has its "clientele," that coalition of organized groups with a major economic or ideological stake in the agency's programs. In general, resource users want to expand their access to resources on the public domain, to use the resource as cheaply as possible, to protect the continuing availability of renewable resources, and to maintain or enhance their influence within the agencies making decisions about resources strategic to them. Sheep and cattle ranchers customarily participate actively in the political struggles over the BLM rangeland regulations; individual timber companies, such as Weyerhaeuser and Crown Zellerbach, and timber trade associations, such as the National Forest Products Association, are involved in Forest Service determinations about allowable timber harvests; Peabody Coal and Climax Coal, two of the largest coal-mining companies in this country, will be found with the spokesperson for the National Coal Association actively attempting to influence the BLM or the Fish and Wildlife Service in writing regulations for coal leasing on land within their agency jurisdictions.

This intimate and historical involvement of clientele in land agency politics often has been criticized sharply, first by the earlier conservation movement and currently by environmentalists. Critics have asserted that agencies are easily "captured" by the clientele, who then promote resource exploitation at the sacrifice of balanced use and, particularly, with little regard for environmental values. Often environmental and conservation groups constitute practically the only politically active and effective force for balanced use within the private pressure group system. Conservationists once dismissed the BLM as the "Bureau of Livestock and Mining"; environmentalists routinely sued the BLM in the 1980s for allegedly failing to enforce surface mining regulations on coal lessees in New Mexico and Wyoming. The Forest Service's exemplary reputation has been no shield from accusations that it sanctions "clear cutting" and other timber practices abhorrent to environmentalists because the Service allegedly has come to define its mission largely as timber production in response to commercial timber company demands. Agency administrators, however, often have a legislative mandate to promote resource use within their jurisdictions, and as a consequence, some community of interest with resource users is inevitable. And, as we have often observed, the right of access by affected private groups to those administrators making decisions affecting such groups is regarded as a fundamental principle in American politics. Both tradition and law make the continued involvement of resource users in agency decisions inevitable and their self-interested pressures on the agencies a continual threat to the concept of balanced use.

Congress and the Public Domain

Congress ultimately decides how the public domain will be used. Although it cautiously shares some of this authority with the president, Congress traditionally has been a jealous and vigilant guardian of its prerogatives to decide finally how the states, federal land management agencies, private resource users, and others shall use the lands it holds in trust for the people of the United States. This authority flows from Article IV of the Constitution and from numerous Supreme Court decisions affirming the primacy of legislative authority in determining the character of the federal lands. Recent Supreme Court decisions have compelled Congress to share with the president the power to withdraw public lands from private use, but Congress has been quick to challenge presidents and their executive agencies when it felt they were usurping a legislative prerogative in land management.

As in other policy areas, congressional control over the public domain is exercised through the committees and subcommittees in each chamber with jurisdiction over federal land management agencies. However, while Congress vigorously defends its authority to define agency programs, it has also left the agencies with enormous discretion, as we have seen, in deciding how lands within their jurisdictions will be used; the many multiple-use laws enacted in the past several decades leave to local land managers great latitude in establishing the character of specific land uses. These agencies, as a result, operate in a politically risky milieu, where discretion is always subject to congressional challenge. When the presidency and Congress are controlled by the same party, conflicts between the two branches over agency decisions are seldom prolonged or serious. But the situation becomes ripe for conflict when differing parties control the White House and one, or both, congressional chambers. Then agency managers, exercising what they believe to be their discretionary authority on behalf of the president's program, may find themselves and their agency under congressional attack. Many of the most publicized conflicts over the Reagan administration's land-use policies erupted as battles between the secretary of the DOI and Democratic-controlled House committees with jurisdiction over the department's land programs. Feeding the conflict were partisan disagreement over which programs the department should implement and traditional disputes over the limits of executive discretion.

In the past several decades Congress has demonstrated an increasing concern for environmental values by enacting legislation requiring federal land management agencies to give conservation greater importance in land-use decisions. The Wilderness Act of 1964, an early manifestation of this growing ecological sensibility, designated by statute for the first time more than 9 million acres of public lands as wilderness and provided for additional future designations. Later, the National Environmental Policy Act of 1970 (NEPA) required federal land management agencies, among many other executive agencies, to create Environmental Impact Statements (EISs) in which the environmental consequences of land-use decisions had to be identified and considered in decisions affecting the public domain. Several major multiple-use laws passed in the 1970s, to be examined later, explicitly required the relevant federal agencies to incorporate ecological protection among the uses to be protected on the affected public domain. This concern for environmental value demonstrated in good part the rising political strength of environmental groups in the legislative process. Congress, particularly the House of Representatives, came to be the principal institutional bastion within the federal government from which environmentalists mounted their attack on President Ronald Reagan's land-use policies at the DOI.

The Environmental Movement and Public Lands

Environmentalists always have given the management of public lands a high priority. Both the National Park Service and the Forest Service were created at the turn of the century in response to vigorous promotion by the great American conservation movement, the ideological and political predecessor of the existing environmental movement. Historical legal and political battles had been waged by the Sierra Club, the Audubon Society, and other environmental groups against ecologically reckless projects promoted by federal water resource agencies long before the environmental era was named. In the 1970s environmentalists achieved a number of legislative and judicial victories that vastly expanded their influence in federal land management activities and compelled even the ecologically primitive BLM to develop, at least fitfully, an environmental conscience.

Among the most important of these achievements was passage of NEPA. As defined by the Council on Environmental Quality, which is responsible for its implementation, NEPA required that EISs be prepared by federal land management agencies for major land-use decisions affecting the environment—in effect, for most major land management planning. Draft statements had to be circulated for public review and comment prior to completion; agency officials were obligated to give the statements careful consideration in all relevant decisions.

In practical terms, the EISs became an early warning system for environmental groups, alerting them to the implications of numerous agency policies whose importance might otherwise have been ignored. Environmentalists had opportunity to organize a political strategy for influencing land management decisions. Further, the statements often forced agencies, such as the BLM, to give greater attention to the ecological impacts of their management practices. Not least important, the EIS was a legally enforceable procedure; environmental groups skillfully exploited many opportunities to use the federal courts to delay or frustrate agency decisions they opposed by challenging the adequacy of impact statements.

Federal courts, often with the explicit approval of Congress, greatly expanded the environmentalists' "standing to sue" federal agencies for alleged failures to give environmental values sufficient attention in land-use planning. This greatly liberalized standing often enabled environmental interests to compel federal agencies to give them a voice in agency proceedings. Critics charged, sometimes justifiably, that environmentalists were seizing on these new strategies primarily to disrupt administrative procedures and thereby to harass their opponents even when their case lacked merit. But the environmental activities inspired by enhanced standing, as well as the impact statement procedures, quite often resulted in valuable ecological improvements in federal land management and greater federal attention to the balanced use of land, to which many agency managers previously had given little more than lip service.

Finally, congressional attempts to encourage greater public involvement in the making of land management decisions by the Forest Service, Park Service, and the BLM also provided environmentalists with effective strategies for influencing federal policies, particularly at the local level at which so many land-use decisions were made. Indeed, environmental groups have perceived correctly that generous provision for public involvement in federal land-use planning has been among the most effective structural means of giving them access and influence in the administrative process generally. For this reason, they have been acutely concerned about the enforcement of these participation provisions in federal land law and convinced that any attempts to narrow such opportunities, by law or administrative manipulation, were covert attacks on their political bases.

In many respects, the 92 million acres of pristine federal land now congressionally protected from development under the Wilderness Act is a monument to environmentalist activism and to the laws and administrative regulations which enormously enlarged their administrative and congressional influence. As political scientist Craig W. Allin observes, provisions for public involvement in federal land use planning at the local level provided wilderness advocates with the incentive and resources to expand their power at the congressional grassroots. "Wilderness advocates quickly overcame their initial organizational disadvantage in local areas. Grassroots organizations sprang up, meeting the demands for public participation and pressing for inclusions of favored areas [in the Wilderness System]. National conservation organizations assisted through local chapters and by publishing information about successful tactics." [11] In a political system where localism dominates congressional life, this ascent of environmentalist power from the grassroots was an instance of capturing the political base from the opposition.

The "Wise Use" Movement Emerges

Out of the political turbulence inspired by the Reagan and Bush administrations' aggressive attempt to promote greater private access to public lands there emerged in 1988 the "wise use" movement. The movement is a loose alliance of public lands user groups: resource developers seeking more public resources such as timber and fossil fuels; grazing and ranching interests opposed to increased user fees on public lands; and a multitude of other economic, regional, and political interests whose assorted agendas share a common desire to diminish severely the federal government's restrictions on access to the public domain. Under the "wise use" banner march groups in other respects as dissimilar as the National Inholders Association (private property owners within public lands), the National Farm Bureau Federation, the Western Cattlemen's Association, the American Freedom Coalition (a part of the Rev. Sun

Myung Moon's Unification Church), off-road vehicle owners, timber interests, petroleum companies, and many others. It is not, however, simply another incarnation of the Sagebrush Rebellion. The idea of property rights as a legal and philosophical basis for action—a strategy which greatly expanded the movement's political appeal beyond the West—gave it a national aura and intellectual depth. "The idea of protection of property rights was borrowed from the property rights movement," explains political scientist Sandra Davis, "which originated in eastern states, and derived its basic concept from the libertarian party. It has been nurtured by intellectual leaders such as Richard Epstein, a law professor at the University of Chicago, and Roger Pilon of the Cato Institute. The Wise Use Movement's adoption of the property rights issue has facilitated its appeals for political support and its likelihood of succeeding in legal cases." [12]

The ideological undergirding of the movement is provided by various economic theories and theorists who argue that private use of many presently protected natural resources—timber, fossil fuels, and grazing lands especially—would constitute a more economically efficient and nationally beneficial policy (or "wise use") than the present restrictions on public resource exploitation. In this respect, "wise use" is in many ways a modern reprise of the Progressive Movement's conviction that the "highest and best use" of the public domain often implied its economic development. By grounding its arguments in economic theory, moreover, the movement gains a measure of intellectual respectability and a breadth of appeal to political and economic conservatives that is lacking in arguments based solely on the often arcane disputes over specific resource economics. The movement also shares a hearty dislike for environmentalists that occasionally erupts into vitriol such as one leader's assertion that the movement intended "to destroy the environmental movement once and for all." [13]

The "wise use" movement packs a potentially powerful appeal but still lacks a charismatic national political leader and proven political impact at the polls. Nonetheless, the environmental movement regards "wise use" with considerable apprehension. Environmentalists recognize that the movement's breadth of political and intellectual appeal could make it a formidable political opponent, especially in the West, if it were able to cohere organizationally behind an effective national leader and a publicly inviting political credo.

The many institutional interests, organized groups, agency programs, and conflicting philosophies of land use involved in managing the public domain mean that conflict and disagreement over policy are inevitable. The 1980s were characterized by unusually open and bitter conflict over management of the public domain triggered by the Reagan administration's vigorous attempts to change land policies in a manner that angered and alarmed conservationist and environmental groups across the nation. At issue were fiercely held and strongly felt convictions on both sides.

Energy and Public Lands

Energy development has been historically inseparable from American public lands politics since the turn of the twentieth century. Energy exploration and production have been powerful justifications for the development of public lands and the related array of organized economic interests embraces many of the nation's largest and most powerful corporations and politically potent state and regional political coalitions, especially those historically identified with the Midwestern and western "oil patch." Between 1980 and 1990 the Reagan administration and its opponents waged a conflict of historic proportions over the fate of energy and related resources on the public lands. The administration began the 1980s with a determination to open public lands to energy and mineral exploration and to transfer tracts of public lands to state and private control on a scale unmatched by any other administration in this century. The responsibility for achieving these ambitious objectives was vested largely in Secretary of the DOI James G. Watt, whose agency controlled the largest portion of the public domain. The administration's aggressive and unapologetic determination to turn much of public land and its resources over to private use was based on a conviction that too many resources, particularly coal, gas, and petroleum, had been locked up on the public domain. "I want to open as much land as I can," Watt remarked in explaining a philosophy that would prevail long after he left the Department. "The basic difference between this Administration and liberals is that we are market-oriented, people-oriented. We are trying to bring our abundant acres into the market so that the market will decide their value." [14]

The Reagan Land Program

What opening up public lands meant to the Reagan administration became evident between 1981 and 1983 in a series of proposals to alter profoundly the character of vast tracts within the public domain. Among the most disturbing to environmentalists follow:

• The DOI's proposed leasing of exploration rights to more than 11 billion tons of coal on federal rangeland, timberland, and wilderness areas in New Mexico, southwest Utah, Montana, and North Dakota.

This plan, opening more coal to exploration than the federal government had done in the previous decade, would affect several hundred thousand acres of previously undeveloped open land.

- The Department proposed opening for gas and petroleum exploration by 1987 about 1 billion acres of the OCS, virtually all the offshore lands within federal jurisdiction, including forty-one lease sales—sixteen off the Alaskan coast—that would likely result in exploration before the end of 1984.

- The DOI proposed a plan to sell to state and private bidders 35 million acres of public land, an area roughly equal in size to Iowa. This property, including abandoned military bases, urban land and parks, and a great diversity of other tracts not included within any of the major federal land-use programs, would have amounted to the largest transfer of public lands to private control in the century. The Reagan administration anticipated receiving $1.3 billion from sales the first year and then $4 billion annually for an indefinite period.

- The Department proposed to permit the Forest Service to open wilderness areas within the national forests to mineral and energy exploration before 1984, when such lands had to be placed beyond exploration in the U.S. Wilderness System.[15]

The scale of these proposals appalled environmentalists; so did the administration's untroubled conviction that resource use, especially energy production, should have a higher priority than any other value on most federal land, including many wilderness areas. The scale also suggests the huge energy stakes involved in decisions over public land development, another reason why public land use conflicts are so persistent and persistently bitter.

The Department in the Middle

The DOI was inevitably the focus of controversy over energy exploration on the public domain. More than 200 billion tons of coal, perhaps a fourth of the nation's coal reserves, lie below western lands under the Department's jurisdiction. Since passage of the Mineral Leasing Act of 1920, the secretary of the DOI has had the discretionary authority to sell leases and to establish conditions for private mineral and energy exploration on public lands. Such leases, to be sold at "fair market value," must be "diligently developed" into mining operations within a decade; both federal and state governments charge royalties for coal production within their boundaries. Until the 1980s, however, the department promoted coal and other resource exploration on its lands rather indifferently, and during the 1970s leasing was virtually suspended while the

Department, Congress, and the White House struggled to fashion a comprehensive leasing program. One finally emerged in the late 1970s but soon was challenged by the Reagan administration's new coal programs.

The change in coal leasing philosophy under the Reagan administration was immediate and dramatic. In 1981 alone, the DOI leased more than 400 times the acreage for coal exploration than it had the previous year. Proponents of a greatly accelerated leasing program asserted that the nation needed the energy resources lying unused on the public domain, that federal regulations could protect the lands from the ravages of surface mining, and that the economic productivity created by private use of the energy resources would generate more jobs and greater prosperity. Many of those within the Department's political leadership would have said a hearty, if perhaps private, "amen" to the summary conclusion on the subject by the president of the American Mining Congress: "Our society is built on the stuff that comes out of the hole in the ground and if we don't unplug the red tape stuffing the hole, this country is going to be in one hell of a mess." [16]

The Department's announced intentions to accelerate the sale of leases for oil and gas exploration on the OCS and its interest in leasing when legally possible even wilderness areas for exploration convinced environmental groups and congressional opponents of the Reagan programs that a massive public campaign to counteract the new policies was imperative. Congress became the institutional weapon.

The Congressional-Environmental Connection

"The probability of our developing any meaningful dialogue with this Administration is low indeed," Russell Peterson, the politically seasoned president of the National Audubon Society, lamented after talking with White House officials less than a year after President Reagan's inauguration.[17] Most environmentalists agreed and turned instead to Congress where they were able to exploit constitutional and partisan rivalries to their advantage in seeking an institutional restraint on the president's land policies. Constitutional checks and balances became one lever with which to move the executive branch, for the issue aroused the institutional rivalries at the heart of the constitutional order. The White House programs awakened among many legislators, particularly those House and Senate committees with oversight of the DOI's programs, a conviction that the Department, with White House blessing, was abusing its delegated authority and subverting congressional intent in handling the new energy programs. Democrats on the oversight committees, especially in the House, sought opportunities to challenge and embarrass the White House by attacking its land programs. In the battle over land policy, the House Interior Committee became the most aggressive congressional antagonist to the White House.

Congressional opposition to Reagan's land programs was most effective when the administration had to draw on discretionary authority clouded by ambiguity and unbuttressed by tradition. Effective opposition also required that environmentalists be able to discover when administrative actions by the Department or the White House amounted to major land-use decisions—administrative language manipulated by skilled practitioners can shroud the intention of an act in a fog of obscurity. Such circumstances did not always prevail. Many land-use policies were implemented in spite of the congressional-environmental coalition.

State and Regional Opposition

Despite Sagebrush Rebellion rhetoric, the states are often guilty of doublethink about resources on the public domain, as the controversy over land policy in the 1980s illustrates. Eager to reap the economic advantages of greater resource use on lands within their domain—more royalties, more severance taxes, greater industrial development, and the like—the states were equally determined not to pay calamitous ecological and economic costs for rapid resource exploitation. The federal government's new public land policies often aroused not enthusiasm but hostility among the western states. These states wanted resource development *and* environmental protection.

Conflict between the federal government and the states was focused most sharply on the federal government's proposal for accelerated leasing of exploration rights to oil and gas on the OCS. In 1978 Congress had passed the Outer Continental Shelf Amendments to increase greatly the environmental safeguards required for OCS exploration; to this end, extensive federal consultation with the states was required prior to any lease sales off their shores. The federal government's announced intention to sell thirty-two oil lease tracts off the central California coast sent California to the federal courts seeking an injunction to prevent the leasing; citing federal failure to consult with the state under terms of the 1978 legislation, the court issued the injunction and the DOI subsequently withdrew most of the disputed tracts from auction.

Responding to pressure from California state officials, including the new Republican governor, most environmental groups, and most of the state's congressional delegation, Congress in 1982 and 1983 further restricted lease sales off the northern and central California coast by denying appropriations to implement the leasing. In 1984 Congress banned leasing in several OCS basins off Florida and Massachusetts. Thus, the OCS states had succeeded in substantially reducing, at least temporarily, the scope of offshore energy exploration through a combination of legal and political strategies. Environmentalists, however, were uneasy about the future, for substantial OCS leasing was still permitted, and the administration seemed determined to press ahead on its OCS development plans whenever it was not massively challenged.

The Continuing Conflict

Watt's resignation as DOI secretary in October 1983 did not end the conflict over land policies initiated by the Reagan administration, nor did it diminish the administration's determination to open up the public domain to further energy exploration. Through the use of existing budgetary authority, established discretionary freedom, and "a thousand small changes," Watt had managed, in the face of formidable opposition, to move federal policy strongly toward more resource development on public lands. The DOI had accelerated the sale of leasing rights on OCS lands, including the largest leasing sale in history: seventy-eight energy companies had bid $3.5 billion to explore about 3.2 million acres of OCS territory off the Louisiana and Alabama coasts. The BLM had issued more than 38,000 leases, covering about 95 million acres, for energy exploration on its territory—about twice the total of the Carter administration. The DOI's Office of Surface Mining Reclamation and Enforcement had been severely depleted of personnel and much of its regulatory responsibility entrusted to the uncertain will and capacity of the states to implement. The BLM had succeeded in opening more than 400,000 acres of recreational areas for mineral exploration, mining, and drilling, including Glen Canyon (Utah) and Lake Meade (Nevada and Arizona).

While Watt's successors, William P. Clark and then Donald P. Hodel, created less public stir than their predecessor, the Department's new leadership pursued the same land policies and objectives throughout the tenure of the Reagan administration. Pressure to develop energy resources persisted. By the beginning of Reagan's second term, more than 1,000 applications for oil and gas exploration rights in wilderness areas and perhaps 50,000 other kinds of mineral claims were pending. During Reagan's second term, Secretary Hodel was especially diligent in quietly seeking to remove restrictions on oil and gas exploration on the OCS. Environmental groups were particularly critical of Hodel's proposal that Congress remove restrictions against oil exploration along 125 miles of OCS land within the Arctic Wildlife Refuge.

In the administration's waning days, the Department attempted a number of actions that convinced environmentalists that the spirit of James Watt still roamed departmental corridors. In the last week of the administration's tenure, for instance, the Department attempted to transfer title to an additional 24,000 acres of western shale oil lands to private owners for $2.50 an acre—228,000 acres had already been sold. This was a "fire sale" price in the opinion of environmental and congressional critics. At the same time, the Department was preparing rules that would lower the royalties paid to the government for coal mined on public land.[18] Congressional opposition and a court injunction obtained by environmentalists thwarted these eleventh-hour initiatives. So the Reagan administration's DOI left as it had entered, embattled with environmentalists.

The Bush administration began on a more conciliatory note, with the president committing himself to an active environmental agenda and implicitly distancing himself from the Reagan public land policies. But the environmental community was not pleased with the administration's new secretary of the DOI. The president's choice, Manuel Lujan, a former congressional representative from New Mexico, had been identified closely with mining, timber, and other corporate resource users during his legislative tenure. He was widely perceived within the environmental community as more antagonist than ally. Lujan's early pronouncements, including advocacy of greater energy exploration on OCS lands, did little to dissipate this image. At the same time, the Department seemed curiously ambivalent and indecisive in its policy agenda, leaving environmentalists unsure about the DOI's future course or priorities.

The Clinton administration arrived in Washington freighted with environmentalist expectations of a major reversal in public lands policies that never occurred. Despite the appointment of Bruce Babbit, an environmentalist paragon, as secretary of DOI and his outspoken commitment to turn away from the pro-development policies of the Reagan and Bush administrations, the White House seemed indecisive and uncertain in its land use policies, frequently leaving Babbitt without the president's apparent support in major clashes with Congress over forest management, energy exploration licenses, and grazing fees on the public domain—all major concerns to public lands activists of all political persuasions—and progressively deflating his, and Clinton's, environmentalist aura. By the time Babbitt left Washington to return to the private sector in 1997, it appeared to many environmentalists that the Clinton administration had been considerably more successful in stifling the pro-developmental momentum of the previous two presidents than in promoting a vigorous, strongly environmentalist land use program of its own.

The Fate of the Forests

More than one in every ten acres on the public domain could be used for commercial timber production. This land, about 89 million acres, lies mostly within the jurisdiction of the Agriculture Department's Forest

Service. Since the end of World War II, pressure has been unremitting on the Forest Service to increase the size of the annual timber harvest from national forests to satisfy the nation's growing demand for wood products. Recently, there has been increased pressure to open many undisturbed "old-growth" timber stands and wilderness areas to commercial logging. Against this economic pressure, the Forest Service is required not only to enforce the doctrine of multiple use, which forbids the service from allowing timber cutting to preclude other forest uses, but it also must manage timber cutting to ensure a "sustained yield" from any forest reserve used for commercial timbering. Congress has left to the Service the difficult and politically contentious responsibility for defining how much timber cutting is compatible with multiple use and sustained yield.

The struggle over competing timber uses is fought in the arcane language of forest economics—"nondeclining, even-flow" formulas, "allowable cuts," and "allowable-cut effects"—but the larger interests and issues at stake are apparent. The struggle represents a collision between preservationist and developmental priorities for timber, between competing definitions of the nation's economic needs, and between differing definitions of the Forest Service's mission. It is a struggle likely to intensify into the next decade.

A Disputed Treasure in Timber

About half of the nation's softwood sawtimber reserves and a very substantial portion of its remaining hardwoods grow today in the national forests. The Pacific Coast region, particularly the timbered hills and lowlands of the Pacific Northwest, contains the largest of these timber stands within the public domain; the Pacific Coast area contains almost half the pine, spruce, fir, and other softwoods in the national forests. These timber reserves, more than three times the size of all the private commercial forests in the United States and currently worth more than $20 billion, will increase in value.

Although timber cutting was permitted in the national forests from their inception, the demand for commercial timber in the forests assumed major proportions only after World War II. In the early 1940s the Service sold about 1.5 billion board feet of timber a year; by 1973 the cut exceeded 12.3 billion board feet. Driven by the nation's ravenous postwar desire for new housing, the demand for wood products rose steadily in the three decades following 1945. Private timber companies, approaching the limits of their own production, began to look increasingly to the national forests as an untapped timber reserve. This demand, if wholly satisfied, would likely result in a doubling of the annual timber harvest from the national forests in keeping with the industry's estimates that the U.S. demand for wood products would double before the turn of the century.

Pressure to expand the allowable timber cut has been particularly intense in the Pacific Northwest. Many of the Douglas fir forests in Oregon and Washington are old-growth stands, virgin forests never touched by a logger's saw, growing in a continuity of development many centuries old. These forests are among the most ecologically diverse and historically unique of all timber stands in North America, reminders of a continent once largely timbered with a profusion of species greater than all of Europe's. Many virgin forests, together with other less spectacular timberlands, are on Forest Service lands still classified, or eligible for classification, as "wilderness." To many environmentalists and to organized preservation groups such as the Sierra Club and the Wilderness Society, these lands are the living expression of the preservationist ethic, the values of the movement made visible. They are, in political terms, "gut issues."

The Greening of Forest Policy

The environmental movement has profoundly changed forest management policies since 1970 by altering its political underpinnings. Prior to the 1970s, as political scientist George Hoberg observed, "the forest policy regime was characterized by a dominant administrative agency, a strong orientation toward the development of timber resources, and little input from the public." [19] By the early 1970s, the organized environmental movement had acquired political muscle and, together with its political allies, had promoted new environmental laws and new federal agencies to implement them. Environmentalists aggressively used their newly expanded judicial access to fashion litigation into a potent political weapon. New statutory and administrative provision for public involvement in the implementation of forest policy and greater congressional oversight of Forest Service policies expanded environmentalist influence in day-to-day forest management. Altogether, this meant a new pluralism in forest management politics in which resource developers no longer dominated and in which environmentalists had become major players whose interests had to be acknowledged, along with their allies, in policy making at all governmental levels.

Once again, as in other aspects of environmental policy, environmental organizations found the courts during the 1970s and early 1980s to be an effective ally. Especially important was the growing trend among federal courts to scrutinize carefully the Forest Service's management decisions to assure they were compatible with newly enacted environmental laws rather than to defer, as the courts had done traditionally, to the Forest Services's professional expertise in cases where the Service's decisions were challenged. It was success in overturning the historic Forest Service practice of "clear-cutting" in the early 1970s, observes Hoberg, that demonstrated how important this shift in judicial attitudes meant for environmentalists. He describes what happened:

> Conservationists found an obscure provision of the original authorizing statute of the Forest Service . . . requiring that harvested trees had to be "dead or matured" and that they had to be marked before being cut. Although these requirements were legislated even before the development of the forestry profession in the United States, the court refused to defer to the Forest Service's interpretation of the statute's meaning and enjoined clear-cutting in the Monoghahela National Forest in West Virginia and the Tongass National Forest in Alaska. By outlawing the most common method for harvesting timber, these rules created a crisis of timber management. Congress was forced to rewrite management laws. . . .[20]

The Forest Service did not respond warmly to most of these early provocations. Professional foresters, and the Service's rank-and-file, often resented the challenge to their professional judgment and the environmentalist insinuations that they were ecologically unenlightened. The rise of politically organized and powerful environmentalism, moreover, spelled the end of the Forest Service's administrative autonomy, especially the customary judicial deference and the congenial congressional oversight it had come to expect. When Congress passed the National Forest Management Act (NFMA) in 1976, it compelled the Service to open its forest management planning process from the lowest levels to environmentalist involvement and set new standards for multiple-use decisions in which ecological values had to be given major consideration. Gradually, however, the Service adapted to the new environmental realities, with the considerable assistance of progressive leaders within professional forestry itself. The academic training and recruitment of Forest Service professionals was transformed to include much greater attention to environmental values and ecologically supportive practices in job preparation. The Forest Service adjusted its organizational structure and decision-making procedures to the new requirements of the National Environmental Policy Act, the NFMA, and other judicial and congressional mandates for greater attention to environmental values in its policy making.

Still, the Forest Service, like other federal land management agencies, must live with multiple-use laws as the fundamental calculus for its land-use decision making, environmentalism notwithstanding. Thus, forest managers are never free of conflicting forces and values pressing constantly upon them whenever major forest management policy must be formulated or implemented. Indeed, multiple-use legislation creates the fundamental political order out of which all forest management decisions must ultimately arise.

Multiple Use and Sustained Yield

Since Congress has chosen not to specify how it expects the foresters to define multiple use or sustained yield in specific jurisdictions, the Forest Service has been left with enormous discretion in translating these formulas into practice. As with the multiple-use doctrine, the congressional definition of sustained yield is open to diverse interpretations, as section 531 of the Multiple Use–Sustained Yield Act suggests:

> Sustained yield . . . means the achievement and maintenance in perpetuity of a high-level annual or regular periodic output of the various renewable resources of the national forests without impairment of the productivity of the land. [16 U.S.C. section 530, 74 Stat. 215 (1960)]

Conflict over interpretation of multiple-use mandates has been intensified by requirements in the Resource Planning Act of 1974, as amended by the National Forest Management Act of 1976, that the Forest Service prepare comprehensive development and management plans for each of the more than 120 management units it operates. The Service began this process in the late 1970s and still has not adopted final plans for all its management units. These management plans often become a catalyst for controversy among interests with competitive demands on particular planning units. Final adoption of a management plan does not necessarily end the controversy, however, for arguments often continue over whether the plan is being properly implemented. The Forest Service often finds itself in the middle of a continuing, and often unresolvable, conflict over what pattern of multiple use is, or should be, implemented in a given forest tract.

Both sustained-yield and multiple-use doctrines are important to the commercial timber industry because they provide the basis for the Service's determination of the allowable cut in a given timber reserve—the amount of timber that can be removed from a particular resource area in a given chronological period. The Service has interpreted sustained yield to require a nondeclining, even-flow policy, which limits the timber cut in a given area to a constant, or increasing rate—but never a declining one. In effect, this has limited severely the cutting of old-growth forests, particularly in the Pacific Northwest, to the ire of the timber industry, local communities, and some forest economists who believe a larger cut of old-growth timber is more economically efficient and compatible with the multiple-use doctrine. Environmentalists, however, generally support protection of old-growth forests and advocate further reductions on the allowable cut elsewhere.[21]

In response to pressure from the timber industry and the Reagan administration's own preferences, the Forest Service began to increase the timber harvest substantially in the mid-1980s and to plan for increasing harvests through the 1990s. Between 1982 and 1989 the total timber cut in the national forests grew from 6.7 to 12.7 million board feet.[22] Forest Service professionals contend that this expansion is consistent with the statutory mandate to maintain a sustained yield. But the timber industry wants more production. With its own reserves rapidly depleting, the industry contends that only a timber harvest from the national forests significantly above the currently projected levels will provide enough wood for the U.S. economy in the next several decades. The Carter administration, responding to the rising cost of new housing, had ordered the Forest Service to depart "in a limited and temporary way" from its general sustained-yield principles and to open up some wilderness areas not specifically included in the Wilderness System for timber harvesting. The Reagan administration, more sympathetic to the viewpoint of the National Forest Products Association, advocated that the Service permanently modify its sustained-yield practices to permit greater timber cuts without violating the balanced-use principle. In keeping with this production bias, the Reagan administration's budgets substantially increased spending for Forest Service activities closely associated with timber production, such as new forest road construction.

The Forest Service asserted that it could meet the higher timber production levels demanded by the Reagan administration only by cutting deeply into the Pacific Northwest old-growth timber, including many of the nation's remaining virgin forests. While towering stands of old Douglas fir and associated species within these forests provide incomparable vistas and sustain a great variety of plant and animal life, they are not particularly productive from an economic viewpoint. About a quarter of the trees will rot once they mature. Most of these forests have already matured and most timber has ceased to grow: they cover highly productive land on which second- and third-growth timber would flourish, producing much greater income over the next century than could be realized from current use. Professional foresters associated with the commercial timber industry have asserted that protecting most of the old-growth forests from commercial cutting largely prevents decaying old forests from being converted to more productive young stands. Moreover, the Service's critics note, higher timber cuts do not mean an end to all, or even most, of the old-growth stands but a selective cutting of some and the conversion of others to second-growth production.

Environmentalists have long opposed the logging of old-growth forests, citing the soil destabilization and ecosystem disruption they assert is almost inevitable. Nor do they find the economic arguments persuasive. The battles tend to be fought on a forest-by-forest basis, as the Service proposes the required long-range plans for each forest and then files the necessary EISs. Environmentalists often challenge the overall adequacy of the impact statements and the specific timber production goals. The struggle over timber use spills into the related issue of wilderness designation, where the Forest Service also exercises discretionary authority. The Bush administration inherited one of these struggles, an especially emotional and public dispute provoked by Forest Service plans to permit greatly expanded timber cutting in old-growth northwestern forests. The plan might have succeeded, except for ecological serendipity in the form of the Northern Spotted Owl.

The Northern Spotted Owl versus the Timber Industry

In the mid-1980s, the Forest Service had planned to permit commercial timber companies to make substantial cuts in the old-growth Oregon forests, whose 2.3 million acres represent the last 1 percent of the nation's original forest cover. In 1985, biologists in the DOI's Fish and Wildlife Service reported to the departmental leadership that the Northern Spotted Owl, whose habitat was almost exclusively northwestern old-growth forests, was fast disappearing and should be designated an "endangered species." Estimates indicated that about 1,500 nesting pairs of owls remained, all in the first-growth stands. One consequence of this designation would be to protect this habitat, if geographically unique, from almost all forms of development. This recommendation was initially overruled by the Department's leadership under considerable pressure from the timber industry and a variety of local Oregon and Washington interests, including timber mills, community leaders, unions, local congressional representatives, and timber industry workers.

Spokespersons for these interests argued that designating the Northern Spotted Owl an endangered species would virtually end logging on 1.5 million acres of old-growth timber in Oregon and Washington. The federal government estimated that between 4,500 and 9,500 jobs would be lost, but the timber industry asserted that the actual figure was ten times that amount. "You're talking about complete devastation of communities," protested Sen. Slade Gorton (R-Wash.). The president of the Northwest Forestry Association, a trade group, repeated a familiar refrain among local economic interests in Washington and Oregon: "To devastate a regional economy over the spotted owl seems absurd. You're talking about affecting half our industry. . . ." [23] The timber industry's outrage was further exacerbated because much of the old-growth, soft-wood timber was exported, primarily to Japan, where it could command several times the domestic price.

Environmentalists had opposed commercial logging in old-growth forests long before the specific tracts in Oregon and Washington entered the dispute. Environmentalists have argued that intensive logging in old-growth forests, with the building of logging roads and disruptive soil practices sure to attend it, greatly reduce the forest's ability to conserve water and to prevent soil erosion, thus violating the principle of balanced use. Spokespersons for environmental organizations have also contended that much of the old-growth timber is found in poor soil—at high elevations and on steep slopes—and exposure to weathering will cause rapid erosion after logging begins. Moreover, they assert, these forests support a unique ecosystem with a great variety of important and irreplaceable flora and fauna. Finally, environmentalists in general challenge the presumption that a major increase in the timber harvest would significantly decrease housing costs. In any case, there are many acceptable substitutes for wood in the U.S. economy that can be had without sacrificing virgin forests, they note.

But for the Northern Spotted Owl, these arguments might have succumbed to the political weight of local, regional, and national interests defending commercial access to first-growth timber. In the fall of 1988, environmental organizations obtained a federal court order that instructed the secretary of the DOI to list the Northern Spotted Owl as endangered and in mid-1989 the DOI complied with the court's demand. The designation appeared almost to end commercial logging in northwestern first-growth forests, but it did nothing to diminish the rancor, or the economic stakes, involved in the continuing controversy over the appropriate use of the national forests.

The Bush Administration and Timber Sales Reform

The Bush administration came into office committed to an active environmental agenda, implicitly distancing itself from the Reagan-Watt era in its goals for public lands. While the environmental community had been displeased with the administration's choice of Lujan as the new secretary of the DOI, it was considerably more receptive to the administration's proposal in early 1990 to reduce substantially timber sales in twelve national forests. The new proposal seemed to repudiate the previous administration's resource policies and to signal a major effort to reform traditional Forest Service sales practices, which had long been criticized by environmentalists. The sales-below-cost controversy—

"political dynamite" in the western states—seemed to set the new administration's public lands policy on a collision course with vast segments of the Forest Service's constituency.

The controversy had been simmering for decades. "The Forest Service typically constructs the roads and assumes other management and administrative responsibilities that allow private companies to harvest [public forest timber] economically," the Conservation Foundation noted. "However, several studies have alleged that the nation actually loses money (as well as valuable wilderness and wildlife habitat) in many cases, particularly in the Rocky Mountain region, because the Forest Service must spend more to allow the harvesting to occur than it receives from the harvests. The Forest Service denies that the economics of sales such as those in the Rocky Mountains and the Northwest are as unfavorable as many critics claim. . . ." [24] Environmentalists, as well as critics within the Service, had long asserted that this practice amounted to public subsidies for the commercial timber industry and a sacrifice of all other multiple-use values, such as recreation or wildlife habitat, to timber sales. "We think the Forest Service overestimates what is sustainable," argued a spokesperson for the National Wildlife Federation. "They overestimate how much timber a given area can produce, they overestimate the potential for the lands to be reforested and they underestimate the impacts on fish and wildlife. The bottom line is they are timber-dominated." [25]

When the Forest Service initiated a new bookkeeping system in 1987, it appeared to demonstrate that the Service was losing money on about two-thirds of its timber sales. [26] Critics cited Alaska's Tongass National Forest as an example of the losses disclosed by the new bookkeeping: the Forest Service had spent about $50 million annually to finance the cutting of 450 million board feet of timber that brought less than $1 million to the government in revenue. [27] Nonetheless, there were many formidable opponents to the new proposal, including loggers, timber companies, state and congressional political spokespersons for the affected areas, and the Forest Service itself. Since much of the Forest Service budget was spent on preparing and auctioning acreage for commercial logging, a reduction in these sales would mean a substantial budget reduction for the Service. In effect, the administration's plan represented the first major assault on a forest management practice that had endured for more than a half century, fortified by a powerful coalition of political and economic interests and defended by one of the federal government's most successful and respected public agencies. The proposal's fate was uncertain at best. In broader perspective, the controversy was evidence that environmentalism had achieved enough political weight to compel a fundamental rethinking of the Forest Service's professional and institutional values.

How Much Wilderness Is Enough?

A substantial portion of the 62 million undeveloped acres under the jurisdiction of the Forest Service—the "roadless regions"—could become part of the National Wilderness System and thereby be forever excluded from timbering. A large portion of this roadless area is eligible for assignment to timber production. Timber producers, environmentalists, the Forest Service, and Congress have disagreed for more than two decades over how much of this roadless area should be designated for multiple use—in other words, how much of the area should be open to timbering, mineral exploring, and other nonrecreational and nonconservation uses. Perhaps as much as a third of the whole national forest system, including many old-growth stands, are in these roadless areas.

Environmentalists have been apprehensive that any multiple-use designation for large undeveloped tracts will be an invitation not only to aggressive timbering but to oil, natural gas, and coal exploring. They predict that energy industries, on locating energy reserves, will seek exceptions to environmental regulations. Air pollution from electric power plants and energy refining operations adjacent to public lands with energy reserves will result, predict environmentalists, and the quality of the lands will be irreversibly degraded. They would prefer that most of the roadless areas under the Forest Service's jurisdiction be included in the National Wilderness System.

With some justification, environmentalists also allege that the Service's strong commitment to its traditional multiple-use doctrine makes it reluctant to turn large tracts of roadless areas over to a single dominant use, such as wilderness preservation. It is this conviction that led environmentalists to criticize the manner in which the Service conducted its first major inventory of roadless areas within its jurisdiction in the early 1970s.

Nonetheless, the Multiple Use–Sustained Yield Act requires the Forest Service to include wilderness protection among other multiple uses of land within its jurisdiction; the National Forest Management Act also requires it to draw up a master plan for the use of land under its jurisdiction that includes consideration of wilderness designation. Thus, the Service was given both ample authority and explicit responsibility to recommend to Congress additional roadless areas for inclusion in the Wilderness System; while Congress alone possesses the authority to assign land to the system formally, the Service's recommendations often influence the decisions. The White House, however, often has proposed its own plans for the roadless areas, sometimes at variance with Forest Service initiatives.

Both the Carter and Reagan administrations offered proposals to Congress for allocating the roadless areas between wilderness and multiple-use categories; both proposals departed in significant ways from the Forest Service's own proposals. The Carter administration's plan, the more conservative, would have allocated about 10 million acres to wilderness and reserved another 10 million for further study. The Reagan administration, committed to increasing the size of territory open to timbering and energy exploring, rejected the Carter proposal. Congress, as it has often done, chose to follow its own agenda for wilderness preservation. During the remainder of the Reagan administration, few new areas were designated for wilderness because Congress and the White House could reach no agreement on priorities.

RARE I and RARE II

The three-sided debate within the federal government over the use of roadless areas—dividing Congress, the Forest Service, and the White House, together with their allied interest groups, into competing coalitions—is a reminder of how pervasively the constitutional dispersion of authority affects resource planning in Washington, D.C. It also illustrates how administrative discretion can be challenged and thwarted by skilled interest groups using the Congress, and even the chief executive, against the professional administrators of an agency.

Twice in the 1970s the Forest Service invested enormous time and money in comprehensive surveys of its roadless areas in an effort to provide Congress with a plan for their future development. The first Roadless Area Review and Evaluation (RARE I) recommended in 1976 about 12 million acres from a total of 56 million for wilderness classification. This study was shelved after environmentalists challenged the plan in the federal courts on grounds that the Service had not prepared adequate EISs and had failed to solicit sufficient public involvement in the plan's preparation.

The Carter administration, attempting to open more public domain to timbering in response to pleas from the commercial timber industry, ordered a second study. RARE II, completed in 1978, recommended more area for wilderness designation (about 16 million acres) but also left more area open to multiple use than had RARE I. RARE II provoked opposition from environmentalists, who still believed too many multiple-use tracts had been proposed, and from the states of California, Oregon, and Washington, which opposed the exclusion of various roadless areas within their boundaries from wilderness designation. Litigation initiated by environmentalists and the state of California kept RARE II in limbo until the end of the Carter administration. President Reagan subsequently ordered the Service to begin yet another study, this time under guidelines intended to maximize opportunities to designate forest areas for multiple use. Further litigation initiated by environmentalists and disagreement between the many congressional committees involved in wilderness designation largely prevented significant growth of the federal Wilderness System during the Reagan administration. The Bush administration, preoccupied with other environmental matters, gave wilderness designation a low priority.

President Clinton had promised that public land protection would be a major concern in his administration, and his appointment of Bruce Babbitt, an outspoken environmentalist, as secretary of the DOI encouraged high expectations for his public land policies among environmentalists. While the Clinton administration's early accomplishments fell far short of environmentalist expectations, they were a significant departure from the public land ethic of the previous Republican administrations. The most important of the early Clinton administration policies included the successful promotion of the California Desert Protection Act in 1994, which designated 9.4 million acres of California's Mojave Desert as a national park and wildlife preserve and a significant reduction in the amount of timber sold from the national forests. To many environmentalists, however, the Clinton administration seemed too timid and indecisive in its efforts to expand the size of the National Wilderness System and to protect other public lands from degradation by ranching and mining interests.

In the 1980s, Congress continued to designate portions of roadless areas for inclusion in the Wilderness System and to order other areas to be reserved for further study, while leaving still other tracts open to multiple use. Congress was planning roadless area development on an ad hoc basis, allocating tracts in response to changing political pressures and circumstances in the context of RARE I and RARE II. As often happens in environmental affairs, Congress became the final arbiter among the contentious White House, environmental, administrative, and private interest factions with a stake in RARE I and RARE II and a determination to change some recommendations to their own advantages.

Areas in Oregon and California not proposed for wilderness designation under RARE II were so designated by congressional committees. Some tracts originally proposed for wilderness were opened to multiple use. In general, environmentalists felt that Congress was a more hospitable arena in which to fight for their vision of roadless area development than either the Reagan White House or the Forest Service operating under White House directives.

The Uncertain Future

Conflict over roadless area management continues, leaving perhaps half the undeveloped areas under Forest Service jurisdiction in limbo, awaiting final assignment to either the wilderness or multiple-use category. The Reagan administration was committed to expanding the multiple-use areas managed by the Forest Service for timbering and for energy exploration but failed in the face of massive congressional and environmentalist opposition.

Although studies by the U.S. Geological Survey suggest roadless areas in the eleven western states, excluding Texas and Oklahoma, are likely to contain relatively small amounts of undiscovered petroleum and natural gas, some tracts may be sufficiently rich in energy reserves to attract massive development should they be opened to multiple use. Others, not only old-growth timber, could be heavily cut for commercial wood products. The wilderness struggle, therefore, is likely to persist well into the next decade and remain intense as long as the need for new energy resources and increased timber harvests are considered credible claims on the public domain.

Conclusion

The struggles over energy exploration, mining, and timbering on public lands reveal a durable structure to the political conflicts over the use of public resources in the United States. The pattern tends to be repeated because it grows from political realities inherent in the U.S. governmental system.

At the center of the conflict is a federal executive agency guarding the resource as a public trust and wrestling with an ambiguous mandate for its management. Most often this agency will be part of the DOI or the Forest Service. The mandates will be vague because Congress must rely on the professional administrator to make expert resource decisions—hence the generality of the mandates—and ambiguous because Congress often shrinks from choosing between conflicting claims on resources. Thus, multiple-use prescriptions for forest or range management appear to offer something to recreationists, conservationists, and resource developers without really settling competing claims. The administrative managers for the public resource inevitably will find their professional decisions politicized as conflicting interests seek to influence technical decisions to their advantages. Technical decisions themselves can often be made and justified in different scientifically defensible ways. All this means that resource administrators sometimes can exercise their professional judgment in the service of their own group and political loyalties. In all these ways, the resource management agency finds itself at the center of a political conflict over the public domain.

Further, both the White House and Congress will become partisan advocates of resource management policy, attempting to influence administrative decisions relevant to resource management and responding to pressure from organized interests with a stake in resource management. We have observed in timber, wilderness, and energy development policies the predictable tendency of Congress to intervene in administrative management in order to protect interests important to legislators. So, too, Presidents Carter, Reagan, Bush, and Clinton, as indeed every president before them for a half century, have directed the DOI and the Forest Service to pursue specific objectives in resource management compatible with their ideological biases and political commitments. Indeed, Congress and the White House often compete in attempting to influence administrative determinations affecting the public domain. The president, despite the illusory title of chief executive, has no guarantee of success in the struggle.

The plurality of organized interests involved in resource decisions means that Congress, the White House, and the administrative agencies all are enmeshed in a process of coalition building with organized groups during resource policy making. These organized interests, moreover, involve not only private interests but also the states within which the public domain resides and for whom the use of the resources on the domain has significant political and economic consequences.

Finally, policy struggles quite often are waged in the technical language of resource economics and scientific management. Perhaps more than most environmental issues, public resource management is an arcane business to most Americans, particularly those living where few public lands exist. In such circumstances specialized private groups, such as environmentalists and resource users, tend to operate almost invisibly to the public; the outcome of the policy struggles depends particularly on their own organizational resources, technical expertise, and political adeptness in the administrative infighting and legal wrangling that often characterize resource policy making. It is a political arena, more particularly, in which organized environmental groups often constitute practically the only expression of viewpoints not associated with resource users or administrators.

Notes

1. Article IV, section 3, clause 2.
2. Congressional Quarterly, *The Battle for Natural Resources* (Washington, D.C.: Congressional Quarterly, 1983), chap. 1.
3. Aldo Leopold, *A Sand County Almanac* (New York: Oxford University Press, 1949), 222.
4. A useful survey of public lands may be found in U.S. Department of the Interior, Bureau of Land Management, *Managing the Nation's Public Lands* (Washington, D.C.: Government Printing Office, 1983).
5. Paul J. Culhane, *Public Lands Politics* (Baltimore, Md.: Johns Hopkins University Press, 1981), 60.

6. James Baker, "The Frustrations of FLPMA," *Wilderness* 47, no. 163 (Winter 1983): 13. See also Jeanne N. Clarke and Daniel McCool, *Staking Out the Terrain: Power Differentials among Natural Resource Agencies* (Albany: State University of New York Press, 1985), chaps. 4 and 5.
7. On the impact of sustained use on the Forest Service, see Culhane, *Public Lands Politics,* chap. 2.
8. Ibid.
9. Council on Environmental Quality, *Environmental Quality, 1979* (Washington, D.C.: Government Printing Office, 1980), 309.
10. Quoted in *New York Times,* June 27, 1981.
11. Craig W. Allin, "Wilderness Policy," in Charles Davis, ed., *Western Public Lands and Environmental Politics* (Boulder, CO: Westview Press, 1997), 179.
12. Sandra K. Davis, "Fighting over Public Lands: Interest Groups, States, and the Federal Government," in *Western Public Lands and Environmental Politics,* ed. Davis, 23.
13. Quoted in World Resources Institute, *The 1994 Information Please Environmental Almanac* (New York: Houghton Mifflin, 1993), 159.
14. *New York Times,* March 21, 1981.
15. Congressional Quarterly, *The Battle for Natural Resources,* chaps. 4 and 5.
16. *New York Times,* July 2, 1982.
17. Ibid.
18. *New York Times,* Jan. 7, 1989.
19. George Hoberg, "From Localism to Legalism," in *Western Public Lands and Environmental Politics,* ed. Davis, 48.
20. Ibid., 53.
21. Culhane, *Public Lands Policies,* chap. 2.
22. U.S. Department of Commerce, Bureau of the Census, *Statistical Abstract of the United States, 1989* (Washington, D.C.: Government Printing Office, 1990), 656.
23. *New York Times,* April 27, 1989.
24. Conservation Foundation, *State of the Environment: A View Toward the Nineties* (Washington, D.C.: Conservation Foundation, 1987), 220.
25. Margaret E. Kriz, "Last Stand on Timber," *National Journal,* March 3, 1990, 509.
26. *New York Times,* Feb. 22, 1988.
27. *New York Times,* Feb. 29, 1988.

Suggested Readings

Clark, Jeanne N., and Daniel McCool. *Staking Out the Terrain.* Albany: State University of New York Press, 1985.
Crawley, R. McGreggor. *Federal Land, Western Anger: The Sagebrush Rebellion and Environmental Politics.* Lawrence: University of Kansas Press, 1993.
Culhane, Paul. *Public Land Politics.* Baltimore, Md.: Johns Hopkins University Press, 1981.
Davis, Charles, ed. *Western Public Lands and Environmental Politics.* Boulder, Colo.: Westview Press, 1997.
Durant, Robert F. *The Administrative Presidency Revised: Public Lands, the BLM, and the Reagan Revolution.* Albany: State University of New York Press, 1992.

Chapter 10

The United States and Climate Diplomacy: The Emerging Politics of Global Environmentalism

Some experts argue the entire notion of what constitutes national security should be redefined, believing that environmental "catastrophe" is as likely to cause chaos in the future as ideological and ethnic conflicts of the past. In response, the CIA, State Department, National Security Council, Defense Department, and the National Intelligence Council have all established "high-level" positions to deal with environmental issues. . . .

—Wall Street Journal, September 25, 1997

What people respond to are things that are directly in front of them—things they can see and touch and smell. Air pollution you can see. Garbage you can touch. Bad water you can smell. But global warming? It's so . . . abstract.

—Peter Hart, Democratic Party pollster

Early in October 1997 the CNN television network suddenly refused to broadcast further advertisements sponsored by the Global Climate Information Network, a coalition of major domestic industries opposing U.S. participation in an international agreement, then being considered in Kyoto, Japan, to limit national emissions of "greenhouse gases" assumed to be responsible for global climate warming. The Climate Network, whose members included the American Automobile Manufacturers Association, the National Association of Manufacturers, and the United Mine Workers, had already spent $1 million for CNN advertising time and expected to spend many millions more. CNN defended the decision by asserting that it was committing significant coverage to the climate-warming debate and had a policy against televising advocacy ads on

334

issues it was extensively covering. Climate Network spokespersons asserted that CNN had canceled the ads because they offended the network's founder, Ted Turner, an outspoken environmentalist.[1] With equal abruptness CNN changed its mind, and the advocacy ads reappeared.

Almost simultaneously, a coalition of national environmental organizations including the Sierra Club, the Natural Resources Defense Council, and the Environmental Information Center launched their own expensive national television advertising campaign that criticized domestic auto makers and petroleum producers for opposing a climate-change treaty. At the same time, the CEOs of Ford, General Motors, and Chrysler used a scheduled White House meeting with President Clinton on trade issues to complain instead about the proposed Kyoto treaty. They were joined by the head of the United Auto Workers in warning the president that such a treaty would discriminate against domestic industries in the international marketplace. The next day, the *Wall Street Journal*'s lead article reported that other U.S. business interests were attracted to the "emissions trading" features of the proposed climate treaty. On the same day, pro-life activists expressed alarm because restrictions on greenhouse gases might encourage population control and increased abortion in developing countries.[2]

It is late 1997. Climate warming has become a dominant issue in American domestic politics. Its rapid trajectory up the U.S. public policy agenda can easily be measured by the enlarging intensity of debate it provokes among the nation's major political and economic interests. But not among the American public. Ted Turner, the Big Three auto makers, the environmentalist establishment, and similar political heavyweights might be deeply engaged, but most Americans are much more concerned about other environmental matters. During the intense public debate immediately preceding the Kyoto meeting, the public considered air and water pollution, or pollution in general, a far more important environmental problem than climate warming. One poll estimated that perhaps one in four Americans were deeply concerned about climate change but far larger proportions were more apprehensive about water pollution, toxic wastes, dirty air, and wildlife destruction. In another poll only 7 percent of the public, when offered a choice, considered climate warming to be the nation's most important environmental problem.[3] And despite President Clinton's pledge to reduce U.S. emissions of greenhouse gas to 1990 levels before the century's end, Department of Energy data released in October revealed that domestic greenhouse gas emissions rose sharply the previous year, virtually assuring that the United States would not come close to Clinton's reduction target.

As a snapshot from environmental history, this one seems misplaced. Unlike important domestic environmental issues, climate warming ascended the national policy agenda unaccompanied by a threatened reactor meltdown, or a dangerously leeching toxic waste site, or other dramatizing events and despite an apathetic public. No sense of urgency about the problem animated American business or labor. Science, not aroused public opinion, has been the prime political mover. In this respect, the global environmental issues advancing on the domestic policy agenda during the 1990s differ from the environmental problems that crowded it in previous decades. As global issues assume greater political and economic importance to Americans, however, the institutions, actors, and processes characteristic of international environmental politics will become increasingly influential in domestic environmental politics. This confluence of domestic and global political forces creates a distinctive "transboundary politics," a style of national environmental decision making likely to grow in importance as the new century unfolds.

Transboundary Environmental Politics

Within the last decade, three global issues—acid precipitation, stratospheric ozone depletion, and global climate warming—have dominated the nation's international ecological agenda and increasingly affected its domestic environmental policies. More than any others, these issues exemplify the internationalization of national environmental politics evolving almost from the first Earth Day.

The United States has been a party to international environmental agreements for more than eighty years, but the scope and pace of this global ecological involvement has increased significantly in the last three decades. Among the 152 multilateral environmental treaties and agreements adopted by the United States through 1990, 20 were signed between 1921 and 1959, 26 during the 1960s, 49 during the 1970s, and 48 in the 1980s.[4] Prior to the 1980s, most of these ecological agreements, like the Law of the Sea Convention signed in 1984, dealt with protection and preservation of the marine environment and fisheries or, like agreements relating to Antarctica and outer space, with freedom of access to common global resources. Until the 1980s, however, transboundary air and water pollution, and especially human-induced ("anthropogenic") changes in global climate, received little, if any, diplomatic attention and remained a largely arcane matter for scientists and public health experts. The rapid rise after the 1970s of scientific concern about cross-national pollution and human-induced climate change, together with a growing volume of information, increasingly sophisticated global environmental monitoring, and the mounting political strength of global environmental organizations, encouraged increased worldwide governmental attention to transboundary pollution problems. As the geographic and climatological scale of scientific analysis expanded, the politics of international environmentalism was transformed. By the mid-1980s, the cross-national transport of pollutants and its global impact had become a major, distinctive issue.

Historic Markers: Stockholm, Rio, and Kyoto

The rapid growth of U.S. involvement in global environmental diplomacy, and especially the nation's increasing engagement in problems of transboundary pollution, can be documented by three historic markers: the Stockholm, Rio, and Kyoto environmental conferences spanning the years between 1972 and 1998. Growing U.S. activism began with the 1972 Conference on the Human Environment in Stockholm, Sweden, the first truly international conference exclusively devoted to environmental issues, attended by 113 states and representatives from 19 international organizations. The theme "Only One Earth" dramatized internationally for the first time the growing gravity and scale of global environmental problems ranging from population growth to outer space pollution. Among the other significant accomplishments of the Stockholm meeting were the creation of the United Nations Environmental Program, initially supported vigorously by the United States, and the enactment of many other, largely symbolic measures that committed the United States to playing a major role in future international environmental activities.[5]

The second major international meeting, the 1992 Conference on Environment and Development, popularly called the "Earth Summit" and held in Rio de Janeiro, was attended by an even larger international delegation comprised of representatives from 179 states, including 116 heads of state. The new conference theme, "Our Last Chance to Save the Earth," invoked the growing sense of urgency about global environmental degradation that characterized the meeting, which focused special attention on the environmental concerns of developing countries. The Rio Declaration on Environment and Development, probably the most widely known of all conference deliberations, proclaimed twenty-eight guiding principles to strengthen global environmental governance. While U.S. delegates attended the conference and actively participated in almost all of its proceedings, the official U.S. delegation, representing the viewpoint of President George Bush and his Republican administration, was widely and severely criticized for its reluctance to assume a leadership role in conference policy making and, in particular, for its refusal to join other industrial nations in agreeing to timetables and reduction goals for the greenhouse gas emissions assumed responsible for global climate warming.

While environmentalists were deeply disappointed in the U.S. delegation's lackluster Rio performance, in a broader perspective the Rio conference did result in a multitude of lesser U.S. commitments to increasing international environmental activism. Most notably, it unleashed powerful domestic and international political pressures on the United States that resulted in the Clinton administration's commitments to the timetables and emissions targets for greenhouse gas reduction incorporated into the 1997 Kyoto Protocol on Climate Change, discussed below.

By the time of the Kyoto meeting, the United States had also signed the 1988 Montreal Protocol limiting domestic production and consumption of chlorofluorocarbons (CFCs) and related chemicals destroying the global stratospheric ozone layer, had resumed financial support for the UN Fund for Population Activities earlier halted by the Reagan and Bush administrations, and had ratified the Biodiversity Treaty and the UN Law of the Sea Convention, again reversing Reagan-Bush presidential policies. Thus, on the threshold of the twenty-first century, the U.S. diplomatic trajectory from Stockholm to Kyoto was leading the United States steadily, if unevenly, toward a broadening and deepening commitment to international environmental governance.

Environmental Diplomacy: Incentives and Disincentives

A multitude of events in the last quarter of the twentieth century, such as the development of satellite earth-monitoring, computer technology, new environmental sciences and, especially, the growth of an international scientific community deeply engaged in ecological research, has compelled national governments to recognize the reality of transboundary pollution while raising a new global consciousness of its scope and impact. Transboundary, or cross-national, pollution eludes the jurisdiction of any national government. Its management often requires local or regional collaboration among governments, such as combating pollution of the Mediterranean Sea. But as science becomes more sophisticated in its ability to monitor and to understand pollution processes, it increasingly frames transboundary environmental problems in terms of complex, intricately related, virtually global causes and effects. This impulse toward comprehensive conceptions of international pollution also animates modern science, however unintentionally, to continually push prospective solutions up the scale of international management.

State Sovereignty vs. Ecological Stewardship. All international diplomacy occurs in a global setting frequently considered "anarchic" in the sense that there is no sovereign political regime—no determinate governmental institutions, laws, processes, or principles—to which national governments give dependable allegiance. In this sovereignless political arena, national relations are governed at different times and places by many principles in various combination: political or economic power, cultural affinities, historical antagonisms, a regional or global super-power, technological and geographic resources, the rule of law, and much else whose nature is a source of unending preoccupation for diplomats and scholars. It is no surprise that the political foundation upon which modern nations are expected to ground their international environmental diplomacy is at best precarious, a structure currently designed to satisfy two dissonant principles, and so inherently insecure.

Embedded in modern environmental diplomacy is a fundamental tension between the concept of national sovereignty over indigenous resources and national responsibility for environmental stewardship. Today, the United States and other nations recognize both principles as stated in Article 21 of the Stockholm Declaration (1972) and later reaffirmed by the Rio Declaration:

> States have in accordance with the Charter of the United Nations and the principles of international law, the sovereign right to exploit their own resources pursuant to their own environmental policies, and the responsibility to insure that activities within their jurisdiction or control do not cause damage to the environment of other states or of areas beyond the limits of national jurisdiction.

Article 21 prudently recognizes the reality of state sovereignty and self-interest and implicitly its primacy in international politics. Virtually all national policy makers, in any case, act as if state sovereignty and self-interest were the higher principle, even while genuflecting in the direction of environmental responsibility toward their neighbors. In effect, the United States conducts its international environmental diplomacy in a global political arena where its own self-interest and sovereignty, and those of every other nation with which it negotiates, are always at risk of conflict with its own environmental goals or with the global policies deemed essential to resolve satisfactorily an international environmental problem. Moreover, the U.S. government, "superpower" or not, cannot routinely or legally assert a sovereign will over other nations in environmental matters as it can often do in domestic political dealings with the states and other domestic political institutions.

National Costs and Benefits.   Transboundary (or transfrontier) environmental issues, like domestic ones, involve an uneven distribution of costs and benefits, but calculated in regional, international, and global metrics that involve money, sovereignty, national prestige, and historic experience.

Virtually all transboundary problems, such as acid deposition, entail the "upstream/downstream" relations in which one nation, or group of nations, disproportionately bears the impact of pollution migration while the polluter is likely to reap the benefits—or to believe it does. This upstream/downstream disjunction is rich in political, social, and economic cleavages sure to erupt whenever issues of pollution management arise.[6] The United States plays both roles in international politics. It is a major source of greenhouse gas emissions associated with the global climate warming and the airborne chemicals responsible for stratospheric ozone depletion, but also shares the ecological and human health risks from both problems with other nations. The United States is also producer and recipient of transboundary acid deposition. International environmental issues are typically first raised, often exclusively, by the downstream pollution recipients, as happened in the case of acid deposition. The problem of acid rain was first brought to international attention in the 1970s by Scandinavian countries experiencing widespread lake and stream damage never previously encountered. Conversely, European nations, such as Great Britain and Germany, which appeared to be a major source for the chemical precursors of Scandinavia's acid precipitation, resolutely resisted diplomatic efforts to reduce their acid rain emissions until new environmental assessments revealed that they, too, were significantly affected by acid precipitation.[7]

Many international environmental problems—climate change or the depletion of commercial fishing species, for example—involve significant cross-generational costs. The cost of this generation's failure to abate the rising depletion of commercial ocean species will be fully experienced by another generation that may be unable to earn a living at all from once-thriving Atlantic commercial tuna or cod fisheries. Rising global sea levels, shifting temperate climate zones, and other major impacts predicted from climate warming may not create significant human problems for several decades or a generation. As with domestic issues, observes Lynton Caldwell, "policies are made or affirmed and implemented by people accountable to the present, not to the future generations. Therefore, the urgency of an issue as an object of policymaking is not necessarily a measure of its ultimate significance."[8] In the case of international issues, the problem of cross-generational impacts is further complicated because many of the most severe cross-generational consequences will be experienced by the world's smaller, or most economically or culturally disadvantaged, nations—those with comparatively meager political leverage on international affairs and least able to mitigate or adapt to prospective ecological change.

Moreover, so-called "developing" or "underdeveloped" nations habitually view international ecological issues through the lens of their political history, infusing their environmental diplomacy with ideologies, passions, and assumptions drawn from their colonial experience, or from past diplomatic, political, or economic associations with Western, industrialized countries. The United States invariably wears distinctive mantles in the perception of such nations engaged in environmental diplomacy. It is "Western," "colonial," or "capitalist," a "superpower," "Northern," or "white"—all perceptions, along with many others similarly derived, that inevitably affect the conduct of any ecological negotiations involving not only the United States but other Western and industrialized nations as well. Post-colonial and other developing nations, for instance, are likely to suspect initially that U.S. or other Western diplomatic initiatives concerning the environment are covert attempts at exploitation or subjugation. Latin American nations may suspect that U.S. environmental initiatives are a newer version of the deeply resented "big stick" diplomacy employed by the United States toward its southern neighbors earlier in the century. Nonetheless, people in developing societies are increasingly aware of and concerned about environmental problems.

Even if history cast no long shadow over environmental diplomacy, the natural rivalries and tensions among sovereign states, and the omnipresent impulse to national power and sovereignty, always threaten a chokehold on national environmental sensibilities; all nations appraise prospective environmental policy first by its apparent impact upon their own sovereignty and power. The surest poison for any international environmental agreement is a national leadership's conviction that their country's sovereignty will be compromised. Thus, opponents launching an early attack on a possible U.S. agreement in Kyoto to limits on U.S. domestic greenhouse gas emissions were quick to conjure images of imperilled national autonomy. "We are taking national sovereignty away from every nation that signs this treaty," charged Republican senator Chuck Hagel (Neb.). "Would [a binding treaty] mean a United Nations multinational bureaucracy could come in and close down industry in the United States?" he queried, adding meddling bureaucrats to the menace.[9]

Almost as potent in shaping environmental diplomacy is national prestige and image: leaders recoil from negotiations that imply national responsibility for an environmental offense or attack the legitimacy of domestic environmental practices. "Any attempt by states or international bodies to alter national [policy] regimes immediately brings into play questions of sovereignty and the competence of a natural bureaucracy. Once allegations are made against countries or their subjects, powerful defensive impulses from those identified as polluters may be expected, " note Sonja Boehmer-Christiansen and Jim Skea.[10] Negotiations get prickly when issues, or apparently impartial scientific data, are construed in a "good guy–bad guy" style that appears to create national villains and victims. As a cautionary tale, political scientist Marc Levy describes the result of this strategy during the 1993 negotiations among European countries over a treaty to reduce acid rain emissions. Using environmental monitoring data, "Swedish and Norwegian officials branded the United Kingdom an irresponsible renegade guilty of damaging Scandinavian resources. In one heated moment, Norwegian environment minister Thorbjorn Berntsen publicly called his British counterpart, John Gummer, a shitbag." [11] Negotiations will be far less impassioned, and usually more productive, when issues and technical data are constructively interpreted to emphasize problem solutions and alternative strategies.

Given the many risks and costs perceived in international environmental diplomacy, national governments are strongly motivated to assume a "wait-and-see" attitude toward environmental initiatives generated elsewhere, especially if they can become "free riders" to multilateral agreements made by other countries when—as in the case of acid rain abatement—benefits cannot be reserved only for those countries signing the treaty. Since international environmental agreements often require some sort of new implementation structure, perhaps a regional or global monitoring system for a pollutant, this may also be an inducement to stay on the diplomatic sidelines. This is particularly likely when the scientific evidence supporting action is not compelling. The evidence may be disputed among experts, or suspected of some political or diplomatic taint, or dramatic proof of a problem may be absent—all situations common to many contemporary international environmental issues like climate warming, global energy resources, or the ecological vitality of coral reefs and their related ecosystems.

Even so, hundreds of environmental treaties exist, and more are being negotiated despite the disincentives. Additionally, a large and complex array of international institutions functions to implement these agreements. Clearly, powerful incentives compel nations to participate in international environmental diplomacy.

Incentives to Cooperation.   Perhaps the most compelling and common incentives for nations to negotiate environmental agreements is recognition of a shared problem or the possibility of mutual advantage. The Montreal Protocol, the 1987 agreement in which forty-seven nations, including the United States, pledged themselves to specific targets and timetables for reducing their production and use of ozone-destroying CFCs, was largely driven by persuasive scientific evidence of a large Antarctic "ozone hole" and predictions of a disastrous depletion of atmospheric ozone in less than a century. Significantly, the original signatories negotiated further agreements in 1990 and 1992 to accelerate the pace and scale of CFC reductions when further scientific data indicated that global ozone depletion was even more serious than originally assumed. These agreements were greatly facilitated by a broad scientific consensus on the problem, by the appearance of a vivid ozone hole, and by recognition that the serious human health and ecological risks of continued stratospheric ozone depletion would be shared globally. Nonetheless, developing nations such as China, India, and the African states were initially reluctant to join the Montreal accords. They were persuaded by a ten-year extension of their compliance deadline and an assurance of financial assistance in finding CFC substitutes through a special multilateral fund established for that purpose. This instance of so-called "side payments"—incentives designed to encourage reluctant nations to join in multilateral agreements—illustrates a strategy often used in environmental, as well as other, international agreements.[12]

Prestige also works to the advantage of environmental diplomacy, as does expediency. Nation's often join international agreements—especially when the apparent costs are minimal—when the perceived gain is prestige, improved national image, or political advantage. France, Belgium, and Italy, for example, signed the 1979 Convention on Long Range Transboundary Air Pollution not only to wear the halo of a good environmental citizen in Europe but also because they anticipated that the national emission reduction goals to which they agreed would have been achieved even without the agreement.[13] In a similar vein, the Clinton administration agreed in 1992 to stabilize greenhouse gas emissions at 1990 levels by the year 2000, thereby reversing the Bush administration's policy, to the approval of environmentalists, and eliminating much of the international censure of the United States for its opposition at the Rio Conference to such goals. However, the administration's implementation plan relied largely on voluntary compliance and other nonregulatory strategies that many domestic critics charged were relatively costless economically or politically and ultimately ineffective.

National security and other military considerations can become potent incentives for international environmental cooperation. The United States, like almost all other nuclear powers, has entered into a variety of international weapons management and disarmament agreements, such as limits on the above-ground testing of atomic weapons and the placement of nuclear missiles, largely for strategic military purposes. Even before environmentalism became a global issue, other, practical considerations had reduced the likelihood of nuclear war, accidental nuclear explosions, and the proliferation of weapons-grade nuclear materials. More recently, U.S. initiatives and agreements to limit the global dispersion of nuclear wastes and to develop technologies for the safe storage or conversion of such material to peaceful uses have been motivated as much by military security as by environmental considerations. In a broader perspective, the growing evidence of global environmental degradation and the concurrent recognition of the mounting capability of technologies to profoundly alter the physical and biological bases of all global life—indeed, to eliminate it in some instances—is promoting a growing perception among policy makers that national security and environmental protection are becoming inextricably linked for virtually all nations.

Political and economic power, often wielded not so subtly, are also common weapons in environmental diplomacy. With its huge presence in the global economy, for instance, the United States can use access to its domestic market as a potent inducement for agricultural exporting nations to accept U.S.-promoted controls on pesticides and other potentially toxic chemicals on commodities shipped abroad. Nor has the United States been reluctant to use foreign aid, or the promise of other kinds of economic or technical assistance, to facilitate environmental agreements on such diverse matters as climate diplomacy, hazardous waste management, the protection of Antarctica, and many other matters.

The Crucial Role of Science.   Scientists and science have assumed an important, and sometimes (in the case of current global climate issues) decisive role in promoting environmental issues to international significance. The relatively recent ascent of environmental science as a crucial force in setting the international environmental agenda has many explanations: the proliferation of and collaboration among scientific organizations at all international levels; the growing technical capability and sophistication of the physical and biological sciences, abetted by increasing national investments in environmental research among the technologically advanced countries; the rapid elaboration of highly efficient global communications systems; and the exponential growth of global environmental monitoring and assessment data.[14]

A striking aspect of contemporary science is not only its capacity to compel international attention to environmental issues but its success in doing so on the basis of predictions, computer models, and other extrapolations whose effect is to project politics and policy issues far into the future, thereby linking present-day decision making in concrete and explicable ways to what has been traditionally treated as a remote, and quite frequently irrelevant, social world. In effect, this amounts to a subtle but ongoing and pervasive redefinition of political time and space for the world's key policy makers, a lengthening of the conceptual horizons in policy thinking, a frequently forced and not necessarily welcome confrontation with the long-term consequences of today's decisions defined in the more or less authoritative language of science.

The resources and authority of modern environmental science originate primarily among the world's technologically advanced and largely Western societies, especially in the United States, Western Europe, and Japan. Because of its enormous scientific infrastructure, American science frequently assumes a major, often dominating, role in Western scientific undertakings. While the environmental science driving global ecological concerns draws considerable strength from its pervasive American and Western character, this becomes an impediment to global environmental diplomacy when non-Western and developing nations suspect, as they often do, that Western science is manipulated to serve Western political and economic interests. As the United States, with other industrialized nations, increasingly strives to include developing and non-Western countries into multilateral agreements concerning climate warming, acid precipitation, and many other matters, establishing the credibility of the scientific assessments upon which such negotiations depend has become a predictable task.

Environmental Diplomacy: The International Structure

U.S. environmental diplomacy occurs within a regime of regional and international organizations, many specifically created to implement environmental agreements, and often tenuous principles of international law established by treaty or precedent to which nations are expected to abide. International negotiations on transboundary pollution have been historically based upon two principles of international law: the "polluter pays" principle and the precautionary principle. The governance that this international structure actually exerts over the conduct of U.S. international environmental affairs is highly variable and often problematic, as it is with all other sovereign nations. Generally, international law and organization exerts as much influence on American ecological policy as the United States chooses to accept. But the fabric of law and organization from which international environmental politics is constituted is not threadbare. The United States and other nations do recognize and accept some measure of global environmental governance, and international environmental organizations exercise a continuing, if often subtle, influence upon the daily conduct of world affairs

Environmental Principles. Several standards of international law are widely acknowledged in defining national obligations in environmental matters. First, the "polluter pays" principle is generally applied. This is interpreted in Principle 16 of the Rio Declaration to mean that

> national authorities should endeavor to promote the internalization of environmental costs . . . taking into account the approach that the polluter should, in principle, bear the cost of pollution, with due regard for the public interest and without distorting international trade and investment.

Second, the precautionary principle dictates that nations take action, even when there is a degree of scientific uncertainty, to abate any potentially harmful pollutants. In recent decades, the rise of international environmental consciousness has led the United States, among other nations, to predicate ecological diplomacy upon appealing, if not predictably compelling, assertions about an international responsibility to "protect the Global Commons," regard intergenerational equity, and respect various "environmental rights" in international affairs. Such principles are, in fact, often recognized and respected in international diplomacy even if they are not yet a constant normative force. Of more practical importance are the explicit obligations to which the United States and other nations agree in specialized environmental treaties, protocols, and other understandings. One measure of their potency is the extent to which they are actually translated domestically into appropriate law and governmental practice. Another is the consistency with which such agreements are honored over significant time periods. That the United States and other nations have accepted the CFC emission controls involved in the Montreal Protocol, for example, or have observed the Law of the Sea regarding national fishing rights in international waters, whatever the reasons, is a reminder that international principles cannot be marginalized as diplomatic windowdressing.

Multilateral Agencies.   A more manifest evidence of international environmental governance is the many permanent organizations implicated in environmental diplomacy. Among the most important to the United States are the major decision-making bodies of the United Nations and, in particular, those UN entities with a primarily environmental mission: the UN Environmental Program (UNEP), the UN Development Program (UNDP), and the UN Commission on Sustainable Development. UNEP, the oldest, was created in 1973 by the Stockholm Conference to "monitor, coordinate and catalyze" international environmental activities. Its most significant activities include environmental monitoring and assessment, such as that undertaken in its highly regarded Earthwatch Program; environmental management; and information dissemination. UNDP, created in 1972, has become an important distributor of multilateral funds to promote biological diversity, aid in the cleanup of international waters, and combat global warming and stratospheric ozone depletion. The UN Commission on Sustainable Development, created in 1992 with a membership of fifty-two nations, is charged with monitoring the implementation of programs initiated by the 1992 Rio Conference, particularly the transfer of financial and technical resources to developing nations.[15]

Beside these UN agencies there is a multitude of other multilateral international organizations important to U.S. environmental diplomacy. Created mostly since World War II, these organizations facilitate and coordinate scientific, economic, and humanitarian activities that have environmental implications. Among them are the World Meteorological Organization, the Food and Agriculture Organization, and the International Atomic Energy Association. In recent decades, European multilateral organizations, particularly the European Union, have assumed great importance in the conduct of environmental diplomacy among industrialized Westerns nations and the Organization for Economic Cooperation and Development. To these can be added hundreds of more specialized and regional entities, often created specifically to implement and monitor the progress of various international and regional agreements. Especially important in shaping the ecological impact of global economic development, particularly among Asian and African nations, are the powerful multilateral economic development agencies such as the World Bank, the Agency for International Development, and many private agencies such as the Ford Foundation.

NGOs and Multilateral Corporations.   By the second day of the crucial Kyoto Conference in late 1997, observers reported that a "carnival" atmosphere prevailed in good part because more than 10,000 persons were crammed into its public meeting space in anticipation of a speech by U.S. vice president Al Gore. More than a third of this human crush represented nongovernmental organizations (NGOs), mostly industry and environmental groups from around the world attempting to influence the deliberating national delegations.[16] Hundreds of organizations constructed displays and information booths encircling the proceedings. Most were competing to capture an audience, like the five-million-member strong international environmental organization Greenpeace, which erected a giant solar array in the parking lot to power an "environmentally correct kitchen." Environmental NGOs created their own daily newspaper for delegates and visitors. Spokespersons for environmental groups, who ordinarily couldn't get a phone call to the media returned, were courted by reporters. For environmental NGOs it was a grand and gratifying demonstration of their importance in international environmental affairs.

The Kyoto Conference was a testimony to the global importance of the NGO sector as a whole in environmental diplomacy. "The importance of NGOs in environmental policymaking can hardly be overemphasized," observes Lynton Caldwell. "NGOs have been essential from its beginning, both within and without nations, and they have been instigators of numerous treaties and international cooperative arrangements." Much of their influence, he notes, rises from their freedom from the constraints of diplomatic protocol and bureaucratic procedure. "In both the forming and execution of international policy," he concludes, "they may act more rapidly and directly, with less risk to national sensitivities, than can official intergovernmental agencies."[17] The number of NGOs of all kinds active in global environmental affairs has continually mounted in the last several decades. Current estimates suggest the number of NGOs has grown from perhaps 15,000 in the early 1980s to over 100,000 currently, including a notable rise in the number of non-Western and "grassroots" organizations representing indigenous peoples. The special importance of proliferating scientific NGOs has already been noted. The rapid emergence of environmental NGOs has somewhat overshadowed the continuing influence and vigor of corporate NGOs and, particularly, the crucial role of multilateral corporations in environmental diplomacy. Multilateral corporate NGOs, a great many originating or based in the United States, represent a rough counterpart to national corporations and other regulated interests in domestic affairs, except that they are often far more powerful and resourceful. This is no surprise considering that the multilateral corporations they serve, including numerous petroleum, industrial, and manufacturing interests, annually produce goods and services economically valued above the gross national products of all but a handful of the world's national economic powers.

Global Politics Is Different

Even a brief depiction of the global political arena illuminates vast differences from the domestic setting of U.S. environmental politics. Unlike the constitutionally sorted and ordered domestic division of governmental power, no sovereign authority, no widely understood, accepted, or explicit apportionment of power predictably directs international affairs. Rather, it is world of competing national sovereignties where power in all forms is customarily the real legitimating and coercive force in international agreements. It is a world of highly pluralized political interests becoming yet more fragmented as traditional nation-states are increasingly forced to accommodate, and often compete for influence with, NGOs, multilateral corporations, regional and international governmental entities, and other entities for diplomatic influence. It is also a world as yet untouched by the moderating influence of a liberal, democratic civic culture or of any common cultural grounding at all. It is a world of dangerous ideological and cultural cleavage, where the hold of environmental governance is still tenuous. In this setting, environmental diplomacy has only just begun to temper the force of power and sovereignty, and a global environmental consciousness is but recently emergent.

Still, within the last several decades two of the most significant environmental agreements in world history have been negotiated, and a third is being deliberated. In each case, the United States has assumed, albeit sometimes reluctantly, a major role. If these agreements achieve their purpose in significant measure, they are likely to be the grounding for an unprecedented climate diplomacy in the next century.

Climate Diplomacy: Ozone Politics and the Montreal Protocols

No issue in climate diplomacy has been driven harder, or more successfully, to international attention by science than has stratospheric ozone depletion. Virtually all national governments now implicitly accept the dominant scientific characterization of the problem. The rapidity with which international agreements have been negotiated to reverse the stratospheric depletion of ozone represents a degree of accord rare to climate diplomacy. Even nature seemed a conspirator, producing a remarkably timely "ozone hole" for a diplomatic backdrop.

The Ozone Issue Emerges

The most common chemicals implicated in stratospheric ozone depletion, chlorofluorocarbons (CFCs), were originally developed in 1931 as a safe refrigerant and subsequently became one of the great success stories in industrial chemistry. For almost a half century thereafter, CFCs were used to make flexible urethane foam for carpeting and furniture; rigid polyurethane foam to insulate homes and refrigeration units; foam for trays, fast-food wrappers, and other convenience items; and, most importantly, as an automobile, industrial, and commercial refrigerant. At the time controls were initiated, annual world production approached 2 billion pounds. The United States produced about 30 percent of the world supply.[18] Other chemicals now known to contribute to the ozone problem include halogenated hydrocarbons ("halons"), used as a flame suppressant; another close chemical relative, hydrochlorofluorocarbons (HCFCs); and possibly methyl bromide, a widespread agricultural chemical used as a soil fumigant.

The first significant scientific warning about the possible danger of CFCs was raised in 1974 by American scientists whose research suggested that CFCs released active chlorine into the upper atmosphere, destroying ambient ozone. If this were true, they warned, adverse consequences would ensue. Upper-atmospheric ozone had long been recognized as important to global human and ecological health, primarily because it reduced the amount of ultraviolet light striking the earth's surface, thus protecting humans from high exposures believed to promote skin cancer and cataracts, among other problems, and affected terrestrial and aquatic plant photosynthesis. The publicity provoked by this announcement among scientists and the mass media encouraged an immediate, sharp increase in public and private support for research which eventually convinced the United States to ban CFCs from all domestic aerosol products in 1978 and to press other nations to take similar action. Concurrently, a new wave of international research and communication about stratospheric ozone among climate scientists began.

In 1985 British scientists in Antarctica were surprised when their research revealed an "ozone hole" over the South Polar region. The ozone hole was political serendipity, arming proponents of an ozone treaty with a powerful psychological weapon. Subsequent analysis of satellite data between 1980 and 1992 indicated an increase in the size and depth of the Antarctic hole by 2.5 percent, plus or minus 1.4 percent, per decade. In 1993 scientists also documented ozone levels at 2 to 3 percent below any previously recorded by satellite in both the Northern and Southern Hemispheres. In 1995 the World Meteorological Organization (WMO) reported that its North American monitoring stations had measured ozone levels 10 to 15 percent below the long-term averages, including a significant decline over the Arctic and a 35 percent decline over Siberia. By 1994, most climate scientists were prepared to accept the verdict from the WMO's major report, *Scientific Assessment of Stratospheric Ozone*: "Anthropogenic chlorine and bromine compounds, coupled with surface chemistry on natural polar stratospheric particles, are the cause of polar ozone depletion."[19] But not all experts agree. Additional causes have been proposed for the ozone depletion, including natural phenomenon and other, more benign consequences. Measured stratospheric ozone decline is apparently nonlinear, at times showing short-run stabilization and even reversal, leading some scientists to assert that the ozone "hole" is a transient matter.[20] Nonetheless, the politics of ozone diplomacy have fallen quickly in step with the prevailing scientific consensus.

Montreal and Beyond

By the mid-1980s, other major global producers of CFCs were persuaded by the scientific evidence to follow the U.S. lead in controlling CFC production and distribution. With considerable support from UNEP, which acted as a clearinghouse for worldwide data about ozone depletion, in 1987 the Montreal Protocol on Substances That Deplete the Ozone Layer was signed by 47 nations, including the United States. Since then, 120 more nations have joined the Protocol. It was among the first international agreements to establish target dates and emission reduction levels for chemical substances believed to harm the global climate. The Protocol was actually a supplement to the Vienna Convention for the Protection of the Ozone Layer, the first of several such Protocols to speed the phase-out of ozone-depleting chemicals.

In its original form, the United States and other signatories to the Montreal Protocol agreed to

1. reduce annual production of CFCs by 50 percent from 1986 levels by June, 1999;
2. stabilize CFC production within seven months after the Protocol came into force and by 20 percent by June, 1994;
3. stabilize the production of halons and other chemicals assumed to be ozone-depleting at 1986 levels by early 1992;
4. allow developing countries up to ten additional years to comply with the deadlines, and to increase their domestic use of the controlled chemicals;
5. restrict trade in restricted chemicals with non-signatories to the treaty; and
6. create a multilateral fund to assist development countries in complying with the treaty. The United States provides about 25 percent of its current budget.

As scientific evidence about the scale of global ozone depletion mounted, the United States agreed to two additional protocols, the London (1990) and Copenhagen (1992) agreements, initiated by Germany and Switzerland, each of which had unilaterally begun to phase out additional chemicals. These agreements accelerated the phase-out of CFCs, methyl chloroform, and carbon tetrachloride to early 1996 and halon to 1995 and established a freeze on methyl bromide consumption for all developing countries. An unusual feature of all these protocols was the extent to which they committed the United States and other signatories to a moving target for chemical phase-outs, the goals changing as scientific research prompted new understandings about reduction schedules. More recently, a working group among the Montreal Protocol signatories has recommended a phase-out of all methyl bromide and HCFC production and other measures to which the United States has not yet agreed.

The primary domestic regulatory instrument for compliance with the Montreal Protocol is Title VI of the Clean Air Act Amendments of 1990, which initially contained chemical phase-out schedules keyed to the original Montreal Protocol and now to the most recent modifications, the Copenhagen Protocols signed by the United States in 1992.

Implementation Issues

The freon smugglers whose story introduced this book are evidence that enforcing the domestic regulation of ozone-depleting chemicals has not been easy. The congressionally created excise taxes passed in the late

1980s and early 1990s drove the price of CFC-12, commonly used in auto air conditioners, from 60 cents per pound to about $25 per pound in early 1997, with further increases expected. A highly profitable international and domestic smuggling business has been created by the regulations and an estimated 10–20,000 tons of smuggled CFC-12 and related gases now enter the United States annually. A second major problem involves international negotiations to ban metered dose inhalers, a major consumer of CFCs used by more than 100 million people internationally to control asthma and other chronic obstructive pulmonary diseases, a rate increasing globally. A number of countries have objected to this prospective ban, as well as some influential domestic interests. Domestic agricultural interests also oppose the total phase-out of methyl bromide, arguing that it should be permitted nationally and internationally for essential uses. Despite these problems, the Montreal Protocols and their successors should be considered at least a qualified success, exemplifying a degree of international agreement and alacrity in managing an environmental problem rare to environmental diplomacy.[21]

Climate Diplomacy: Acid Precipitation

In the early 1990s, a national opinion poll estimated that more than three-fourths of the public ranked atmospheric damage, forest destruction, and air pollution among the nation's "very serious or extremely serious" environmental problems.[22] By the late 1990s, acid precipitation had become commonplace on the public's agenda of environmental ills. A decade earlier, acid precipitation lacked not only public visibility but scientific credibility and political force. The transformation of acid precipitation into a salient public issue demonstrates clearly how scientific advocacy allied to national media capable of magnifying and dramatizing the scientific issues can powerfully shape the public's environmental sensibilities and, thereby, the public policy agenda. It is the politics of acid precipitation, as much as the science, that has advanced the issue from scientific speculation to public policy. Despite continuing scientific debate about the character and severity of the ecological impact of acid precipitation, the weight of the political constituency demanding public measures to abate acid precipitation made a policy response inevitable. As James L. Regens observed in his careful study of the issue's development, once acid precipitation became politically sensitive, other aspects of the issue become secondary. "Sensitive environmental issues, by their very nature, create controversy. Once they find a niche in the policy-making process, the existence of scientific, technical, or economic uncertainty may forestall action but ultimately is not likely to preclude regulatory interventions."[23]

The Scientific Evidence

There is now little disagreement among all concerned over the existence of acid precipitation. But disagreement persists about practically every other aspect of the matter, including how much industry, utilities, and automobiles contribute to the problem; how injurious such precipitation is to humans and the environment; and who should bear the costs for abating air emissions causing acid precipitation—if, in fact, abatement is necessary.

The most common chemical precursors of acid precipitation are sulfur and nitrogen oxides emissions from fossil fuel combustion and metal smelting. These gases can be captured by high-altitude winds and transported hundreds of miles from their point of origin. In the process, these gases become sulfate and nitrate aerosols, then join with other airborne chemical compounds, including ozone and hydrogen peroxide, volatile organic compounds, and water, to become the complex chemicals that return to earth dissolved in water or fixed in ice crystals. Microscopic solids of heavy metals, termed microparticulates, may also become acid deposition. Based on estimates made in several eastern watersheds, between 60 and 70 percent of acid precipitation found in rain or snow is sulfuric acid and the remainder mostly nitric acid.[24]

Scientists have been aware for more than a century that some acid precipitation occurs naturally. However, in the past century acid precipitation has become increasingly widespread and acidic. It now occurs throughout much of the world as well as the United States and is believed to be ten to thirty times more acidic in many U.S. industrialized regions than it would be naturally.[25] Scientists attribute most of this increase to growing fossil fuel combustion, particularly by electric utilities and industry. The United States, currently discharging about 41 metric tons of nitrogen and sulfur oxides annually, is the global leader, but acid precipitation is a world issue because all industrialized nations and many developing ones discharge significant amounts of the precursors of acid precipitation.

The first warning that acid precipitation might be an impending global problem came in the early 1970s when scientists discovered that hundreds of previously normal Swedish lakes had become too acidic to maintain normal biological processes: the usual plant and animal life was absent or dying. Many lakes were deceptively beautiful: "The water is sparkling clear because acid had destroyed everything in it, including the color. It is abnormally peaceful because its natural aquatic life, from fish to crayfish to snails, has ceased."[26] Much of the acid precipitation in Sweden's lakes originated in Eastern and Western Europe and other parts of Scandinavia. By the middle 1980s, evidence had accumulated rapidly that lake acidification and other ecologically disruptive effects of acid precipitation were increasing at an alarming rate in Scandinavia, Eastern and Western Europe, Great Britain, and North America. By the late 1980s, high levels of acid precipitation had been discovered for the first time over rain forests in Central Africa. Moreover, wherever acid precipitation was significant, it appeared to be damaging forests, forest soils, agricultural lands, and their related ecosystems. Large-scale forest dieback can be extremely costly. As a report by the United Nations Environment Program noted, "A 1990 study put the cost of pollution damage to European forests at roughly $30 billion per year—about equal to the revenues from Germany's steel industry, and three times as much as Europe's current financial commitment to air pollution abatement."[27]

By the 1990s, evidence was mounting that acid precipitation was economically as well as ecologically costly and increasingly pervasive throughout the United States. The evidence became daily news:

A massive dying of red spruce and other trees was documented in 1988 along the crest of the Appalachians from Maine to Georgia. Researchers asserted it was "90 percent certain" that the pollution originated in the Ohio and Tennessee River valleys.

After surveying almost half the 2,700 lakes in New York's Adirondack Mountains, the New York State environmental agency reported in 1989 that one-quarter were so acidic that the vast majority could not support fish and an additional one-fifth were so acidified they were "endangered."

Scientists employed by the Environmental Defense Fund reported in 1988 that acid precipitation, primarily oxides of nitrogen from automobiles and utilities, accounted for one-quarter of the nitrates entering the Chesapeake Bay. Nitrogen oxides were found to be degrading not only the bay but the waters of Long Island Sound, the New York Bight, and North Carolina's Albemarle-Pimlico Sound.[28]

The Politics

The Reagan administration, asserting that insufficient evidence existed about the distribution and dangers of acid precipitation, refused to propose more than further research on the issue. Political pressure continued to build, however, not only from environmentalists but from northeastern states claiming environmental damage from Midwestern air emissions. Complaints also came from Canada, where 20 to 40 percent of the acid precursors appeared to come from the United States. The Reagan administration belatedly conceded the seriousness of the acid precipitation problem by signing an international protocol in 1988 that committed the United States to limit its nitrogen oxide emissions in 1994 to 1987 levels. The Bush administration, taking an aggressive stance that earned the president a rare accolade from environmentalists, agreed to provisions in Title IV of the Clean Air Act Amendments of 1990 that committed the United States to reducing sulfur dioxide emissions from electric generating plants by 10 million tons per year and nitrogen oxides by 2 million tons per year and set a cap on the amount of sulfur oxides emitted by the year 2000—altogether, a potential 50 percent reduction of 1990 emission levels. An innovative feature of Title IV was the creation of a market-based system, discussed in Chapter 5, for trading emissions allowances among regulated interests to finance cleanup costs.[29]

While the U.S. decision to initiate controls of its sulfur oxide emissions was welcomed in Canada and other nations, a long-term solution to acid precipitation domestically and internationally is not yet assured. Regulating the other major precursor of acid precipitation, oxides of nitrogen (NO_x), has been far more difficult because the domestic political costs are steep. Most of the nitrogen precursors arise from mobile sources—automobiles, utility vehicles, light trucks—cherished by average Americans. The mounting number of these vehicles, even with required pollution control devices, is a major reason why nitrogen oxides remain a major urban air quality problem. In contrast, sulfur oxides (SO_x) are emitted from a relatively small number of large sources, such as electric power plants and industrial smelters, which are, as John E. Carroll remarks, "a regulator's dream" because a culprit can be named. But NO_x control "threatens politically unacceptable changes in lifestyles and points an accusing finger at most of the population vis-à-vis its lifestyle. . . . Lawmakers who are also politicians invariably see opportunities in SO_2 control and only political danger in any effort toward NO_x control." [30]

Additionally, regional political conflict has not subsided between northeastern states and Midwestern "smokestack" regions over the distribution of regulatory costs for sulfur oxide control.

Climate Diplomacy: Climate Warming

In mid-1988, James E. Hansen, director of the National Aeronautics and Space Administration (NASA) Goddard Institute for Space Studies, testified to members of the Senate Energy and Natural Resources Committee that it was "99 percent certain" that the unusually hot summer of 1988 was evidence that a global climate warming was underway.[31] That remark instantly caught the attention of Congress and the media. Suddenly, global warming, often called the Greenhouse Effect, bore the imprimatur of NASA science; it was speculation no more. Hansen accomplished what the environmental movement could not despite many years of labor. Global warming had acquired political credibility. "The scientific evidence is compelling," concluded Sen. Tim Wirth (D-Colo.). "Now the Congress must begin to consider how we are going to slow or halt that warming trend. . . ."[32]

In fact, the scientific evidence was less than compelling but global climate warming had arrived politically on a wave of international scientific advocacy and presidents were compelled to act as if it were imminent. Both the Bush and Clinton administrations, uneasy with the science and politics of climate warming, initiated measures, albeit irresolutely, to mitigate its impact. Since the United States is the leading producer of the carbon dioxide emissions believed to be the most important cause of climate warming, this U.S. initiative is essential to any worldwide scheme to prevent climate warming.

Is the Climate Warming? Yes

Predictions of an impending global warming are based primarily on evidence that the amount of carbon dioxide in the atmosphere has been steadily increasing since the Industrial Revolution in the mid-nineteenth century. Until the middle of this century, fossil fuel combustion, mostly from worldwide coal burning and motor vehicles, was the principal source of these emissions. In the past several decades, deforestation (particularly in the South American and Asian tropics) is estimated to have created additional carbon dioxide emissions varying from 12 to 50 percent of that released by fossil fuel combustion.[33] The Greenhouse theory asserts that increasing levels of carbon dioxide, methane, nitrogen oxides, and other gases will progressively trap more of the earth's heat; various studies project a global climate warming by an annual average of 1 to 4° F.

A 1997 report from the Intergovernmental Panel on Climate Change (IPCC), the most internationally influential scientific entity currently involved with climate change research, provides what many experts consider a prudent assessment of future climate alterations, including

• an annual mean global surface temperature rise of 1 to 4° F by the year 2100;
• a global mean sea level rise of approximately 1 foot, largely from the melting of polar ice caps; and
• a shift in spatial and temporal patterns of precipitation globally with a net increase of about 7 percent globally.[34]

Changes of this magnitude without mitigation would profoundly, and possibly catastrophically, affect much of the world. Low-lying areas, including many economically underdeveloped countries in Africa and Asia as well as island nations, would be inundated by seawater, their economic and ecological sustainability severely jeopardized. Economically and technologically advanced nations with exposed seacoasts or levee-protected lowlands would also confront formidable economic, engineering, and logistical problems in adjusting to rising seas. Generally, the world's temperate zones would likely shift further north, accelerating the desertification and deforestation of many continental areas in Asia, Africa, Europe, and North America, while transforming agricultural production in many others. Along with these transformations would come predictable but difficult to characterize shifts in regional ecology and a multitude of other natural changes. Not all the predicted changes would necessarily be adverse. Some experts have also predicted longer and more productive growing seasons for many crops as a result of increased ambient carbon dioxide, the transformation of some northern latitudes into new agricultural "breadbaskets," and other benign consequences. In any event, the profound global alterations attending significant climate warming, however characterized, would apparently create a relatively swift, pervasive transformation of human societies and world ecosystems unprecedented in modern human history.

Will There Be a Climate Warming? No and Maybe

Not all atmospheric scientists or other experts find predictions of an imminent climate warming convincing. The ongoing scientific debate swirls around a multitude of complex technical issues certain to confuse the public. The critics' favorite target has been the computer models used to generate climate warming predictions, which have been assailed continually for faulty assumptions and inadequate data about current climate trends. Some experts have asserted that many computer models are based upon inaccurate measures of historic temperature change, that climate warming models fail to describe the long-range physics of climate change, that other historic climate data is misconstrued or misapplied in climate modeling, and much more. Some experts cite other causes, such as solar activity and terrestrial volcanos, to explain climate warming. Others rely on different models suggesting that the Greenhouse Effect is not inevitable. Still others do not believe sufficient evidence exists to make *any* responsible judgment about future climate warming. Media reports often mystify. In November 1997, for instance, national news media reported that a Columbia University scientist had discovered evidence in ancient ocean sediments that global warming might be part of a longer natural climate cycle. The same day, another report in the same paper described findings by federal government scientists that satellite data indicated, contrary to most climate warming predictions, a current increase in Antarctic water. In early 1998, however, another federal agency reported that global temperatures in the previous year reached their highest level since records were kept, adding credibility to the warming hypothesis.[35]

The Evolving Politics

The United States produces about one-third of the total global carbon gas emissions believed responsible for climate warming and must therefore be an active participant in any global agreements intended to mitigate the Greenhouse Effect. A great diversity of domestic political interests are caught up in the regulatory battle over greenhouse gas emissions, including electric utilities, which account for 80 percent of all domestic coal combustion; automobile manufacturers and petroleum producers, whose products create significant carbon emissions; agricultural crop and livestock producers; and almost any other fossil fuel-consuming industries. Throughout the 1990s, the domestic campaign for national and international controls on greenhouse gas emissions was led primarily by scientists, environmentalists, and segments of the national media. They were strongly supported by most European nations and Japan, who were prepared to negotiate a tough climate treaty by the early 1990s and brought considerable diplomatic pressure on the United States to act similarly.

Most potentially regulated segments of the U.S. economy, led by the utilities, car manufacturers, and petroleum producers, were joined by organized labor in very early opposition to any domestic or international agreements setting compulsory timetables and targets for cutbacks in fossil fuel emissions associated with climate warming. This domestic opposition was joined by most developing nations, which collectively account for 30 to 40 percent of current global greenhouse gas emissions. Some believed that the largely Western scientific community advocating climate controls could not speak to the interests of the developing world. Some poorer nations, for instance, resented calculations produced by the IPCC indicating that deforestation and livestock in developing nations contributed to global climate warming. From the Third World perspective, this unfairly stigmatized their difficult economic circumstances. In their view, "deforestation is a matter of desperation, not choice, and subsistence animals who provide a variety of useful functions cannot be compared with surplus, overfed stock in rich countries."[36] Third World countries also asserted that greenhouse gas abatement should be the industrialized nation's responsibility because developing nations needed all their resources for survival. "How can we devote our precious resources toward reducing emissions," asked Malawi's Minister of Forestry, Fisheries and Environmental Affairs at the Kyoto Conference, "when we are struggling every day just to feed, clothe and house our citizens?" [37] Nor did developing countries find most economists helpful. Economists who asserted that developing countries could abate their fossil fuel emissions far more cheaply than could developed ones seemed to be feeding the appetites of privileged nations for thrusting the abatement burden as much as possible onto others.

In any event, the estimated costs to the United States alone to reduce its carbon dioxide emissions would be enormous. An EPA economist has estimated that the replacement of beaches washed away by rising oceans—to mitigate the effects on coastal tides, damage done to saltwater estuaries and the shellfish breeding for which they are responsible, not to mention major coastal cities such as New York, Boston, and Los Angeles—would cost from $10 to $50 billion.[38] The cost of abating carbon dioxide emissions in the United States would fall heavily on coal users and producers, particularly electric utilities, and the auto industry. The capital cost of installing control technologies for carbon dioxide emissions—and no commercially proven technology yet exists—is estimated to be 70 to 150 percent of the entire cost of a new electric-generating facility. This cost, in turn, could raise the average American's electric bill by 75 percent.[39] Every American would feel some impact of abatement policies on lifestyle and pocketbook.

Until the early 1990s, scientific discensus and public passivity forced policy makers to become scientific judges and scientists to become salespeople in the struggle to determine whose data would govern policy decisions. By the end of the Bush administration, however, the combined scientific and diplomatic pressures, together with a gradually emerging public concern about climate warming, forced the White House to confront the Greenhouse Effect diplomatically. At the 1992 Rio Conference the U.S. delegation reluctantly agreed to reduce voluntarily its greenhouse gas emissions to 1990 levels by the year 2000. When it was evident two years later that neither the United States nor several other industrialized nations would meet the voluntary emission abatement targets they had set in Rio, President Clinton agreed to negotiate a binding treaty at the 1997 Kyoto Conference, convened at the initiative of the parties to the UN Framework Convention on Climate Change. Thus, the United States for the first time was apparently committed to a compulsory target-and-timetable agreement. But no consensus on the need for such a treaty existed within either congressional party or among the public as the negotiations began, leaving the outcome very much in doubt.

The Kyoto Agreement

By the time the Kyoto Conference convened in December 1997, national opinion polls indicated strong public support for U.S. action to limit climate warming, even unilaterally if necessary, and the recently released IPCC scientific report added further impetus for action.[40] Nonetheless, the Clinton administration, facing an unsympathetic congressional Republican majority and continued domestic opposition from almost all of the prospective regulated interests, seemed irresolute and confused, leading environmentalists and their allies to doubt that the United States would agree to tough greenhouse gas emission controls despite previous promises. Because any agreement signed at Kyoto would require Senate approval, the congressional mood constantly occupied the American negotiators. The Senate characteristically viewed the proceedings through political bifocals, continually scrutinizing the international implications for U.S. sovereignty and then the likely domestic economic impacts, particularly in home states. With Senate Republicans generally skeptical and Democrats divided on a treaty's merits, the U.S. delegation knew that eventual Senate approval of any agreement would be problematic.

With 120 nations attending and worldwide media coverage, Kyoto became one of the century's historic international environmental conferences. To the considerable surprise of environmentalists and others expecting an indecisive performance, the U.S. delegation eventually committed to what many observers believed to be a rigorous schedule of emission reductions. By agreeing to the draft treaty, the United States had pledged to

1. join other industrialized nations in a set of binding emission targets for all six major greenhouse gasses, which for the United States amounted to a 7 percent overall emission reduction;

2. achieve emission targets over a set of five-year "budget periods" beginning with the years 2008–2012;

3. join with other countries accepting emissions targets in an "emissions trading" regime through which such nations could buy and sell emission allowances for greenhouse gas so long as all kept within the overall emissions targets to which they agreed;

4. permit "joint implementation" through which countries with emissions targets could get credit toward their targets through project-based emission reductions in other such countries; and

5. encourage developing countries to join voluntarily in the emissions trading regime and, through other parts of the protocol, to secure a meaningful commitment from developing countries to set timetables and targets for their own emissions reductions.[41]

The Kyoto Protocol would enter into force when at least fifty-five countries, accounting for at least 55 percent of the total 1990 carbon dioxide emissions of developed countries, ratified the agreement.

After Kyoto

The Kyoto Protocol is freighted with many uncertainties for the United States. It will have little domestic impact unless ratified by the Senate, to which the president has promised a submission within three years of signing the draft agreement. Proponents hope that Clinton can rally the necessary two-thirds Senate majority for the treaty, but the outcome is problematic. Numerous members of both parties have pledged their opposition unless the developing nations also agree to mandatory domestic emission cutbacks, which they have as yet vigorously rejected. Other major senatorial concerns involve fears of lost sovereignty and adverse domestic economic impacts. Somewhat unexpectedly, tentative support emerged for the agreement among some segments of the automobile manufacturing, petroleum, and electric utility industries, but powerful opposition remains. Further, many scientists believe that the Kyoto Protocol is at best a first step toward what must be a greatly accelerated timetable with much greater emission reductions among all major industrial nations if the worst impacts of a future climate warming are to be averted.

Conclusion: The End as the Beginning

Something profound, and as yet but vaguely conceived, has happened to political cognition in the latter third of the twentieth century. To this phenomenon we have ascribed the inadequate word "environmentalism." The artifacts are the most visible and, ultimately, the least important. Beginning with Earth Day in 1970 in the United States and comparable political stirrings elsewhere in the industrialized world, a structure of domestic laws, institutions, and cultural practices has evolved in the United States to translate "environmentalism" into a social force and presence. This already large and elaborate national structure—the focus of most of this book—has become one national pediment among many throughout the world upon which a new regional and international regime of environmental management—the focus of this chapter—is emerging. This incipient "globalization" of environmental management is extremely tenuous and as yet largely unproven, still more symbol than monument. Yet it does exist, and it has never existed before in the history of human civilization. It is worth reflecting upon the profound historic implications of an international protocol to manage climate change in the twilight of the twentieth century.

On the cusp of the new century, however, a better perspective on the future path of environmentalism might be gained by looking beyond its current political and governmental architecture, important as they may be, to its implications for our evolving national conceptions of political time, space, and causality. From this perspective, one of environmentalism's most profound impacts has been to accelerate the way in which science is transforming public policy making. Environmental science, embodied in the technical underpinnings of current understandings of climate warming, ozone depletion, and inter-generational equity is compelling policy makers to think in terms of policy problems and impacts, of the consequences of present decisions and future undertakings, on a time scale almost unthinkable a few decades ago and unavoidable in the future. The genie of anticipatory environmental science is out of the bottle and, like the secrets of nuclear power, cannot now be ignored, however disconcerting it may be. While our national political language has always been afflicted with the vaporous rhetoric "the future" or "concern for future generations," science today is providing policy makers with the intellectual tools and a scientific metric for characterizing the future impact of present public decision making that imposes a responsibility quite new to public life.

Added to this increasingly sophisticated ability to describe and anticipate the environmental consequences of present policies, environmentalism has also made us aware, sometimes acutely, of the need to think deliberately about the long-term risks of technological innovation. As the U.S. experience with nuclear power amply demonstrates, it is not only the scientific risks of technology development that need to be appraised, but also the institutional risks—the questions about whether we have, or can develop in appropriate ways, the institutional means of managing satisfactorily the technologies we create domestically and internationally.

Most important, the evolving impact of environmentalism on our politics and culture has made an especially persuasive case, for those who will listen, that we are approaching a new century not only with the technological ability to destroy the cultural and biological conditions for the survival of human life on earth, but also with the capability to alter the genetic foundations of human life and thus consciously shape human evolution in materially and spiritually beneficial ways. Environmentalism at its best is a challenge to develop the moral and ethical sensibilities to leaven this power with an enlightened stewardship of the earth.

Notes

1. Howard Kurtz, "CNN Pulls Industry Anti-Treaty Ads," *Washington Post,* Oct. 3, 1997.
2. *USA Today,* Oct. 3, 1997.

3. John H. Cushman, Jr., "Public Backs Tough Steps For a Treaty On Warming," *New York Times,* Nov. 28, 1997, A36.

4. Marvin S. Soroos, "From Stockholm to Rio and Beyond: The Evolution of Global Environmental Governance," in *Environmental Policy in the 1990s,* 3d ed., ed. Norman J. Vig and Michael E. Kraft (Washington, D.C.: CQ Press, 1997), 283.

5. For the history of international environmental negotiations, see Lynton Keith Caldwell, *International Environmental Policy: Emergence and Dimensions,* 2d rev. ed. (Durham, N.C.: Duke University Press, 1990).

6. See, for example, Jill Jager and Tim O'Riordan, *The History of Climate Change Science and Politics* (London: Routledge, 1996); Sonja Boehmer-Christansen and Jim Skea, *Acid Politics* (New York: Belhaven Press, 1991); Duncan Liefferink, *Environment and the Nation State: The Netherlands, the EU and Acid Rain* (New York: Manchester University Press, 1996); and Oran Young, *International Governance: Protecting the Environment in a Stateless Society* (Ithaca, N.Y.: Cornell University Press, 1994).

7. Boehmer-Christansen and Skea, *Acid Politics,* Part II.

8. Caldwell, *International Environmental Policy,* 14.

9. "Four U.S. Senators Lobbying in Kyoto," *Washington Post,* Dec. 3, 1997, A35, A42.

10. Boehmer-Christansen and Skea, *Acid Politics,* 19–20.

11. Marc A. Levy, "International Co-operation to Combat Acid Rain," in *Green Globe Yearbook 1995,* ed. Helge Ole Bergesen and Georg Parmanis (New York: Oxford University Press, 1996), 63.

12. See Richard Elliot Benedick, *Ozone Diplomacy: New Directions in Safeguarding the Planet* (Cambridge, Mass.: Harvard University Press, 1991).

13. Levy, "International Co-operation," 60.

14. On the role of science in international climate diplomacy, see Bert Bolin, "Science and Policy Making," *Ambio* 23, no. 1 (Feb. 1994): 25–29; Peter Haas, "Introduction: Epistemic Communities and International Policy Coordination," *International Organization* 46, no. 1 (Winter 1992): 1–35; Joseph Alcamo, Roderick Shaw, and Leen Hordik, eds., *The RAINS Model of Acidification* (Boston: Kluwer Academic Publishers, 1990); and John E. Carroll, ed., *International Environmental Diplomacy: The Management of Transfrontier Environmental Problems* (New York: Cambridge University Press, 1988).

15. On UNEP, see Peter M. Haas, "United Nations Environmental Program," in *Conservation and Environmentalism: An Encyclopedia,* ed. Robert Paehlke (New York: Garland Publishing, 1995), 653–656; for UN environmental organizations generally, see Caldwell, *International Environmental Policy,* chap. 4.

16. Traci Watson, "It's a Full-On Circus in Kyoto," *USA Today,* Dec. 4, 1997.

17. Caldwell, *International Environmental Policy,* 313.

18. Larry Parker and David E. Gushee, "Stratospheric Ozone Depletion: Implementation Issues," *CRS Issue Brief for Congress,* No. 97003 (Washington, D.C.: Congressional Research Service, Jan. 16, 1998).

19. Cited in Parker and Gushee, "Stratospheric Ozone Depletion."

20. See, for example, S. Fred Singer, "(N)O3 Problem," *The National Interest* (Summer 1994): 73–76; Pamela S. Zurer, "Complexities of Ozone Loss Continue to Challenge Scientists," *Chemical and Engineering News,* June 12, 1995, 20–23; and U.S. Congress, House, Committee on Science, Subcommittee on Energy and the Environment, *Stratospheric Ozone: Myths and Realities,* Hearings, 104th Cong., 1st Sess., Sept. 20, 1995.

21. Parker and Gushee, "Stratospheric Ozone Depletion."

22. The poll, conducted by Environmental Opinion Survey in June 1991, is cited in Environmental Protection Agency (EPA), *Securing Our Legacy,* (Washington, D.C.: EPA, 1992). See also *New York Times,* Sept. 25, 1988.

23. James L. Regens, "Acid Deposition," in *Keeping Pace with Science and Engineering: Case Studies in Environmental Regulation,* ed. Myron F. Ulman (Washington, D.C.: National Academy Press, 1993), 185.

24. Government Accounting Office (GAO), "The Debate over Acid Precipitation: Opposing Views, Status of Research," Report no. CMD 81-113 (Sept. 11, 1981). See also Sandra Postel, *Altering the Earth's Chemistry: Assessing the Risks* (Washington, D.C.: Worldwatch Institute, 1986), 25–33; and James L. Regens and Robert W. Rycroft, *The Acid Rain Controversy* (Pittsburgh: University of Pittsburgh Press, 1988), chap. 2.

25. Sandra Postel, *Air Pollution, Acid Rain, and the Future of the Forests* (Washington, D.C.: Worldwatch Institute, 1984), 18.

26. Ross Howard and Michael Perley, *Acid Rain* (New York: McGraw-Hill, 1982), 19.

27. World Resources Institute, *World Resources: 1992–93* (New York: Oxford University Press, 1992), 193.

28. *New York Times,* July 24, 1988, July 7, 1989, and April 25, 1988.

29. For an analysis of Title IV's political history, see Gary C. Bryner, *Blue Skies, Green Politics, 2d ed.* (Washington, D.C.: CQ Press, 1995), chaps. 3, 4.

30. John E. Carroll, "Acid Precipitation: Legislative Initiatives," in *Conservation and Environmentalism,* ed. Paehlke, 6.

31. *New York Times,* June 24, 1988.

32. Ibid.

33. Postel, *Altering the Earth's Chemistry,* 8.

34. *New York Times,* Dec. 1, 1997, F4.

35. These stories were reported in William Stevens, "Study Suggests Natural Weather Shifts," *New York Times,* Nov. 18, 1997; Malcolm Brown, "Ice Shifts Confound Warming Models," *New York Times,* Nov. 18, 1997; and "Scientists See Weather Trend as Powerful Proof of Global Warming," *Washington Post,* Jan. 9, 1998, A8.

36. Jill Jaeger and Tim O'Riordan, "The History of Climate Change Science and Politics," in *Politics of Climate Change,* ed. Tim O'Riordan and Jill Jaeger (London: Routledge, 1996), 5.

37. Calvin Sims, "Poor Nations Reject Role On Warming," *New York Times,* Dec. 13, 1997, A7.

38. *New York Times,* June 26, 1988.

39. *New York Times,* Aug. 28, 1988.

40. John Cushman, "Polls Show Public Support for Treaty," *New York Times,* Nov. 11, 1997; see also "Public Backs Tough Steps For a Treaty on Warming," *New York Times,* Nov. 28, 1997, A36.

41. EPA, "The Kyoto Protocol on Climate Change" (Fact sheet released by the U.S. Department of State, Bureau of Oceans and International Environmental and Scientific Affairs, January 15, 1998) (http://www.epa.gov/globa.../kyoto_dosfs_011598.html).

Suggested Readings

Benedick, Richard E. *Ozone Diplomacy: New Directions in Safeguarding the Planet.* Cambridge, Mass.: Harvard University Press, 1991.

Haas, Peter, et al., eds. *Institutions for the Earth.* Cambridge, Mass.: MIT Press, 1994.

Johnson, Beverly Rose. *Who Pays the Price? The Socio-cultural Context of the Environmental Crisis.* Washington, D.C.: Island Press, 1994.

Meyers, Norman. *Ultimate Security: The Environmental Basis of Political Stability.* New York: W. W. Norton, 1993.

Porter, Gareth, and Janet Welsh Brown. *Global Environmental Politics.* Boulder, Colo.: Westview Press, 1991.

Susskind, Lawrence E. *Environmental Diplomacy: Negotiating More Effective Global Agreements.* Cambridge, Mass.: MIT Press, 1994.

List of Abbreviations

AEC	Atomic Energy Commission
AID	Agency for International Development
AQCR	Air Quality Control Region
BCA	benefit/cost analysis
BLM	Bureau of Land Management
CAA	Clean Air Act of 1970
CEQ	Council on Environmental Quality
CERCLA	Comprehensive Environmental Response, Compensation, and Liability Act of 1980 ("Superfund")
CFCs	chlorofluorocarbons
CPI	consumer price index
CWA	Clean Water Act
DOD	Department of Defense
DOE	Department of Energy
DOI	Department of the Interior
EDS	Endangered Species List
EIS	Environmental Impact Statement
EO	Executive Order
EPA	Environmental Protection Agency
ESA	Endangered Species Act of 1973
FAO	Food and Agricultural Organization
FIFRA	Federal Insecticide, Fungicide, and Rodenticide Act of 1947
FWPCAA	Federal Water Pollution Control Act Amendments of 1972
FWS	Fish and Wildlife Service
GAO	General Accounting Office
GNP	gross national product
HCFCs	hydrochlorofluorocarbons
IAEA	International Atomic Energy Agency

IPCC	Intergovernmental Panel on Climate Change
LRTAP	International Convention on Long Range Transboundary Air Pollution
LUST	liquid underground storage tank
MCL	maximum contaminant limit
NAAQS	National Ambient Air Quality Standards
NASA	National Aeronautics and Space Administration
NEPA	National Environmental Policy Act of 1969
NGOs	nongovernmental organizations
NIMBY	Not in My Backyard
NO_x	nitrogen oxides
NOAA	National Oceanic and Atmospheric Administration
NPDES	National Pollution Discharge Elimination System
NPL	National Priority List
NRC	Nuclear Regulatory Commission
NRDC	Natural Resources Defense Council
NSPS	New Source Performance Standards
NWPA	Nuclear Waste Policy Act of 1982
OCS	outer continental shelf
OECD	Organization for Economic Cooperation and Development
OMB	Office of Management and Budget
OSH Act	Occupational Safety and Health Act
OSHA	Occupational Safety and Health Administration
OSMRE	Office of Surface Mining Reclamation and Enforcement
PCBs	polychlorinated biphenyls
PPM	parts per million
PSD	prevention of significant deterioration
R&D	research and development
RARE	Roadless Area Review and Evaluation
RCRA	Resource Conservation and Recovery Act
RIA	Regulatory Impact Analysis
SARA	Superfund Amendments and Reauthorization Act of 1986
SDWA	Safe Drinking Water Act
SIP	State Implementation Plan
SMCRA	Surface Mining Control and Reclamation Act
SO_x	sulfur oxides

TCDD	2,3,7,8-tetrachloridibenzodioxin
TRI	Toxic Release Inventory
TSCA	Toxic Substances Control Act
UNCS	United Nations Commission on Sustainable Development
UNDP	United Nations Development Program
UNEP	United Nations Environmental Program
VOCs	volatile organic compounds
WIPP	Waste Isolation Pilot Project
WMO	World Meteorological Organization

Index